PRESIDENTS
IN
CRISIS

Also by Michael K. Bohn:

Nerve Center: Inside the White House Situation Room

The Achille Lauro Hijacking: Lessons in the Politics and Prejudice of Terrorism

Money Golf: 600 Years of Bettin' on Birdies

Heroes & Ballyhoo: How the Golden Age of the 1920s Transformed American Sports

Mount Vernon Revisited, with Jessie Biele

PRESIDENTS
IN
CRISIS

Tough Decisions inside the White House
from Truman to Obama

M ICHAEL K. B OHN

Arcade Publishing
New York

First Edition

Arcade Publishing books may be purchased in bulk at special discounts for sales promotion, corporate gifts, fund-raising, or educational purposes. Special editions can also be created to specifications. For details, contact the Special Sales Department, Arcade Publishing, 307 West 36th Street, 11th Floor, New York, NY 10018 or arcade@skyhorsepublishing.com.

Arcade Publishing® is a registered trademark of Skyhorse Publishing, Inc.®, a Delaware corporation.

Visit our website at www.arcadepub.com.
Visit the author's site at www.bohnbooks.com.

10 9 8 7 6 5 4 3 2 1

Library of Congress Cataloging-in-Publication Data

Bohn, Michael K.
  Presidents in crisis : tough decisions inside the White House from Truman to Obama / Michael K Bohn. — First Edition.
pages cm
  ISBN 978-1-62872-431-8 (hardback) — ISBN 978-1-62872-475-2 (Ebook)
1. Presidents—United States—Decision making—Case studies. 2. United States—Foreign relations—1945–1989—Case studies. 3. United States—Foreign relations—1989—Case studies. 4. Political leadership—United States—Case studies. 5. Executive power—United States—Case studies. I. Title.
E840.B647 2015
327.73—dc23   2014038861

Cover design by Brian Peterson
Cover photo credit: Shutterstock

Printed in the United States of America

To my wife Elin in thanks for her forty-two years
of love and support

CONTENTS

LIST OF MAPS AND CHARTS

PREFACE

Only a few hundred people alive today understand the difficulties facing an American president during an unanticipated international crisis—the presidents themselves and their closest advisers. Luckily for me, my experiences as the director of the White House Situation Room enabled me to at least recognize their challenges and reach some of them for interviews. However, as participants' memories dim with passing time, I had to turn to written accounts, including the minutes of key decision-making meetings, or in some cases audio tape transcripts. Memoirs from presidents and their advisers were crucial sources, but my West Wing knowledge helped me scrub away any remaining image polish from self-serving accounts. In several instances, advisers told conflicting stories about a crisis, and I took the common denominator from the different accounts. Recollections from National Security Council staff members—the note takers in critical meetings—were important and usually objective, as were observations from the dozens of Situation Room staff members who have served since the facility's 1961 creation. Presidential biographers provided keen insights into presidential character and personality, but I had to season some books with grains of salt. Information on President Obama's crisis decision making, at least beyond that parceled out to the news media by his team, was hard to find. Even third-party accounts of Obama's crisis management by reputable publications—Michael Lewis's article in the October 2012 issue of *Vanity Fair* and

David Remnick's January 2014 piece in *The New Yorker*, for example—
were carefully orchestrated and vetted by administration officials.
Last, I had the advantage of writing a 2003 book, *Nerve Center, Inside
the White House Situation Room*, and the information I gathered for it
from former presidents and national security advisers helped with this
project.

Two developments prompted me to consider writing a second
book about presidential crisis management. First was the opportunity
to write individual newspaper stories about several of the crises in this
book. I detailed two of the most dangerous situations for McClatchy
Newspapers, a chain of twenty-nine dailies from the *Miami Herald*
to the *Anchorage Daily News*. In 2011, using firsthand accounts from
those involved, I re-created what happened on September 11, 2001,
in the White House Situation Room and aboard Air Force One with
President George W. Bush. The following year, the fiftieth anniversary of the 1962 Cuban Missile Crisis, I took McClatchy readers into
John Kennedy's tense White House meetings. I wrote a third piece in
2013 for the *Washington Post* magazine about the Washington-Moscow
Hot Line, a crisis-managing communications tool that arose from the
Cuban Missile Crisis. The Hot Line figured in several emergency situations after its installation in 1963. Researching these stories inspired me
to analyze other crises, some of which I had touched on in *Nerve Center*.

The second issue has been the enormous amounts of partisan and
ill-informed second-guessing from the sidelines by critics of a sitting
president during a crisis. The phenomenon has arisen during every
presidency that I studied, starting with Truman's. President Obama's
handling of the Arab Spring crises that began in early 2011 drew ran-
corous partisan reactions, for example, just as armchair quarterbacks
blasted the two Bush presidents and Reagan. Politicians and partisan
news media stars naturally exploit most everything to their own advantage, with some presidents even attempting to use a crisis to quiet critics and boost poll ratings. But putting aside election-year posturing,
no one on the sidelines can possibly appreciate how hard it is to make
sensible decisions when time is short and lives are at stake. The titles of
two recent memoirs, whether you agree with the authors or not, reflect
those circumstances—*Decision Points*, by George W. Bush, and *Hard
Choices* by Hillary Clinton.

I want to acknowledge the help people have given me during this project, starting with my literary agent, Julia Lord, and my TV/film agent Judy Coppage. Cal Barksdale provided keen insight and editing at Arcade, and Don McKeon and Vicki Chamblee helped superbly when I was drafting the book proposal. A number of others contributed ideas and thoughts along the way: The *Washington Post*'s Jim Hoagland, Professors Mark Rozell and Jim Pfiffner at George Mason University, Professor Denise Bostdorff at Wooster College, Professor William Quandt at University of Virginia, Professor Stephen Wayne at Georgetown University, Professor Amos Kiewe at Syracuse University, and James Kitfield at the Center for the Study of the Presidency & Congress.

Photo archivists at several presidential libraries helped greatly: Pauline Testerman, Truman; Kathy Struss, Eisenhower; Margaret Harman, Johnson; Jon Fletcher, Nixon; Polly Nodine, Carter; Michael Pinckney, Reagan; Mary Finch, Bush 41; Herbert Ragan, Clinton; Sarah Barca, Bush 43. Thanks also to Lisa Crunk at the US Naval History and Heritage Command, and the staff in the White House Photo Office.

September 15, 2014, was the cutoff date for this book's assessment of President Obama's handling of the Syrian civil war, as well as the rise of the Islamic State and its control of areas of Syria and Iraq. The fluid nature of the confrontation between Russia and Ukraine at time of writing inhibited an analysis of Obama's reaction to that crisis.

A NOTE ON THE WHITE HOUSE SITUATION ROOM

The White House Situation Room is not just a room. It is a complex of multiple spaces manned 24/7 by rotating teams of duty officers and communications specialists. Team members are on loan from intelligence agencies, the State Department, and the military services. The facility, which John Kennedy created in 1961, serves as the president's intelligence and alerting center. The staff, which includes both watch-standers and "day workers," monitors international developments, writes daily summaries of world events, and connects the president and his immediate national security team to the federal government's multiple communications systems. There has always been at least one conference room in the facility, and the changes over the years in the décor and information display systems are evident in the photo section of the book. While technically in the West Wing basement, the "Sit Room" is actually on the ground-floor segment of the building and has discreetly covered windows facing west. When I was the director, I had a window box full of geraniums in the summer and a nice view of the Old Executive Office Building next door.

The communications and information processing capabilities of the Situation Room have helped presidents seize control of the foreign policy apparatus and thus create a true "operational presidency." Until Kennedy's time, the White House staff depended on State, Defense, and the CIA to send over classified information on international incidents and trends. Since 1961, all of the appropriate Washington agencies and departments generally get most every diplomatic cable and intelligence alert at the same time. However, the most sensitive information—video from the unfolding raid to kill Osama bin Laden, for example—is often routed solely to the Situation Room.

INTRODUCTION

"This is a national disgrace," former California governor Ronald Reagan said of President Jimmy Carter's handling of the Iran hostage crisis. The actor turned GOP presidential hopeful frequently castigated Carter during March and April of 1980. The presidential primary election season that spring yielded plenty of potshots aimed at the president, especially from Republicans exploiting the stalemated crisis in Tehran. By that time, fifty-three people from the US embassy had been held by Iranians for over five months.

"I'm not a jingo thinking about pushing the war button when it wouldn't do any good," Reagan said to the media regarding the hostage situation. "But this administration has dillied and dallied for five months now." On March 27, Reagan urged Carter to block the shipment of food and oil to Iran and use the US Navy to blockade Iranian ports. Had he been president, Reagan said that he would have given Iran a private ultimatum to free the Americans and set a deadline. If Iran failed to meet the deadline, he would have threatened "very unpleasant action."

Fast forward to June 1985. Iranian-backed Hezbollah terrorists hijacked an American airliner, TWA Flight 847, in Europe and during the ensuing crisis killed a passenger, a US Navy sailor. The hijackers had demanded that Israel release hundreds of Palestinian prisoners. With no forceful options available to free the hostages, President

Reagan found himself standing in Carter's shoes, and the irony was pinching from heel to toe.

Reagan ultimately made a "no-deal deal" with the Israelis to release their prisoners and promised Syria's leader Hafez al-Assad that the United States would not retaliate against Hezbollah targets in Lebanon. That led to the TWA passengers' release. Reagan didn't play a Hollywood action figure in this drama but rather a cautious negotiator. A week after the TWA crisis resolution, the headline for a July 7 *Washington Post* op-ed piece by *Post* reporter Lou Cannon read, "What Happened to Reagan the Gunslinger?" The subhead added to the point: "Now His Problem Is Convincing Skeptics He Isn't a Pussycat." Cannon reminded readers of Reagan's promise of "swift and effective retribution" against terrorists after his inauguration in January 1981 and noted that Reagan's conservative supporters "would prefer a president who has more than talk in his antiterrorist arsenal." The *Wall Street Journal* editorial page called the president "Jimmy Reagan."

As all newly elected US presidents have learned in the past sixty-five years, handling the 3:00 a.m. phone call is hard work. And no experience could have prepared him for White House crisis decision making. Nothing he said as a candidate or as a sideline critic will work in the Situation Room. Talk was cheap when he didn't have any skin in the game. All of the no-fly zones that looked so easy to implement from the campaign trail become deadly battle spaces after a presidential order.

After that first nighttime call—it's always then because most bad international situations erupt in someone else's daytime—the new president swears to himself that he will take bold and decisive action. When American lives or vital interests are at stake, the public—and especially the news media and political opponents—expect aggressive leadership. But given the difficulties facing a president during an emergency, immediate and conclusive action only happens in the fairy tale model of crisis management espoused by opposing politicians and crank pundits. *New York Times* columnist David Brooks has recognized a president's dilemma in confronting an unanticipated incident. "Everybody wants to be a striding titan," Brooks wrote in 2009. "Almost all alpha leaders want to be the brilliant visionary in a time of crisis—the one who sees the situation clearly, makes bold plans, and delivers the faithful to the other side." He noted that it never happens that way: "In real crises, the successful leaders are usually the ones who cope best with ignorance and error."

Americans rarely see forceful action used effectively in crises. In the seventeen incidents I have analyzed in this study, only one president successfully resolved a crisis with bold and decisive action, and some critics want to put an asterisk on the file. A few strong reactions backfired, and others created a messy long-term situation afterward. And at least three presidents who faced a scandal or political problem used bold action in a crisis to distract the public and media—"a tail wagging the dog," in Hollywood parlance. A fourth overreacted to demonstrate his presidential timber. Regardless, every president from Truman through Obama encountered pressures and pitfalls that hampered a straight-ahead, win-win resolution of a crisis. On the other hand, many presidents resolved a crisis through cautious pragmatism and incremental action.

A range of factors inhibit presidents from forcefully acting in an unexpected crisis. Foremost is the "fog of war," the blanket that smothers desperately needed information about what happened. Faulty intelligence, or worse, faulty interpretation of intelligence, adds to the cloud cover shrouding the crisis landscape. Bickering and turf wars between senior advisers get in the way of bold action. Worse, cabinet secretaries and military leaders who ignore presidential orders or secretly conspire with the president's political opponents hinder forthright crisis resolution. Any incident involving Israel will unleash a storm of political pressure in America and can severely limit action alternatives. A White House sex scandal can undercut bold action if the public perceives the president is changing the subject. A reelection campaign gets in the way because doing the right thing in a crisis isn't always synonymous with raising money and winning a second term. And during much of the time since 1950 there was a far more robust reason for caution—the risk of a nuclear holocaust.

Lack of US leverage in an incident is another common brake on bold action. Can the president affect a crisis outcome? If not, he immediately pushes aside blunt or forceful options and sticks with diplomacy and perhaps economic sanctions. During the 1956 Suez crisis involving Great Britain, France, and Israel, for example, the Soviets invaded Hungary to reestablish a communist government. Eisenhower knew that he had no leverage short of all-out war, so he retreated to rhetoric. In 2008, Russia intervened in Georgia to support pro-Russian separatists, and President George W. Bush (Bush 43) didn't have risk-free means to bolster democracy in the country. Obama had few effective options in Ukraine beyond economic sanctions on Russia in the spring and summer of 2014. On the other hand, Reagan had leverage in a backyard mini-crisis in the Caribbean nation of Grenada in 1983, and so did President George H. W. Bush (Bush 41) in his 1989 military intervention in Panama.

Kennedy acknowledged the frequent scarcity of American clout in international situations in an interview two months after the 1962 Cuban Missile Crisis. "Well, I think in the first place the problems are more difficult than I had imagined they were," he explained. "Secondly, there is a limitation upon the ability of the United States to solve these problems."

Group dynamics among a president's advisers can influence decision making in diverse manners. Reagan never reconciled his warring advisers, and his acceptance of dissonance yielded watered-down policies and actions. Conversely, Carter countenanced policy chasms between advisers and lost his principled secretary of state in the middle of a crisis. Truman and his advisers fell victim to "groupthink," a phenomenon created by harmony and the absence of devil's advocates. That led to bold action in Korea that backfired and resulted in a three-year war.

A fear of leaks has forced several presidents to minimize the number of their crisis advisers. That invites groupthink, and the late presidential scholar James David Barber addressed the trade-offs: "The group locks itself in, locks other counselors out. The risk of leaks is worth taking in such cases, compared to the risk of groupthink." Barber wrote that only the president can create balance among these factors while guarding against a serious problem—"galloping consensus in the Oval Office."

George Reedy, a Johnson intimate, observed that strong presidents affect group dynamics differently than weak ones. Those with forceful personalities "weed out ruthlessly those assistants who might persist in presenting him with irritating thoughts." A president considered weak or "wishy-washy" is "less ready to eliminate strong-minded people from his immediate vicinity."

Domestic political concerns affect every decision made in the White House, including those made in a crisis. Serious Truman students assert that the president's overreach in Korea arose from domestic pressures. Ike's advisers warned that his decisions during the 1956 Suez War would negatively affect his reelection chances. The appointed president, Gerald Ford, appeared to overreact in a 1975 incident to prove he was a viable candidate in the 1976 election. General Colin Powell urged Bush 41 to continue sanctions against Iraq in 1990 instead of quickly moving to forceful ejection of Iraqi military forces from Kuwait. Bush said that approach wasn't politically feasible.

Domestic considerations have often led to what longtime *New York Times* correspondent R. W. "Johnny" Apple called a "presidential rite of passage." At the time of Bush 41's 1989 invasion of Panama, Apple wrote that most newly elected presidents since World War II had followed an initiation rite of shedding blood to demonstrate a willingness to defend US national interests. "All of them," Apple wrote, "acted in the belief that American political culture required them to show the world promptly that they carried big sticks."

Mutual distrust or misunderstanding between White House civilians and the uniformed military leadership has hindered crisis management. The worst case had White House staff members ordering military operations as if they were playing a battleship board game. In the Pentagon, that's called using a 10,000-mile screwdriver from the White House to adjust the tactical levers of military power. Secretary of Defense Robert Gates criticized the White House of just that during the 2011 intervention in Libya. But presidents worried about their political future have been hesitant to give a military commander a long leash. Truman let General MacArthur overextend himself in Korea, but Bush 41 held a tight rein on General Norman Schwarzkopf in the 1991 Persian Gulf War.

Regardless of the threat a crisis poses to America or the forcefulness of a president's response, presidential rhetoric has been an important factor in every crisis. Primarily, it's a crisis because he says so. Political rhetoric expert Theodore Windt described the birth of a crisis in this way: "Situations do not create crises. Rather, the president's perception of the situation and the rhetoric he uses to describe it mark an event as a crisis." While some incidents need no characterization—the

9/11/2001 terrorist attacks—the public usually must look to the president for an incident's significance. For example, when a Soviet fighter jet shot down a Korean Airlines 747 in September 1983, President Reagan called it a "wanton misdeed" and lamented the horrible loss of life. On the other hand, in June 1985, he called the hijacking of TWA Flight 847 in the Mideast an "attack on all citizens of the world" and a "dangerous and volatile situation."

Following a president's declaration of a crisis, he has to attempt to garner the American people's support for his proposed response. A common theme is that a dangerous and evil man/country/terrorist organization is threatening the United States and other peace-loving countries. Kennedy accused the deceitful Soviets of deploying nuclear ballistic missiles to Cuba and described the action as a "clandestine, reckless, and provocative threat to world peace." Bush 41 characterized Saddam Hussein as the new Hitler, who sanctioned rape and pillaging. The Bush 43 administration played on the public's alarm by deceptively ascribing to al-Qaeda a motive—the destruction of America's way of life, democracy, and Western civilization—that made the president's response seem apolitical and unassailable.

Tough-sounding rhetoric at the outset of a crisis has backfired on presidents. President Kennedy, under intense scrutiny by Republicans on Capitol Hill just before the 1962 midterm elections, drew a red line on the introduction of Soviet offensive missiles in Cuba. He later admitted that the ultimatum had narrowed his options when push came to shove. In August 2012, President Obama ad-libbed a warning on Syria's use of chemical weapons. Obama later tried to adjust that line as the chemical weapons crisis deepened and tough decisions loomed. An Obama aide said at the time of the line drawing, "We're kind of boxed in."

Presidents may fine-tune public perceptions of a situation by carefully selecting the location of a crisis meeting. For example, Tony Lake, Clinton's first national security adviser, believed that keeping Clinton out of the Situation Room was the best approach for managing public perceptions. "The president meeting his advisers in the Situation Room could suggest to the public that we had a crisis that needed managing," Lake told me. "Meeting in the Cabinet Room suggests thoughtful, deliberate consideration."

On the other hand, Brent Scowcroft, adviser to both Ford and Bush 41, thought the media were intrigued with the mystique that the Situation Room brings to an event. "I believe that the fact that the president meets with his team in the Situation Room adds gravity to the situation in the eyes of the news media," Scowcroft told me in 2001. "It shows that the president is seriously concerned about an issue or event."

Public expectations of bold presidential action in a crisis arise from cultural touchstones. The 1776 Revolution was certainly bold, as were the frontiersmen who tamed the West and the rugged individuals prized in American history. Folks remember Washington, Lincoln, Wilson, and the two Roosevelts for their transformative actions. Another source is the public's "collective memory," which presidents often exploit, according to Denise Bostdorff, Wooster College professor of political rhetoric. She points to celebrations of World War II—Tom Brokaw's books on the greatest generation and dramatizations such as *Saving Private Ryan* and *Band of Brothers*—as reinforcing examples of a collective memory that feeds public expectations in a crisis.

James David Barber of Duke University examined the cultural expectations that the public thrusts up to the presidency. Barber grouped them into reassurance in the face of fear, legitimacy that holds a president above politics, and the action of a take-charge doer. Barber noted that expectations change in cycles. For example, when a president overdoes action to the point his policies become too political, public expectations shift to legitimacy and reassurance.

Political analyst Charlie Cook has elaborated on the cycles of expectations. "After President Nixon's fall in the Watergate scandal, we opted for former Georgia governor Jimmy Carter, who exuded honesty and promised that he would never lie to us. After the Iranian hostage crisis, when Carter seemed weak and indecisive, we elected Ronald Reagan, the closest we could come to John Wayne." Additionally, Cook noted, after Bush 41 focused on foreign policy, Clinton ran on the theme, "It's the economy, stupid." And we don't need Cook to understand that people voted in Barack Obama when they tired of Bush 43's wars.

Presidents pay attention to public hopes and want to act accordingly. George Mason University professor of public policy Mark

Rozell summarized the bottom line: "Our definitions of what it means to be a successful leader drive presidents to behave in certain ways and to make certain types of decisions. No one wants to be known as the caretaker, or the one who consolidated the achievements of his predecessors."

But more often than not, presidents discover that bold action in a crisis is too risky from either a national security or political standpoint. As a result, as columnist Brooks wrote, they opt for "wise muddling through." A real-life example of his thesis involved President Clinton, and Secretary of State Madeleine Albright highlighted the strategy on January 15, 1999. Clinton's top advisers were considering how to respond to a Serbian massacre of ethnic Albanians during the Balkan hostilities. Albright told her colleagues that they had three alternative courses: Step back from the situation, muddle through, or take decisive action.

Muddling through in this context is not by any means confused decision making or foolish dithering. Charles Lindblom established the "Science of Muddling Through" in 1959. In layman's terms, it is an incremental crisis management process, one in which decision makers take a small step, judge its efficacy, and then act again. Setbacks will occur, but the process helps to avoid the "Big Error," or an avoidable escalation of the situation to a catastrophe. For generations, British leaders have favored this approach, which is optimal for crisis decision making in a democracy. The mainstays of government by the people—majority rule and minority rights, civil-military relations, the rule of law, and human rights, for example—are frequently best managed and protected by muddling through a crisis.

Although some journalists love the phrase "muddling through," it has a negative connotation outside the media and a small circle of behavioral and political scientists. Today, it is better to character-ize not-so-bold crisis reactions by the White House as "cautious," "incremental," "selectively engaged," "pragmatically realistic," or "interest-based." Kennedy successfully followed this approach in the Cuban Missile Crisis, as did Johnson in the 1967 Six-Day War, and Nixon (actually Kissinger) in the 1973 October War. Obama gener-ally opted for incremental or cautious steps during the Arab Spring, alternating between idealism and realism on a case-by-case basis. He almost took bold action with a planned military strike on Syria because of its use of chemical weapons, but his muddling-through instincts—plus a threat—produced a deal with Russia and Syria to remove Assad's chemical weapon stockpiles.

As a president looks for an option that won't blow up in his face, his muddling-through phase draws accusations of wavering and weakness. Critics who shout, "Do something!" usually haven't a clue that every forceful action in the crisis du jour can have untoward consequences. Muddling reflects the reality of crisis decision making, but it doesn't readily fit popular perceptions of leadership, especially when magnified or distorted by the jagged edges of domestic politics.

President Obama defended his cautious approach to managing crises while talking with reporters in late April 2014 and described his strategy of pulling economic and diplomatic levers before the one for bombs away. "That may not always be sexy," he said. "That may not always attract a lot of attention, and it doesn't make for good argument on Sunday morning shows. But it avoids errors." The president then slipped into his sports metaphor mode. "You hit singles, you hit doubles; every once in a while we may be able to hit a home run. But we steadily advance the interests of the American people and our partnership with folks around the world."

Some Obama critics have faulted the president for not having a consistent approach to emerging crises, a strategy that generally worked during the Cold War. From Truman through Reagan, presidents usually pursued a one-size-fits-all solution to crises arising from communist expansionism. But after the Cold War ended for the first time in 1989, only Bush 43 clung to the "good versus evil" and "you're either with us or against us" dictums. More nuanced foreign policy practitioners, however, have acknowledged that increased globalization and shifting sources of tension and violence demand more realism and less idealism in crisis resolution. *Washington Post* columnist David Ignatius wrote in 1989 that containment had given way to a strategy of "hedging your bets."

More recently, foreign affairs journalist Fareed Zakaria wrote in 2011 that people should stop looking for an Obama Doctrine. "The doctrinal approach to foreign policy doesn't make much sense anymore," Zakaria wrote. "In today's multipolar, multilayered world, there is no central hinge upon which all American foreign policy rests. Policymaking looks more varied, and inconsistent, as regions require approaches that don't necessarily apply elsewhere."

Regardless of a president's approach to a crisis, re-creating his decision making depends on insider accounts, and most are biased toward positive descriptions of presidential actions. A memoirist who

Grading Crisis Management

Notes: 1. Hostage rescue attempt appeared to be a wag-the-dog moment. 2. DEFCON change was for domestic consumption. 3. In the context of 1981–1988 tit-for-tat series. 4. Afghan ops vs. al-Qaeda/Taliban only.

was in the Oval Office during a crisis was there because of mutual trust between the future writer and the president. However, negative accounts can arise from leaks by a disgruntled adviser whose recommendations had been spurned, and thus prove the point that wholly objective interpretations from participants are hard to find. Even third-party narratives such as those from the well-connected Bob Woodward depend on insider versions of crisis meetings. Those presidents who secretly taped crisis decision-making sessions should be applauded for their "deceitful" practices.

Most presidents had to face multiple crises during their presidencies, so, for this book, I chose the crises that best illustrate the decision-making process. For example, the 1990 Iraqi invasion of Kuwait will tell us more about Bush 41's decision making than his nice little war in Panama. The same can be said of Reagan's actions before and after the 1983 Marine barracks bombing in Beirut versus his simultaneous invasion of Grenada. Eisenhower's 1958 intervention in Lebanon exposes less of his crisis management strategies than the 1956 Suez War. Moreover, this book does not offer a critique of the overall foreign policies of twelve presidents, but rather insights into how presidential crisis decisions are made. The American public can generally see only the product of Sit Room deliberations, the sausage if you will, without ever going inside the sausage factory to see how it's made.

The graph on the facing page displays an assessment of how each president from Truman through Obama managed the selected crises. The individual grades arose from my aggregation of conclusions from foreign affairs experts, but I assigned the placement of each crisis in the four quadrants by subjectively comparing each affair to the others. There is no quantitative scale for measuring crisis decision making.

None of these crises offered much more than an isolated light moment or gesture that brought a smile to a participant. However, Henry Kissinger told me about one of these rare incidents, which occurred late in the 1973 October War. Washington and Moscow had exchanged serious messages on the Hot Line on October 23 when Israel ignored United Nations cease-fire resolutions in an attempt to capture or neutralize the Egyptian Third Field Army in the Sinai Peninsula. Kissinger called Israeli ambassador Simcha Dinitz from the

White House Situation Room and demanded that Dinitz urge Israeli prime minister Golda Meir to immediately stop the hostilities. Henry momentarily lost his composure.

"Jesus Christ!" he yelled. "Don't you realize how important this is?"

Kissinger quietly listened to Dinitz's deadpan reply.

"Henry, my government might be more persuaded if you invoke the name of a different prophet."

PRESIDENTS
IN
CRISIS

CHAPTER 1

HARRY TRUMAN

Korean War, 1950

Bold Action, Overreach

President Harry Truman's housekeeper, Vietta Garr, announced that dinner was ready. Truman, his wife Bess, and daughter Margaret walked to the dining room of their home in Independence, Missouri. It was 6:30 p.m. on Saturday, June 24, 1950, and Missouri's summer heat had prompted Vietta to open most of the windows in hopes of catching an evening breeze. The first family had escaped from the Washington merry-go-round for what they hoped would be a restful weekend respite.

After dinner, Truman began to tire and talked of going to bed early. The peaceful evening suddenly ended when the hall telephone jangled. Dean Acheson, Truman's secretary of state, was calling from his home in Maryland.

"Mr. President," he said, "I have very serious news. The North Koreans have invaded South Korea."

Acheson briefed the president on available details and recommended that the State Department seek a cease-fire resolution from the United Nations Security Council. Truman readily agreed. The president then asked if he should return immediately to Washington, and Acheson counseled against that, primarily because he did not know the extent of the aggression. Further, Truman's unscheduled return might unnecessarily prompt public anxiety. But that didn't stop apprehension from affecting the Truman family "None of us got much sleep that night," Margaret recalled later. "My father made it clear from the moment that he heard the news, that he feared this was the opening round of World War III."

The next morning, Truman asked Bess and Margaret to act as if nothing had happened. The two women went to church, and the president and his Secret Service escort made a previously scheduled visit to the family farm in nearby Grandview. When he returned home, a military aide gave him a cable with bad news from John Muccio, the US ambassador to the Republic of Korea (ROK, or South Korea).

IT WOULD APPEAR FROM THE NATURE OF THE ATTACK AND MANNER IN WHICH IT WAS LAUNCHED THAT IT CONSTITUTES AN ALL-OUT OFFENSIVE AGAINST ROK. MUCCIO

Shortly after noon, Acheson called again with updates and confirmed the action to be a full-scale invasion. Truman responded forcefully: "Dean, we've got to stop the sons of bitches no matter what."

Truman decided on the spot to return to Washington. His aides hustled to get the plane and crew ready for departure within an hour. At the Kansas City Airport, just ten miles from the Truman home, reporters besieged the president and his party with questions about wire reports on Korean hostilities. The president's physician, Brigadier General Wallace Graham, responded to *New York Times* writer Anthony Leviero and *Time*'s Edwin Darby, "The boss is going to hit those fellows hard."

While Truman and his party prepared to board the president's plane, *Independence*, a modified Douglas DC-6 airliner, his family, who remained behind, watched silently from the tarmac. "Mrs. Truman was calm but serious," Leviero reported that night. "She looked much as she appeared on the fateful evening of the late President Roosevelt's death."

During the three-hour flight to Washington, Truman solidified within his mind his initial impulse to confront the North Koreans. The appeasements in Europe and Asia in the 1930s shaped his thinking.

"Communism was acting in Korea just as Hitler, Mussolini, and the Japanese had acted ten, fifteen, and twenty years earlier," Truman wrote in his memoir. He also surmised that if the North Korean aggression went unchecked, the communists would target other countries. "If this was allowed to go unchallenged, it would mean a third world war, just as similar incidents had brought on the second world war." Throughout his political career, Truman prided himself for trying to do the "right" thing, and he believed that a strong response was just that.

The president had his staff radio ahead to Acheson, asking that he assemble the top civilian and military leaders at Blair House for a dinner meeting. The central part of the White House, including the family quarters, was undergoing extensive repairs, so the first family was living across Pennsylvania Avenue in the chief executive's official guesthouse.

At 6:00 p.m., the UN Security Council passed a Korean cease-fire resolution, which also called for all member countries to withhold any assistance to North Korea. The vote was 9-0, with Yugoslavia abstaining. The Soviet representative, Jacob Malik, was not present. He had been boycotting Security Council meetings since the previous January in protest of the Council's refusal to replace one of its members, Nationalist China, with Communist China. Malik's absence surprised US diplomats, but unknown to them, Soviet general secretary Joseph Stalin had personally directed Malik's inaction. Later revelations have disclosed that Stalin knew that acting under the UN umbrella would limit possible American escalation. The United States would need to keep its allies within the coalition and thus refrain from overly aggressive operations.

Independence landed at National Airport at 7:15 p.m., and Acheson, Undersecretary of State James Webb, and Secretary of Defense Louis Johnson were there to meet Truman. As they drove downtown in the president's limousine, Acheson briefed Truman on the UN action. While exiting the limo, Truman demonstrated the resolve he had formulated that morning and aboard *Independence*: "By God," he declared, "I'm going to let them have it!"

At Blair House, several assistants from State and Defense joined Acheson and Johnson, as well as the secretaries of the Army, Navy, and Air Force, chairman of the Joint Chiefs, General Omar Bradley, and the three service chiefs. Missing was Averell Harriman, Truman's newly appointed assistant for foreign policy. The former ambassador to the UK and Soviet Union was in London on a personal visit. The president asked the men to withhold all substantive matters until after dinner.

Chief White House butler Alonzo Fields and his tuxedo-clad assistants served the fourteen men a dinner of fried chicken, shoestring potatoes, asparagus, tomatoes, hearts of lettuce, dessert, and coffee. Once the butlers had cleared the table and retreated, Truman stated that he wanted to focus that evening on immediately needed decisions. He then turned the meeting over to Acheson, the tall and aristocratic representative of the Eastern Establishment.

Secretary Acheson began with what he termed a "darkening" report of situation in Korea and then covered the early diplomatic developments. The taciturn Bradley spoke next and immediately hewed to Truman's hard line: "We must draw the line somewhere." But the chairman, a steely World War II combat commander, questioned the advisability of committing US ground units. Army chief General Joe Collins, Army secretary Frank Pace, and Secretary of Defense Johnson interjected, agreeing that US actions should be limited to air and sea power.

General Bradley continued speaking and assessed the possibility of a Soviet escalation to global war. Noting that the Soviets had yet to recover from World War II, he asserted, "Russia is not yet ready for war." Air Force chief General Hoyt Vandenberg, who agreed that the US must stop the North Koreans, disagreed and said the group should not "base our action on the assumption that the Russians would not fight."

That statement prompted Truman to ask about the strength of Soviet naval and air forces in the Far East. The respective service chiefs gave thumbnail sketches of the capabilities and numbers, with Vandenberg mentioning that the Soviets based large numbers of jet aircraft near Shanghai, China. Truman then asked, "Can we knock out their bases in the Far East?"

"It might take some time," Vandenberg replied. He then mentioned an issue that would arise again during the crisis, "It could be done if we used A-bombs."

The subject then turned to the military chain of command in Asia. Johnson noted that General Douglas MacArthur was the commander of US Army forces in the Far East and the likely candidate to lead the US defense of South Korea. MacArthur had accepted the Japanese surrender to end World War II and had stayed in Tokyo as the commander of US occupying forces. Secretary Johnson spoke of appointing MacArthur to handle the military side of the crisis, but urged caution because of MacArthur's well-known propensity to follow only his own counsel. "Instructions to General MacArthur," Johnson said, "should be detailed so as not to give him too much discretion." Truman said nothing at this point but was well aware of the general's haughty and arrogant demeanor. The president had previously referred to MacArthur as "Mr. Prima Donna" and a "stuffed shirt."

By the end of the meeting, Truman had formally decided to confront the North Koreans militarily, but only under the auspices of the UN. Until Acheson could gain a UN resolution to provide that authority, the president ordered several preparatory actions: MacArthur was to resupply South Korean forces and send a survey group to Korea to assess the hostilities; provide air cover for the evacuation of Americans; reposition naval forces; create contingency plans for the destruction of Soviet Far East air bases; and assess the next potential targets for Soviet expansion. He also banned both explicit statements and background comments to the press until he spoke publicly in two days. The president closed with an invitation: "Now let's all have a drink. It's been a hard day."

Truman had committed to repulse the North Korean invasion even if it meant war, but he turned contemplative after the first bourbon. "I have hoped and prayed that I would never have to make a decision like the one I have just made today," he said. "But, I saw nothing else that was possible for me to do except that."

A Secret Communist Plan

Cold War historian John Gaddis, writing about the Korean War in 1997, noted in general terms how seemingly unrelated events proceeding along parallel tracks had converged all at once with results that had been unpredictable. More specifically, Gaddis added, ". . . What is striking about the Korean War is the extent to which its outbreak, escalation, and ultimate resolution surprised everyone."

Upon the defeat of Japan in World War II, the Soviet Union accepted the surrender of Japanese forces north of the 38th parallel of latitude and occupied that part of the Korean peninsula; the United States took control south of the line. The Soviets installed a communist government in the north, led by Kim Il-sung. He had been a resistance leader during the Japanese occupation and a major in the Soviet Red Army during World War II. Kim led the creation of the People's Republic of Korea in 1948 and became prime minister. In the south, Syngman Rhee, a US-backed anticommunist, was elected the first president of the Republic of Korea. Kim and Rhee wanted to unify the country, but only on their individual terms. Those ambitions created a potentially explosive dynamic, which prompted both sides to mount cross-border raids prior to 1950.

Neither Rhee nor Kim, however, could successfully invade the other side without support from their superpower sponsors. In the case of North Korea, this meant that any thoughts of invading the South had to fit into Stalin's overall plan for communist expansion. Many in the West believed at the time that Stalin exercised rigid control over all communist states, although such hegemony was far from complete. What Truman and his advisers didn't know was that in early 1950, Stalin concluded the time was right for a possible move by Kim. The West had stymied communist expansion attempts in Europe through the formation of NATO's collective defense, and the Marshall Plan's economic rebuilding efforts helped strengthen Western Europe. Further, the 1948–1949 US airlift to an isolated West Berlin in communist East Germany showed Stalin the West's resolve. In Asia, however, the communist forces led by Mao Zedong had taken control of China in 1949 and pushed their opponents, the Nationalists, offshore to the island of Formosa. Perhaps another Asian nation could be next. Stalin was also emboldened by the development of his own atomic weapons, and if a Korean initiative prompted a US-China war, the conflict would give him time to increase Soviet military strength. The United States added to Stalin's expansionist thinking by withdrawing its military from South Korea in 1949. But the clincher for Soviet action came from an oversight by Acheson.

While speaking at the National Press Club in Washington on January 12, 1950, the secretary of state described the American "defense perimeter" in the Western Pacific. He inadvertently left Korea and Formosa (now Taiwan) off the list of countries that the US military would protect. Already primed for communist expansion in Asia, Stalin quickly approved a plan by communist China's chairman Mao Zedong to invade Formosa, and he entertained Kim's proposal for forceful Korean reunification. Kim pressed his case personally when he visited Moscow in April and gave Stalin assurances that "America would never participate in the war. We are absolutely sure of this."

Stalin conditionally approved Kim's invasion, pending approval by Chairman Mao. "If you should get kicked in the teeth," Stalin told Kim, "I shall not lift a finger. You have to ask Mao for all the help."

Kim, the grandfather of North Korea's current ruler, traveled to Peking (now Beijing) in April while the Soviet general staff prepared detailed war plans for the North Korean military. Kim exaggerated Stalin's support when he approached Mao and said that he would not need Chinese help. The Chinese gave Kim a green light, and Mao, focusing on preparations for attacking Formosa, appeared thereafter to pay little attention to Kim's war preparations.

President Truman knew nothing about the secret coordination between Stalin, Mao, and Kim. While Truman's advisers assumed Moscow's control of China and Korea, they misjudged the readiness of Stalin and Mao to intervene, and the forcefulness of that intercession. That intelligence deficit and the resulting misjudgment yielded a potentially disastrous trap.

The Commander in Chief Acts

On Monday, June 26, the day after Truman returned to Washington, MacArthur cabled bad news. "Tanks entering the capital city of Seoul . . . South Korean units unable to resist determined Northern offensive . . . Our estimate is that a complete collapse is imminent." Truman immediately met with his advisers that evening at Blair House. He decided to beef up US forces in the Philippines, increase aid to Indochina, another potential communist target, and to commit US air and naval forces in support of the South. However, the president banned operations above the 38th parallel. Both Bradley and Acheson remained skeptical about introducing US ground troops, and Bradley counseled, "Let's wait a few days."

The president and his Blair House crisis team met with congressional leaders on the 27th in the White House West Wing. The delegation fully supported the president's actions thus far and agreed that Truman could act under his authority as commander in chief and did not need a congressional resolution. However, this approval from the Capitol Hill leadership didn't extend throughout the ranks. Robert Taft (R-Ohio), a frequent critic of Truman, spoke up on the Senate floor the next day. He said that he would have voted for a resolution, but Truman needed congressional approval to send aid to South Korea. Taft, who often faulted Acheson as the source of America's international problems, also pointed to "the bungling and inconsistent foreign policy of the administration." Taft called for the secretary of state's resignation.

At his weekly news conference on June 29, the president told reporters that American military aid to South Korea would help the republic maintain its independence. Truman refused to talk about sending US ground troops or comment on the possible use of atomic bombs, which he had employed in Japan to end World War II in Asia. At one point, however, a reporter asked, "Mr. President, everybody is asking in this country, are we or are we not at war?"

"We are not at war," Truman responded tersely. After an exchange about what Truman labeled a "bandit raid" by North Korea, another reporter angled back toward the nature of America's possible military actions. "Mr. President, would it be correct, against your explanation, to call this a police action under the United Nations?"

"Yes. That is exactly what it amounts to."

Some have viewed as a mistake Truman's acceptance of a journalist's words to describe the conflict. However, in the circumstance, Truman wanted to avoid a congressional declaration of war given the scant five years since the last one; the police term handily fit his strategy. But the exchange did fit a pattern he had established during his regular dialogues with the press. Acheson later reflected on Truman's extemporaneous conversations with reporters: "He was not good in the fast back-and-forth of a press conference. President Truman's mind is not so quick as his tongue." Truman often responded to a question before a reporter finished it and trapped himself with an off-kilter answer. "This tendency was a constant danger to him," Acheson wrote, "and bugbear to his advisers."

In a meeting after the news conference, Truman clearly reiterated his war aims to his advisers: "Push the North Koreans back behind the 38th parallel . . . Restore peace and restore the border." Those tasks became more complicated the following morning.

"Frank Pace called at 5 a.m. EDT," Truman wrote in his diary, referring to the Army secretary. "I was already up and shaved. Said MacArthur wanted two divisions of ground troops." In his full report to the Pentagon that morning, MacArthur elaborated on his conclusion: "The only assurance of holding the present line and the ability to regain later the lost ground is through the introduction of US ground combat forces into the Korean battle area."

President Truman immediately approved MacArthur's request. He also granted permission to the US Air Force to attack North Korean bases and supply lines, and directed the US Navy to blockade the North's coastline. He then invited congressional leaders to the White House and updated them. Republican Kenneth Wherry, the Senate minority leader, repeatedly asked the president when he planned to consult formally with Congress. As many future presidents also would do, Truman deflected the point and said of his decisions that morning: "I just had to act as commander-in-chief, and I did."

Leapfrog and Mission Creep

MacArthur had scant resources from which to draw two divisions of US troops. The US military had demobilized after World War II, and his only choice was to take troops from the Eighth Army. That unit occupied postwar Japan, and its soldiers lacked combat training. On July 7, the UN created the United Nations Command, with MacArthur as its chief. Ultimately, fifteen countries contributed men and weapon systems. Since South Korea was not a UN member, its military forces served under US Army command. But all of this reinforcement and organization didn't help on the battle lines. By late July, the North Koreans had pushed the South's army and elements of the

Eighth Army to the southern tip of the peninsula. The defenders were preparing to make their last stand at the port city of Pusan.

By this time, US intelligence indicated the Chinese were massing forces on the coast for what the Pentagon assumed was an invasion of Formosa. Truman decided to protect the island with units of the Navy's Seventh Fleet and forego the use of other American forces. Many in the military, including Johnson and the Joint Chiefs, pushed for more aggressive actions, including offensive military operations against the communist mainland. MacArthur also sought an all-out military response and undertook two initiatives that not only infuriated Truman, but also foreshadowed the undoing of Truman's management of the crisis.

The general traveled to Formosa on July 31 and made public statements there about arming the Nationalist leader Chiang Kai-shek for a return to the mainland. This was sharply at odds with Truman's decision to merely defend Formosa. The president sent his assistant, Averell Harriman, to Tokyo to instruct the general to get in line with the president's policy, and MacArthur agreed. Truman assured the press that he and MacArthur "saw eye-to-eye on Formosa." Nevertheless, MacArthur further irritated the president by writing a letter in late August to the annual meeting of the Veterans of Foreign Wars. In his message, MacArthur impugned Truman's cautious approach to Mao's threat to Formosa. "Nothing could be more fallacious," MacArthur wrote, "than the threadbare argument by those who advocate appeasement and defeatism in the Pacific that if we defend Formosa we alienate continental Asia." Bradley viewed the message as "the height of arrogance."

Outraged at MacArthur's latest affront, Truman met with Acheson, Johnson, Harriman, Bradley, and the service chiefs on August 26. Had anyone known about this beforehand? the president asked. No one had. The president told Johnson, whom Truman blamed for MacArthur's off-the-reservation activities, to order MacArthur to withdraw the letter. Johnson tried to "weasel out" of the task, according to Bradley, and in the end Truman dictated the letter to Johnson over the phone.

MacArthur's escapades prompted a shift in Truman's view of the general from one critical of the general's pompous personality to distrust. The events also marked the end of Johnson's term as defense secretary and a member of the president's crisis management team. Johnson's evasion on the MacArthur letter was, according to Margaret Truman, "close to the last straw." Truman had been trying since May to determine how to fire Johnson, especially when he became aware that Johnson had been scheming with congressional Republicans to oust Acheson.

"Louis Johnson was causing huge problems," wrote Truman aide George Elsey years later. "Johnson loathed Acheson and despised anyone associated with the State Department." In addition, Johnson had political ambitions. He wanted to cut Pentagon funding and run for the Democratic presidential nomination in 1952 as a "dollar-saving strong man who could whip the military into shape." Harriman tried to mediate between Johnson and Acheson, a job presidential assistants have routinely undertaken since, even in the middle of crises. Johnson in turn made a bid to recruit Harriman to help force out Acheson, assuring him that he would become the new secretary of state. With that, Harriman went to the Oval Office, where the desk plate read THE BUCK STOPS HERE.

Truman, true to his direct, "Give-him-hell, Harry" personality, called in Johnson on September 11 and fired him. He then walked down the hall and told press secretary Charley Ross and Elsey what had happened. "When he came in," Truman said, "I had a letter of resignation ready. I handed him a pen and told him to sign it. He broke down and cried." Truman described how he waited a bit and then said, "Lou, you've got to sign."

At this point in the Asian crisis, Truman received some good news: Intelligence suggested China's threat to Formosa had begun to wane, and in Pusan, reinforced US and South Korean forces finally held firm. (Truman was unaware that Mao had decided to cancel the Formosa invasion.) With total defeat avoided in Korea, MacArthur proposed a daring breakout maneuver, a leapfrog amphibious assault on the western flank of the North's forces at Inchon, near Seoul. The Joint Chiefs were quite cynical about the plan's chance for success but consented. In orders approved by Truman, MacArthur was to "extend his operations north of the parallel and to make plans for the occupation of North Korea." The directive also banned ground operations north of the

38th parallel if either the Soviets or Chinese entered the war. These expanded objectives for MacArthur reflected Truman's enlargement of his war aims beyond the late June mission of merely restoring the border; now reunification of Korea was on the horizon.

On September 15, the First Marine Division and the Army's Seventh Infantry Division landed at Inchon and quickly recaptured Seoul. That cut off the North Korean forces in the South, and restored the

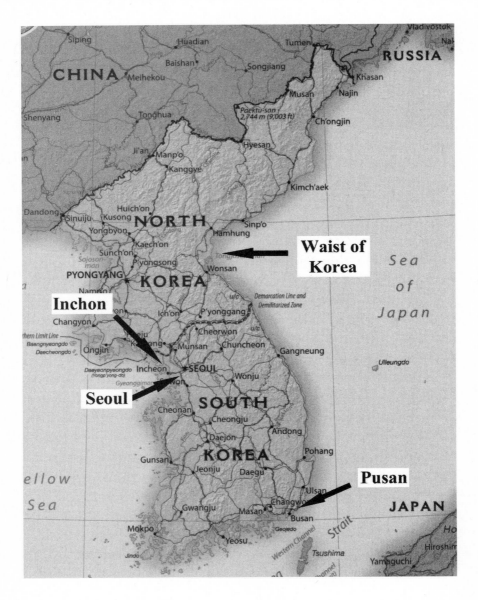

Republic of Korea's government. MacArthur asked permission to pursue retreating North forces beyond the 38th parallel. On September 27, Truman ordered MacArthur to destroy the North Korean armed forces, provided there was "no threat by Russian or Chinese communists to counter our operations militarily." The new secretary of defense, George Marshall, also loosened MacArthur's reins: "We want you to feel unhampered tactically and strategically to proceed north of the 38th parallel." By October 1, South Korean troops crossed the border in pursuit of the retreating remnants of the North's army.

The Korean mission creep moved yet another notch on October 7, when the UN General Assembly approved a US-written resolution on Korea. It reaffirmed the goal of a unified and democratic Korea and authorized "all appropriate steps to be taken to assure stability" throughout the peninsula. The following day, Truman amended Mac-Arthur's guidance. The general was to "continue the action as long as, in your judgment, action by forces under your control offers a reasonable chance of success."

China Joins the War

As MacArthur's battlefield victories mounted and Truman enlarged his war aims, the Chinese prepared to set a trap for UN forces. Mao had foreseen a possible US victory in the South. "They may get so dizzy with success that they may threaten us," Mao said at an August 4 meeting in Peking. He then declared that China would intervene at the timeliest moment, perhaps when MacArthur was in a vulnerable situation.

Kim appealed to Stalin for help on September 29 as UN forces neared the North-South border. Rather than answer Kim directly, Stalin asked Mao two days later to send Chinese soldiers, remarking, "The situation of our Korean friends is getting desperate." Stalin and Mao then began a two-week negotiation about how to respond to the UN's expanded offensive. The two men discussed the possibilities of a "big war" with the United States. "Should we fear this?" Stalin asked rhetorically. "In my opinion, we should not. . . . If war is inevitable, then let it be waged now, and not in a few years when Japanese militarism will be restored."

Mao instructed Foreign Minister Zhou Enlai to pass a warning to the West through the Indian ambassador: the Chinese would intervene if UN troops crossed the parallel. However, intelligence analysts—both in theater and in Washington—believed the Soviet Union did not want global war and that it could control the Chinese, and Truman's advisers discounted Zhou Enlai's statement as a bluff. Based on those assessments, on October 9, MacArthur broadcast a surrender ultimatum to the North. Kim, with Chinese help looming, rejected the demand.

Mao, with assurances of Soviet air cover from Stalin, decided on October 13 to defend North Korea. The next day, he ordered the movement of an estimated 80,000 soldiers of the Chinese Fourth Field Army across the Yalu River, which marked the border, into North Korea. Much of the force had been near the border since July, but American intelligence and reconnaissance operations had failed to detect their staging and preparations.

Wake Island. A Stunt?

MacArthur's successful maneuver at Inchon amplified his already heady self-confidence. "He was itching to overrun all of North Korea and take on China if she entered the fight," Elsey wrote later. Elsey believed that Truman had begun to wonder if MacArthur might disobey orders or ignore restraint. He and another staff member suggested that the president fly to Wake Island in the Pacific west of Hawaii to meet with MacArthur and size up the man face-to-face. Truman agreed.

"I begged to be excused," Acheson later wrote of what he described as the president's "pilgrimage" to Wake Island: "While General MacArthur had many of the attributes of a foreign sovereign, I said, and was quite as difficult as any, it did not seem wise to recognize him as one." With the midterm elections just a few weeks away, Republican strategists viewed the trip as a political stunt, and it likely was.

Contrary to early accounts of MacArthur arriving after Truman, the general met the president's plane when it landed on Wake on October 15. MacArthur was respectful, and the two men generally agreed on a course of action. During the meeting, Truman asked, "What are the chances for Chinese or Soviet interference?"

"Very little . . . We are no longer fearful of the intervention." The general later added, "If the Chinese tried to get down to Pyongyang, there would be the greatest slaughter."

Assistant Secretary of State for Far Eastern Affairs Dean Rusk, who had subbed for Acheson, became alarmed at how quickly Truman ran through his agenda items during the meeting. He knew too short a session would add to the speculation already in the press that Truman's trip to Wake Island was a political act. Rusk passed a note to the president, requesting that he slow down. The president wrote on the back and returned it to Rusk: "Hell no! I want to get out of here before we get into trouble."

Upon his return to the States, Truman triumphantly spoke about the harmony between himself and MacArthur at Wake Island in a radio speech in San Francisco on October 17. "The San Francisco report on Wake was to be the high-water mark of the second term," Elsey wrote later of Truman's time in office. "All went downhill thereafter."

The widely perceived political nature of Truman's pilgrimage to Wake Island reflected the tense mixture of domestic politics and war in Washington in the months leading up to the November 1950 midterm elections. Historian Richard Lebow examined the period and wrote in 1981, "The Korean War only temporarily restored bipartisanship in foreign policy. By August, bipartisanship began to break down under pressure of the upcoming elections; the Republicans had too good an issue in Korea not to exploit it to their advantage." MacArthur's criticism of Truman's policies in August, and the subsequent politically inspired scheming by Secretary of Defense Johnson added to the political divisions. The Republicans previously had cast the Democrats as the party that lost China, and now the GOP labeled the Korean conflict as Truman's War.

Outside of Washington, the Democratic Party faced opposition from the public, and opinion polls showed that unhappiness. Many people had suffered through the Depression, World War II, the meager production of consumer goods in the immediate postwar years, and the 1949 recession. People wanted to get back to the good times, and the GOP preyed on public concerns, to say nothing about the communist witch hunts that drove Washington politics at the time—Commies are in the State Department! Truman increased public discontent in

September when he and Congress established the Defense Production Act of 1950, which allocated many potential consumer materials to the Korean War effort.

In light of both political and public criticism, a victory in North Korea was an appealing prospect to the Democrats. The successful Inchon landing and subsequent encirclement of parts of the North Korean army enhanced that possibility. "The pressures on the administration to liberate North Korea were almost irresistible," Lebow concluded. Truman's authorizing MacArthur to cross the 38th parallel on September 27 reflected the apparent dual goals of military and political triumph. "At this juncture," Lebow wrote, "a stunning victory over the communists must have appeared to Truman, Acheson, and their supporters as the administration's hope for political salvation."

Nevertheless, the Democrats suffered losses in the November 7 midterm elections, but clung to slim majorities in both houses of Congress.

An Entirely New War

MacArthur's offensive in the North met an ominous obstacle on October 25. Elements of the Chinese forces that had deployed to North Korea in mid-October attacked three South Korean divisions 60 miles south of the Chinese border and routed two of them. MacArthur was undeterred by what he considered a small group of 15,000 to 20,000 Chinese "volunteers," but his concerns grew when aerial reconnaissance discovered more Chinese troops crossing the Yalu River bridges into North Korea. When MacArthur ordered air strikes on bridges, his air component commander saw that as a provocative act and informally alerted Washington; Truman ordered the air assaults canceled.

The Joint Chiefs met November 6 and agreed that MacArthur should withdraw to the "waist" of Korea near the North Korean capital of Pyongyang. The military leaders believed, now that the Chinese had entered the war, that the administration should seek a cease-fire through diplomacy. Yet their position was not fully presented to President Truman at an NSC meeting on November 9. Chairman Bradley elected instead to defer to MacArthur by allowing the theater commander to choose tactics. Truman agreed with him and decided not to rescind or change MacArthur's orders from October 8—continue aggressive offensive action, pending further review. Bradley came to regret not stepping in to stop MacArthur. "Unfortunately," Bradley wrote later, "we reached drastically wrong conclusions and decisions." The chairman blamed MacArthur's "wildly erroneous estimates of the situation . . . as well as . . . too much wishful thinking of our own."

Chairman Mao now had MacArthur's armies where he wanted them. "To hook a big fish," one of Mao's generals said, "you must let the fish taste your bait. MacArthur boasts that he has never been defeated. We'll see who is going to wipe out whom." Mao ordered the covert staging of five armies near the border, and when that movement was completed, he added more bait to the hook. He created the illusion of a Chinese retreat on November 8 when he ordered a number of Chinese and North Korean units to withdraw from the battle lines. That move added energy to MacArthur's offensive, and reinforced the earlier US conclusion that the Chinese were bluffing.

By mid-November, MacArthur's forces were in a vulnerable position. The Eighth Army had separated from the Tenth Corps, exposing the former's right flank. (An Army corps then consisted of two or more divisions, and multiple corps constituted a field army.) MacArthur had ordered the disposition in order to occupy all of Korea and blamed the rugged terrain of a mountain range for keeping the two forces separated.

Key Truman advisers—Harriman, secretaries Acheson and Marshall, Bradley, the Joint Chiefs, and others—met without the president in the Pentagon on November 21. Chairman Bradley later called the session "our last real chance to stop MacArthur's proposed ground offensive," which was scheduled to begin in three days. He and the service chiefs disapproved of the risky force disposition and saw a potential disaster in the offing. Coincidently, British military officials also considered MacArthur's forces to be vulnerable to counterattack and urged a pullback. But when these dissenting views were not presented in full to the president, MacArthur's orders remained unchanged. Accordingly, the theater commander readied his armies to kill or capture all remaining enemy forces in North Korea.

On November 24, MacArthur flew from Tokyo to Eighth Army headquarters near the Chongchon River, about fifty miles south of the

China-North Korea border. He toured the battle lines and witnessed the start of his big, end-the-war offensive. He also told reporters in his press contingent, "If this operation is successful, I hope we can get the boys home for Christmas."

Just after sunset on the next day, a massive Chinese military force counterattacked near the spot MacArthur had been the day before. By the 28th, the UN armies were in retreat and his offensive in shambles. Bradley called Truman at dawn that morning with the bad news: "We face an entirely new war."

The President Misspeaks

At 10:00 a.m. on Tuesday, four hours after Bradley's ominous call, President Harry Truman met with his West Wing staff. After coolly dispensing with routine business, Truman changed both the subject and his demeanor. He said in a grave voice, "We've got a terrific situation on our hands. General Bradley called me at six-fifteen this morning. He said that there were two hundred and sixty thousand Chinese troops against MacArthur. MacArthur says he has to go over to the defensive. The Chinese have come in with both feet."

The staff stiffened in silence. The success enjoyed in Korea up until then suddenly seemed illusory. The chance for a quick victory had evaporated, and the chance for general war loomed. After a few beats of stunned stillness, Truman, who was normally ebullient, continued with a downbeat tone. "I'm going to meet with the cabinet this afternoon. General Bradley will be there to discuss the situation. Acheson is informing the congressional committees." Truman paused again, yielding to the tension that had built within him in the previous four hours. His expression grew even more grim, and he seemed to be gripped by powerful emotions. "This is the worst situation we have had yet," he said. "We'll just have to meet it as we've met all the rest."

Truman convened an NSC meeting at 3:00 p.m. in the West Wing's Cabinet Room. Attendees included Acheson, Marshall, Bradley and the Joint Chiefs, and others including Vice President Alben Barkley. In one of the most important meetings of his presidency, Truman decided to do everything possible to keep the Korean conflict from escalating into a world war. Secretary of Defense Marshall seconded that policy, saying America must slow the hostilities and "get out with honor."

The White House scheduled a press conference for Truman on November 30 at 10:30 a.m. in the Executive Office Building across from the West Wing. In the ornate Indian Treaty Room, over two hundred reporters rose as one when Truman arrived. He wore a dark blue suit and a tie that sported a colorful Paul Bunyan carrying a tree on his shoulder. Truman initially read a prepared statement, a bland roadmap of planned next steps in Korea, with no mention of honorable withdrawal. He then took questions from reporters. In testimony to the tense situation and his own taut emotions, Truman cut off each reporter mid-question and offered a terse answer. As Acheson had noted, Truman occasionally let his mouth race ahead of his mind. He also condescendingly addressed each correspondent by either his first name or nickname and made clear that there would be no news that morning. *New York Daily News* reporter Jack Doherty nevertheless tried to dig out a reportable nugget and asked, "Mr. President, will the United Nations troops be allowed to bomb across the Manchurian border?"

"I can't answer that question this morning." After another question about specific battlefield tactics, Truman assured the press that the United States would take all necessary steps to meet the military situation. Doherty bored in again.

"Will that include the atomic bomb?" Startled, the other reporters looked up from their pads.

"There has always been active consideration of its use. I don't want to see it used. It is a terrible weapon, and it should not be used on innocent men, women, and children who have nothing whatever to do with this military aggression."

"Mr. President, you said this depends on United Nations action," NBC's Frank Bourgholtzer asked. "Does that mean that we wouldn't use the atomic bomb except on a United Nations authorization?"

"No, it doesn't mean that at all," Truman snapped. He then made two badly worded points, with the first implying the UN's lead role: "The action against communist China depends on the action of the United Nations." The second was untrue: "The military commander in the field will have charge of the use of the weapons, as he always has." Suddenly, the reporters had some news. By law, only the president could direct the use of atomic weapons.

After a few more questions, Truman's impatience and anger with the press for what he considered falsehoods from journalists about his administration's actions tumbled out. "All these attacks and speculations and lies that have been told on the members of this government have not helped that situation one little bit," he said. Truman continued his scolding and ended the press conference with a testy statement. "I am getting tired of all this foolishness."

Within minutes of the press conference's conclusion, the news wires overheated. The United Press carried this bulletin at 10:47 a.m.:

WA10A WASHINGTON NOV 30—(UP)—PRESIDENT TRUMAN SAID TODAY THAT THE UNITED STATES HAS UNDER CONSIDERATION THE USE OF THE ATOMIC BOMB IN CONNECTION WITH THE WAR IN KOREA.

The White House quickly issued a correction to Truman's statement about the bomb. Truman and his advisers had never considered its use, and they put the option aside after Truman's gaffe. However, the British reacted strongly, and Congressional Republicans loudly added to the tempest. Already stunned by the consequences of his overreach in Korea, the president further damaged his handling of the crisis when his emotions caused him to misspeak dangerously in a critical moment.

The Chinese forced an immediate and bloody retreat by UN forces, and the Pentagon scrambled to find a way out of the dire military situation. Lieutenant General Matthew Ridgway, Army deputy chief of staff for operations, spoke alarmingly from a backbench at a December 3 Joint Chiefs meeting about MacArthur's dangerous circumstances. He recommended an immediate direct order to MacArthur to "correct a state of affairs that was going rapidly from bad to disastrous"; none of the chiefs responded. Afterward, Ridgway approached Air Force chief Vandenberg, an old friend. "Why don't the Joint Chiefs send orders to MacArthur and tell him what to do?"

"What good would that do?" Vandenberg asked back. "He wouldn't obey orders. What can we do?"

"You can relieve any commander who won't obey orders, can't you?" Ridgway countered. Vandenberg did not reply.

Throughout December, UN forces, including the US Eighth Army and Tenth Corps, retreated with heavy losses to a broad area southeast of Seoul. Upon the accidental death of the Eighth Army's commander, Lieutenant General Walton Walker, Ridgway assumed command of the Eighth on December 26. He energized the troops and began to stabilize his sector of the front, despite the introduction of Soviet air support for the Chinese and North Korean troops. By February 1951, the Chinese military force had outrun its logistic support tail, and Chinese commanders eased their operational pace. Ridgway countered with a successful offensive push back toward Seoul.

President Truman fired MacArthur in April 1951. The president had had enough after the general repeatedly defied orders and communicated his opposition to Truman's policies to a Republican congressman. MacArthur's recall, however, proved to be a political disaster for the president. Republicans called for Truman's impeachment, regardless of the president's prerogatives as commander in chief. Nevertheless, MacArthur's successor, General Ridgway, provided successful leadership on the battlefront, and American troops and their allies eventually recaptured lost ground and gained a stalemate near the 38th parallel. UN and Chinese/North Korean representatives began truce talks in July 1951, although many bloody battles ensued while the lengthy negotiations dragged on. The two sides signed an armistice two years later.

Dwight Eisenhower broke the twenty-year Democratic hold on the White House in the 1952 election, and the GOP also won small majorities in the House and Senate. The MacArthur saga had added to the public's discontent with Truman's War and the Democratic Party.

Assessment

Truman acted boldly and decisively in his initial reaction to the North Korean invasion of the South. However, faulty decision making during the fourth and fifth months of the crisis led to a disastrous setback on the battlefield. US and UN military forces eventually overcame that tactical defeat, but a bloody three-year war ensued.

President Truman's crisis management errors have become textbook examples of "groupthink," a term coined by Yale research psychologist Irving Janis. The expression has worked its way into the lexicon of crisis analysis because the dynamic has also challenged presidents who followed Truman. Janis defined the malady as "the psychological drive for consensus at any cost that suppresses disagreement and prevents the appraisal of alternatives in cohesive decision-making groups."

Groupthink arose from conditions within the Truman team that to a casual observer might seem intuitively valuable—the team enjoyed significant solidarity and little friction. Each man respected the others and valued consensus. However, this circumstance stifled healthy disagreement. Team harmony only increased when Secretary of Defense Johnson was fired and replaced by George Marshall. As a former secretary of state and chairman of the Joint Chiefs, Marshall was reluctant to second-guess his successors.

Additionally, any dissent within a department about proposed actions never made it up the stovepipe to the president if the secretary or general discounted advice from subordinates. Examples of this include the two occasions in November when Bradley didn't fully brief Truman on the Joint Chiefs' grave concern about MacArthur's overreach. Also adding to the harmful harmony was another seemingly illogical dynamic—MacArthur's success at Inchon. This led to euphoria and optimism among the team members, the "intoxication of success," which in turn led to "wishful thinking" that no dissenting voice was available to puncture.

From the start, Truman forcefully favored an aggressive response. The president stated in passing at the first NSC meeting that he had an open mind but then proceeded to espouse his belligerent position. "By God," he said to his secretaries of state and defense, "I'm going to let them have it!" His crisis advisers fell in line, not necessarily through sycophancy but rather because of the group dynamics. It was in this context that the president fostered the mission creep within military operations. The president's main crisis goal started with restoration of the North-South border in June. By early October, after MacArthur's shift to offensive operations, reunification of Korea was the target. Total destruction of the enemy in North Korea followed in

November. Periodic enlargement of crisis objectives, without full consideration of potential untoward consequences, led to ever more risky
situations. Also, wishful thinking about the unlikelihood of a Chinese
counterattack led Truman and his team to discount very real battlefield
risks. On the other hand, MacArthur's sweep into North Korea looked
great for Democratic strategists in the run-up to the November midterm elections. As in all crises, domestic politics have flavored virtually
everything done in the White House, a constant that will be evident in
subsequent chapters.

Truman diverted his ire after the Chinese counterattack to the press
and political foes, especially during his November 30 press conference.
This too is a symptom of group solidarity—the president didn't want
to blame a team member for the dangerous mess, so he picked on the
press. And yet he had many reasons to fault his advisers by November
1950. During the two-week period in November before the start of
MacArthur's end-the-war offensive, Acheson, Marshall, and Bradley
saw what was coming. Political scientist Richard Neustadt captured
the quandary: "No one went to Truman because everyone thought
someone else should go." Acheson agreed: "We were all deeply apprehensive. We were frank with one another, but not frank enough."

Looking back nearly sixty-five years, there is irony in the way the
nation's perception of President Truman has changed. The public and
his political opponents faulted Truman for poor crisis decision making
during the Korean War, as have political scientists since then, but his
stock over time has risen nonetheless. Multiple polls in recent years
have ranked Truman in the "near great" category of presidents following those in the top group—Washington, Lincoln, and Franklin
Roosevelt. He appears in the top ten in virtually all polls. History has
proven that Truman deserves credit for containing Soviet expansion on
several fronts, including Korea, despite his missteps during the crisis.

CHAPTER 2

DWIGHT EISENHOWER
Part 1. 1956 Suez War
Confronting Allies

With the 1956 presidential election only eight days away, President and Mrs. Eisenhower traveled from Washington, DC, to Florida on the morning of October 29 for campaign appearances in Miami and Jacksonville. Later in the day, the couple and staff flew to Richmond, Virginia, for another reelection rally. President Eisenhower was in the midst of that event when an urgent wire service report reached the State Department in Washington. "FLASH-FLASH-FLASH. MAJOR ISRAELI FORCES HAVE INVADED EGYPT AND HEAVY FIGHTING IS UNDERWAY."

As Eisenhower hurriedly flew back to Washington, his staff organized a White House crisis meeting at 7:15 p.m. Joining the president were Secretary of State John Foster Dulles, Undersecretary of State Herbert Hoover, Jr., Secretary of Defense Charles Wilson, Chairman of the Joint Chiefs of Staff Admiral Arthur Radford, CIA director Allen Dulles, and several Eisenhower staff members.

President Eisenhower started the meeting mad. He immediately directed Secretary Dulles to contact the Israelis. "All right Foster, you tell 'em, goddamn it, we're going to apply sanctions, we're going to the United Nations, we're going to do everything that there is so we can stop this thing."

Admiral Radford counseled patience: "This will be all over in a few days."

Why is that? the president asked.

"The Israelis will be to the Suez Canal within two or three days."

"It is far more serious than that," Dulles interjected. "The canal is likely to be disrupted, and oil pipe lines through the Middle East broken. If these things happen, we must expect British and French intervention. In fact, they appear to be ready for it and may even have concerted their action with the Israelis." Dulles added that US communications with the French and Britain had dried up during the last ten days. When Radford urged that US action be guided by principle, Eisenhower instantly agreed and adopted that point as his personal attitude during the meeting—principled US reaction to the Israeli attack.

"We should let the British know at once our position," the president stated flatly. "And nothing justifies double-crossing us," he added, angry with America's closest allies. He went further and stated that the United States must act honorably, even if that meant opposing the British. "I don't fancy helping the Egyptians, but I feel that our word must be made good."

America's "word" in this case referred to the 1950 Tripartite Declaration (or Agreement) that bound the United States, Great Britain, and France to guarantee the borders between Israel and its Arab neighbors. In the aftermath of the creation of the state of Israel in 1948 and the Arab-Israeli War that immediately followed, the three allies wanted to limit sales of arms to both Israel and the Arab states in order to reduce the chance of future violence, and they needed an alternate arrangement to stabilize the region. To that end, the central tenet of the declaration that applied to Israel and the Arab states declared that if "any of these states was preparing to violate frontiers or armistice lines," the three powers "would immediately take action, both within and outside of the United Nations, to prevent it." In the present circumstances, the Tripartite called for the three allies to act in concert against Israel.

The minutes of the meeting show that the participants used the word "pledge" nine times when referring to the Tripartite. For example, Ike observed at one point: "In these circumstances perhaps we cannot be bound by our traditional alliances, but must instead face the question how to make good on our pledge." With that remark, Ike defined the pickle he found himself in—choosing between two of his basic instincts. He was an "unabashed believer in conciliation and compromise," according to his adviser Emmet Hughes, yet his principles tugged him in the opposite direction. Perhaps his anger with his allies' deceit tipped him toward principle. Regardless, the moral high ground seized by the former World War II Army general at this early point in the crisis would later prove to be challenging terrain. The president's declaration of his preferred solution at the start of the incident only added to the potential for problems during the crisis by virtually eliminating alternative options from consideration.

Later that evening, Eisenhower met with several Republican politicians, who told the president his campaign was at risk. The men suggested that forceful US opposition to the Israeli aggression would backfire on Ike politically. Eisenhower later wrote of their message: "With many of our citizens of the Eastern Seaboard emotionally involved in the Zionist cause, this, it was believed, could possibly bring political defeat."

Background

The origins of what became known as the 1956 Suez War were complex, but a few key points and events stand out. After defeating Germany and its allies in World War I, the Allied Powers—Great Britain, France, Russia, the United States, and others—dictated the breakup of their major opponents, the German, Austro-Hungarian, and Ottoman Empires. The newly formed League of Nations, a predecessor to the UN, mandated Great Britain in 1923 to control Ottoman Syria, and the British subsequently divided the territory into two sectors, Palestine and Transjordan. The British governed Palestine and allowed the Hashemite family to rule what later became Jordan.

Great Britain terminated its mandate in May 1948, and the nongovernmental Jewish Agency immediately declared the formation of the state of Israel. The United States quickly recognized the new country. However, military forces from Egypt, Jordan, Syria, and Iraq just as rapidly began attacking Jewish settlements. The ensuing

1948 Arab-Israeli War ended the next year with individual armistices between Israel and her neighbors. Israel gained control of nearly 80 percent of the former Palestine. Egypt controlled the Gaza Strip, a small enclave on the Mediterranean coast between Egypt and Israel. Jordan gained East Jerusalem and the West Bank, a 2,200-square-mile area sandwiched between Jordan and Israel that is west of the Jordan River. The UN agreed to monitor the cease-fire and armistice agreements. A flood of Jewish immigrants began to populate the new nation, but cross-border raids and Egypt's blocking of Israeli shipping through the Suez Canal kept tensions simmering.

In this volatile situation, the Soviet Union and the West jockeyed for influence. Egypt's president, Gamal Abdel Nasser, had sought arms from the West to counter Israel's increasing military power. But he became disappointed with the amount of weapons offered by Great Britain and France, and he viewed France's growing arms sales to Israel as destabilizing. Nasser then turned to the United Sates, counting on Eisenhower's recently declared "even-handed" Arab-Israeli policy to facilitate US arms transfers. Eisenhower initially agreed in November 1955 but asked in return that Egypt enter into a Western-sponsored mutual defense agreement. When Nasser balked, the Eisenhower administration withdrew the weapons sale offer. Seizing that opening, the Soviets engineered a $200 million arms deal via Czechoslovakia in return for Egyptian cotton. Political scientists Edward Drachman and Alan Shank in their 1997 book, *Presidents and Foreign Policy*, concluded that the Czech deal changed the regional balance of power, opened the door for Soviet influence, and started a chain of events that led to the 1956 Suez War.

Though he declined to sell arms, Eisenhower had offered in late 1955 to join Great Britain in helping fund Nasser's grand plan to increase agriculture production in Egypt through the construction of the Aswan Dam on the Nile. But opposition to the offer arose in Congress, especially from senators representing cotton-producing states and the Israel lobby. Distracted by illness in June 1956, Ike allowed Secretary Dulles to withdraw the Aswan assistance offer on July 19. That prompted Nasser to play his highest card—the Suez Canal.

French engineers using Egyptian labor had built the Suez Canal, and upon its 1869 opening, the Suez Canal Company controlled its operation. French investors owned 66 percent of the company's stock, the ruler of Egypt, Mohammed Said, who governed under the suzerainty of the Ottoman Empire, held 44 percent. Said's successor sold Egypt's stake in 1875 to Great Britain, which had found the canal to be critical for shipping to and from its Asian colonies.

When civil unrest in 1882 threatened the Egyptian ruler, Khedive Tewfik, Britain invaded Egypt and wrested the country from the Ottomans. Egypt became a British protectorate in 1914, thus ensuring

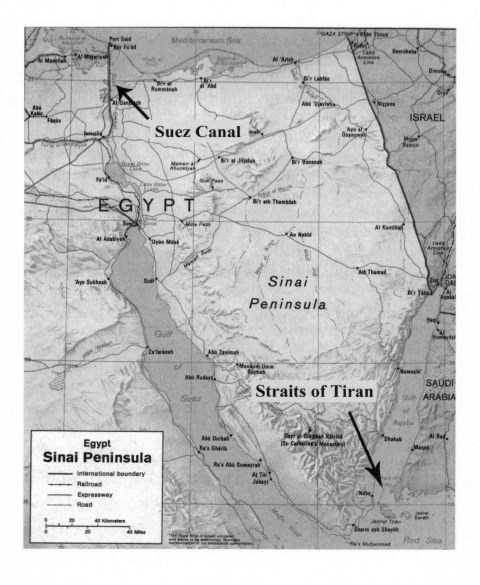

continued British and French control of the canal. British troops occupied Egypt through 1936, when most withdrew except for 10,000 soldiers left to guard the canal. The 1954 Anglo-Egyptian Treaty directed the withdrawal of the remaining units but allowed Britain the right to intervene if the canal was threatened. Given that oil tankers en route to Europe made up two-thirds of canal traffic, its continued operation in a manner sympathetic to Britain and France was critical to those countries. The remaining British troops left Egypt in mid-June 1956.

Nasser nationalized the Suez Canal on July 26, 1956, and closed the Straits of Tiran, which Israeli shipping needed for access to the Red Sea from the Gulf of Aqaba. Britain and France immediately began to rattle their neocolonial sabers. Eisenhower responded with "a strategy of delay, cooling off, playing for time, diplomacy, and negotiations." That made sense, given Ike's proclivity for conciliation and compromise. What he didn't know was that Britain, France, and Israel had devised a secret plan to redress their individual grievances with Egypt.

The three countries hatched their plot that summer, agreeing to coordinate military operations to regain control of the Suez Canal. During October, the conspirators conducted several hoaxes to obscure their planning and preparations. For example, Israel acted as if it was preparing to assault Jordan, and France and Britain went through the motions of searching for diplomatic guarantees of international passage through the canal. On October 24, representatives of the three countries met in Sèvres, near Paris, to sign off on the final plan. Israel would invade Egypt's Sinai Peninsula, a 115-mile stretch of desert that separated Israel's southwest border from the Suez Canal, and thus appear to threaten the canal. Britain, with assistance from France, would intervene in accordance with the 1954 Anglo-Egyptian Treaty and reassert control of the canal.

On Saturday afternoon, two days before the secretly planned October 29 Israeli invasion, Eisenhower checked into Washington's Walter Reed Army Hospital. He was there for a scheduled overnight physical, and his White House physician, Dr. Howard Snyder, was relieved to have him there. He had found Ike exhausted the previous day, with his pulse at 100 and irregular.

Eisenhower underwent multiple tests on Saturday, most of which were routine, but the sixty-six-year-old president's health problems required extended examinations. He had suffered a heart attack the year before, and on the previous June 9, surgeons removed a blocked section of his intestine. Nevertheless, the physicians reported that he was doing well, and the president returned to the White House on Sunday afternoon. His political advisers rejoiced and hoped they had removed the president's health from the debate surrounding his reelection bid.

Eisenhower went directly to the Oval Office to prepare for his trip to Florida and Virginia. He had not campaigned extensively, so this trip to Dixie was important to match the interest there for his Democratic opponent, Adlai Stevenson. Once at his desk, Ike called in Emmet Hughes, his speechwriter and confidant, to help him make final edits to his stump speeches.

Hughes arrived to find the president in a foul mood over breaking news from the Middle East. Israeli armed forces had mobilized, and Mideast hostilities, perhaps with Jordan, appeared likely. Ignorant of the secret British, French, and Israeli plans, Eisenhower could only guess what was afoot: "I just can't figure out what the Israelis think they're up to. . . . Maybe they're thinking they just can't survive without more land . . . But I don't see how they can survive without coming to some honorable and peaceful terms with the whole Arab world that surrounds them." During their conversation, other aides brought more bad news—the Brits were joining France in encouraging Israel to attack Egypt, another facet of the secret strategy.

Ike's temper rose again. "I just can't believe it," Ike said of Britain. "I can't believe they would be so stupid as to invite on themselves all the Arab hostility to Israel." He then turned to the intervention's impact on America. "Are they going to dare us—dare us—to defend the Tripartite Declaration?"

Hughes understood that two other simultaneous challenges had the president's attention. The Soviets faced a grave situation in Hungary, one of their East European satellite states behind the Iron Curtain. A few days before, the Hungarian people had revolted and ousted the Soviet-imposed communist government. Surprisingly, the Soviets publicly agreed to negotiate with the populist revolutionary leaders, but Western experts viewed the move as a likely delaying tactic before a Soviet military intervention. Eisenhower worried about what the

United States and NATO should do if violence ensued in Hungary. Closer to home was the presidential election campaign, now in its final days.

The president wearily arose from his chair and started to walk slowly toward the chrysanthemum-filled Rose Garden. The normally optimistic and cheerful man seemed depressed. "Well, I better get out of here—or despite all those doctors—these things will have my blood pressure up to 490."

The looming crisis in the Middle East would test more than his heart. Also at risk were his principles and his leadership of the NATO allies.

Great Britain and France Join the Hostilities

On October 30, the day after Israel invaded Egypt and Eisenhower hurriedly returned to Washington, the president met with Secretary Dulles, Deputy Secretary Hoover, and several staff members in the Oval Office. Hughes noted Ike's haggard appearance as he arrived— "His face drawn, eyes heavy with fatigue, worry, or both."

Though unaware of the secret Britain-France-Israel war strategy, Dulles briefed the president on a number of indicators of such a possibility; Hoover agreed that a coordinated operation was likely under way. That tentative conclusion led to a discussion of how the president should respond. "There's the danger of our being drawn into the hostilities as we were in World Wars I and II," Dulles said, "with the difference that this time it appears that the British and French might well be considered the aggressors in the eyes of the world."

"In my judgment," the president responded, "the French and the British do not have an adequate cause for war. Egyptian action in nationalizing the canal was not enough to justify this."

The men speculated that the United Kingdom and France may have assumed the United States would side with them instead of the Arabs. Dulles argued along that line: "Their thinking might be that they will confront us with a de facto situation."

"I don't see much value in an unworthy and unreliable ally," the president said, "and that the necessity to support them might not be as great as they believed."

The meeting broke up after less than an hour, and several of the men offered encouragement to Secretary Dulles, who had become ill with an undiagnosed intestinal ailment. The problem would grow worse during the unfolding crisis and eventually become life-threatening. Considering Ike's heavy reliance on Dulles, the secretary's health would impinge on the president's crisis decision making.

Later that day, the president exchanged a series of cables with British prime minister Anthony Eden and French prime minister Guy Mollet. In the first message to Eden, Eisenhower raised their Tripartite commitments, but Eden brushed that aside and blamed Egypt for the problem. Mollet advised Eisenhower that he and Eden would soon issue an ultimatum to Israel and Egypt—withdraw their troops from the Canal Zone in twelve hours, or France and Great Britain would "assume temporary control of the canal." Ike finished the day-long cable exchange by expressing to both Eden and Mollet his "deep concern at the prospect of this drastic action." Shortly afterward, Britain and France vetoed a UN Security Council resolution asking all UN members to stay out of the fighting. Although Eden and Mollet acknowledged their intentions of seizing the canal to Eisenhower, they said nothing of their coordination of the entire operation with Israel.

Eisenhower also spoke that day with Arthur Flemming, head of the Office of Defense Mobilization, about oil supply and transport. They discussed how the crisis might affect US needs but generally focused on the possibility of the British and French asking the US to send oil tankers. "They may be planning to present us with a fait accompli," Ike said, "then expecting us to foot the bill." His emotional temperature began to rise when he discussed his allies' behavior. "I am inclined to think that those who began this operation," Eisenhower said, "should be left to work out their own oil problems—to boil in their own oil."

In his bedroom that night, Eisenhower talked about the crisis with his son John. "Well," he mused, "it looks as if we're in for trouble. If the Israelis keep going—and if the UN says so—I may have to use force to stop them. . . . Then I'd lose the election. There would go New York, New Jersey, Pennsylvania, and Connecticut, at least."

"Wowie," John gasped. "Couldn't you hold off taking action until after the election is over?"

"That might be too late. We'll just have to see."

Dawn on October 31 brought a tough decision for the president. Nasser asked the United States to direct the Sixth Fleet, which the US Navy based in the Mediterranean Sea, to stop what he saw as an impending British-French invasion of Egypt. Since Eden and Mollet had threatened such action the day before, Eisenhower found himself in a corner. He had pledged support under the Tripartite, but military action against his NATO allies was unthinkable. The president ducked Nasser's request, and gave the Egyptian a vague answer: The United States "would do everything we can in the United Nations."

Adlai Stevenson, Eisenhower's Democratic opponent in the election, eagerly second-guessed the president as the crisis grew. Stevenson charged that the administration's foreign policy was "at an absolute dead end," and pointed to Ike's many failures. The influential newspaper columnists, brothers Joseph and Stewart Alsop, declared that Eisenhower's Middle East policy "has been a dismal and desperate failure."

Britain and France commenced air attacks late that afternoon. The secret plan had called for the assault twelve hours earlier, but fifteen American transport aircraft, lined up at Cairo-West Airport, one of the primary targets, caused the delay. The US Air Force had deployed the planes there to evacuate Americans from Egypt, a measure that the Soviets seized upon to claim American collusion. British prime minister Eden frantically postponed the first wave of British attack aircraft until the American aircraft had departed. Once the attacks commenced, Nasser sank a ship loaded with rocks and concrete in the canal to block its use. He would go on to sink thirty-two vessels in the canal but claimed British aircraft had bombed them.

President Eisenhower decided to address the nation on live television about the crisis in Egypt. Due to speak at 7:00 p.m., Eisenhower received a draft speech at 3:15 p.m. from Dulles, whose condition had worsened, and didn't like it. He told Hughes to start over and gave him broad guidelines. Hughes embarked on a frantic two-hour speech-writing crisis within a crisis. "We go past 6:00 still dictating, typing, pencil-editing with Dulles reviewing text as it came back from the typewriter," Hughes recalled the secretary's condition later. "He is ashen gray, heavy-lidded, strained. His shoulders seem to sag as he murmurs: 'I'm just sick about the bombings . . . the idea of planes over Cairo right now!'"

In the Cabinet Room, Hughes underlined key words in the speech text, and then passed one page at a time to Eisenhower for his first read-through. At 6:56, the president stood up to walk into the Oval Office and said to Hughes, "Boy, this is taking it right off the stove, isn't it?"

Internal Debate

At 9:00 a.m. on Thursday, November 1, President Eisenhower met with his full National Security Council in the Cabinet Room. The UN General Assembly had scheduled a 5:00 p.m. session that day to consider the Suez crisis. Ambassador Henry Cabot Lodge, Jr., planned to introduce a cease-fire resolution, and the main objective of the NSC meeting was to discuss the wording of the resolution. The gravely ill Dulles laid out his proposal to assert American leadership against colonialism and keep newly independent countries from turning away from the United States to the Soviet Union. He urged that the resolution wording reflect the theme the president had espoused from the start: stop the French and British intervention.

In the discussion that followed, Harold Stassen, Ike's staff aide for arms control, repeatedly raised objections to Dulles's arguments. He maintained that while Britain and France had erred badly, US relations with the two countries were preeminent. "It seems to me that the future of Great Britain and of France is still the most important consideration for the United States, and that all our efforts should now be directed toward a cease-fire." He proposed a simple cease-fire resolution, one that did not castigate the aggressors. Dulles disagreed, and the men debated back and forth. Ike joined the talk at several points and in one instance emphatically offered his assessment of Britain and France: "I believe these powers are going downhill with the kind of policy that they were engaged at the moment in carrying out." Ike ordered a carefully worded draft resolution. During the night of November 1–2, the UN General Assembly adopted the American resolution, which called for the simple cease-fire and withdrawal of forces endorsed by Stassen.

The Suez crisis deepened the next day. Britain, France, and Israel ignored the UN resolution and continued their military operations.

By then Israeli forces controlled most of the Sinai Peninsula and had destroyed the Egyptian air force. Additionally, one hundred British and French warships and troop transports neared the Egyptian coast. On Saturday, saboteurs blew up three oil pipelines that crossed Syria from Iraq to the Mediterranean Sea. At the same time in Washington, Dulles entered Walter Reed Hospital for emergency surgery for a perforated colon caused by cancer. While Ike would subsequently accept advice from Dulles's deputy Hoover, the president generally acted as his own secretary of state as the crisis continued.

On November 4, the UN turned to another crisis, with the Security Council voting on a resolution that called for Soviet withdrawal from Hungary. The Soviets vetoed the measure, and within hours the Soviet Red Army invaded Hungary with 200,000 troops and 4,000 tanks. The Hungarian government fled, and the Soviets installed a new government. Eisenhower wrote later that any intervention by the United States against the Soviets in Hungary would have led to general war. He had no choice but to stand aside.

Cease-Fire

At dawn on November 5, British and French paratroopers jumped into key areas near Port Said, Egypt, at the mouth of the canal. Other forces followed them ashore during the day, and Port Said quickly fell to the Europeans. In response, Soviet premier Nikolai Bulganin cabled Eden, Mollet, and Israeli prime minister David Ben-Gurion, warning that he was prepared to counter their aggression with military force and restore peace. He proposed joint operations with the United States to stop the fighting, but also issued a threat to Eisenhower that would be common in future Mideast conflicts: "If this war is not stopped, it is fraught with danger and can grow into [a] third world war."

Eisenhower immediately met with his advisers to determine a response to the Soviet Union. The president made clear that he wanted no joint operations with the Soviets and would work through the UN on all actions. Eisenhower also suggested that the Bulganin overture was an attempt to divert attention from their mess in Hungary, though he was not unconcerned about a possible Soviet intervention in the Mideast crisis. "We have to be positive and clear in our every word, every step. And if those fellows start something, we may have to hit 'em—and, if necessary, with *everything* in the bucket."

On Election Day, November 6, the president and Mrs. Eisenhower traveled by limousine to their home in Gettysburg, Pennsylvania, to vote. While they were en route, ominous news reports filtered into Washington about possible Soviet military flight activity to the Mideast. US ambassador Chip Bohlen in Moscow cabled that the Soviet attitude had grown ominous and that he thought the Soviets might actually do something if a cease-fire didn't take hold immediately. That led the president's aide, Colonel Andrew Goodpaster, to arrange for the president to take a helicopter to Washington after voting.

In London, Prime Minister Eden was under attack from multiple opponents of the war—the press, political opponents, and his own cabinet. Public pressure on the pound and gold reserves severely tested the government's financial liquidity. British Deputy Prime Minister Rab Butler called his friend, US treasury secretary George Humphrey, and asked for a $1.5 billion loan. Humphrey said the money was available but only if Britain observed the UN cease-fire resolution and withdrew from Egypt. Eden soon capitulated, and he and his cabinet decided to accept the cease-fire that night. Prime Minister Mollet agreed after some back and forth. The invasion forces had been ashore in Egypt for only a day and a half, and Israel had already stopped fighting.

Upon Eisenhower's arrival at the White House, his staff briefed him on the cease-fire decisions by Eden and Mollet. The president reached the beleaguered Eden on the phone. "First of all," Ike said, "I can't tell you how pleased we are that you found it possible to accept the cease-fire."

"We are going to cease firing tonight," Eden said with a hint of equivocation. Without conditions? the president asked.

"We cease firing tonight at midnight provided we are not attacked," Eden said, continuing his ambiguous tone. The president felt his anger well.

"If you don't get out of Port Said tomorrow," Eisenhower said firmly, "I'll cause a run on the pound and drive it down to zero!"

Eden and Mollet conferred shortly thereafter and both ordered their respective forces to cease hostilities at midnight, London time. The president's next task was to force Britain, France, and Israel to withdraw their military forces from Egypt, and get UN peacekeeping units quickly into the conflict area. While the president and Hoover sent firm demands to the Israelis, Ike turned to oil supply as a means for ensuring European withdrawal. It was a dicey strategy because the United States needed to keep the primary Arab oil exporter—Saudi Arabia—on good terms with the West and not imperil the European economies in the long term. To that end, Eisenhower made a deal with the Saudis. If they continued to pump oil through an intact pipeline to the West, he promised to ensure that none of it would go to France and Great Britain until they withdrew their troops. And the president understood the stakes: "I am quite certain that unless we can restore very soon the Mideast as the principal source of oil supply, there is nothing we can do to save Western Europe."

The last of the British and French forces departed Egypt on December 22. Forcing Israel to withdraw was harder, despite multiple UN resolutions condemning Israel's intransience. Eisenhower, battling the American Jewish community and members of Congress, finally prevailed. The last Israeli troops withdrew from their positions near the canal and the Straits of Tiran on the Red Sea and returned to Israel on March 16, 1957. National boundaries were thus returned to pre-crisis conditions—status quo ante. A month later, salvage crews had removed all sunken ships from the canal, and the severed pipelines in Syria were repaired soon afterward.

Assessment

Eisenhower managed the crisis with bold and principled action, and in the short term achieved successes—stopping the fighting and forcing the UK, France, and Israel to withdraw from Egypt. He publicly sought collective action through the UN but privately pressured his former World War II allies and NATO partners, Britain and France. Ike risked domestic political backlash by reining in the Israelis but did so anyway. At the most critical moment, Eisenhower used geopolitical levers at his disposal and American heft in the international oil and financial markets, to gain a cease-fire.

Nikita Khrushchev, then first secretary of the Soviet Communist Party, quickly claimed the Soviets had terminated the crisis by forcing

British and French compliance with the UN cease-fire resolution. But he later conceded in his memoir the saber rattling was a bluff. One of Eden's cabinet members, Anthony Nutting, also discounted the Soviet impact. In his memoir, he listed the most important reasons for the cease-fire: political opposition to the war in Britain, which included Nutting himself, who had resigned during the crisis; the closing of the canal and reduced oil supplies; and, most importantly, the run on the pound.

The American public approved of Eisenhower's actions. He won reelection in a landslide, winning 57 percent of the popular vote and a huge Electoral College majority. Further, an early December Gallup poll found 75 percent of respondents supported Eisenhower, up from 67 percent the previous August. However, some Washington insiders criticized Eisenhower's decision to oppose his NATO allies and spoke up vigorously at the time. These included, among others, Dean Acheson, Truman's secretary of state; George Kennan, the architect of the American postwar policy of Soviet containment; the Alsop brothers; and newspaper columnists Walter Lippmann and Chalmers Roberts.

Over the longer term, however, Eisenhower's crisis decisions had several adverse effects on US international interests. In Britain, Eden's government collapsed, and the war signaled the end of the country's reign as a world power. In France, Mollet lasted until the following spring. The absence of American support for France in Egypt echoed the US refusal to help that country retain control of Indochina in the mid-1950s. In light of the perceived threat from the Soviet Union during the crisis, France began to question whether the US nuclear umbrella extended to its territory. Charles de Gaulle, when he came to power in 1958, aggressively pursued France's development of her own nuclear weapons. In 1966, France withdrew from the integrated NATO military command. When the United States got bogged down in Vietnam, Britain and France offered little help.

Nasser became an Arab hero in the Middle East, and his anti-US rhetoric gained even more stridency. The Soviets gained substantially from the emergency too. In the years that followed, they claimed to be the pro-Arab counterweight to Western neocolonialism in the Mideast. The late Kenneth Thompson, the longtime director of the University of Virginia's Miller Center of Public Affairs, wrote about

Eisenhower's actions: "He understood the principle of what was right for America . . . but was somehow unprepared for the advantages that the Soviet Union gained when the United States turned against its allies in the Suez Crisis."

As the years passed, two people quite close to the crisis joined critics of Eisenhower's Suez decisions—Richard Nixon and Eisenhower himself. Nixon criticized Eisenhower in his 1978 memoir: "In retrospect, I believe that our actions were a serious mistake. . . . The most tragic result was that Britain and France were so humiliated and discouraged by the Suez crisis that they lost the will to play a major role on the world scene." Nixon also blamed Eisenhower for planting the seeds for the 1967 Arab-Israeli War. Concluding his argument, he offered the following assessment without further explanation: "I have often felt that if the Suez crisis had not arisen during the heat of a presidential campaign a different decision would have been made."

In 1987, Nixon revealed that Eisenhower, after he had left office, had told him that Suez was his "major foreign policy mistake." Ike said the same thing to Israeli ambassador Avraham Harman during a 1967 meeting in Gettysburg.

Finally, the two Dulles brothers had secretly pulled for Britain, France, and Israel to succeed. Allen, the CIA director, cabled his station chief in London when the Brits were pondering the cease-fire order: "Either way, we'll back 'em up if they do it fast." After the crisis subsided, several European officials including British foreign secretary Selwyn Lloyd visited Foster at Walter Reed Hospital.

"Why didn't you go through with it and get Nasser down?" Dulles asked.

"Foster," Lloyd responded, "why didn't you give us a wink?"

"Oh. I couldn't do anything like *that!*"

Part 2. U-2 Shoot-down, 1960

Crisis Mismanagement

Nikita Khrushchev awoke in his home in Lenin Hills above the Moscow River to the sound of a ringing telephone. Shaking the sleep from his eyes, the Soviet premier picked up the receiver and heard a voice say, "Minister of Defense Marshal Malinovsky reporting." It was 5:00 a.m. on May 1, 1960.

The marshal informed him that a high altitude American aircraft had crossed the southern border with Afghanistan and was headed northwest; the flight profile repeated those of other similar flights detected over the previous four years. Khrushchev ordered Malinovsky, as he had during the last flight on April 9, to shoot it down. The marshal replied that he had already given the order, but in view of the May Day holiday, he worried aloud about a repeat of April 9 when lax missile crews failed to engage the aircraft.

Later in the day, the annual May Day celebration featured Soviet tanks and mobile missile launchers rumbling across Red Square, a scene often shown in those days on US newsreel clips. Under cloudy skies and with temperatures in the forties, Khrushchev and other officials watched and saluted from the reviewing stand atop Lenin's Mausoleum. At one point, Marshal Sergei Biryuzov snaked his way through the men and approached Khrushchev. Nearby, foreign diplomats, including American ambassador Llewellyn Thompson, noticed the commotion. All of the military dignitaries on the stand were wearing their finest uniforms and decorations; Biryuzov had on his workaday tunic.

"Jesus," remarked Thompson to his wife, Jane, "I wonder what's happening now."

Biryuzov whispered in Khrushchev's ear: *We've shot down the intruder! The pilot has been captured!*

Closing Gaps

President Eisenhower authorized the manufacture of the U-2 reconnaissance aircraft in 1954 under the auspices of the CIA. Lockheed's famed Skunk Works produced the plane, which was more of a powered glider than an ordinary jet. The U-2 could cruise at 70,000 feet using unique fuel and special pilot life-support systems. The first cameras had been developed to produce a resolution of 2.5 feet at an altitude of 60,000 feet.

This remarkable aircraft proved to be of enormous significance during the Cold War. The intelligence it provided from overflights of the Soviet Union erased a widespread American fear that the Soviets held a commanding lead in the arms race in effective long-range bombers and intercontinental ballistic missiles. The perceived Soviet lead prompted the phrases "bomber gap" and "missile gap" to describe the degree by which America purportedly trailed the Soviets in the technology of Armageddon. Instead, the U-2's imagery gained from nearly two dozen overflights of the Soviet Union from 1956 through April 1960 proved the United States to be firmly in the lead.

On April 25, Eisenhower approved the twenty-fourth U-2 overflight, but only if launched on or before May 1. Despite the proximity to the planned May 16 four-power summit in Paris—between the United States, Soviet Union, Great Britain, and France—Ike felt comfortable in okaying the mission because of the many successful earlier flights.

At 6:26 a.m. local time on May 1, Francis Gary Powers, a CIA employee, began his takeoff roll at a secret airstrip near Peshawar, in western Pakistan. His 3,788-mile mission would take him over the Soviet missile test site at Tyuratam near the Aral Sea, across the Ural Mountains, and over multiple targets in European Russia. His destination was an airstrip in Bodø, Norway. In addition to his parachute, he carried a knife, pistol with silencer, and survival gear. His kit also included inducements for the locals to help him if he had to bail out: 7,500 rubles, two dozen gold coins, and gold rings and watches.

In Washington later that day, Eisenhower first learned of what Biryuzov had told Khrushchev. "Mr. President," the recently promoted brigadier general Andrew Goodpaster said on an unsecure telephone, "one of our reconnaissance planes on a scheduled flight from its base in Adana, Turkey, is overdue and possibly lost." Eisenhower immediately assumed it was a U-2. The next morning, May 2, Goodpaster confirmed the loss. "There was nothing further to do about it that May morning," Ike wrote later, "so I asked General Goodpaster to keep me informed."

President Eisenhower's decision to do nothing led to a chain of poor decisions and outright deceptions during the crisis. Historians believe the resulting calamity extended the Cold War for years.

Lies and Cover-Up

The administration had done little to plan for losing a U-2 over the Soviet Union. CIA director Allen Dulles and others believed that if the U-2 was shot down or crashed, the Soviets would remain silent because of their embarrassing inability to counter the platform. Further, the aircraft's fragility prompted most of Ike's team to believe it would disintegrate in an engagement, and the pilot would perish. Just in case, however, the plane carried a demolition explosive device. Each pilot carried a small pin coated with a powerful poison should he choose duty and country over life. Based on these assumptions, on May 3 the Eisenhower administration began a four-day charade of falsehoods, fabrications, half-truths, and spin to keep the U-2 program hidden from view:

Lie number one. The National Aeronautics and Space Administration, in a statement approved by the president, declared the U-2 had been on a weather research flight.

Meanwhile, in Moscow, Khrushchev devised his plan: announce the shoot-down but temporarily withhold information on the pilot's fate. He wanted to take credit for the downing, make the Americans lie more and put them on the defensive, reveal that the pilot was in captivity, force an Eisenhower apology, and arrive at the Paris summit as the propaganda winner. On May 5, Khrushchev revealed the shoot-down to the 1,300-member Supreme Soviet meeting in Moscow. "Shame to the aggressor!" the audience shouted. "Shame to the aggressor!"

Lie number two. In response to the Moscow revelation, Jim Hagerty, the president's press secretary, read a statement to reporters: "At the direction of the president, a complete inquiry is being made."

Lie number three. Dulles and Undersecretary of State Douglas Dillon fabricated a longer statement for release at State. It claimed the weather-mission pilot had oxygen equipment problems and passed out. The autopilot inadvertently had flown the plane into Soviet airspace.

On Saturday, May 7, Khrushchev told the Supreme Soviet that the pilot was alive and the military had collected much of the plane's wreckage. News reports of Khrushchev's announcement flashed across the Atlantic. Goodpaster called his new assistant, Major John Eisenhower, who was with the president at his Gettysburg home. John broke the news to his father and thus spared the staff from Ike's predictable rage.

Lie number four. Secretary of State Christian Herter, who had replaced Foster Dulles, recommended a half-truth statement to a reluctant Eisenhower, who said, "It is worth a try." The State spokesman acknowledged to reporters that a civilian U-2 had overflown the Soviet Union to gather intelligence that might ease "apprehension over a surprise attack with weapons of mass destruction." However, a caveat was included—it was an unauthorized flight.

The allegation of an "unauthorized" flight added, in the minds of the press and opposing politicians, to the popular perception that Ike left decisions to his staff while he played golf. The *New York Times'* James Reston wrote on Sunday about the American reaction to the bumbling: "This is a sad and perplexed capital tonight, caught in a swirl of charges of clumsy administration, bad judgment, and bad faith."

On Monday, May 9, Eisenhower convened an NSC meeting at the White House. He got right to the point. "Well, we're just going to have to take a lot of beating on this—and I'm the one who's going to have to take it," he said. "Of course, one had to expect that the thing would fail at one time or another. But that it had to be such a boo-boo and that we would be caught with our pants down was rather painful."

The president held a news conference on May 11 in the Indian Treaty Room in the Executive Office Building next to the West Wing.

In a time-honored Washington tradition, Ike tried to spin the press about a bad situation. Reading a prepared statement, he stressed four points: the need for intelligence—"No one wants another Pearl Harbor"; intelligence gathering activities must be secret; intelligence work "is a distasteful but vital necessity"; and the Soviets are the problem—"The emphasis given to the flight of an unarmed nonmilitary plane can only reflect a fetish for secrecy."

The president's public statements hardened Khrushchev's position. "Eisenhower's stand canceled any opportunity," the premier wrote later, "for us to get him out of the ticklish situation he was in. . . . He had, so to speak, offered us his back end, and we obliged him by kicking it as hard as we could."

Summit Disaster

While en route to Paris, Khrushchev decided to disrupt the four-power summit. Upon arrival on May 14, he called on host Charles de Gaulle at Elysée Palace and rudely handed the French president a written set of prerequisites for his participation in the meetings. Prominent among them was an ultimatum that Eisenhower apologize, but de Gaulle made no commitments.

Eisenhower arrived in Paris the following day. His motorcade moved through a city packed with reporters, diplomats, and VIP watchers. After a nap and lunch at American ambassador Amory Houghton's residence, Ike drove to Elysée and met with de Gaulle, UK prime minister Harold Macmillan, and West German chancellor Konrad Adenauer. Afterward, the president met with his traveling party to decide how to handle Khrushchev's demands. State Department counselor Chip Bohlen urged firmness: "The Russians are trying to get us to grovel—or to assert a legal right to overfly, which they will challenge as untenable." Livingston Merchant, undersecretary of state for political affairs, set the tone for Eisenhower: "All things considered, it would be better to have Mr. Khrushchev walk out of the conference than the president."

At 11:00 a.m. on Monday, May 16, the four leaders and their entourages entered a large, high-ceilinged room on the second floor of the Elysée. Each delegation sat on one side of a square group of tables.

De Gaulle and his party sat on the east side, with Eisenhower across the table. The Soviets were on de Gaulle's left, opposite from the British. The French president welcomed everyone and then invited Ike to speak first, since he was a formal head of state and the other two were not. An excited Khrushchev stood up and shouted that he had asked the previous day to speak first. When the interpreters had finished, de Gaulle silently turned to Ike, who nodded his assent.

Khrushchev rose, and with a sheaf of papers in his hand—the statement he had read to de Gaulle previously—and began shouting and berating America and Eisenhower. De Gaulle interrupted and, using his own interpreter, spoke to the Soviet: "The acoustics in this room are excellent. We can all hear the chairman. There is no need for him to raise his voice." Khrushchev quieted a bit, but then worked himself into another frenzy about the U-2 overflights. Raising his clenched right fist, he shouted, "I have been overflown!"

The six-foot-five de Gaulle rose to his feet and towered over the short and paunchy Khrushchev. The Frenchman said that he had been overflown as well. "Yesterday that satellite you launched just before you left Moscow to impress us overflew the sky of France eighteen times without my permission." De Gaulle asked if the satellite had cameras.

"Bog minya vidit. Moi rukhi chesti," Khrushchev replied sharply— God sees me. My hands are clean.

Eisenhower watched and listened patiently, but his flushed face and neck betrayed his barely controllable anger. Khrushchev ended his talk after forty-five minutes of vitriol, with a stern declaration. Unless Eisenhower apologized, he would not attend any more sessions.

Before Eisenhower rose to speak, Herter slipped him a note: "Do not let K interrupt you, as he will try to." President Eisenhower then made a few mollifying remarks, including a promise not to overfly the Soviet Union any more. Khrushchev interrupted him and again demanded an apology. With that, de Gaulle lectured Khrushchev, as he might an errant schoolboy, about wasting everyone's time by waiting until then to announce his conditions for carrying on the summit. The Soviet premier responded by storming out of the room.

The four-power summit ended the next day when Khrushchev declined de Gaulle's invitation for another meeting. Eisenhower departed Paris on May 19 in a profoundly depressed mood. Upon his arrival at Andrews Air Force Base outside Washington, newspaper reporters among the welcoming throng noticed his grim and weary deportment. Despite the encouraging approval from the crowd, the president's disappointment was obvious.

In February 1962, the United States and the Soviet Union exchanged Francis Powers for William Fischer, a.k.a. Rudolf Abel, a convicted Soviet intelligence agent. A thick layer of irony hovered over the Glienicker Bridge between East Germany and West Berlin on the day of the prisoner swap. Abel was the classic spy, while Powers reflected the new trend toward technical means of intelligence collection.

Assessment

Both Khrushchev and Eisenhower made serious mistakes in the U-2 affair. The Soviet leader had a chance to handle the incident in a manner that could have helped US-Soviet relations, but instead he felt he had to exploit the shootdown to strengthen his position within the Soviet leadership. This was his way of offsetting the humiliation wrought by the U-2 technology and the doubts it created among Khrushchev's opponents in the Politburo. Domestic political pressures filled the hallways of the Kremlin then as they did in Washington. Regardless, Khrushchev's opponents later criticized his aggressiveness during the incident, with one saying, "That was no way to deal with Eisenhower. Khrushchev engaged in inexcusable hysterics."

For his part, Ike offered a case study for future presidents on how not to handle an unanticipated crisis. In rapid order, he elected to do nothing, fabricated a cover-up that changed in detail daily, and set up himself and the country for humiliation by his Cold War opponent. The incident halted the slight thaw then under way in US-Soviet relations and put the two countries on a track to the Cold War's most dangerous time, the Cuban Missile Crisis. In view of the definition I have given the term "muddling through"—taking thoughtful incremental steps—I have to say that Eisenhower "stumbled through" the U-2 crisis.

Ike recognized his mistake. "The big error," he wrote in his memoir, "was, of course, the issuance of a premature and erroneous cover story." In an interview after leaving office, Eisenhower reiterated that the biggest regret of his presidency was "the lie we told about the U-2. I didn't realize how high a price we were going to pay for that lie."

In the years since, rule number one in crisis management, whether in the White House or during run-of-the-mill Washington scandals, has been "Tell the truth and tell it early."

CHAPTER 3

JOHN KENNEDY

Cuban Missile Crisis, 1962

Thirteen Days to Armageddon

The Joint Chiefs of Staff walked into the White House Cabinet Room, where President John Kennedy shook hands with each man. The four generals and an admiral, including the chairman, General Maxwell Taylor, and Secretary of Defense Robert McNamara circled the table and stopped at the seat by his nameplate. The officers stood erect and silent, with chests full of ribbons that reflected their wartime valor and long service. Kennedy pulled out his chair along the middle of the table and sat down with his back to the windows that faced the Rose Garden. The date was October 19, 1962, and tension filled the room.

The president had summoned his uniformed military leaders to seek their advice on a burgeoning international crisis, one that seemed destined to heat up the Cold War between the United States and the Soviet Union. American high-altitude aerial photography taken on October 14 had revealed the presence of Soviet ballistic missiles in Cuba. Senior intelligence officials had briefed Kennedy at the White House on the sixteenth. Since then, the president and a select group of his advisers had held secret and near-continuous discussions about how the nation should respond to this threat, barely ninety miles from Florida. On this Friday, the fourth day of the crisis, the alternatives included diplomatic maneuvers, a naval blockade of Cuba, and an invasion of Cuba.

Taylor, a cerebral Army general whom Kennedy had sworn in as chairman less than three weeks before, explained that the chiefs were united in their support of bold military action. Taylor then suggested that each man add his own comments. "Let me just say a little, first, about what the problem is, from my point of view," Kennedy responded. He was not about to let the generals dictate the terms of the session, largely because he didn't trust them. He also knew that these men viewed him as a youngster with a liberal and elitist background.

Kennedy emphasized his key point: he feared that the situation could escalate into war with the Soviet Union. The Soviets, for example, might seize West Berlin, which was isolated in communist East Germany, in response to a US attack on communist Cuba. "Which leaves me with only one alternative," Kennedy said, "which is to fire nuclear weapons—a hell of an alternative."

"We don't have any choice except direct military action," General Curtis "Bombs Away" LeMay gruffly interjected and then stuck his cigar back into the corner of his mouth.

"What do you think the Soviet reply would be?" asked the president.

"I don't think they're going to make any reply," the head of the Air Force said and then blew a puff of smoke across the table. "I see no other solution. This blockade and political action, I see leading into war. This is almost as bad as the appeasement at Munich." Kennedy took the comment exactly as LeMay intended—as a cheap shot at the president's father. Joseph Kennedy, Sr., had been the US ambassador to the United Kingdom in 1938 when that country had tried diplomatic initiatives to blunt German leader Adolf Hitler's aggressive territorial demands, steps that most believe emboldened Hitler.

The other chiefs spoke in succession: Admiral George Anderson, Jr., of the Navy; the Army's Earle Wheeler; and Marine Corps commandant David Shoup, then an ad hoc JCS member. All pushed for an immediate attack. The president acknowledged the potential for such steps, despite his instinctive opposition to their proposals. He asked when the forces would be ready to launch an air strike if he were to approve it. LeMay said perhaps on Sunday, October 21, but Tuesday, the 23rd, would be better.

The president also explored the details of a naval blockade to keep Soviet ships away from Cuban waters. He thought a limited first step might give Soviet premier Nikita Khrushchev room to counter with actions short of war. Finally, LeMay, notorious for his intimidation of civilians and subordinates, leaned forward in his chair and verbally thrust his point at the president. "I think that a blockade, and political talk, would be considered by a lot of our friends and neutrals as being a pretty weak response to this." The general then gestured at Kennedy and said, "You're in a pretty bad fix, Mr. President."

"What did you say?" Kennedy calmly asked, but he bit his lip at LeMay's bald impertinence.

"You're in a pretty bad fix."

"You're in it with me," Kennedy parried, "personally."

After the officers left, Kennedy walked to the Oval Office and spoke with his personal assistant, David Powers. "These brass hats have one great advantage in their favor," the president said. "If we do what they want us to do, none of us will be alive later to tell them that they were wrong."

In the fifty-odd years since Kennedy feared the worst outcome of the crisis, most historians have agreed that his concerns were well founded. Kennedy's court biographer and intimate, Arthur Schlesinger Jr., described the Cuban Missile Crisis as "the most dangerous moment in human history." Independent experts have offered less sensational assessments, but most consider the situation to be America's closest brush with nuclear war. The US military's lust for a showdown with the Soviets and Khrushchev's adventurism heightened the threat of Armageddon. Kennedy, caught in the middle, worked his way through the predicament with cautious and incremental steps.

The Soviet installation of ballistic missiles in Cuba had surprised President Kennedy. With the benefit of a half century of hindsight, however, one can say that Kennedy was as much to blame as Khrushchev in provoking the crisis. After a rocky start, the two men would work together to resolve the situation.

Cold War Context

The late 1950s and early 1960s proved to be one of the most dynamic and riskiest periods of East-West competition and confrontation during the Cold War. Eisenhower's handling of the 1960 U-2 incident sparked the worsening situation, and the Fidel Castro–led revolution in Cuba added to the friction. After chasing dictator Fulgencio Batista from office in 1959, Castro became a Soviet-sponsored communist client quite close to Florida. The CIA-backed invasion of Cuba in April 1961—the Bay of Pigs operation that failed badly—also warmed the Cold War. Kennedy inherited the Eisenhower plan to use Cuban exiles to assault Cuba from the sea and by parachute to overthrow Castro. The accompanying air strikes by painted-over US aircraft failed badly, and the Cuban counterattack killed one hundred of the 1,400-man landing team and captured 1,200.

The Berlin Crisis had tested Kennedy during the summer and fall of 1961. The Soviets and the western allies had divided Germany after World War II, and the former German capital, Berlin, was isolated in East Germany. It too was divided into east and west sectors, and by 1961 millions of East Germans had fled west. Losing population and economic vitality, the Soviets and East Germans responded by erecting the infamous wall to stop the exodus. Kennedy initially talked publicly about a military response, but he ultimately acquiesced to the barrier.

As we know now, Kennedy had undertaken several actions that influenced Khrushchev's decision to deploy ballistic missiles to Cuba. The first was Operation Mongoose, a covert, CIA-sponsored campaign to assassinate or depose Castro. As the sabotage and raids in Cuba by Cuban exiles intensified, Castro and Khrushchev assumed another invasion loomed. Khrushchev believed that Kennedy wanted revenge for the Bay of Pigs fiasco. The US military added to the perception of an American threat to Cuba by holding a series of exercises in the spring of 1962 that tested contingency plans for invading Cuba. Secretary McNamara later declared that Kennedy had no plans beyond Mongoose to force Castro out, but to Khrushchev, the exercises looked like rehearsals.

The Kennedy administration had taken another tension-inducing step in October 1961. Deputy Secretary of Defense Roswell Gilpatric declared in a speech that America held an overwhelming advantage over the Soviet Union in strategic nuclear weapon systems. Eisenhower had thought the United States badly trailed the Soviets in long-range missiles, but by 1961 the "missile gap" proved to be a baseless claim by Khrushchev. Thus exposed, the Soviet leader sought in the spring of 1962 a means to redress the Soviet vulnerability. He found a solution by looking at the medium-range ballistic missiles that the United States and NATO had deployed to Italy and Turkey. He would do the same in the US backyard.

Kennedy's Red Line

Official news of the discovery of offensive missiles in Cuba reached the White House at 8:00 a.m. on the first day of the thirteen-day crisis, Tuesday, October 16, 1962. National Security Adviser McGeorge Bundy walked briskly to the residence and then upstairs to the president's bedroom. Kennedy, in his pajamas and robe, had the *New York Times* opened to a story headlined "Eisenhower Calls President Weak on Foreign Policy."

Bundy described the Soviet medium-range ballistic missiles in San Diego de los Baños in western Cuba. He explained that analysts had spotted the weapon system, designated SS-4 by NATO, in photography taken two days earlier by a U-2 reconnaissance aircraft from an altitude of 72,500 feet. The missile, which carried a one-megaton nuclear warhead, had a maximum range of 1,292 nautical miles, an arc that threatened the US Eastern Seaboard. Kennedy's anger erupted at that point. Khrushchev had personally assured the president that he would not introduce offensive weapons into Cuba. Kennedy fumed, "He can't do this to me."

As Kennedy dressed, he reviewed in his mind the developments of the previous few months. In July rumors had begun seeping out of Cuba about Soviet ships arriving with soldiers aboard. At an August 22 press conference, Kennedy had conceded the presence of Soviet shipments of "supplies" but offered nothing on Soviet troops. Poor weather had grounded U-2 flights after August 5, thus denying valuable intelligence on Soviet activities. But a mission on August 29 revealed the presence of Soviet surface-to-air missiles in eastern Cuba.

On September 4, Kennedy told the press there were no indications of a significant Soviet offensive capability in Cuba. He had said, "Were it to be otherwise, the gravest issues would arise."

Later in the morning, the president and his advisers gathered in the Cabinet Room. Included were Bundy; Taylor; McNamara; Gilpatric; Secretary of State Dean Rusk and his undersecretary, George Ball, and two other State Department officials; Robert "Bobby" Kennedy, the attorney general and the president's younger brother; Secretary of the Treasury Douglas Dillon; Theodore Sorensen, a trusted Kennedy aide on the White House staff; and Lieutenant General Marshall Carter, the CIA deputy director. The men first discussed the alarming intelligence reports and then shifted to the capabilities of the SS-4 system and when the weapons might be operational. They soon turned to alternative responses to the Soviet initiative. Kennedy initially supported a punitive air strike to destroy the missiles but didn't press his views too hard as others offered alternatives.

From day one of the crisis, Kennedy and his team felt the need for an urgent response to the Soviet missile deployment. A traditional explanation for the time factor was the perceived need to act before the weapons became operational. "The air strike advocates," George Ball said years later, "were using the issue of the missiles becoming 'operational' to buttress their case for urgency." But there were other forces at work. Ball also talked of the need for a quick decision before a possible leak alerted the public. Douglas Dillon later seconded the point: "There was real concern to control the agenda and keep it from being set by some newspaper."

Further, Kennedy and his advisers recognized immediately that once the missile deployment became known, the Republicans would demand action. When the August 29 U-2 mission found surface-to-air missiles, Kennedy told the CIA what to do with the imagery—"Put it back in the box and nail it shut." Later, after the president had acknowledged the presence of SAMs in Cuba, Senator Homer Capehart (R-IN) called for an immediate invasion of the island. Senator Kenneth Keating (R-NY) criticized Kennedy for his "do-nothing" approach to the matter.

In the face of growing GOP criticism, Kennedy tried to get in front of the Cuban situation. At a press conference on September 13, he had repeated that the Soviet military buildup was not a serious threat to the United States. "Rash talk is cheap," he said, "particularly on the part of those who do not have the responsibility." He then drew a red line around the Soviet offensive missile bases in Cuba. If Cuba became "an offensive military base of significant capacity for the Soviet Union," Kennedy declared at the press conference, "then this country will do whatever must be done to protect its own security and that of its allies." Later in the crisis, Kennedy acknowledged that he had to respect his own red line. If he hadn't acted on the missiles, he told Bobby of his expected fate: "I woulda been impeached."

The domestic political ramifications of the crisis concerned the president's advisers from the start. For example, Secretary McNamara spoke of the issue in the evening meeting on the first day. "I don't think there is a military problem here," he said of the relative insignificance of the missiles. "This is a domestic, political problem." A number of "revisionists," critics of Kennedy's management of the crisis, used McNamara's comment to claim that the president inflated the situation to bolster the Democratic Party's chances in the coming election.

From the beginning, Kennedy wanted to adhere to his previously announced schedule to keep the crisis out of the news as long as possible. The president had scheduled multiple political trips to campaign for key Democratic candidates as part of the run-up to the November midterm elections. On Wednesday, October 17, he flew to Connecticut to campaign for Senate candidate Abraham Ribicoff. He had another planned trip to the Midwest that would start on Friday.

His group of advisers—they later called themselves the ExComm, for the Executive Committee of the National Security Council (NSC)—met twice without the president on Wednesday, day two. The hawks called for offensive actions and argued that a naval blockade alone would not affect the missiles already in Cuba. The outnumbered doves talked of less aggressive actions. All agreed that inaction meant an accommodation of Soviet blackmail. Gradually, five alternatives surfaced: Follow an ultimatum to Khrushchev with an air strike on the missile sites; launch surprise but limited air strikes; lodge diplomatic threats, initiate a naval blockade, and engage allies; stage large-scale air strikes after limited diplomatic preparation; or invade Cuba.

While the ExComm deliberated, photo interpreters in Washington discovered another startling development as they analyzed new U-2 photos. They found facilities in Guanajay and Remedios associated with a larger, intermediate-range ballistic missile system. The more capable SS-5, with a maximum range of 2,400 nautical miles and a one-megaton warhead, could threaten all major American cities except Seattle. This discovery raised the stakes, but the group didn't fully appreciate the strength of the entire Soviet military contingent in Cuba.

On October 17, there were four Soviet infantry regiments there, as well as an integrated air defense system that had 144 SAM launchers and forty-two MiG-21 interceptors. Also deployed were cruise missile batteries for coastal defense, twelve cruise missile-equipped patrol boats, and forty-two IL-28 light bombers. The missile deployment plan called for forty-eight SS-4 missiles and thirty-two SS-5s. All of the SS-4 missiles had arrived, but only some of the SS-5 launchers, less missiles, were in Cuba. Also in country were eighty tactical nuclear warheads and bombs for the cruise missiles, short-range ground-to-ground rockets, and the Il-28s. Soviet military personal in Cuba totaled a staggering 42,000.

On Thursday, the ExComm met with the president at 11:00 a.m. in the Cabinet Room. The debate moved in circles, and participants changed positions as others made well-reasoned arguments. Bobby Kennedy raised the moral question of launching a surprise, unilateral action and cited the reviled Japanese attack at Pearl Harbor. All agreed, meanwhile, that the president should take his planned political trip to the Midwest the next day. Likewise, the president stuck to his schedule at 5:00 p.m., when he kept a previously arranged appointment with Soviet foreign minister Andrei Gromyko. The two spoke about the Soviet weapons deployed in Cuba, and the Russian claimed they were strictly defensive. Later revelations, however, proved that Gromyko was fully informed about the ballistic missile deployment. The president made no mention of the intelligence discoveries in order to safeguard his options for a surprise attack. "I was dying to confront him with our evidence," he said of Gromyko, whom he called "that lying bastard."

Gromyko's conversation with Kennedy also concealed Khrushchev's objectives in deploying the missiles to Cuba. Those came to light during meetings between former US, Russian, and Cuban officials during the period from 1983 to 1992, which disclosed that Khrushchev's aim was to prevent an American invasion of Cuba, offset US superiority in strategic weapons, and subject the United States to the close-in threat that US medium-range Jupiter missiles created for the Soviets in Turkey.

Former Soviet participants in the crisis also described Khrushchev's planned sequence for the missile deployment. He wanted to install the weapons secretly in September and October, and then reveal their presence after the midterm elections in November. Gromyko told Khrushchev that the deployment would cause a "political explosion in America." Khrushchev pressed forward regardless. Conversely, Ted Sorensen wrote later that the missile installation "was a probe, a test of America's will to resist." That line sells books, but we know now that Khrushchev had larger objectives.

Kennedy met with the ExComm during the evening, and nine of them jammed themselves into Bobby's government car to dodge the media. Afterward, Kennedy sat alone in the Oval Office and dictated his thoughts into his secret audio recording system. Among other subjects, he remarked about increased support within the ExComm for a naval blockade. McNamara, for example, began to promote such a limited first step but cautiously urged contingency plans for air strikes. Bobby Kennedy also had begun to move toward a blockade.

The Quarantine Decision

After his testy consultation with the Joint Chiefs on Friday morning, October 19, Kennedy turned to his brother and Sorensen before his flight to Cleveland for a political rally. He asked them to forge a consensus on the blockade in his absence. The ExComm deliberated the remainder of the day and night, and the unanimity that the president sought gradually emerged. By the next morning, the president's advisers were ready for him to make a decision on the implementation of a naval "quarantine." International norms held a blockade to be an act of war, so the group chose the less hostile term, one that did not require a congressional declaration of war. Regardless, the US Navy would stop ships en route to Cuba and search their cargo for offensive weapons.

Accordingly, Bobby called the president at the Blackstone Hotel in Chicago and told him they were ready to meet with him. Press Secretary Pierre Salinger told the media that the president had a cold and Kennedy returned to the White House. When the president entered the Oval Room in the family quarters for a 2:30 p.m. meeting with his advisers, he explained that he wanted to make a final decision on US actions. "Gentlemen," he said, "today we're going to earn our pay."

"I shall never forget that scene," Ed McDermott, head of the Office of Emergency Planning, wrote in his journal. "President Kennedy asked each person present, twelve of us, for his personal recommendation on alternative actions." Kennedy was especially adept, according to his many biographers, at listening to others. He tried not to skew the discussion up front by flatly announcing his own preferences. He had a flexible and analytical mind and easily absorbed vast quantities of information. Throughout his presidency, he impressed others with his restraint and prudent choices, at least those outside of his voracious sex life.

Although most of the discussion focused on previously debated options, UN ambassador Adlai Stevenson offered a new idea. He suggested trading US missiles in Italy and Turkey for the Soviet missiles in Cuba. Stevenson also proposed giving up the US naval base at Guantanamo Bay, Cuba, which the United States held through a binding lease agreement with Cuba. Kennedy reportedly rejected both ideas, but Bobby later spoke about Stevenson's idea with Arthur Schlesinger: "We will have to make a deal in the end; but we must stand absolutely firm now. Concessions must come at the end of negotiations not at the beginning."

After everyone spoke, the president stepped out onto the Truman Balcony to think by himself. McDermott recalled the atmosphere: "All twelve in the room sat silently and one could hear a pin drop." Bobby and Sorensen soon joined the president, framed as they talked by the massive columns and wrought iron balustrade. They returned to the group, and the president said, "I know each of you is hoping I didn't take your advice." He went on to announce his decision to proceed with the quarantine.

Kennedy began the ultimate resolution of the crisis by choosing to initiate the maritime operation, a step between diplomacy and instant killing. He wanted this incremental first step not to be his last; he wanted room to take follow-on action. Moreover, the quarantine gave Khrushchev an avenue to back away. In taking this approach, Kennedy set a fine example for presidents who followed.

McDermott, whose position was equivalent to the head of today's Federal Emergency Management Agency, began to prepare the non-military parts of the government for nuclear war in case the situation spun out of control. He initiated secret Continuity of Government procedures, which, among other actions, arranged for a possible evac-uation of the president and hundreds of key officials to safe sites away from Washington.

The ExComm wrestled, in near-continuous sessions on Sunday, day six, with myriad decisions required to implement the quarantine on October 24. The State Department notified allies, and Defense ordered 180 naval combatants under way and firmed contingency plans for air strikes and troop movement. Aides prepared a speech for Kennedy to deliver to the nation Monday night, and others drafted an ultimatum to Khrushchev. "Everybody was given a specific assignment to discharge," McDermott wrote later. "The president's problem was to prepare for diplomatic and military actions, but not panic the Amer-ican people. There was a sense that anything could happen."

All of the activity over the weekend had caught the attention of reporters in Washington. Kennedy successfully appealed to the pub-lishers of the *New York Times* and *Washington Post* to hold the story until after his planned Monday speech and concurrent ultimatum to the Soviets.

On Monday, October 22, the president invited congressional lead-ers to the White House for a private briefing. Knowing that three weeks before he had publicly promised an aggressive response to offensive weapons in Cuba, Kennedy expected some blowback from the opposition leaders about his naval quarantine decision; he got it. Senator Richard B. Russell (D-GA), chairman of the Senate Armed Services Committee, gasped when Kennedy told the group that some of the missiles were ready to fire. He urged an immediate air strike and invasion. "We're either a world-class power or we're not," he declared. Senator J. William Fulbright (D-AR) strongly agreed with his colleague and told Kennedy, "A blockade seems to me the worst alternative." Dean Rusk countered that argument by pointing to Kennedy's incremental approach to the crisis. "We do think this first step," referring to the quarantine, "provides for a brief pause for the people on the other side to have another thought before we get into an utterly crashing crisis."

Late in the day, Rusk called in Soviet ambassador Anatoly Dobrynin and handed him a copy of the president's ultimatum. "Dobrynin aged at least ten years right before my eyes," Rusk wrote later. "He reacted as a man in physical shock and said, 'This is a terrible situation.' Judging by his reaction, Dobrynin didn't know about the missiles." Coincidently, the Defense Department raised its worldwide readiness level to Defense Condition 3, two notches short of actual combat. McNamara ordered the Strategic Air Command to assume DEFCON 2, but the commander, General Thomas Power, did so in an unauthorized manner to "rub it in" the Soviet faces. He transmitted all his commands in the clear as he kept one-eighth of all nuclear-armed B-52 bombers continuously in the air.

Kennedy spoke to the American public about the crisis via radio and television at 7:00 p.m. Kennedy critic R. J. Walton called the speech "probably the most dramatic and most frightening presidential address in the history of the republic." Communications professor Denise Bostdorff is less harsh, but still explains how Kennedy spun useful themes in the speech. To cast the Soviets as evil disruptors of international order, he emphasized issues that would legitimize US actions. "I call upon Chairman Khrushchev," Kennedy said, "to halt or eliminate this clandestine, reckless, and provocative threat to world peace."

Bostdorff has studied the crisis rhetoric of presidents from Kennedy through Reagan. "More so than any other president in this study," she wrote, "Kennedy used fear-arousing language to construct a ghastly scene that dominated his discourse." She went on to explain that by doing so, Kennedy preempted talk of US Jupiter missiles threatening the Soviet Union in the same manner, or the Operation Mongoose plan to kill Castro.

Khrushchev and his colleagues stayed up for the speech. The president's announcement of a quarantine was serious, and, according to Khrushchev's son Sergei, the Soviet leadership viewed the action as a threat. Nevertheless, Khrushchev and his inner circle were relieved that Kennedy had put aside an immediate attack. But the Soviet leadership still had to decide their next step. Khrushchev's son later wrote, "If Soviet missiles in Cuba were attacked, he had no retaliatory actions in reserve." The United States enjoyed vastly superior forces in the Caribbean, reciprocal action in Berlin was too dangerous in Khrushchev's mind, he couldn't change the balance of missile power, and nuclear war was out of the question. Further, Kennedy appeared ready to escalate the quarantine to include oil shipments, Cuba's lifeblood.

Khrushchev responded directly to Kennedy with letters on October 23 and 24. Both were threatening, but, according to Vasily Kuznetsov, a foreign ministry official at the time, the letters masked Khrushchev's indecision on what to do next. Again, revelations from the late 1980s suggest Khrushchev eventually settled on a dual strategy at this point. First, he would keep up the bluster toward Kennedy in hopes of gaining concessions for withdrawing the missiles. At the same time, he sought to convince his Soviet presidium colleagues that removing the missiles would forestall an American invasion of Cuba.

As Kennedy read the two letters, he thought about one of his greatest concerns during the standoff—the chance of a miscalculation, a step toward a dangerous escalation of the crisis. Already Kennedy had made one miscalculation—he thought the Soviets would never deploy nuclear weapons to Cuba. Khrushchev also had erred by assuming the United States would ultimately accept the missiles. Further, both men worried about an accident that might start a war, and Kennedy drew upon the lessons of Barbara Tuchman's history of World War I, *The Guns of August*. She described how misinformation and missteps unleashed the "war to end all wars." As many have observed, Kennedy did not want an error to precipitate a sequel, *The Missiles of October*.

Two Versions of the Eyeball-to-Eyeball Moment

The Navy implemented the quarantine at 10:00 a.m., Washington time, on day nine, October 24. Kennedy and the ExComm gathered in the Cabinet Room to monitor Soviet reactions. In his brief on the maritime situation, McNamara told Kennedy that several Soviet cargo ships were near the quarantine line in the Caribbean Sea and that several Soviet submarines were in the vicinity. The men talked about the possibilities of maritime hostilities if the submarines tried to protect the cargo ships from the US Navy's intervention. The tension in the room rose noticeably, especially when Kennedy sharply questioned the Navy's plan to use practice depth charges to warn off the submarines.

What the men didn't know was that Khrushchev already had decided to defuse any quarantine problems. The previous day, he had ordered all ships en route to Cuba to stop. More importantly, sixteen vessels carrying weapons, including the SS-5 missiles, were ordered to return home. However, the Kremlin directed one ship, *Aleksandrovsk*, to make for the nearest Cuban port. She carried twenty-four nuclear warheads for the SS-5 and forty tactical nuclear warheads. *Aleksandrovsk* arrived at La Isablea at dawn on October 23. Khrushchev not only wanted to avoid a confrontation at sea, he wanted to prevent losing Soviet weapons technology to US Navy boarding parties.

But at the White House, Kennedy and his team continued operating without the full situational awareness gained by others twenty-five years later. CIA director John McCone, when handed a note, interrupted the discussion, "We've just received information that all six Soviet ships currently identified in Cuban waters—and I don't know what that means—have either stopped or reversed course." Dean Rusk and Kennedy peppered McCone with questions, and the director stepped outside to seek more details. A few minutes later, McCone reappeared. The president impatiently asked, "Whadda ya have, John?"

"The ships were all westbound, all inbound for Cuba. They either stopped them, or reversed direction."

After a period of immense tension, the men sensed a glimmer of hope. "We're eyeball to eyeball," Rusk offered, "and the other fellow just blinked."

Khrushchev actually had blinked the day before, but this scene became central to the story line created by Kennedy associates who wrote about the president's heroic measures during the crisis. Two films about the crisis, *The Missiles of October* (1974) and *13 Days* (2000), dramatize the eyeball-to-eyeball statement.

Back to 1962. On the next day, October 25, Kennedy replied to Khrushchev's harsh letter of the twenty-fourth, "I repeat my regret that these events should cause a deterioration in our relations." That nonthreatening tone impressed Khrushchev, but so did another development. That day's *Washington Post* carried a column by one of the administration's favorites, Walter Lippmann. He suggested trading the Jupiter missiles in Turkey for the Soviet's Cuban arsenal. The *New York Times'* Max Frankel reported simultaneously that Washington had "unofficial" interest in dismantling US bases near the Soviet Union. Moscow likely saw these stories as trial balloons.

With Khrushchev's position unknown to anyone in Washington, Ed McDermott's activity reached a fevered pitch as he prepared the government for a possible Soviet attack on Washington. His staff notified Vice President Lyndon B. Johnson and congressional leaders where to meet helicopters that would fly them to safety at COG evacuation sites. In a meeting with Supreme Court Chief Justice Earl Warren, McDermott briefed him on the justices' evacuation procedures. Warren, who said that he spoke for the other eight justices, told McDermott that they wouldn't go without their families. The justice pointed to a photo of his wife and said, "If she's not important enough to save, neither am I."

Secretary of State Rusk had a similar response, and after McDermott gave the COG packet to Kennedy aides Powers and Kenneth O'Donnell, both worried about the fate of their families. Powers later wrote of his wife Helen's reaction: "While you're safe with the president under a rock somewhere, what am I supposed to do with your five children?" Another of Kennedy's aides told the president that he had no plans to leave. "That's OK," Kennedy said. "Neither do I. I'm staying right here."

On Friday, October 26, Navy destroyer USS *Joseph P. Kennedy* stopped and boarded the first ship to cross the quarantine line, a freighter named *Marcula*. The Soviets had chartered the former Liberty ship, which was owned by Panama and registered in Lebanon, for a general cargo run to Cuba. Kennedy handpicked the merchant vessel to show that the United States meant business. The Navy chose not to order one of its nearby ships to intercept *Marcula*, electing instead to enhance its public image by using a ship named for the president's late brother. Finding no weapons, the Navy allowed *Marcula* to continue to Cuba.

At an ExComm meeting Friday morning, the president and his advisers struggled with their fundamental challenge—getting the Soviet missiles out of Cuba. The discussion gradually turned to trading Jupiter missiles in Turkey—which, before the crisis, Kennedy had talked of removing because of their obsolescence—for the Soviet SS-4s and SS-5s. "Well, our quarantine itself won't remove the weapons," Kennedy said. "So we've only got two ways of removing the weapons. One is to negotiate them out or trade them out. And the other is to go over and just take them out."

Bobby Kennedy and Ambassador Dobrynin held a significant meeting on Friday. None of the first generation crisis reconstructions reported this appointment. Former State Department official Raymond Garthoff wrote that Bobby told Dobrynin the president intended to remove the Jupiters once the current situation stabilized. Dobrynin, who confirmed this account in 1989, cabled Moscow that evening, and his message likely arrived soon after summaries of the Lippmann and Frankel newspaper stories.

Khrushchev replied initially to Kennedy's nonthreatening October 25 letter in a rambling cable that arrived in Washington in four parts between 6:00 p.m. to 9:00 p.m. Friday evening, October 26. In what is called the "Friday letter," Khrushchev suggested that if Kennedy foreswore invading Cuba the need for Soviet missiles there could be eliminated. However, Khrushchev did not specifically commit to missile removal. Although US Army and Marine units continued to prepare for an invasion, the ExComm members suspected that this development might be the crisis's pivot point. Bobby said that night, "I had a slight feeling of optimism." But then the crisis took a new direction.

Compromise Versus War

On what should have been a day of eased tensions—Saturday, October 27—events quickly turned it into what Bobby Kennedy later called "Black Saturday." First, the FBI reported that Soviet personnel at the UN in New York had begun to destroy sensitive documents. Also, aerial reconnaissance showed Soviet crews still at work on missile sites and partially assembled Il-28 bombers.

The ExComm gathered at 10:00 a.m. to debate how to reply to Khrushchev's Friday letter, which had arrived too late the previous evening for a detailed discussion. But less than an hour into the meeting, a second letter from Khrushchev arrived. This "Saturday letter" demanded that the United States withdraw its Jupiter medium-range missiles from Turkey in exchange for the Soviet's dismantling of their weapons in Cuba. "It was like a dose of cold water in the face," recalled Dillon. "I thought, we are back to square one."

Most early analysis of the two letters was wrong. More recent information from former Soviet officials has helped revise previous accounts. Khrushchev had felt his first letter should have contained a promise to remove the missiles, hence the need to follow up. Second, Walter Lippmann's column and Dobrynin's Friday report of Bobby Kennedy's willingness to talk turkey on the Jupiters had reached Khrushchev. Third, Bundy later argued that Khrushchev, already committed by this time to removing the missiles, saw the Turkish weapons as a further concession, a "haggle," within his reach; the trade would help cover his retreat domestically. Last, to ensure that his Saturday letter quickly reached the White House, Khrushchev had the text broadcast over Radio Moscow in parallel to diplomatic transmission. Public knowledge of the Soviet terms, however, would soon haunt Kennedy.

Khrushchev also took another significant step that was unobserved by US intelligence and diplomatic resources. He sent firm instructions to Soviet commanders in Cuba "absolutely forbidding" the use of nuclear weapons, including the tactical warheads. This reaffirmed his similar order on October 23 after Kennedy's speech. But other events that day proved that accidents can happen.

Earlier that morning, Washington time, Air Force Captain Charles Maultsby accidentally flew his U-2 off his prescribed reconnaissance route in the Arctic and strayed into Soviet air space. On a routine air-sampling mission that morning to detect fallout from an unrelated Soviet nuclear test, Maultsby's errant flight path on his return leg prompted intense concern in both American and Soviet command centers. Given the crisis in Cuba, Soviet air defense forces scrambled six interceptors, thinking the U-2 was a precursor to an American attack over the North Pole. Luckily, the American pilot corrected his course, and landed safely in Alaska. But then came the blackest of events.

A Soviet SA-2 surface-to-air missile brought down a US Air Force U-2 aircraft over Banes in eastern Cuba, killing the pilot, Major Rudolf Anderson. Moscow had explicitly ordered Soviet forces not to engage US aircraft, but the Cuban military had fired at low-level US reconnaissance planes that day, which alarmed the commander of Soviet air defense forces in Cuba, Lieutenant General Stepan Grechko. Thinking the war had started and unable to reach his superior, Grechko authorized the launch of two SA-2 missiles at the U-2. News of the downing reached the Pentagon at about 2:30 p.m. The Joint Chiefs reacted aggressively to Major Anderson's death and urged an air strike on Cuba on Monday, followed the next day with a ground force invasion. At a 4:00 p.m. meeting, most of the ExComm agreed, but Kennedy urged caution. "It isn't the first step that concerns me, but both sides escalating to the fourth or fifth step."

In the face of all of this tension, Kennedy had to decide how to respond to the two letters. During the late afternoon ExComm meeting, Kennedy said of the Soviet missiles, "We can't very well invade Cuba, with all its toil and blood . . . when we could have gotten 'em out by making a deal on the same missiles on Turkey. If that's part of the record . . . then you don't have a very good war." Khrushchev's public disclosure of the "Saturday" letter put Kennedy in a politically treacherous corner. How the president got out of that box is the subject to two differing accounts. Traditional descriptions have Kennedy replying only to the Friday letter and ignoring the Saturday demand for Jupiter removal. That became known as the "Trollope ploy"—a construct in novels involving reactions to contradictory statements. Kennedy's letter promising not to invade Cuba in return for UN–observed missile removal from Cuba was transmitted at 8:05 p.m.

But more recent accounts cast light on what actually happened. After the ExComm meeting ended, Kennedy invited a few key members to meet with him in the Oval Office. The group quickly agreed to send Bobby to see Soviet ambassador Dobrynin with a secret oral offer to remove the Jupiters as a means of replying to the Saturday letter. Bobby was to warn Dobrynin that any Soviet reference to the offer would nullify it. As the others left the Oval Office, Rusk stayed behind. He and Kennedy devised a back-up plan, also secret, to approach UN secretary general U Thant. If the oral message to Dobrynin failed, Kennedy would ask U Thant to propose Turkey-Cuba missile trade.

In 1989, Dobrynin verified his conversation with Bobby, saying their conversation centered on an explicit trade. Bobby died before the publication of his account of the crisis, *Thirteen Days*. Ted Sorensen had used Bobby's diary of the event to make the final edit, but admitted in 1989 that he had deleted the reference to the Jupiter deal, claiming it was still classified.

While Kennedy waited for Khrushchev's reply, he ordered all potential attacks on Cuba delayed until Tuesday. But he still authorized the call-up of the Air Force reserves needed for a Cuban invasion. In Moscow, Khrushchev showed similar restraint by waving aside the incident of the wayward U-2 in the Arctic. "The plane violating our airspace was probably lost," he said. The U-2 that was shot down over Cuba was another matter altogether. He felt the situation "slipping out of his control," according to his son. "Today one general had decided it was a good idea to launch an antiaircraft missile," the chairman thought at the time. "Tomorrow, a different one might decide to launch a ballistic missile—also without asking Moscow's permission."

Later, Khrushchev, upon reading Dobrynin's report of his second secret conversation with the president's brother, declared victory. He had won an American promise not to invade Cuba, and another to remove the Jupiters from the Soviet border. The latter concession garnered the Soviet Union a measure of equality regarding short-range nuclear threats. Accordingly, the Soviet leader urgently sent to the White House his agreement to dismantle and remove the missiles from Cuba with UN supervision and inspection. He sent his message via three paths to ensure rapid and certain transmission to Kennedy before US air strikes began.

McGeorge Bundy called Kennedy with the news of Khrushchev's decision before the president attended Sunday Mass at St. Stephen Martyr Catholic Church in the District. "I feel like a new man," the president said to his aide Dave Powers. "Do you realize that we had an air strike all arranged for Tuesday? Thank God it's all over."

True to form, however, the military brass called the Soviet offer a charade and grumbled at the lost chance for war. Kennedy met with the Joint Chiefs late Sunday and sought to reestablish a functional relationship with the men. Surprisingly, the chiefs didn't back down an inch. The chief of naval operations told the president, "We've been had." LeMay added his two cents, growling, "It's the greatest defeat in our history." Their brazen disrespect stunned Kennedy.

In the following months, the Soviets allowed US reconnaissance aircraft to monitor the removal of the ballistic missiles and IL-28 bombers. But both Moscow and Castro refused to permit UN observers to monitor weapon systems withdrawal, which caused Kennedy to withhold any formal pledge not to invade Cuba. US crews completed disassembly of the Jupiter missiles in Turkey in April 1963. Kennedy terminated Operation Mongoose, the CIA plot to eliminate Fidel Castro, after the crisis subsided.

Assessment

Traditional Kennedy biographers have cast his management of the Cuban Missile Crisis as a bold display of American might and right. By waving a big stick in the face of a deceitful communist menace, they say, Kennedy provided a model of crisis decision making for future presidents. A few days after the crisis ended, *Time* magazine wrote that when Khrushchev had seen Kennedy's steely resolve, "the bellicose premier of the Soviet Union first wavered, then weaseled, and finally backed down." Not quite true. On the other hand, some revisionists claim Kennedy magnified the situation for his political gain—a gross case of wag-the-dog machismo. That's not quite true either.

It is true that Kennedy waved a big stick through all of this. That bludgeon consisted of more than 100,000 Army and 40,000 Marine combat troops; 579 tactical aircraft; and 183 ships, including eight aircraft carriers, on station. The air-strike plan called for 1,190 sorties on the first day. The vast US superiority in conventional forces in the Caribbean theater did influence Khrushchev, especially since the Russian had ruled out nuclear war.

With that big stick at the ready, Kennedy successfully muddled through the crisis, or in other words, acted with incremental steps, with the naval quarantine being the most important. He also wisely followed a rule from military theorist Carl von Clausewitz: Don't take the first step without thinking about what may be the last. And he took those steps coupled with a healthy dose of realism, a willingness to understand the other fellow's problem, and the good sense to compromise. Both leaders made concessions while maintaining an appearance of resolve, and thus became coconspirators. Both men blinked.

Kennedy and Khrushchev each claimed achievement of their major crisis goals at the end. The president got the missiles out of Cuba, and the Soviet leader turned to his Presidium critics and claimed he had saved Cuba and gotten the Jupiters out of Turkey. Each man espoused rigid positions at the onset and created the crisis, but both feared nuclear war enough to moderate their stances. Both trapped the other near the end. Kennedy faced a political disaster if he started a war when a publicly offered compromise was within reach. Khrushchev had no options beyond war or making a trade with Kennedy.

Nevertheless, the Kennedy administration carefully scrubbed references to the Jupiter deal in contemporary accounts of the crisis. Sources leaked a flattering portrait of Kennedy's crisis management to Stewart Alsop and Charles Bartlett. The journalists wrote an inside-the-White-House account for the *Saturday Evening Post* in December 1962 that had no mention of compromises with Khrushchev. The authors painted UN ambassador Adlai Stevenson as the sole proponent of pulling the Jupiters out of Turkey and quoted an ExComm attendee as saying, "Adlai wanted a Munich." Bobby refused to accept an October 28 letter from Khrushchev, via Dobrynin, that formalized the missile swap. Bobby didn't want any evidence in the presidential papers collection. In his memoir, presidential assistant Bundy acknowledged the cover-up: "We misled our colleagues, our countrymen, our successors, and our allies."

Both leaders miscalculated. Kennedy sent threatening signals before the crisis: the October 1961 speech by Deputy Secretary of Defense Gilpatric that boasted of America's advantage in strategic weapons; Operation Mongoose; bellicose rhetoric; and invasion-threatening military exercises. Khrushchev failed to anticipate the US reaction to the missile deployment—"The Americans will make a fuss, make more of a fuss, and then accept," he had said—and misunderstood the domestic pressures on Kennedy that would demand a forceful US reaction.

Les Gelb, a former *New York Times* correspondent and State Department appointee, and now president emeritus of the Council on Foreign Relations, recently wrote about the Kennedy crisis myth. He believes presidents after Kennedy learned the wrong lessons from the Cuban Missile Crisis. "Compromise is not a word that generally makes political hearts flutter, and it is even less loved when it comes to the politics of US foreign policy," Gelb wrote in 2012. "The myth of the missile crisis strengthened the scorn. The myth, not the reality, became the measure for how to bargain with adversaries."

CHAPTER 4

LYNDON JOHNSON

Two Crises Beyond Vietnam

Part I. Six-Day War, 1967: A Green Light

A buzz from a desk-top phone in Secretary of Defense Robert McNamara's office interrupted his careful reading of morning intelligence reports on the ongoing Middle East crisis. It was his direct line to the on-duty general in the National Military Command Center in the Pentagon's basement. The time was 7:15 a.m. on June 5, 1967, and to McNamara, a call from NMCC meant trouble.

"Mr. Secretary, Soviet Prime Minister Kosygin is on the Moscow Hot Line and he wishes to speak to the President. What should I tell him?"

"Why did you call me, General?" McNamara asked.

"Well, sir, the Hot Line ends at the Pentagon," duty officer said.

"General, you'd better take a few thousands of dollars of our huge military budget and get this thing extended over to the White House quickly. You call the Situation Room, and I'll call the president and decide what to do."

McNamara hung up and reached for another handset, one connected to a secure, or encrypted line to an Army switchboard in the White House. He asked the operator to ring the Air Force sergeant on duty outside Johnson's bedroom in the residence.

"Sergeant, this is Secretary McNamara and I want to talk to the president."

"He's asleep, sir."

"Hell, I know he's asleep, but wake him."

"He doesn't like to be awakened, sir."

"Wake him."

After a few minutes, Johnson came on the line.

"Mr. President, Prime Minister Alexei Kosygin's on the Hot Line. How do you wish to respond?"

"What did you say?"

Walt Rostow, Johnson's national security adviser, had already awakened the president earlier that morning at 4:35 a.m. with news reports of Israeli military attacks on Egypt. Johnson also had spoken with Secretary of State Dean Rusk about the Israeli action, but neither Rusk nor Rostow were aware of the Hot Line activation.

"What do you think I should do?" Johnson asked.

"I will respond and say that you'll be down in the Situation Room in fifteen minutes. In the meantime, I'll call Dean and we'll meet you down there."

"Fine."

The crisis that became known as the Six-Day War had been brewing all spring in 1967, and the Hot Line's activation should have been the only surprise that June morning. Johnson had actively sought to defuse the building tensions, but he was unable to avert the war.

Prewar Actions

Johnson and Rusk had sought an evenhanded approach to Arab-Israeli matters in the mid-1960s while still supporting Israeli security. That aim, however, proved difficult because of the intense feelings within the American Jewish community about the US role in protecting Israel. "They look upon anything less than an all-out pro-Israel stance," Rusk wrote in his memoir, "by the State Department and the US government as betrayal."

Growing opposition to the Vietnam War among American Jews added instability to Johnson's Mideast balancing act. Johnson saw commonality between containing communist expansionism in Southeast

Asia and blunting Soviet encroachment in Mideast Arab states, with the latter increasing the threat to Israel. He was troubled that Jewish intellectuals and activists who joined antiwar demonstrations seemed unappreciative of his strong public support for Jews and Israel.

Cross-border violence between Israel and Palestinian Fatah guerrillas dramatically increased in 1966–1967 and it upset Johnson's policy calculations. A serious clash in April 1967 prompted Egyptian leader Gamal Abdel Nasser to mobilize his military in May and immediately

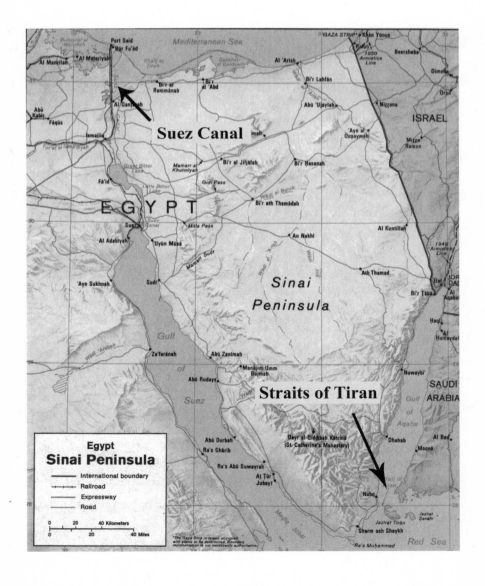

deploy units into the Sinai. He asked UN secretary general U Thant to withdraw a portion of the UN peacekeeping force in Sinai, which was a leftover from the 1956 Suez War. U Thant startled the United States and Israel by ordering the withdrawal of all UN troops in Sinai, and those forces were gone by May 18. Four days later, Nasser closed the Straits of Tiran, the narrow passage between the Red Sea and the Gulf of Aqaba that he had closed during the 1956 Suez War. It was a vital route for Israeli shipping to Africa and Asia, and Nasser's action provided a casus belli for Israel.

Johnson and his advisers moved quickly to restrain Israel. The president also wrote Kosygin, asking for help moderating the situation, and consulted with the French and British. London suggested forming a UN-sponsored multinational naval task force to break Nasser's obstruction of the Straits of Tiran. Johnson made the proposed operation, derisively termed the "Red Sea Regatta" by opponents, a centerpiece of his strategy to prevent a war. But difficulties quickly arose. Although the State Department liked the plan, Defense objected. The Pentagon had the Navy busy with Vietnam operations, and rapidly getting US ships to the Red Sea without access to the Suez Canal would be difficult. Further, the types of ships available for the flotilla were incapable of fully defending themselves in confined waters from Egyptian aircraft. Last, organizing combatants from different countries would be a daunting order for a task force commander.

Johnson would not entertain either "unleashing" Israel or unilateral US action. Letting Israel open the straits on her own might lead to another war. If Israel fared poorly, Johnson would have to lead America into the hostilities. The latter option was off the table because of the Congressional backlash he had incurred after the 1964 Gulf of Tonkin incident. The president had used the North Vietnamese attack on US naval ships off the North's coast to gain Congressional approval for broad military actions to stem communist aggression in Southeast Asia. He had then leveraged that authority to start the Vietnam War, and many believed that Johnson had misled Congress by exaggerating details of the Tonkin incident.

On May 26, ten days before the start of the war, Israeli foreign minister Abba Eban visited Washington in what proved to be a key point in both US and Israeli prewar strategies. Israeli prime minister

Levi Eshkol sent his emissary with the ostensible purpose of seeking Johnson's affirmation of the president's previously declared intent to reopen the Straits of Tiran. At the same time, though, the Israeli cabinet was ready to go it alone and preemptively attack Egypt, and Eshkol wanted to convince Johnson that he had a justifiable reason—the Egyptians were about to attack. As Eban arrived in Washington on the 25th, Eshkol cabled him instructions to exaggerate the Egyptian threat: "All to create an alibi."

At about the same time, the CIA sent to Rusk, McNamara, and Walt Rostow a skeptical assessment of Israeli cries of an Egyptian wolf. "We think it is probably a gambit intended to influence the US to do one or more of the following: (a) provide military supplies, (b) make more public commitments to Israel, (c) approve Israeli military initiatives, and (d) put more pressure on Nasser."

Johnson gathered all of his advisers together at 1:30 p.m. on Friday May 26, to discuss how he should handle Eban. "Around sundown I'm going to have to bell this cat," Johnson said. "I need to know what I'm going to say." He encountered mixed reactions, as the following examples from the ensuing discussion show.

"Whatever we do we're in trouble," Assistant Secretary of State Lucius Battle said of America's standing with the Arabs.

"Israel's existence is at stake," declared Vice President Hubert Humphrey.

"The United States cannot let Israel stand alone," offered Judge Abe Fortas, a Johnson confidant and a member of the Supreme Court at the time.

"If Israel fires first, it'll have to forget the United States," Rusk countered. McNamara agreed.

Mindful of this mix of opinions among his advisers, the president welcomed Eban in the Yellow Oval Room in the living quarters of the White House at 7:15 p.m. on May 26. Also present were Rusk, McNamara, Joint Chiefs chairman General Earle Wheeler, Rostow, and several others. The guest sat on a plush yellow sofa, with Johnson in an armchair under an ornate chandelier. After some preliminaries, Eban got to the bottom line: "Do you have the will and determination to open the straits? Do we fight alone or are you with us?" Johnson responded with talk about a multinational fleet and aspirations for UN action, but said he needed time to coordinate such actions. He said nothing about US unilateral action. However, he added that he, the Congress, and the country "will support a plan to use any and all measures to open the straits."

McNamara briefed Eban on the Pentagon's assessment—equal to CIA's—of Egyptian forces and intentions, which contradicted Israeli conclusions that an Egyptian attack was looming. The president then went beyond that point by declaring, "If [Egypt] attacks, you will whip the hell out of them." The president also stated his concern about Israeli preemptive action: "If your cabinet decides to do that they will have to do it on their own." Johnson said with emphasis, "*Israel will not be alone unless it decides to go it alone.*" The president repeated that statement during the remainder of the session.

During the following days, the Israelis carefully parsed Johnson's words for a green light, or even a blinking yellow, for an Israeli assault on Egypt. Some hint, perhaps, to go along with Johnson's declared intention "to use any and all measures to open the straits." Secretary Rusk appeared to offer such support on May 31 with the public remark, "I don't think it's our business to restrain anyone." But Walt Rostow sent a conflicting signal by telling Israeli ambassador Avaham Harman that Johnson saw no workable resolution to the crisis. That point worried the Israeli cabinet in Tel Aviv, leading them to suspect Johnson could find an unhelpful compromise with Nasser regarding his blockade of the Straits of Tiran. The Israeli need for a clarification of Johnson's position became more acute when Jordan and Egypt signed a mutual defense pact, making an Israeli preemptive attack on its Arab neighbors seem more urgent than ever.

Eshkold resorted to a dual approach to clarify the confusing messages emanating from Washington. First, he immediately sent the head of Israeli intelligence, Meir Amit, to Washington to probe Secretary McNamara and CIA director Richard Helms for at least implicit approval for offensive Israeli operations. Amit gained nothing substantive from either American, but in separate conversation with a Helms assistant, James Angleton, he heard a supportive remark. "Meir, if you crush Nasser," Angleton said, "the Americans will cheer you on." Upon his return to Israel, Amit told the Israeli cabinet, "The United States won't go into mourning if Israel attacks Egypt."

Prime Minister Eshkold's second initiative involved using well-established private communications channels between President Johnson and Israeli politicians and diplomats. Minister Ephraim Evron, the second-ranking official in Israel's Washington embassy, called on Justice Fortas on June 1. Johnson's close friend, assuredly speaking for the president, thanked Eshkold and Eban for allowing the president to explore nonmilitary means to defuse the situation. "If they had not done so," Fortas said, "it would have been difficult to secure the president's sympathy." Evron reported this oblique statement to Eshkold and Eban as a greenish light. The next day, Israeli ambassador Avraham Harman spoke with Fortas in his Supreme Court chambers. The justice, who had just talked with Johnson, offered more support: "Rusk will fiddle while Israel burns. If you are going to save yourselves, do it yourselves."

The US ambassador to the UN, Arthur Goldberg, sent a stronger signal to his Israeli counterpart, Gideon Rafael. Goldberg wrote that the Regatta idea was off the table, and only Israel herself could challenge Nasser. "I understand that if you act alone," Goldberg wrote, "you will know how to act." This message, when added to those gleaned by Amit, Evron, and Harman, convinced the Israeli cabinet on June 4 to start the war the next day. In their view, President Johnson had decided to stand aside. Essentially, Johnson had changed the red light he had given Eban in the White House on May 26, to a yellow-green signal by June 2.

In 2007, political scientists John Mearsheimer and Stephen Walt, using recent Israeli studies, confirmed that Israel's intent from the beginning was to launch a preventive war. In keeping with Eshkold's instruction, "All to create an alibi," the Israeli leadership had to mask their real intentions. Cabinet member Menachem Begin called the hostilities a "war of choice." Begin said of Nasser, "We decided to attack him."

Israel Attacks, the Hotline, and USS *Liberty*

Israeli strike aircraft flew west out to sea on the morning of June 5 before turning back toward the Egyptian coast and making low-level approaches to Egyptian airfields. Within two hours, Israel had destroyed much of the Egyptian air force, the primary hindrance to quick victory. Those operations also removed one of President Johnson's main concerns—a need for the United States to join the hostilities.

Johnson thus cast aside the assumptions of the pre-hostility period of his crisis management and his public stance of cautious planning. Instead, he shifted to strong support of Israel and turned to his most important objective during the actual hostilities—deterring Soviet intervention. Another primary focus would be avoiding a cease-fire that returned control of the Straits of Tiran to Egypt. The four-year-old Washington-Moscow Hot Line facilitated both of Johnson's crisis goals beginning on the first day of the actual war. Created in the aftermath of the clumsy communications during the 1962 Cuban Missile Crisis, the Hot Line allowed Johnson and Kosygin to exchange views, proposals, and threats. For example, in his initial message to Johnson that triggered McNamara's phone call on June 5, Kosygin wrote, "We hope that the Government of the United States will . . . exert appropriate influence on the Government of Israel particularly since you have all opportunities of doing so."

As Johnson and his team prepared a reply to the Soviet premier, Rostow had the Hot Line technicians query their counterparts in Moscow regarding how the president should address Kosygin in the message. The answer: "Comrade Kosygin." Johnson replied with a Hot Line message dutifully addressed to Comrade Kosygin. He wrote that he too was seeking a cease-fire and added, "We feel it is very important that the United Nations Security Council succeed in bringing this fighting to an end as quickly as possible and are ready to cooperate with all members of the Council to that end." The Situation Room staff transmitted the reply via the hastily arranged White House Hot Line connection at 8:47 a.m.

Ambassador Llewellyn Thompson, temporarily home from Moscow and called to the Situation Room that day, said in a 1968 interview that Soviets initially believed Johnson was "making fun of them in some way" with the "Comrade" salutation. However, the Soviet ambassador to the United States, Anatoly Dobrynin, later told Thompson that he had guessed that the seemingly condescending salutation had been an innocent mistake.

The early Hot Line exchanges did not deter Nasser from claiming US aircraft had joined the Israeli forces in the initial strikes. Egypt and several other Arab states broke diplomatic relations with the United States as a result. American officials later determined that the Egyptians based their allegation on the unusual direction from which the Israeli aircraft attacked. The Egyptian radar tracking would have matched that of carrier-based US Navy strike aircraft. Regardless, the Arab reaction to Nasser's assertion quickly triggered one of the most damaging political mistakes of the Johnson administration during the war.

At the June 5 press briefing at State, spokesman Robert McCloskey stressed the US neutrality in the conflict. "We have tried to steer an even-handed course through this. Our position is neutral in thought, word, and deed." McCloskey's statement elicited a storm of protest from American Jews, a wind that blew into the White House office of Johnson's special assistant, Joseph Califano. He contacted Rusk later in the afternoon, saying, "McCloskey's statement was killing us with the Jews in this country." When Johnson heard of the gaffe, he quickly ordered his press secretary, George Christian, and Rusk to back away from the McCloskey remark.

Israeli ground forces surged into the Sinai after the initial wave of air attacks against Egypt. Soon Israel began combat operations against Jordan. With Israeli success on the battlefield expected, Johnson concentrated on preventing a superpower confrontation. He began spending many of his waking hours in the Situation Room conference room with his closest advisers. The location gave him immediate access to the government's broadest range of communications, and he often made decisions on the spot. Similarly, the Soviet Politburo, of which Kosygin was first among equals, remained in continuous session.

On day three of the war, June 7, Israel seized all of Jordan's West Bank territory. The Israelis then heeded Johnson's call for a cease-fire with Jordan to stabilize the rule of King Hussein. Israel also offered to accept a full UN-ordered cease-fire on the Egyptian front, but Egypt refused. Although Syria had pummeled Israeli settlements with artillery fire and Israel had retaliated, neither country had attempted to invade the other.

President Johnson and his staff continued to battle the fallout from the McCloskey neutrality statement two days previously. Speechwriter

Ben Wattenberg and domestic legislative counsel Larry Levinson sent a memo to Johnson late on the 7th to notify him of a planned rally the next day in front of the White House, sponsored by the Anti-Defamation League of the B'nai B'rith. The two men suggested Johnson send a supportive message to the gathering. "It would neutralize the 'neutrality' statement and could lead to a great domestic political bonus—and not only from Jews," the memo read. "Generally speaking, it would seem that the Mid-East crisis can turn around a lot of anti-Viet Nam anti-Johnson feeling, particularly if you use it as an opportunity to your advantage."

Johnson, when he saw Levinson later in the West Wing, vented his frustration with domestic political issues that were interfering with his management of the Arab-Israeli crisis. Johnson raised his fist and shouted, "You Zionist dupe! You and Wattenberg are Zionist dupes in the White House. Why can't you see I'm doing all I can for Israel?" The president stormed off to the residence, leaving Levinson, as he said later, "shaken to the marrow of my bones."

The outburst reflected Johnson's complex character, which author Robert Dallek placed in perspective in an essay for PBS. "Johnson was much loved and greatly hated—not just liked and disliked but adored by some and despised by others. Some people remember him as kind, generous, compassionate, considerate, decent, and devoted to advancing the well-being of the least advantaged among us. Others describe him as cruel, dictatorial, grandiose, and even vicious."

On June 8, unidentified aircraft and torpedo boats inexplicitly attacked an American intelligence-gathering ship, USS *Liberty*, in international waters off the Israeli coast. Johnson and his advisers immediately thought the Soviets were responsible and had to wait over an hour before word reached the White House that Israeli forces had severely damaged *Liberty*. When the US Sixth Fleet rushed assistance to the ship, Johnson sent Kosygin a Hot Line message, one of five exchanged that day, which assured the Soviets the US Navy was not joining the hostilities. The Israelis claimed they had made a mistake, but the administration was quite skeptical. Dean Rusk said later, "I didn't believe them."

The Johnson administration declined to dispute vigorously the "accident," although thirty-four *Liberty* crewmembers died and 171 were wounded. Johnson didn't need a crisis with Israel at this point. That has not stopped others from speculating that the reason for the Israeli attack, especially in view of its timing, had something to do with Syria. Syria had shown little interest in joining the war through June 8. Within the Israeli cabinet, however, a debate raged on the costs and benefits of punishing Syria for its support of deadly operations against Israel in the 1960s. Defense minister Moshe Dayan opposed the proposal, but others wanted retaliation for the hundreds of Israelis killed over the years by Syrian gunners on the Golan Heights. The latter group finally won Eshkold's support for a Syrian front, but the attack was delayed until the morning of June 9. Critics of Israel's claim of an accident suggest the Israelis feared that *Liberty* would intercept pre-assault radio communications and alert Washington of the pending attack; hence the strikes on *Liberty*.

On June 9, Israel, Syria, and Egypt agreed to a UN cease-fire, but Israel kept fighting to drive the Syrian army from the Golan Heights, a strategically important area of western Syria. Rusk threatened UN sanctions, but the Israelis appeared to be within a day or two of a clean sweep of their three Arab neighbors and were reluctant to stop. The Soviet Union, an aggressive supporter of Syria since 1956, weighed in at this point by pressuring the UN and America to rein in the Israelis. With his patience wearing thin, and his concern for Syria's fate growing, Comrade Kosygin hit on a means to get the attention of Johnson and Israel.

A Soviet Threat and Resolution

"On the morning of June 10 we thought we could see the end of the road," Johnson wrote later. "But new word from Moscow brought a sudden chill to the situation." The Hot Line was up again, and a message clattered out of the White House terminal. "Mr. Kosygin wants the president to come to the equipment as soon as possible."

Johnson was in the Situation Room when the message arrived. With him were McNamara, Rostow, Helms, Thompson, former national security adviser McGeorge Bundy, and Under Secretary of State Nicholas Katzenbach. The Kosygin message arrived at 8:48 a.m., and the men pored over the version translated by the Hot Line operators. Thompson translated aloud as he read parts of the Russian copy, saying Soviets warned of a grave catastrophe if the United States did not force Israel to stop fighting immediately. If it failed to do so, the Soviet premier threatened military intervention. Johnson pushed aside his half-eaten breakfast of chipped beef on toast. The room, according to Helms, "went silent as abruptly as if a radio had been switched off."

Just five years after the superpower confrontation over Soviet missiles in Cuba, the threat of a larger war had erupted again. Richard Helms later recalled the moment: "Tension in the room was as taut as a violin string. One feels a visceral physical reaction. Our voices were so low we might have been speaking in whispers."

"Where is the Sixth Fleet now?" Johnson asked McNamara. The president had instructed the ships to stay well clear of the hostilities, but he wanted to know their exact location.

McNamara picked up a phone and called the National Military Command Center. In a moment, he lowered the handset to his chest to keep the line open and answered, "Three hundred miles west of the Syrian coast."

"How fast do these carriers normally travel?"

"About twenty-five knots. They are some ten to twelve hours away from Syria."

The group knew that Soviet surveillance ships and submarines had been keeping close track of the carriers USS *America* and USS *Saratoga* and their escorts. The Soviet units would instantly report any change in US operations to Moscow. Johnson felt an incremental step would signal America's resolve in the face of a Soviet threat. The men discussed the advantages and risks associated with moving the naval forces. Everyone agreed with the idea, and Johnson ordered, "Send them east, but no closer to the Syrian coast than fifty miles."

Rostow organized a reply to Kosygin, which emphasized US efforts to halt the Israeli fighting, and the Situation Room staff sent the message at 9:39 a.m. Although Johnson and his team assumed the worst from the Soviets, Ambassador Dobrynin later downplayed Soviet intentions at that point. "The Kremlin did not actually plan any definite military action against Israel," he wrote in his memoir. "It only considered further airlifting of armed supplies to Arab countries at their request." Dobrynin cited similar actions by the United States as the reason.

Regardless of the signal conveyed to the Soviets by the carrier movement, Johnson knew that he had to force the Israelis to stop fighting. He instructed Katzenbach to deliver a stern message to the chargé at the Israeli embassy in Washington. The undersecretary returned to the State Department and called in Minister Ephraim Evron, who appeared immediately. "President Johnson says it is time for a cease-fire to be in place," Katzenbach said, "and he is not prepared to accept any delays."

"I understand," Evron responded. He offered no protest or argument.

"Do you want to inform your government, or do you want me to have our ambassador in Israel do so?"

"Your communications may be faster," said Evron. "Let's do both."

The Israelis accepted the cease-fire within two hours. The tone of the final two Kosygin Hot Line messages softened considerably, which Johnson's team viewed as a result of the Sixth Fleet maneuvers. Dobrynin instead credited the continuing Hot Line exchanges for cooling the crisis.

Johnson and Kosygin exchanged nineteen Hot Line messages during the Six-Day War. President Johnson wrote later of the link's value during the crisis: "The Hot Line proved a powerful tool not merely, or even mainly, because communications were so rapid. The overriding importance of the Hot Line was that it engaged the heads of government and their top advisers, forcing prompt attention and decisions." Rostow told me in 2001 that he was pleased the Hot Line only had a teletype connection. "I'm glad the circuit had not been a telephone line or we might have inadvertently said the wrong thing."

Assessment

Conventional wisdom holds that President Johnson eschewed bold and decisive action to either prevent or manage the crisis of the 1967 Six-Day War. He felt severely constrained by the ongoing Vietnam War, understood the widespread reluctance in Congress for unilateral US action, and dreaded the ever present possibility of a confrontation with the Soviet Union. Further complicating the complex mixture of forces and factors was the constant pressure from Jewish Americans and sympathetic congressmen to back Israel to the hilt regardless of the situation. As a result, Johnson *appeared* to have struck a middle course in which he focused on restraining Israel and a far-fetched plan to assemble a multinational fleet to challenge Nasser's blockade of the Straits of Tiran, a scheme wholly opposed by the Pentagon.

Johnson didn't have to seriously contemplate bold moves since both the Pentagon and CIA predicted an easy Israeli victory. Instead, in the words of Bundy, the president sought to "watch closely, watch against escalation, watch out for the safety of the Israelis, and try not to let it get out of control." Johnson opted for a cautious, muddling-through approach, or so it seemed.

Bundy's reasoning may be a bit too pat and sidesteps the possibility that Johnson operated at two levels during the crisis, public and very private. William Quandt, an NSC staffer in the 1970s, was critical of Johnson's public actions during the pre-crisis period, claiming that Johnson had locked himself into a narrow range of actions and put himself into a period of "wishful thinking." Now the Edward R. Stettinius Professor of Politics at the University of Virginia, Quandt saw Johnson's activity before the shooting started as "cautious, at times ambiguous, and ultimately insensitive to the danger that war might break out at Israel's instigation." But all of that from a normally bold and decisive Johnson may have been merely spin for Congress, the media, and public. It may also have formed a smokescreen for Johnson's private and unspoken greenish light to Israel to strike Egypt, and then Jordan and Syria. Johnson's statements to Eban on May 26 in the White House, when taken collectively, should have showed the latitude that the president would tolerate: "Any and all measures to open the straits"; "whip the hell out of them"; and "Israel will not be alone unless it decides to go it alone." Perhaps Johnson, an ardent supporter of Israel, simply meant, "Go it alone." No one is alive today to support this theory, but the private communications between Johnson and the Israelis via Fortas and Goldberg appeared to have switched on a "winking" green light.

Quandt faults the Johnson administration for not linking crisis decisions during the hostilities to possible postwar outcomes. What would Israel do with the Sinai, West Bank, and Golan Heights? Eisenhower had forced Israel to withdraw from those areas after the 1956 War, which didn't yield peace. Johnson, who later called those arrangements "temporary and hasty," didn't press for the same action after the Six-Day War. On one hand, Johnson understood that wherever territorial lines were drawn, the enmity created by the Arabs' humiliating defeat, coupled with Israel's overconfidence in victory, could not be a basis for a lasting peace. Conversely, and cynically speaking, Israel's long-term occupation of the seized territories may have been part of the private arrangement to allow the Israelis to strike and keep the spoils of war.

Whether Johnson cautiously muddled through the 1967 War or adroitly stayed on the sidelines out of Israel's way, the crisis did not mark an end to Arab-Israeli conflict. Nor did it change the manner in which the United States approached the problem or forestall the next Arab-Israeli war six years later. Soon after the 1967 war's end, President Johnson asked for a thorough review of US interests in the Mideast. A bland consensus report later reached the president, the product of interdepartmental inertia and bureaucratic biases. Johnson, leafing through the review, turned to an aide and asked, "Same old shit isn't it?"

Part II. USS *Pueblo* Seizure, 1968

Few Good Options

"Captain to the bridge!" squawked the ship's public address system. Commander Lloyd Bucher arose from his lunch shortly before noon and strode briskly up to the signal bridge. Quartermaster First Class Charles Law pointed at an unidentified vessel headed straight toward USS *Pueblo*. The coastline of North Korea loomed on the hazy horizon behind the contact.

The ship's executive officer, Lieutenant Edward Murphy, joined Bucher and suggested the vessel was a North Korean submarine chaser, a small coastal combatant. Bucher then sent Murphy one deck down to the pilothouse to confirm *Pueblo*'s exact location. As the craft closed at forty knots, the quartermaster of the watch confirmed that it was a Soviet-built SO-1 class sub chaser. The North Korean crew was at battle stations and had their twin 57 mm guns rigged for action.

Pueblo was on station in the western Sea of Japan on January 23, 1968, to collect signals intelligence (SIGINT) emanating from North Korean military facilities and operations. The Navy had disguised the ship as an oceanographic research vessel, but it actually carried a 29-man detachment from the Naval Security Group, the service's SIGINT collection and exploitation arm. The team operated intercept and recording equipment in a boxy structure built on the deck of the World War II coastal logistics ship. Inside the SIGINT "hut," Cryptologic Technician First Class Don Bailey turned to a teletype circuit and typed a quick message to the Security Group's regional center in Kamiseya, Japan, COMPANY OUTSIDE. Lieutenant Murphy reported to Bucher that *Pueblo* was fifteen and nine tenths nautical miles off the North Korean island of Hug Do. North Korea claimed that their territorial waters extended to twelve nautical miles.

The SO-1 slowed and began to circle *Pueblo*, which was dead in the water. The North Korean vessel hoisted international signal flags that spelled out, WHAT NATIONALITY? Bucher had his signalman raise the American Flag. On the third time around, the SO-1 replaced its signal flags with HEAVE TO OR I WILL FIRE. *Pueblo* replied, I AM IN INTERNATIONAL WATERS. Bucher ordered a formatted emergency message transmitted that reported the North Korean harassment. Bailey sent it at 12:54 p.m.

Meanwhile, four P-4 North Korean torpedo boats arrived on the scene. All of the crews were on deck with weapons pointed at *Pueblo*. Bucher immediately ordered Lieutenant (junior grade) Carl Schumacher to transmit a second emergency message, a CRITIC, the military's highest priority warning of danger. Bucher then asked how long it would take to scuttle the ship—two hours—and then asked for water depth—thirty fathoms (180 feet). Too shallow to thwart North Korean divers.

The SO-1 neared *Pueblo*, and it was clear to Bucher that the North Korean crew, armed with automatic weapons, meant to board his ship. He ordered the ship under way on a course away from the coast. But as *Pueblo* gained speed, the sub chaser fired a salvo with her 57s, and the P-4s rattled off a six-second burst of machine gun fire. The rounds shattered the plastic windshield on the bridge and riddled the superstructure. Bucher and others dove to the floor, and the captain, wounded by shrapnel, shouted, "Commence emergency destruction of all classified pubs and gear!" With his ship armed only with two .50 caliber machine guns, which were mounted in exposed locations, Bucher decided not to fight. He ordered, "All stop," to the engine room.

The SO-1 signaled, FOLLOW ME. I HAVE A PILOT ABOARD. Bucher complied. Bailey sent an update at 1:45 p.m., WE ARE BEING ESCORTED INTO PROB WONSON REPEAT WONSON. Some of the men in the SIGINT hut began beating equipment with sledgehammers, while others shredded and burned documents. The officer-in-charge, Lieutenant Stephen Harris, didn't want to throw weighted laundry bags of material overboard in such shallow water. Accordingly, Bucher decided to gamble a bit to gain more time to destroy classified material, and ordered the ship to stop. That prompted another salvo from the sub chaser that raked the *Pueblo*'s starboard side. The exploding shells mortally wounded Fireman Duane Hodges. On the bridge, Bucher hesitated, but then ordered, "Ahead one-third."

Pueblo's first emergency message took two hours to reach the headquarters of the US Fifth Air Force, the command tasked with providing support in the event of trouble. The Fifth had four aircraft stationed at Osan, South Korea, which was thirty minutes flying time from *Pueblo*'s location. All were configured to carry nuclear weapons, though, and could not be converted in time to help. Twelve F-105 Thunderchief fighter-bombers launched from Okinawa but had to abort and land in South Korea because of darkness. Other tactical aircraft based in Japan were unavailable, largely because of US-Japanese agreements limiting US offensive operations from Japanese territory. US authorities restrained South Korea from launching fighters because of concerns of a possible North-South engagement that might escalate. Theater authorities had not assigned either maritime or airborne escorts for *Pueblo* for three reasons: Accompanying forces could elicit a like response and prompt an engagement; such an escort would dampen the signals that *Pueblo* hoped to collect; and the threat to *Pueblo* had been judged as minimal by the Commander, Naval Forces Japan.

Early Decisions and Actions

Just after midnight on January 23, Washington time, the senior duty officer in the White House Situation Room received *Pueblo*'s CRITIC and called Walt Rostow at home. Rostow came into the Sit Room and at 2:24 a.m., nearly two hours after the boarding report, awakened Johnson. The president took no immediate action; *Pueblo* had already moored in a North Korean port.

In the early afternoon, Johnson began his weekly Tuesday luncheon with his national security advisers. Joining him were Secretaries Rusk and McNamara, JCS chairman Wheeler, Director Helms,

Rostow, and Secretary of Defense–designate Clark Clifford. Johnson first asked about possible Soviet involvement in the *Pueblo* incident, and Rusk reported that they had denied participation. The president asked about action alternatives but then proceeded to tick off his own ideas: "Hitting the North Koreans with US forces, getting a thorough explanation, and capturing one of their ships." The forceful and strong-willed Johnson rarely let his team tee up options without first giving his opinion, an approach that has stifled alternative thinking in presidential crises.

The discussion quickly turned to an issue that would prove tricky for the administration in the coming weeks—*Pueblo*'s location at the time of the confrontation. Wheeler used a map to show that *Pueblo*'s noon position report had it twenty-five miles offshore and sixteen from the nearest North Korean island. But McNamara hedged by saying it was "unclear whether or not the ship had strayed into waters near the coast of North Korea prior to the incident."

Helms reminded everyone that two days before, North Korean infiltrators had attacked the Blue House, the residence of South Korea's president, Park Chung Hee. Further, North Korean military units had recently violated the Demilitarized Zone that separated North and South Korea. Johnson picked up on those events later in the meeting and voiced a theory that he would doggedly embrace throughout the crisis—an integrated, worldwide communist plot to attack US forces and interests.

After *Pueblo* had docked in Wonson Harbor, the North Koreans removed the crew and Hodges's body. Guards repeatedly beat the men and immediately began interrogating Bucher and demanding a confession of espionage operations. The North Koreans eventually transported the crew to Pyongyang.

On January 24 (Korean time), the day after *Pueblo*'s seizure, Rear Admiral John Smith entered a building that sat precisely astride the border between North and South Korea near Panmunjom. As the chief negotiator for the United Nations Command, he was there to meet with his North Korean counterpart, Major General Pak Chung Kuk. Smith demanded that the North return *Pueblo* and crew and apologize for the illegal action. Pak, after a diatribe against America that was quite common in such meetings, listed his country's demands—acknowledge that *Pueblo* had been in North Korean territorial waters, apologize for the illegal incursion, and promise never to do it again.

On the same day in Washington, President Johnson and his advisers convened again. News reporting of the incident was the first agenda item. Primary among them were criticisms from Capitol Hill about the absence of a rescue attempt. "Were there no planes available which were prepared to come to the aid of this vessel?" Johnson asked. "Every press story I have seen this morning said that US planes were only thirty minutes away."

"Air defenses in the Wonsan area are extensive," McNamara replied. "If we had sent airplanes to support and intercept, it is likely that these extensive air defense measures would be brought into play. In addition, it is necessary to consider the time of day and the approach of darkness." Later in the day, the president and his team met again to consider action options. But no effective alternatives emerged that didn't endanger the crew or precipitate another East Asian war. Johnson did authorize a strong message to Premier Kosygin in Moscow but stopped short of using the Hot Line. Johnson announced that he wanted to meet again the next morning, January 25.

The general unpopularity of Johnson and the Vietnam War made it easy for politicians, regardless of party affiliation, to make hay over an international setback to the United States. Senator Stuart Symington (D-MO) asserted that the American commitment to Vietnam let other nations challenge the United States with impunity. Representative Bob Wilson (R-CA) asked semi-rhetorical questions: "Why wasn't air cover sent? Why wasn't there protection for the patrolling *Pueblo*? Why wasn't the ship scuttled . . . before it was boarded?" Representative Durwood Hall (R-MO) called for an immediate and forceful response. Editorial writers likened the *Pueblo* seizure to Johnson's Tonkin Gulf incident—the August 1964 engagement between US and North Vietnamese military forces that some believed Johnson had embellished.

At a breakfast meeting on the 25th, Johnson and his team discussed the need for diplomatic initiatives that might gain the time needed to send military reinforcements to the theater, seek support in Congress, and convince the Soviets to help with North Korea. Other subjects included possible Soviet, North Korean, and Chinese reactions to aircraft and ship movements, a reserve call-up, and extending military enlistments to keep units at full strength.

The men met again for lunch, and the president got down to brass tacks. Johnson repeatedly asked, "How do we get the ship and the boys back?"

"Mr. President, the only way to get that ship out with the crew is talking through diplomatic channels," Undersecretary Katzenbach bluntly answered. "We must make it clear that this is the wiser course for North Korea." Katzenbach then argued for an incremental approach: "I think we should take our steps fairly slowly. We should see how we are doing in the United Nations before we ask for broader authority in Korea."

Secretary Rusk agreed: "We cannot shoot the men out of there. The North Koreans do not have vessels on the high seas that we can seize."

"Clark," the president asked Clifford, "what is your judgment on this whole situation?"

"If anything, I have a feeling that we need to proceed with caution. . . . I am not comfortable with this large military build-up." He then added, "If it appears we pose a threat to North Korea and do nothing, we are in a very difficult situation.

"I am deeply sorry about the ship and the eighty-three men," Clark concluded, "but I do not think it is worth a resumption of the Korean War."

"But this still leaves us," Katzenbach responded, "with the fact that they took a tug at Uncle Sam's beard and got away with it."

At a third meeting that day, the discussion turned back to possible reaction by the Soviets and Chinese to military actions. "I think a measured show of force supports our diplomatic efforts," Clifford said. "We can start by saying that no North Korean shipping will come out of two or three harbors. By blocking them off, we take reversible steps." Clifford surely recalled Kennedy using the naval blockade, a reversible step, in the Cuban Missile Crisis. Eventually, the group decided to call up selected reserves and move reinforcing forces to the western Pacific.

Toward the meeting's end, Helms asked a tough question about an ultimatum. "What is wrong in telling the North Koreans they must get the ship to us by a certain date or face the consequences?"

"The simple answer to that," Johnson said, "is that we do not want a war with the Chinese and the Soviets."

On January 26, the news media became aware of Johnson's decisions on reserves and reinforcements. On the same day, the president addressed the nation on TV and stated that the military steps were for contingency purposes. He also described his approach to the UN and talked in general terms of other diplomatic initiatives.

Later that day, Washington time, North Vietnam escalated the Vietnam War by launching coordinated military operations throughout the South—the Tet Offensive. While US and South Vietnamese forces ultimately dealt a severe defeat to the North, the public's perception about positive outcomes in Vietnam began to erode rapidly. Even Johnson aides questioned the president's long-standing optimism about the war.

The confluence of events mounted enormous challenges for Lyndon Johnson. The widely reported North Vietnamese Army's siege of the US Marine Corps base at Khe Sanh in South Vietnam, the Tet Offensive that followed that battle, and the *Pueblo* seizure collectively led Johnson to see a coordinated communist push against America. These challenges weighed heavily on the president, and his staff saw weariness and despair in his eyes and body language. At times during this trying period, Johnson's emotions yielded to the pressures. Often unable to sleep at night, he walked down to the Situation Room in his robe and pajamas to check the status of operations in Vietnam. Author Robert Mann wrote that in early 1968, Johnson "often cried uncontrollably."

The public's rising distrust of Johnson on military matters gained further momentum eleven days into the *Pueblo* crisis. McNamara and Rusk appeared on NBC TV's *Meet the Press* on February 3 and seemed to backpedal on *Pueblo*'s location at the time of seizure. The administration had maintained to this point that the ship was in international waters, and US ambassador Arthur Goldberg followed that line at the UN on January 26. However, McNamara told the NBC audience that *Pueblo* had kept radio silence January 10–21. "In that period," he said, "we lack knowledge of its moves." The news media seized on the waffling as more evidence of the administration's duplicity.

On February 7, Major General Pak handed Rear Admiral Smith a casualty list from *Pueblo*. By the next day, the news media reported Hodges's death and the wounding of two other sailors and a Marine.

Resolution

Johnson declined on March 31 to run for another term. Subsequently, he appeared to feel less pressure to "do something" about *Pueblo*, leaving him the freedom to do what was best for the crew—work through negotiation for their release. This approach irritated the families of the crew, especially when the administration failed to regularly share news and developments with them. Commander Bucher's wife, Rose, and other wives began writing letters to their representatives and senators, as well as to the White House. The resulting publicity prompted Republicans on Capitol Hill to ratchet up election-year criticism of Johnson and the Democratic Party. Representative Bob Michel (R-IL) called the *Pueblo* affair, "still another failure of the United States foreign policy during the past eight years." Representative Louis Wyman (R-ND) urged the administration to "get off its duff." Sadly, though, the crew's imprisonment dragged on throughout much of 1968.

An idea for breaking the impasse between the UN and North Korea arose not in the halls of the State Department but in a private residence in nearby Bethesda, Maryland. In late November, James Leonard, State's Korea country officer, talked with his wife, Eleanor, about how the US government might trick the North Koreans by signing a false apology, yet not pay the price on the world stage. Mrs. Leonard had an idea. "If you really make it clear beforehand," she argued, "that your signature is on a false document, well, then you remove the deception." Just tell the world that the paper you are about to sign contains falsehoods.

Leonard and former South Korean ambassador Winthrop Brown approached Undersecretary Katzenbach with the idea. They reasoned that North Korea could use the written confession of illegal operations and apology internally and not care about what the Americans said about the document around the world. The undersecretary endorsed the plan for "prior refutation," which became known as the "Leonard proposal." Johnson approved it in hopes of getting the crew home by Christmas or the end of his term.

Major General Gilbert Woodward, who had replaced Admiral Smith at the Korean DMZ, immediately liked the idea and on December 17 met with his counterpart, General Pak. Woodward explained the process, and Pak soon approved. On December 23, Woodward signed a document prepared by North Korea, which the United States repudiated both before and afterward. The North Korean authorities released the crew at 11:30 a.m., Korea time, and the men of USS *Pueblo* walked across North-South border on the Bridge of No Return.

Assessment

> There is a time for everything,
> > and a season for every activity under the heavens;
> > . . . a time to tear and a time to mend,
> > a time to be silent and a time to speak.
> > > > > > > > > Ecclesiastes 3:7

Johnson initially thought of boldly rescuing *Pueblo* and crew, and early discussion centered on those options. He ordered reinforcements to the theater to support possible military solutions, but within days, his advisers highlighted the lack of any option for forceful action that would protect the hostages' lives. Dean Rusk frequently cited Ecclesiastes 3:7, saying that as long as the crew remained imprisoned, it was not a time for aggressive action but rather a time for patient diplomacy. Nicholas Katzenbach offered sound advice that would be useful to any president when hostages are involved—use an incremental approach and take steps that you can reverse. Clark Clifford also counseled caution. When options are limited, he said, don't worry about the loss of a tuft of Uncle Sam's beard.

Factors beyond the immediate *Pueblo* crisis, primarily the poisonous atmosphere surrounding his handling of the Vietnam War, further limited the range of options available to Johnson. As biographer Robert Dallek wrote in 2004, the administration's "false hopes, self-generated illusions, and paranoid fears of domestic opponents" didn't inspire confidence within the public or Congress in Johnson's crisis decision-making." Given that atmosphere, Capitol Hill opponents of the president, as they are wont to do during any administration, heaped abuse on the man. In this case it was for not protecting the ship in the first place and not rescuing it upon the attack.

Johnson's advisers largely united behind a negotiation-first approach, but Johnson invited enough outsiders into his crisis deliberations to allow for a helpful range of opinions. Although the families of the *Pueblo* crewmembers would disagree, Johnson successfully muddled through a tricky situation.

In another example of the value of hindsight, more recent reporting on Soviet and North Korea relations in 1968 undercut Johnson's presumption of their coordinated actions on *Pueblo*. The Soviet Union was "not only uninvolved in the planning but they were also exceedingly unhappy with both the attack itself and Kim's unwillingness to accept an early resolution." A Soviet official reportedly said at the time, "When we try to moderate this warmongering state of mind, our position is not taken into account."

A few of Johnson's advisers lived long enough to witness succeeding presidents wrestle with hostage crises. Some of those commanders in chief would later point to Johnson's handling of the matter as something to avoid, while others understood and appreciated his approach. Men and women in the Oval Office would speak of USS *Pueblo* many times in the future.

CHAPTER 5

RICHARD NIXON

The October War, 1973

Watergate and the Mideast

Assistant Secretary of State Joseph Sisco knocked loudly on the bedroom door of Henry Kissinger's suite at the Waldorf Towers in Manhattan. Waiting only a few seconds, Sisco unceremoniously opened the door and followed the shaft of light from the anteroom into the darkness. He awoke the secretary of state, and as soon as Kissinger became alert, announced that Egypt and Syria were about to start a war with Israel. The time was 6:15 a.m. on Saturday, October 6, 1973—Yom Kippur, the Day of Atonement in the Jewish religion and the holiest day of their year.

Sisco told Kissinger that the State Department in Washington had received an alert from Kenneth Keating, the US ambassador to Tel Aviv. Israeli prime minister Golda Meir was convinced that Egypt and Syria were about to assault Israeli military positions in the Palestinian, Egyptian, and Syrian territories that Israel had been occupying since the 1967 war. Keating's message thoroughly surprised US intelligence and diplomatic officials. The ambassador also relayed Meir's request that the US government notify immediately the Soviet Union and Israel's Arab neighbors that Israel had no plans to attack preemptively either Egypt or Syria.

Kissinger, who was in New York to attend the annual UN General Assembly meeting, quickly told his communications people to call Anatoly Dobrynin, the Soviet ambassador in Washington. Once on the line with Dobrynin, the pajama-clad secretary described the situation and passed on Meir's promise not to initiate hostilities despite the looming threat. Kissinger also commented on the potential impact of an Arab-Israeli war on the recent thaw in the Cold War, which the United States and the Soviet Union called détente, French for "easing of tensions." "This is very important for our relationship," Kissinger said to Dobrynin, "that we do not have an explosion in the Middle East right now."

At 8:35 a.m., after a number of other calls, Kissinger phoned President Richard Nixon's chief of staff, General Alexander Haig, who was with Nixon in Key Biscayne, Florida. Nixon had retreated to his vacation house for a brief respite from the Washington theatrics surrounding the investigation of White House involvement in the 1972 break-in at Democratic Party offices in the Watergate office building. "We may have a Middle East war going on today," Kissinger said as Haig got on the line.

"Really?" Haig replied, reflecting the general surprise in the United States that morning.

"I am sending a report to the president and to you of the events this morning. We got a report at 6:00 this morning that the Israelis were expecting a Syrian and Egyptian attack within six hours."

"Yes," Haig acknowledged, and then asked about a major potential problem. "What is your view of the Soviet attitude?"

"My view is that they are trying to keep it quiet and they are surprised," Kissinger replied.

"Do you believe that?"

"Yes. I think it is too insane for them to have started it."

"You never know," Haig said, and then added a separate thought: "A lot of difficulties here."

The general was lamenting the grand jury investigation of Vice President Spiro Agnew for extortion and bribery during his time as Maryland governor. Also, Nixon was in the middle of a constitutional crisis involving the Watergate prosecutor's subpoena of secret audio tapes from Nixon's two White House offices.

Next, the men addressed coordination matters, including Henry's return to Washington and scheduling a meeting of Nixon's crisis management team, the Washington Special Action Group (WSAG). Kissinger concluded with a warning about public comments and Nixon's role.

"Don't let Ziegler shoot off at the mouth without our knowledge," Kissinger said, referring to White House press secretary Ron Ziegler. "Your position is that the president is on top of the situation and getting regular reports."

"I will say the president received a report at 6:00," Haig responded.

"Say 6:30. Say I have been in contact with all of these people."

"Okay," Haig said, and then prepared to speak with Nixon.

Background

"Deceptively calm" is how former NSC Mideast staffer William Quandt described the Middle East from September 1970 to October 1973. "In the absence of acute crises, American policymakers paid comparatively little attention to the area," Quandt wrote later. Moreover, Washington did not understand that Egyptian president Anwar Sadat had hatched a plan to restore the Arab stature that had been lost in the 1967 War. "I had to win back honor and prestige for my people," Sadat wrote in his memoir, "not only in Egypt but throughout the Arab world." He had perceived that the Israelis were not as unbeatable on the battlefield as they seemed, nor were Arab countries surrounding Israel as inept as America and Europe supposed. That confidence, he later explained, led him to his long-term strategy: "Paradoxically, I went to war to make peace."

Sadat's first step was to expel 15,000 Soviet military advisers in July 1972. He expected their presence at the start of his planned assault on Israel to complicate military operations, plus Soviet aid to Egypt had declined in response to the US-Soviet détente. The need for Egypt to maintain good relations with the Soviets, Sadat asserted, had decreased in response. According to Quandt, Nixon's attention to his 1972 reelection prevented exploiting the Soviets expulsion to strengthen US-Egyptian ties.

Sadat and Syria's leader, Hafez al-Assad, agreed to a coordinated attack on Israel, and both began war planning in the fall of 1972.

Beyond the goal of reestablishing Arab standing, they sought to regain control of the territories occupied by Israel since 1967. According to Sadat, he undertook a series of military, diplomatic, and rhetorical feints to disguise his war preparations, including two massive military exercises in May and August of 1973. Israel mobilized its reserves each time, which were costly endeavors. Sadat explained later that, when he began actual hostilities, Israel would likely conclude that the activities represented another war game and wouldn't mobilize.

Unlike Washington, Moscow saw danger ahead. In a May 1973 meeting with Kissinger, Soviet leader Leonid Brezhnev warned that Egypt and Syria planned to retake lost land through war and claimed that he could not stop them. Soviet foreign minister Andrei Gromyko, in the United States for the UN General Assembly meeting on September 28, told Nixon the same thing. "We could all wake up one day and find there is a real conflagration in that area." Further, Brezhnev warned Sadat on four occasions before October not to attempt to regain the Sinai Peninsula, lost six years earlier.

President Nixon swore in Henry Kissinger as the secretary of state on September 22 and thus added a second hat to that of national security adviser. It was an unparalleled concentration of power and was subject to both praise and suspicion. Many authors have noted that the two men made an odd couple. Nixon was a loner and misanthrope who hated multiple groups: journalists, Ivy League liberals at the CIA, and Jews, for example. Kissinger was a socially adept bon vivant who enjoyed partying with celebrities. The president placed the Fourth Estate high on his enemies list, while his foreign policy adviser schmoozed and spoon-fed his favorite reporters. Yet the two suffered equally from paranoia and its handmaiden, secretiveness.

A few accounts of the October War hold that Sadat advised Brezhnev on September 22 that the war would start on October 6. On the other hand, Victor Israelyan, a Soviet foreign ministry diplomat, wrote in 1995 that the Kremlin had no notice before October 4. On that date, the Soviet ambassadors in Cairo and Damascus gained permission for Soviet aircraft to land and evacuate Soviet dependents. Simultaneously, the Israeli cabinet met repeatedly to consider intelligence reports of Egyptian and Syrian military activities and dispositions. As Sadat had expected, the Israel Defense Forces and military intelligence analysts viewed developments as exercises or defensive in nature.

Finally, at sunrise on October 6, when all indications were that the Arabs were about to attack, IDF chief of staff Lieutenant General David Elazar demanded a reserve call-up and urged Meir to attack Egypt and Syria preemptively. Both the prime minister and Minister of Defense Moshe Dayan refused, knowing that the United States would not fully support Israel if it struck first. "Don't ever preempt!" Kissinger previously had told Israeli ambassador Simcha Dinitz. "If you fire the first shot, you won't have a dogcatcher in this country supporting you. You won't have presidential support. You'll be alone, all alone." Meir indeed held firm, and the war started at 2:00 p.m., four hours earlier than expected.

Israel on the Defensive

Major General Brent Scowcroft, who had become Kissinger's White House deputy in August, convened a WSAG meeting at 9:01 a.m. on October 6. Attendees in the Situation Room included Secretary of Defense James Schlesinger, Chairman of the Joint Chiefs Admiral Thomas Moorer, Deputy Secretary of State Kenneth Rush, Director of Central Intelligence William Colby, and several others, including Quandt. The discussion centered on traditional questions in initial crisis management meetings: What's going on? Who started it? Are American citizens at risk? What should the president do? What are the president's objectives? What should we say to the news media? As in virtually all incidents such as this, the fog of war predominates and answers were scarce. The session lasted only an hour.

Quandt later wrote about why the Arabs had caught the United States by surprise. Foremost was the existing Mideast balance of power, which heavily favored Israel. The volume of 1971–1973 US military aid to Israel had led Quandt to the conclusion: "It would be an act of folly for the Arabs to initiate a war."

Four hours after their first telephone conversation that morning, Haig called Kissinger and announced Nixon's plans to return to Washington. The two men talked about the signals Nixon might send to either the Soviets or the combination of the news media and political opponents by cutting short his vacation. "If he returns early," Kissinger said, "it looks like a hysterical move." He later added another thought about helping the president with his tarnished image. "We should use the president when it will do him some good." Kissinger also counseled Haig to dampen any of Nixon's ideas of taking aggressive actions in the Arab-Israeli conflict, or perhaps exploiting a foreign crisis to ease the domestic pressures. In his recent anxious state, Nixon occasionally had fantasized with Haig and Kissinger about taking bold action in a crisis, along the lines of the popular fictional character Walter Mitty, who escapes reality in dreams of personal triumphs. Kissinger pointedly warned Haig, "I would urge you to keep any Walter Mitty tendencies under control."

After returning to Washington from New York, Kissinger chaired a WSAG meeting at 7:22 p.m. Participants were roughly the same as in the morning but with the addition of Treasury Secretary William Simon. The president did not attend, which was the case throughout the crisis. It was not Nixon's style to meet with his advisers to discuss policy options. Haig told me in 2001 that Nixon didn't like group meetings that might turn unscripted and spontaneous. "He preferred to let his advisers meet without him, and then study their written evaluation of a crisis and recommended actions." NSC staffer Peter Rodman seconded that point: "He basically hated people. He would much rather communicate by written memos than in any kind of discussion."

Director Colby started the WSAG meeting with what little information he had—Syria was pushing into the Israeli-occupied Golan, and Egypt was attacking Israel's defensive line in the Sinai east of the Suez Canal. Discussions then turned to Nixon's order through Kissinger to move units of the US Sixth Fleet in the Mediterranean Sea to a point near Crete as a show of force. Discussion of the evacuation of American citizens from potentially dangerous spots continued from the morning session.

Soon, Kissinger attempted to crystallize the issues. "Our major problems are the position of the UN; the general US stance; and the Soviet Union. Ideally, we would like to deal with the matter jointly with the Soviet Union to get a ceasefire and a restoration of the status quo ante." Further, Kissinger and the others clung to an assumption that would persist through the first week of the crisis, that Israel would quickly counterattack and finish off the Arabs in short order.

At one point, the group turned to a matter that would dominate White House crisis management during the war's first phase—if, when, and how to resupply Israeli military forces. Kissinger, Schlesinger, and Rush agreed they could wait a few days on the matter. This initial hesitancy was rooted in a concern by Nixon and Kissinger about the potential downside of an overt tilt toward Israel. The men had spoken earlier on the matter, with the president saying, "One thing that we have to have in the back of our mind is we don't want to be so pro-Israel that the oil states—the Arabs that are not involved in the fighting—will break ranks."

Political horse-trading, both international and domestic, often continues during crises. The United States and the Soviets were then engaged in negotiating a trade pact that would grant "most favored nation" status to the Russians. But Senator Scoop Jackson (D-WA) wanted to amend the agreement to force the Soviets to ease restrictions on Jewish emigration. Kissinger told Dobrynin on October 7 that he would continue to push for a Soviet MFN designation if Dobrynin's bosses would show restraint in the Middle East war. To Jewish leaders, Kissinger said that in return for an American resupply of Israel he wanted them to drop their support of the Jackson amendment. He also broached the subject with Dinitz, telling the Israeli that he planned to mention the MFN issue in a speech October 8. "I hope to God this is not a week when every Jewish league will start attacking me on this position."

Israel's standing army suffered a series of setbacks during the first two days of fighting, especially against Syria in the north where there was no buffer zone such that the Sinai provided. Israel frantically transported mobilized reserve forces into blocking positions, north and south, but the situation was dire on October 8. That evening Meir and her kitchen cabinet met through the night to consider their options. They decided to place the IDF's nuclear weapons on alert. They had assembled by that time thirteen twenty-kiloton devices, which the Jericho missile and F-4 Phantom jets could deliver. This move generated a debate in America after the war, with positions ranging from the literal—Dayan feared for Israel's existence—to the cynical—it was a move to blackmail America into full-bore support or signal-sending to the Arabs via the Soviet Union.

Meir also instructed Dinitz to contact Kissinger and warn that Israel was on the verge of defeat. Dinitz and the Israeli defense attaché, Major General Mordechai Gur, met with Kissinger and two NSC staffers in the White House Map Room early in the morning of October 9. They detailed Israel's staggering losses to that point—forty-nine combat aircraft, including fourteen F-4s, and five hundred tanks. Dinitz asked that the numbers be given only to Nixon, and he pleaded for an immediate and robust American resupply effort. But organizing and executing the resupply turned into a messy affair and a crucial turning point in the crisis.

The Resupply Gambit

Historians and biographers have created a cottage industry analyzing the dynamics of the US resupply activities during the war. On one hand, some believe Kissinger heroically overcame Pentagon resistance and established an air bridge to a desperate Israel. Others maintain that the Machiavellian secretary of state, in cahoots with Schlesinger, arranged to slow the resupply. Kissinger wanted to further his geopolitical goals of keeping the Soviets at bay and not alienating the Arabs. All of this would help him negotiate a permanent peace after the war but still ensure that Israel remained secure. "The best result," Kissinger told Schlesinger early on, "would be if Israel came out a little ahead but got bloodied in the process, and the US stayed clean."

Reconstructing the resupply episode depends on sorting through multiple sources—contemporaneous reporting, memoirs, and biographies—and deciding which are accurate and which are image-polishing half-truths. For example, Nixon's memoir is of little value for reasons cited throughout this chapter. Kissinger's many volumes have extraordinary detail, but he appears to have excluded key points on the critical resupply initiative. Some Kissinger biographers push one version, while others seem more objective. And so on.

From October 7 through 11, Ambassador Dinitz pestered Kissinger for commitments on replacing destroyed equipment and expendables. The secretary dissembled, dodged, and blamed the Pentagon for not being forthcoming. Additionally, he slowed the process by quibbling over possible aircraft platforms—cargo planes from the Israeli airline El Al, charters, or US military transports. All evidence points to Kissinger and Schlesinger creating a charade to give Kissinger time to exploit the crisis for larger Mideast peace objectives.

The starkest description of Kissinger's gambit came from an insider, Admiral Elmo "Bud" Zumwalt, the chief of naval operations at the time and a member of the Joint Chiefs. In his memoir, Zumwalt recalled a chiefs meeting on October 10 in which they received resupply guidance from Schlesinger. Their services were to be "overtly niggardly and covertly forthcoming." Zumwalt later asked Schlesinger directly about the scheme. The secretary replied that his "hands were tied" and that national policy was "to maintain a low profile and avoid visible involvement." Alarmed that Kissinger appeared to be usurping power from the distracted president, Zumwalt privately advised Senator Jackson about the Kissinger scheme. "I told him that I believed Israel was going to lose if the United States did not get equipment aloft at once." Schlesinger confirmed his comments to Zumwalt in a piece that Les Gelb wrote in the *New York Times* the following year. Schlesinger told Gelb that the delay was a "national policy."

On the 12th, Pentagon officials described to Dinitz the logistical and political impediments to an aggressive resupply effort. That caused Dinitz to threaten his big gun—appealing publicly to the American Jewish population, a tactic within his capability. In fact, the Israeli ambassador to Washington has been called the de facto leader of Zionist Jewry in America, and Dinitz called the vociferous American Zionists his "shock troops." Their likely response would have been so widespread and severe that Nixon might have resigned in 1973 instead of the following year.

Besides Dinitz's threat, two other developments on October 11 and 12 brought an end to the apparent Kissinger-Schlesinger scheme. The Soviets were sending giant AN-22 transports full of war supplies in a stream of nose-to-tail flights to Syria and Egypt. Further, the Soviet general staff placed their seven airborne divisions on alert, adding to the pressure to support Israel.

Regardless of motives and manipulation, Nixon and his team got a full-scale airlift off the ground on Saturday, October 13, seven days into the war. True to form, there are several versions of that decision process. Those providing differing details of the decision included Nixon; Kissinger; several Kissinger biographers, among them Walter Isaacson, Roger Morris, and the brothers Marvin and Bernard Kalb; author Edward Sheehan; and Israeli insider Matte Golan. It is as if a bunch of people reached into the Mr. Potato Head kit and fabricated wholly different characters with exactly the same plastic pieces. Yet, however Nixon's team reached consensus on the airlift, US military aircraft were moving a thousand tons a day to Israel by October 14. On that same day, Israel had regained lost ground in Golan and won a decisive battle in Sinai. The following day, the IDF, now unhindered by resupply concerns, initiated a bold counterattack across the Suez Canal aimed at splitting the Egyptian Second and Third Field Armies.

During the resupply theatrics, multiple domestic developments limited Nixon's attention to the Israeli crisis. Agnew resigned under pressure on October 10, and two days later Nixon nominated House Republican Gerald Ford to replace him. Also on the 12th, the House passed the War Powers Resolution, a bill that would limit the president's

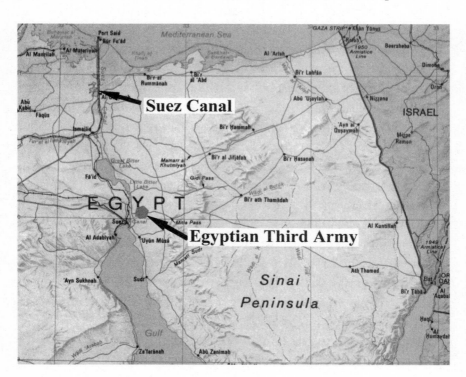

ability to commit US armed forces in a conflict without congressional approval. The Senate approved the War Powers bill two days later. Congressional leaders had chosen to push this legislation during a time when the Watergate scandal had weakened the presidency. Nixon later vetoed the bill, but both houses quickly overrode his veto.

Cease-Fire Maneuvering

On October 16, in a perfect example of a legislator bridging the separation of powers during a crisis, Senator J. William Fulbright called on Ambassador Dobrynin. The powerful chairman of the Senate Foreign Relations Committee described a secret Pentagon briefing for congressmen that suggested that Egypt was about to get shellacked by the Israelis. Fulbright told Dobrynin that the United States and the Soviet Union should impose a cease-fire to save both Sadat and détente.

After Fulbright's warning, the Soviets quickly became interested in a cease-fire to stem the Syrian and Egyptian losses. Premier Alexi Kosygin flew to Egypt on October 16 to coordinate with Sadat. Hafiz Ismail, Sadat's adviser, urged Kissinger through their back channel to formulate a US cease-fire proposal, reflecting an Egyptian distrust of the Soviets to help with a settlement. At about the same time on another front, Arab oil ministers in Kuwait announced 5 percent monthly cuts in oil production until Israel vacated the territories occupied in 1967. On October 20, Saudi Arabia declared an immediate 10 percent production cut and banned all oil shipments to America.

On October 19, the Soviets began pressing for a cease-fire. Brezhnev, acting on a back-channel suggestion from Kissinger, invited the secretary of state to fly to Moscow; Nixon agreed. "The trick would be to get a cease-fire at just the right moment," Quandt wrote later. "Until then, Israel should continue to advance on the ground, but, Kissinger felt, Israel must be prepared to stop once the superpowers reached agreement on a cease-fire." On the same day, the Nixon administration sent Congress a proposed $2.2 billion aid package for Israel to pay for the resupply, further adding to Soviet concerns.

The Watergate investigation drama reached a new crisis point on October 20, when Nixon ordered Attorney General Elliot Richardson to fire the special Watergate prosecutor, Archibald Cox. Richardson resigned rather than carry out the order, as did his deputy, William Ruckelshaus. The number three at the Justice Department, Solicitor General Robert Bork, agreed to discharge Cox. The news media dubbed the event the Saturday Night Massacre.

As Kissinger flew to Moscow, Nixon severely undercut the secretary's negotiating position, at least in Kissinger's view. The president cabled Brezhnev, writing, "Dr. Kissinger speaks with my full authority." That message infuriated Kissinger, who had planned to stall by begging consultations with Washington before agreeing to anything. He wanted to give the IDF more time as they encircled the Egyptian Third Army. Nixon also sent in-flight instructions to Kissinger, telling him to negotiate a deal in which the superpowers would impose a long-term settlement of the Arab-Israeli problem independent of Israel and the Arabs. Nixon understood the potential blowback from Jewish Americans on such a strategy. "I want you to know," the president wrote, "that I am prepared to pressure the Israelis to the extent required, regardless of the domestic political consequences." Kissinger ignored the instructions.

Nevertheless, by noon Washington time on the 21st, Kissinger and Brezhnev had agreed on the wording of a proposed UN cease-fire resolution. Haig quickly obtained Meir's grudging agreement. At 12:50 a.m. on October 22 in New York, the Security Council adopted Resolution 338, which called for a cease-fire in twelve hours and follow-on negotiations. At Meir's request for consultations, Kissinger detoured to Tel Aviv, arriving just before 1:00 p.m., Middle East time, on the 22nd.

With the UN cease-fire set for 7:00 p.m., Kissinger tried to ease Israeli concerns that the IDF wasn't ready to stop fighting. He gave them a green light to ignore the cease-fire temporarily. He told Meir that if the IDF engaged "during the night while I'm flying" home, there would be "no violent protests from Washington." Since Kissinger and Brezhnev had failed to establish cease-fire observation procedures, the secretary thought the Israelis could keep fighting. Kissinger reportedly hinted that two or three days might be available. Little did he know on October 22 that in two days his allowing some slippage in the cease-fire would create what many perceived at the time to be the most dangerous moment in the crisis.

Watergate and Changing the Subject

Nixon sought chances to wag the dog during the period of October 13 to 22, the second phase of the crisis. In the negotiations leading up to the Saturday Night Massacre, Nixon announced that he would not appeal a court order to hand over the audio tapes secretly recorded as Nixon discussed covering up the Watergate break-in. The president suggested such a move might inhibit his management of international dangers. Further, when he confronted Richardson, he asked the attorney general to delay his resignation until after the Middle East crisis was resolved. He added, "Brezhnev would never understand it if I let Cox defy my instructions."

Before Kissinger's departure for Moscow, Haig advised that Nixon wanted Henry to announce his trip to the media in order to draw attention to the bold presidential action. "My honest opinion is that is a cheap stunt," Kissinger responded. "It looks as if he is using foreign policy to cover a domestic thing." Although Haig argued otherwise, Kissinger persisted. "I would not link foreign policy with Watergate. You will regret it for the rest of your life." Kissinger provided these ethical pronouncements in his account of the crisis, but they seem at odds with some of his other machinations during the war.

The third phase of the crisis began on October 23 when the IDF took advantage of Kissinger's cease-fire slippage. Military leaders attempted to finish off the Third Army, which was isolated on the east side of the canal at a point south of the Great Bitter Lake. Kissinger quickly engaged in a back-and-forth with Dinitz and the Soviet chargé in Washington, Yuli Vorontsov. Brezhnev then weighed in with a cable addressed to Kissinger, not Nixon. Vorontsov read the text of the letter to Kissinger over the phone at 10:40 a.m. Brezhnev was incensed with Israel's reengagement: "This is absolutely unacceptable. All this looks like a flagrant deceit on the part of the Israelis."

Kissinger's complex web of maneuvering had gotten sticky again. "We were now in a serious predicament," he wrote later. ". . . If the United States held still while the Egyptian Third Army was being destroyed after an American-sponsored cease-fire and a secretary of state's visit to Israel, not even the most moderate Arab would cooperate with us any longer. We had to move quickly." Among other actions,

Kissinger had Haig call Dinitz and, in Nixon's name, formally demand Israel halt all offensive military operations.

Just after noon, to show his seriousness Brezhnev fired up the Washington-Moscow Hot Line for the first time since 1967. He used it to complain again of Israeli treachery and added, "Too much is at stake, not only as concerns the situation in the Middle East, but in our relations as well." Nixon replied within an hour, also via the Hot Line, and claimed that he was insisting that Israel stop fighting. That prompted a second Hot Line message from Brezhnev that urged US cooperation on another Security Council cease-fire resolution.

The UN did indeed pass another cease-fire resolution on October 24. In response, Sadat continued to communicate with Nixon, and Kissinger with Dinitz and Dobrynin. Kissinger pushed for an Israeli stand-down and safe passage of food and water for the Third Army, but the Israelis fought on. The Hot Line was quiet, however Brezhnev sent a note to Nixon via Dobrynin in the early afternoon. He was alarmed that the Israelis had broken the second cease-fire and insisted that the United States do something about it.

During the afternoon, Sadat precipitated the most critical point in the crisis. He asked that the Soviet Union and the United States jointly send military forces to enforce the cease-fire. Dobrynin and Kissinger exchanged several phone calls in the early evening about Sadat's appeal, and in one, the Russian said that his government would seek UN approval for joint peace-making operations. Kissinger replied, saying the United States would veto any such proposal.

In response, Brezhnev sent a message to Nixon via Kissinger that arrived at the State Department at 10:00 p.m. He threatened unilateral Soviet military action: "I will say it straight that if you find it impossible to act jointly with us in this matter, we should be faced with the necessity urgently to consider the question of taking appropriate steps unilaterally." Nixon's team suddenly faced the most dangerous point of the crisis. Kissinger immediately called Haig.

"I just had a letter from Brezhnev asking us to send forces in together or he would send them in alone," Kissinger said.

"I was afraid of that. Where are the Israelis at this point?"

"They've got the Third Army surrounded."

"I think they're playing chicken," Haig responded, speaking of the Russians. "They're not going to put in forces at the end of the war. Do the Israelis know? I mean, have you brought them along?"

"I've kept them informed. Should I wake the president?" Kissinger asked.

"No."

Twenty minutes later the two men spoke again. "Have you talked to the president?" Haig asked.

"No, I haven't. He would just start charging around—until we have analyzed it," Kissinger said, referring to Brezhnev's letter. They talked for several minutes about the risk of an armed confrontation with the Soviets, and then Kissinger explained that he had scheduled a WSAG meeting in the coming hour.

"Are you meeting at the White House or . . . ?"

"The State Department."

"He has to be a part of everything you are doing," Haig said, as a caution of blatantly excluding Nixon.

"Should I get him up?" Kissinger asked. Haig did not answer. He shifted the point to the meeting location.

"I wish you would hold it at the White House."

"All right."

The WSAG convened in the Situation Room at 10:30 p.m. on Wednesday, October 24. Attendees included Schlesinger, Admiral Moorer, Director Colby, Kissinger, Haig, Scowcroft, and Commander Jonathan Howe, Kissinger's military assistant. The group agreed the first order of business was to get Sadat to withdraw his request for joint Soviet and American forces. Accordingly, Kissinger had a back-channel message sent immediately. The primary concern, however, was that the Soviets might intervene with their on-alert airborne troops at first light the next day. Moorer pointed to the fact that the Soviet airlift flights had stopped and the aircraft may be preparing to carry troops instead. All discussed possible Soviet motives for threatening escalation. Kissinger and Haig pointed toward Nixon's precarious political position and suggested that the Soviet leadership saw an opportunity to exploit.

The discussion then turned to drafting a tough response and backing it up with signals of resolve. They decided to take several immediate actions: (1) Raise the worldwide defense readiness condition level from DEFCON 4 to DEFCON 3, the highest peacetime condition. (2) Move one carrier into the Mediterranean from the Atlantic, and position two other carriers in the eastern Mediterranean. (3) Order a Navy/Marine amphibious group to get under way from the island of Crete. (4) Put the US Army's 82d Airborne Division on alert. (5) Recall seventy-five B-52 Stratofortresses from Guam to the United States. The group knew that Soviet intelligence and surveillance assets would quickly detect these actions. They then completed drafting the response to Brezhnev. The DEFCON alert needed little amplification, so the letter was a mix of firm positions, accommodation, and polite words. The group decided to hold the response for several hours to give the Pentagon time to initiate its actions. The finished letter, "sent in Nixon's name," was delivered to the Soviet Embassy at 5:40 a.m. on October 25.

Nixon did not attend the WSAG meeting, although he later claimed that he did. Haig afterward asserted that the president had no intention of attending, and that he had visited Nixon in the residence several times during the meeting to coordinate Nixon's orders. British author Alistair Horne compiled a detailed survey of those who maintain Nixon played no role that night and was likely drinking. On that list is Roger Morris, biographer of Haig and Kissinger and former NSC staffer. He wrote of Larry Eagleburger and other Kissinger aides telling "a frightening story of Nixon upstairs drunk." Author Walter Isaacson wrote that Nixon was "not part of the decision-making process that night, nor was he briefed. Kissinger never even spoke to him, nor did Haig or anyone else."

Was Nixon ill or drunk? Horne asked Schlesinger. "I don't know," Schlesinger said. "Haig would know." Scowcroft told Horne that Nixon was "off the wall. . . . He had had a very bad day."

Was he drunk?

"I can't rule it out," Scowcroft responded. ". . . Two martinis and he changed . . . he couldn't hold his liquor."

By the afternoon of the twenty-fifth, Brezhnev sent a bland letter to Nixon that offered cooperation with the United States on a nonmilitary cease-fire observation team. After an all-night cabinet meeting, October 25–26, the Israeli government accepted the third and latest cease-fire, Resolution 340, which called for cease-fire monitors from non-superpowers. The Egyptian Third Army was spared, and the worst of the crisis was over.

At a press conference that Kissinger held on October 25, reporters bored in on the idea that the worldwide alert had been a manufactured diversion from Nixon's Watergate woes. Kissinger replied, "It is a symptom of what is happening to our country that it could even be suggested that the United States would alert its forces for domestic reasons." Despite Kissinger's scolding, the major newspapers harped on the timing of the alert. James Reston of the *New York Times*, for example, wrote the next day from Washington, "This town is seething with doubt and suspicion." Reston argued that Nixon's stonewalling on the secret Watergate audio tapes had poisoned the atmosphere surrounding the Mideast war. "But now if he hands over the tapes, people will say that he doctored them, and even when he staggers from one move to another, he is met with the cynical remark: 'A crisis a day keeps impeachment away.'"

Debate on the need for the US military alert and its efficacy continued for years afterward. Kissinger had his view: "The Soviets subsided as soon as we showed our teeth." Kissinger's chest thumping, however, doesn't jibe with other accounts of the October War. For example, Richard Lebow and Janice Stein published a study on the crisis in 1994, which was based on their interviews with Soviet Politburo members and accounts from Kremlin insiders. They portray a different Soviet reaction. First, Brezhnev had no intention of sending Soviet troops into the war. He made that clear to his Cairo ambassador on October 8 and again to Kosygin before the latter left to consult with Sadat in Egypt. According to Lebow and Stein, Brezhnev's October 24 threat to consider unilateral action was a bluff, issued in frustration at the failure of diplomacy to stop the fighting, and in anger at what Brezhnev considered Kissinger's "duplicity."

Once the US alert took effect, Brezhnev called a Politburo meeting. The DEFCON change confused the members, and they struggled to understand how one sentence in Brezhnev's 10:00 p.m. letter to Kissinger on October 24 could have caused such a US overreaction. The officials debated the real reason behind the alert, with Brezhnev and others seeing it as a manifestation of Nixon's desire to show that he was a strong president, despite the Watergate crisis. Others pointed out that the alert was inconsistent with the near continuous dialogue between Moscow and Washington. The top Washington analyst in Moscow, Georgi Arbatov, told Lebow and Stein, "The American alert was for home consumption."

Nevertheless, several powerful and hawkish Politburo members urged a Soviet mobilization in response to the US alert. Marshal Andrei Grechko proposed ordering Soviet troops to occupy the Golan Heights in response to the American attempt at intimidation. Kosygin argued against that idea: "It is not reasonable to become involved in a war with the United States because of Egypt and Syria." Finally, Brezhnev, unwilling to undercut his positive stance on détente, ruled out any military response. "Nixon is overreacting," he said, "and we need to give him an opportunity to calm down."

Lebow and Stein argue that Moscow's initial attempt at compelling the United States to stop the fighting backfired. For seventeen hours, Kissinger and the WSAG put aside leaning on the Israelis to deal with Brezhnev's perceived threat of "taking appropriate steps unilaterally." When the mini-tempest with the Soviets died down, US policymakers got back to the goal that they shared with Moscow—get Israel to adhere to the UN cease-fire.

Anatoly Dobrynin, in his 1995 memoir, wrote that Kissinger had asked him not to take the alert as a "hostile act," but rather a White House move "mostly determined by 'domestic considerations.'" Kissinger had asked Dobrynin to inform Brezhnev accordingly and that the alert would be canceled after twenty-four hours. Further, Dobrynin wrote that Kissinger later conceded that the White House "had made a mistake putting its forces on high combat alert." Dobrynin believed the Americans had created a myth that they had saved the Middle East from a Soviet invasion.

Sadat viewed the outcome of the war as a win for Egypt. "Our military efforts brought about the immediate restoration of Arab pride," he wrote later. "We destroyed the myth of an invincible Israeli military." He also reflected, perhaps self-servingly, on the impact of the war on his long-term goals: "Our victory gave me the power to later pursue peace with Israel despite protests from our Arab friends."

Assessment

The Nixon administration took two decisive, albeit incremental actions during the October War to manage the crisis. The first was the commitment to a full-scale resupply of Israel on October 13. The Soviet resupply of the Arabs had forced a US balancing action. But the shenanigans that Kissinger used to stall the full resupply operation in order to pursue non-crisis, geopolitical goals detracted from the resupply's ultimate success. The second decisive action was what Kissinger called his deliberate overreaction to what appeared to be a possible Soviet intervention in the war on October 24–25. We know now that Brezhnev's threat was a bluff, and Kissinger, acting in Nixon's name, responded with his own bluff. The remaining actions and decisions during the crisis, some of which involved the president, were cautious muddling-through steps aimed at containing and ending it. They included cease-fire proposals, consultations with the Soviets, Israelis, and Egyptians, and conferring with allies.

A number of issues and pressures inhibited bold and sweeping actions to resolve the October War crisis. Détente or not, the possibility of a superpower confrontation provided a dangerous backdrop throughout and limited America's range of response. Jewish American pressure was constant, and Ambassador Dinitz and Kissinger conferred repeatedly during the war in an attempt to manage the issue. Simultaneously, both Nixon and his advisers, especially Secretary of Defense Schlesinger, measured crisis decisions against possible reactions from the Saudis that might affect their oil exports. Both Nixon and Kissinger tried to exploit the crisis to establish a long-term peace process in the Middle East, but that often complicated the day-to-day management of the crisis.

But the 800-pound gorilla in the Oval Office—the Watergate investigation—vastly inhibited decisive action and caused the public and news media to question anything Nixon said or did. Mistrust was so widespread that observers had difficulty in determining which decision or initiative was a wag-the-dog moment or a legitimate crisis management undertaking. Steven Ambrose captured the circumstance in his monumental biography of Nixon. "A president, any president, expects—can count on—the people to rally behind him in the midst of a crisis. Yet what Nixon got in the October crisis was not support, but sneers, suspicions, and skepticism. . . . All of his action and statements had become suspect." Sadly, Nixon understood his predicament, and in private conversations with Haig and Kissinger he repeatedly asked them to spin the press and Congress on his "forceful" crisis leadership.

This tangled collection of pressures forced the president's team to employ several risky strategies that had the potential to backfire. For example, the alleged friction between Kissinger and Schlesinger that was cited as the reason for the resupply delay helped Kissinger with his complex dialogue with the Israelis. Conversely, the alleged Pentagon foot-dragging became a potential target for Dinitz's Jewish-American shock troops. The American resupply boosted Israel's successful counterattacks, but it triggered the Arab oil embargo. Allowing Israel slippage in the cease-fire deadline aided Kissinger's overall plan, but Israel's use of that leeway backed Kissinger into a tight spot with the Soviets on October 24–25. Additionally, Zumwalt called Kissinger naïve for attempting to use the slippage maneuver to coordinate cease-fire initiatives with Israeli military operations. "Any attempt to fine-tune the course of a battle in progress, particularly somebody else's battle, is almost laughably academic."

Another factor complicating Nixon's handling of the crisis was his management style. He preferred to remain aloof from the deliberations of his crisis team, a departure from the approach largely taken by the other presidents in this study. Choosing to read written recommendations from his senior national security advisers deprived him of the back-and-forth exchange of views that benefited other recent presidents in crisis, perhaps with the partial exception of Reagan. Haig and Kissinger kept the president informed, at least until the end of the crisis, but that gave Kissinger the chance to put his spin on every issue. Also, Nixon's growing stress levels and depression deepened his isolation. He appeared to withdraw from the crisis at key points, including the exchange of bluffs on the penultimate day of the crisis. The president's key advisers nevertheless acted on their own in accordance with Nixon's principles, a process that would be repeated in the second Reagan administration (chapter 8). This was not, however, a usurpation of presidential powers but rather an apparent honest attempt to take action.

   While Nixon and his team resolved the crisis, the October War undermined the nascent thaw in East-West relations created by détente, which became a partial casualty of the war. The Arabs responded with an oil embargo that created economic problems in the United States for several years. Israel solidified its control of the territories it seized in the 1967 War, and that occupation, in the view of many, remains an impediment to a lasting Israeli-Palestinian peace. On the positive side, the October War led to the 1979 agreements that Sadad had sought between Israel and Egypt, known as the Camp David Accords, and the associated Egypt-Israel Peace Treaty.

CHAPTER 6

GERALD FORD

SS *Mayaguez* Seizure, 1975

Bold Action, Second-Guessed

MAYDAY, MAYDAY, MAYDAY. SS MAYAGUEZ. HAVE BEEN FIRED UPON AND BOARDED BY CAMBODIAN ARMED FORCES AT 9 DEGREES 48 MINUTES NORTH AND 102 DEGREES 53 MINUTES EAST. SHIP IS BEING TOWED TO UNKNOWN CAMBODIAN PORT. MAYDAY.

CALL THE AMERICAN AUTHORITIES. CALL ANY-WHERE YOU CAN. MAYDAY.

The SOS from the American merchant ship SS *Mayaguez* landed on President Gerald Ford's Oval Office desk at 7:40 a.m. on May 12, 1975. Earlier, John Neal of Delta Exploration Company in Jakarta, Indonesia, had heard the ship's call for help on his radio at 3:18 a.m., Washington time. Neal called the US embassy in Jakarta, and the staff there sent a series of six cables beginning at 4:54 a.m. to several military commands and federal entities, including the National Military Command Center in the Pentagon. A duty officer there relayed the SOS to the White House Situation Room. Deputy national security adviser, Lieutenant General Brent Scowcroft, arrived in the Sit Room at 7:00 a.m. and quickly scanned the morning intelligence summaries and reports, including the *Mayaguez* SOS. He then walked to the Oval Office for his regular meeting with the president, accompanied by David Peterson, Ford's daily CIA briefer.

Scowcroft and Peterson briefed the president on the *Mayaguez* situation and included a bit of information that had not been part of the SOS. Scowcroft said that the ship reportedly was headed for the Cambodian port city of Kompong Som, now also called Sihanoukville. The Jakarta embassy had apparently added that news, and it would become an important factor in Ford's decision making as the crisis unfolded.

Three hours later, the President met with his press secretary, Ron Nessen, and displayed the frustration that was already building. "Would you go in there and bomb the Cambodians and take a chance of the American crew members being killed?" he asked, more thinking out loud than seeking Nessen's theories. "Would you send helicopter to rescue them? Would you mine every harbor in Cambodia?"

Speak English?

At the time Ford and Nessen spoke, *Mayaguez* rode at anchor in the overnight darkness near Poulo Wai, a Cambodian-claimed island in the Gulf of Thailand about sixty miles off Cambodian coast. The previous afternoon, Khmer Rouge troops aboard former US Navy Swift boats had intercepted the ship in the Gulf of Thailand as it made a routine transit. When one of the gunboats fired its machine guns across the bow of *Mayaguez*, Captain Charles Miller cut his speed. The Cambodians pulled alongside, and Miller had the pilot ladder lowered down the ship's side. Miller, a gray-haired, sixty-two-year-old veteran of thirty-two years at sea, said to himself, "Well, we'll find out soon enough what these bastards want."

Seven Cambodians, all armed with AK-47s and clad in black pajama-like clothing favored then by the communist Khmer Rouge, scampered up the ladder and then to bridge. "Speak English?" Miller asked. Nothing. "Parlez-vous français?" Nodding no, a Cambodian pointed at the chart table and motioned for Miller to join him. With a pencil, he drew the shape of an anchor next to Poulo Wai. As Miller prepared to get under way, other patrol boats arrived and a total of forty KR soldiers came aboard. Miller called for full ahead and followed the boats to a point just off Poulo Wai. *Mayaguez* dropped anchor at 4:55 p.m., 5:55 a.m. Washington time. The Cambodians were generally civil, especially after the ship's cooks fed them and led them to the crew's showers.

Mayaguez was a World War II–era freighter that in 1960 had been lengthened and converted to carry 274 containers. The Sea-Land Corporation used her on Southeast Asia routes, and on May 12, she was en route from Hong Kong to Sattahip, Thailand, with general cargo ranging from clothing to chemicals, as well as materials destined for US military facilities in Thailand.

We Will Act Quickly

President Ford convened an NSC meeting in the White House Cabinet Room at 12:05 p.m. on May 12. Joining him were Vice President Nelson Rockefeller; Henry Kissinger, then still both secretary of state and national security adviser; Secretary of Defense James Schlesinger and his deputy, William Clements; acting chairman of the Joint Chiefs, General David Jones (Chairman George Brown was traveling in Europe); Director of Central Intelligence William Colby; Ford's chief of staff, Donald Rumsfeld; Scowcroft; and several others.

Director Colby shared the meager available information on the ship's status, but it was based solely on the Jakarta embassy amplification and thus erroneous. "At last report," Colby said, "the ship was being taken to the port of Kompong Som, about sixty miles away, under escort by a Khmer communist gunboat." Schlesinger added to the bad information: "When I left the Pentagon, the ship was already only about ten miles out." This issue was key because the men immediately saw a parallel to the 1968 USS *Pueblo* incident, when the North Koreans forced the Navy ship into a mainland harbor and thus eliminated an array of military responses. Ford and his team suspected this would soon be the case with *Mayaguez* as well.

Colby did have some information, however, on potential Cambodian motives for what Ford immediately called piracy. The communist Khmer Rouge had taken control of Cambodia less than a month before and straightaway began asserting a claim of territorial waters extending out ninety miles from the coast. On May 4, for example,

Cambodian patrol craft had fired upon and chased a South Korean vessel near Poulo Wai, and three days later the Cambodians had held a Panamanian ship for twenty-four hours before releasing it. At the same time, Vietnam and Cambodia were jousting over undersea oil rights claims. At the crisis meeting, the discussion turned to the availability of military assets that might be near the Gulf of Thailand. Aircraft carrier USS *Coral Sea* was en route to Australia and could be diverted, but nevertheless was thirty-six hours away from the presumed location of *Mayaguez*.

Rockefeller, whom Ford had appointed as vice president when he succeeded Nixon, broke through the back-and-forth with a bold stand: "I think a violent response is in order. The world should know that we will act and that we will act quickly. . . . If they get any hostages, this can go on forever." Kissinger agreed, "At some point the United States must draw the line." Kissinger then defined two goals for any action: Get the ship back and give the appearance of a strong United States. President Ford agreed and ordered several immediate steps: Turn around *Coral Sea*, conduct continuous aerial reconnaissance of the Poulo Wai–Kompong Som area, deliver a strong protest to Cambodian government via the Chinese, issue a statement to the press, and develop military options to free *Mayaguez*.

The crisis presented Ford, the appointed president, with the opportunity to demonstrate decisiveness and prove that he deserved to be president. Further, he could help dissipate the embarrassing images of US military helicopters evacuating American citizens from atop the embassy in South Vietnam only two weeks earlier. The simultaneous Khmer Rouge assumption of power signaled America's ignoble retreat from Southeast Asia, prompting many to see the United States as a helpless giant. Nixon's resignation the previous year had already damaged America's reputation.

Ford's communications handlers wanted to use the incident to distinguish the president from his conniving predecessor. They didn't have to work hard, for Ford was the antithesis of Nixon, according to Scowcroft. "He had a very straightforward personality," Scowcroft said in 1996, "simple in the best sense of the word. There is no guile, no convolution, no complexity in Gerald Ford."

Gunfire

A Navy patrol aircraft identified *Mayaguez* at anchor near Poulo Wai early May 13. The Cambodians let loose a fusillade of small arms fire but hit the plane only once. In response, the officer in charge of the KR troops ordered Captain Miller to get under way. By 8:44 a.m., *Mayaguez* was gathering speed on a north-northeast course toward the mainland. After several hours, the KR officer had Miller heave to and anchor one mile north of Tang Island, which lay thirty-four miles from the Cambodian coast. Miller, who was aware of *Pueblo*'s plight seven years before, was relieved that they weren't headed immediately to Kompong Som. The anchor hit the water at 1:26 p.m. A flight of US Air Force F-4 Phantoms from Thailand arrived at 3:45 and strafed the sea surface near the ship. The signal to the KR was clear: Don't get under way!

At 5:00 p.m., the KR guards ordered the crew off the ship and onto two fishing boats alongside. After moving to shallow water to anchor overnight, a KR gunboat joined the nest. An officer disembarked and

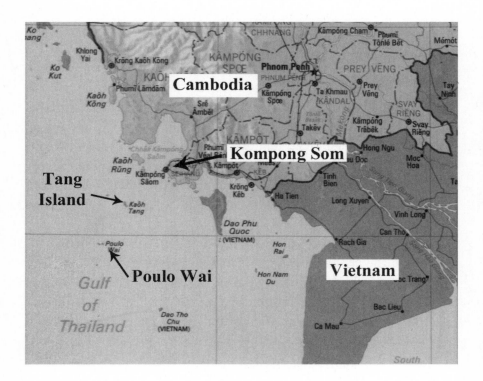

sought out Miller. "No worry," he said in broken English. "Cambodians no hurt you. Go back to ship in morning."

Do Something!

Scowcroft briefed Ford shortly after 9:30 p.m. on the sighting of *Mayaguez* anchored off Poulo Wai. Soon afterward, the Situation Room duty officer received the report that *Mayaguez* was under way, steaming toward the mainland. On Ford's order, General Scowcroft tasked the Pentagon with employing Air Force F-4s to use gunfire to dissuade the KR from taking *Mayaguez* to Kompong Som. The Phantoms and the ship had come together at Tang Island.

The president called for an NSC meeting for the morning of May 13 in the Cabinet Room. Kissinger was traveling in the Midwest on a trip that he didn't cancel for "business-as-usual" perceptions, and Undersecretary of State Joseph Sisco sat in for him. Schlesinger summarized military options for rescuing the crew and ship. Primary among them was sending 1,200 Marines from Okinawa to Thailand. Air Force helicopters would then carry the Marines to the Tang Island area for both an assault on the ship and the KR forces on the island. A Navy destroyer escort, USS *Holt*, was on the way to assist with boarding *Mayaguez*. *Coral Sea* and another carrier would also be available soon to support the Marines landing on the island. Schlesinger said that a Cambodian defector had reported sixty KR troops on Tang Island. Rockefeller twice remarked that time was against them. They had to do something quickly, he said. Robert Hartmann, Ford's counselor, agreed with the vice president. "We were all haunted, of course, by the *Pueblo* affair," Hartmann wrote later. "Ford wasn't sure at the outset what he would do, but he was sure he had to do *something*."

Near the meeting's end, the president reviewed the rough plan that had begun to form. First, use aircraft to stop any boats en route to or leaving the island. Second, stage the Marines to U-Tapao, Thailand. Third, board *Mayaguez*, and fourth, insert the Marines on Tang Island. After a few more exchanges, Ford directed specific actions: "I think the first two steps can be done. Let us take them." Nevertheless, Schlesinger and General Jones repeatedly spoke of the difficulty of some of the possible or proposed military operations. Although

Kissinger was absent, he wrote later of his exasperation with Defense's lack of enthusiasm for any *Mayaguez* operation. "The Pentagon dutifully assembled the forces as it was ordered to do. But it was clearly reluctant, offered no ideas of its own, and left it to the civilians to prod it into action."

The meeting highlighted two issues that came to dominate Ford's management of the crisis. The chance that the KR might take the crew or the ship to the mainland in a *Pueblo* scenario made time a critical factor. Rescue the crew before that happens was the byword. Second, Ford seized on the time constraint to centralize command and control of rescue operations, however improvised they might be, at the White House.

The US military suffered its first casualties associated with the *Mayaguez* crisis in the late evening of May 13 in Thailand. A US Air Force helicopter crashed shortly after takeoff in Thailand, killing eighteen Air Police and five crewmen. They were en route to U-Tapao for possible use in retaking *Mayaguez*. At about the same time, the Chinese liaison office in Washington—the two countries had yet to establish formal diplomatic relations—refused to accept the State Department's letter asking for help with the Cambodian government. George H. W. Bush, the American liaison in Peking, met the same resistance. Additionally, the Thai government refused to permit US combat operations to be launched from bases in that country. Ford and his team would ignore the restrictions but apologize afterward.

Tear Gas

Sunrise on May 14 greeted a stiff and poorly rested *Mayaguez* crew. Aboard two fishing vessels anchored fifty yards off a Tang Island beach, the men hoped the Cambodian officer's promise the night before to return them to the ship would prove true. The KR guards consolidated the men on one of the larger fishing boats, and nine armed Cambodians came aboard as well. The trawler got under way at 8:00 a.m. with an escort of two Swift boats. At first, Miller could see that they were steering for *Mayaguez*, but the craft abruptly turned northeast. "Hey, Skipper," yelled third mate Dave English, "looks like we're headed for Kompong Som."

Minutes later, six US attack aircraft roared over the boats and then climbed, banked, and came back in pairs on strafing runs. They fired their twenty-millimeter cannons and pod-mounted rockets and dropped bombs in front of the three boats. It was clear to Miller that the aircraft were attempting to force the vessels to return to Tang Island. The crew and their guards were exposed on deck and soon three crewmembers had been slightly wounded by shrapnel from nearby exploding bombs. Ultimately, one of the Swift boats peeled away and retreated to the island. The jets sank the second. A KR guard held his AK-47 at the head of the fisherman at the helm of the trawler and had him maintain his course toward Kompong Som.

Suddenly, the American jets stopped firing and began dispensing exploding tear gas canisters. Both the KR guards and the crew gagged as the gas seared their lungs and winced from the hot canister fragments striking their skin. One *Mayaguez* crewman, a cook named Kassem Saleh, thought to himself, *I can't breathe*. He passed out briefly, and, when he regained consciousness, he said to a shipmate, "If they do that again, I am going to jump overboard."

Commander in Chief's Orders

At 9:48 p.m. on May 13, Schlesinger's military assistant called Scowcroft with startling news. During a strafing run, a Navy A-7 Corsair pilot reported seeing possible Caucasians aboard a fishing boat headed toward Kompong Som. The pilot, whose radio had been patched through to theater commanders, the Pentagon, and the Situation Room, presumed that he might have seen *Mayaguez* crewmembers and asked for instructions. When Scowcroft passed this update to the president, Ford ordered an immediate NSC meeting. When all hands had arrived, Scowcroft quickly got to the point.

"We do not have much time," Kissinger's deputy said. "Our aircraft has used riot control agents twice. That has delayed the boat but it has not stopped it. It is now about six miles from Kompong Som, according to the pilot. He is not at all sure that he can disable the boat without sinking it."

"Tell them to sink the boats near the island," Ford directed. "On the other boat, use riot control agents or other methods, but do not

attack it." Scowcroft slipped away from the table and walked down-
stairs to the Sit Room. Scowcroft passed Ford's orders to everyone on
the improvised radio battle net, including the pilot. Ford said a few
years later that he felt compelled "to take strong, decisive action—as
opposed to the incremental use of force—even though the odds might
be against us. It was far better than doing nothing."

Welcome to Cambodia

On the president's orders, tactical aircraft had attempted to use riot
control gas to stop the fishing boat carrying the *Mayaguez* crew. But
as the vessel neared Kompong Som harbor, the aircraft withdrew. The
trawler tied up at the base of a twenty-foot-tall quay wall, one intended
to handle large freighters.

But soon the fishing boat cast loose its lines and motored southeast. It anchored off a beach, and guards fed the crew—steamed
rice with vegetables. They quickly got under way again and made a
ninety-minute run due west to Rong Sam Lem Island in the company
of a Swift boat. At 2:15 p.m., the fishing boat moored at a pier, and
a guard motioned for Miller to step ashore. A Khmer Rouge officer
held out his hand toward Miller, smiled, and in decent English said,
"Welcome to Cambodia."

"I'm Captain Miller," the American responded.

"We'll go ashore and have some hot tea. Then we'll fix some food."

Later, the same man, whom Miller called the "English-speaker,"
started questioning the captain. "Do any members of your crew work
for the CIA?"

"No."

"Are any of your crew members of the FBI?"

"No. We are all merchant sailors."

The questioning continued, and toward the end of the session, the
Cambodian asked about the American response to the ship seizure.
"Why did so many planes come? Three of our boats have been sunk
and one hundred friendly Cambodian people have been hurt." Miller
had no answer. As dusk fell that evening, the English-speaker finally
said to Miller, "Wait till morning. Then you can all go."

Congressional Grumbling

Eight hours later, President Ford convened his fourth and last NSC meeting of the crisis. Joining him in the Cabinet Room at 3:52 p.m. on May 14 were fourteen other men, including the council principals—Vice President Rockefeller, Kissinger, Schlesinger, Jones, and Colby. Director Colby summarized available information on the situation, some of which was erroneous. "The Cambodians have apparently transported at least some of the American crew from Tang Island to the mainland, putting them ashore at Kompong Som port at about 11:00 last night, Washington time." Colby added that the crew members might have been moved inland, but added, "At present there is no way of telling where they may be."

For nearly two hours, the president and his civilian advisers grilled acting chairman Jones, who was accompanied by Chief of Naval Operations Admiral James Holloway. They asked extraordinarily fine-grained questions about operational planning. Gradually, the group agreed on the final plan. The first wave of eight Air Force helicopters would land 175 Marines on Tang Island in an attempt to seize the island, thought to be defended by a few dozen KR troops, and seek out crewmembers thought to be held there. The aircraft would return to U-Tapao to pick up the next wave of Marines.

Three separate helicopters would drop forty-eight Marines on *Holt*'s miniscule helicopter pad. *Holt* would then approach *Mayaguez* and send over a Marine boarding party to take control of the ship and free any crewmembers onboard. *Coral Sea* aircraft would conduct simultaneous strikes against Kompong Som targets—Ream Airfield, naval facilities and vessels, and the civilian port.

Ford then asked about a sticky wicket—Congressional liaison. At issue was the War Powers Resolution (or Act) and its requirement for the president to consult with Congress before initiating combat. Many lawmakers viewed merely "advising" Congress as unacceptable. "Last night," counselor Hartmann said, "we gave the leadership information on your actions. They agreed. They said that they were advised but not consulted. We reported the attacks to them. Again, they supported you. Today, in the House, people are saying that there was no consultation under the War Powers Act."

Another at the table noted that the resolution required the president to notify Congress within forty-eight hours of a hostile act. That period, which had started with the aircraft warning fire on the patrol boats, expired that evening. In response, Ford directed his staff to invite the Congressional leaders to the White House immediately. He then told Schlesinger to execute the military plan.

An hour later, President Ford entered the Cabinet Room to the bipartisan applause of the assembled Congressional leadership. Ford outlined the planned military operations aimed at rescuing the *Mayaguez* crew but struck a nerve when he briefed them on the air strikes against the Cambodian mainland. Senate Majority Leader Mike Mansfield and Democratic senators Robert Byrd and John McClellan harshly criticized that part of the plan. "I thought we were going to use minimum force," grumbled McClellan. "Can't we wait and see if the Cambodians attack?"

"It's too great a risk," Ford replied.

"Frankly, I have grave doubts about this move," said Mansfield.

"Why weren't the leaders brought in when there was time for them to raise a word of caution?" Byrd asked testily.

"We have a government of separation of powers," Ford responded. "In this case, as commander in chief, I had the responsibility and obligation to act."

At this point, available intelligence indicated that at least some of the *Mayaguez* crew were on the mainland. Ford, however, had ordered four waves of air attacks on targets in and around Kompong Som, potentially putting the crew members' lives at risk. This suggests that signaling presidential resolve at a time when Ford was struggling to become a viable GOP candidate for 1976 was in competition with the crew rescue. Historian John Robert Greene offered his assessment of Ford's actions. "It can be argued that Ford threw caution to the wind when he agreed to a plan to retrieve the crew of *Mayaguez*—a plan that was a punitive operation born of a political need."

Let's Look Ferocious!

Cambodian authorities had decided to release the *Mayaguez* crew before the first wave of helicopters approached Tang Island. Virtually all of the subsequent activity undertaken by one protagonist was unknown to the other at the time.

Cambodia (local time)	**Washington** (local time)
6:07 a.m. May 15. Cambodian minister of information Hu Nim begins a radio speech in which he announces that *Mayaguez* is free to depart Cambodian waters.	7:07 p.m. May 14.
6:09 a.m. The first wave of five helicopters attempt to insert Marines on Tang Island. Two are immediately shot down, one ditches, one retreats, one makes emergency landing.	
7:09 a.m. Second wave of three helicopters approach Koh Tang, two of which land under withering KR fire with fifty-four Marines. The third retreats for refueling.	
	8:15 p.m. Sit Room gives Cambodian radio text to Scowcroft.
	8:23 p.m. A tuxedo-clad Ford arrives in the Red Room for drinks before a working dinner for Dutch premier Johannes den Uyl.
7:25 a.m. Marines on *Holt* board *Mayaguez*. No one onboard.	

7:29 a.m. Crew departs Rong Sam Lem on fishing boat en route *Mayaguez*.

7:45 a.m. *Coral Sea* aircraft drops first ordnance on mainland targets.

9:35 a.m. Navy aircraft sights fishing boat carrying crew waving white flags.

9:49 a.m. USS *Wilson* recovers *Mayaguez* crew.

8:29 p.m. Kissinger and Scowcroft brief Ford on Cambodian radio speech. Ford orders continuation of strikes because crew's status is unknown.

9:15 p.m. At Kissinger's urging, Ford's press secretary Ron Nessen issues a statement to news wires that US will cease military operations if Cambodia releases crew.

By the time the Dutch premier left the White House, reports of the crew sighting had reached the Situation Room. The president, Kissinger, Scowcroft, Rumsfeld, and a young Marine officer named Bud McFarlane celebrated in the Oval Office. The second, third, and fourth planned waves of attack on the mainland had yet to begin, but the Marines were in a fierce firefight. "Is there any reason for the Pentagon not to disengage?" Scowcroft asked the group.

"No, but tell them to bomb the mainland," Kissinger replied. "Let's look ferocious! Otherwise they will attack us as the ship leaves." The second and third attacks proceeded, but Schlesinger unilaterally canceled the fourth.

Schlesinger's press officer announced the rescue of the *Mayaguez* crew, thus usurping the President's chance to make the announcement. Furious, Nessen decided to trump the Pentagon with the only card he had left. He paraded the president outside the West Wing in front of the assembled TV cameras. Ford, who had changed into a business suit but kept his patent leather dress shoes, read a statement about the bold and successful operation to free the crew.

The Marines had landed in a hornets' nest on Tang Island. Instead of a token KR force, they faced nearly two hundred well-trained troops armed with assault rifles and machine guns. The landing zones became killing fields for men and helicopters. Seven of the eight helicopters assigned to the Marine assault were shot down while landing or disabled. Eighteen Marines and airmen died and forty-one were wounded. The withdrawal later in the day was as perilous as the initial assault, and on-scene commanders accidently left three Marines behind. The KR captured the men days later as they attempted to steal food from KR camps; they were summarily executed. Counting the victims of the helicopter crash on May 13, forty-one men died attempting to rescue forty *Mayaguez* crewmembers.

Assessment

Ford acted boldly from the start of the *Mayaguez* incident. However, he appeared to exaggerate the severity of the crisis and then overreacted in an apparent attempt to showcase his presidential timber for the following year's election. The Cambodians had decided to free the crew after the initial harassment and strafing from US combat aircraft, not because of the deadly assault on Tang Island and the heavy-handed bombing of the mainland. Ford centralized command and control of the situation at the White House, claiming that the urgency of the moment demanded it. Yet Ford, despite his naval service as a junior officer in World War II, had no experience in directing military operations. Both Ford and Kissinger pushed the Pentagon to act faster than they considered the situation merited and than their post-Vietnam disposition of forces allowed. The president made the *Mayaguez* incident his crisis, but in doing so he dove too deeply into the details, ordering about Navy attack pilots.

Scowcroft later rationalized Ford's long-distance crisis management style. "The president's political neck is on the line," he said in a 1990 retrospective. "As a matter of course, he is going to be very reluctant to leave in the hands of some unknown military commander decisions which have a great impact on his political well-being."

But practically speaking, President Ford's version of the president in crisis as a striding titan met with an enormous blanket of war fog and lousy intelligence. Despite their rapid-fire actions, Ford and his team always seemed half a day behind the crew's movement and Cambodian activity. The team marshaled excessive military force largely because of poor situational awareness, and this drew media characterizations like "Used a sledgehammer to swat a fly" and "The US should have paused to think before overreacting." Ford and his team nevertheless charged boldly into the night. The *Mayaguez* crewmen regained their freedom, but at a disproportionate loss of life and largely through good fortune. As Scowcroft said later, "We were lucky."

The American public generally praised President Ford's aggressive response to the *Mayaguez* crisis. Polls indicated his approval rating increased from 39 percent before the incident to 51 afterward. Virtually all private citizens, however, likely remained ignorant of the high casualty rate. GOP politicians supported Ford's actions, while liberal journalists peppered post mortems with words such as "overreaction" and "disproportionate."

In June 1975, Representative Dante Fascell (D-FL) asked the General Accounting Office to review the administration's management of the *Mayaguez* crisis. The GAO completed the study in May 1976, but the report's security classification prohibited public release. However, an unclassified version of the report, which was critical of Ford's crisis management, miraculously appeared in the news at a politically sensitive time during the 1976 presidential election. Ford and his Democratic challenger, Jimmy Carter, were scheduled to have a foreign policy debate in San Francisco on October 6, and the news media picked up the GAO's hot potato the day before.

Administration officials cried foul, with Kissinger's aide Lawrence Eagleburger implying the report's release was meant to embarrass Ford during the election. *Mayaguez*'s Captain Miller loudly criticized the

GAO report, but his involvement smacked of political maneuvering. Ford's deputy press secretary had contacted Miller the day before the Carter debate and asked the captain to come to San Francisco. Upon his arrival, Press Secretary Ron Nessen introduced Miller at a news conference at 1:00 p.m. on the afternoon of the debate. Miller said that the early interdiction attacks had convinced the Khmer Rouge to release him and his crew prior to the assault on Tang Island and Kompong Som. His claim was indeed true, but Miller skirted the ineffectiveness of the air attacks and Marine assault that transpired after Cambodia had decided to free the crew.

Everyone in the leadership team, Ford included, had other goals during the crisis that they pursued in parallel to the crew rescue. Ford wanted to demonstrate his fitness to be president. Schlesinger and Jones wanted to show military competence with a clean success. Kissinger wanted to draw lines and send signals. Presidential historians Richard Neustadt and Earnest May assessed the achievement of those goals as follows: "Neither Ford, nor Schlesinger and the military, nor Kissinger harvested from the *Mayaguez* incident much of what they hoped for."

CHAPTER 7

JIMMY CARTER

Iranian Hostage-Taking, 1979–1981

A Hostage President

On October 1, 1979, President Jimmy Carter had yet another problem. As if skyrocketing inflation rates and gasoline shortages weren't enough, Mohammed Reza Shah Pahlevi, the exiled monarch of Iran, was seriously ill. Since his abdication from the Peacock Throne the previous January, the shah had presented a continuing and thorny dilemma to Carter. After fleeing the wrath of his rioting Iranian subjects, the shah had flown to Cairo, Egypt, then sought refuge in the Bahamas, and finally settled in Cuernavaca, Mexico. The president knew that if the shah asked to enter the United States, approval would severely impact American efforts to open a dialogue with the new Iranian government. But a new facet of the problem had arisen and complicated the matter—the shah was suffering from an as yet undiagnosed but serious illness and needed sophisticated medical treatment. Carter's national security team was split on how to handle the situation, and they gathered to consider the president's options.

"It would be a sign of weakness not to allow the shah to come to the States to live," argued National Security Adviser Zbigniew Brzezinski. "If we turned our backs on the fallen shah, it would be a signal to the world that the United States is a fair-weather friend." Along with Secretary of State Cyrus Vance, Carter disagreed. "It makes no sense to bring him here," the president said, "and destroy whatever slim chance we have of rebuilding a relationship with Iran. It boils down to a choice between the shah's preferences as to where he lives and the interests of our country."

The president's position at this meeting reminded Vice President Walter Mondale and Brzezinski of what he had said a few weeks earlier. "Fuck the shah!" Carter shouted in a meeting. "I'm not going to welcome him here when he has other places to go where he'll be safe." As Carter knew, the million demonstrators in the Tehran streets saw the shah as an American puppet and a co-conspirator with Carter and the devil against them. The shah's move to America would be evidence in their minds of a joint plan for the shah's resumption of the throne.

The division among Carter's advisers eased later in October when they learned that the shah had been diagnosed with malignant lymphoma and a blocked bile duct. The shah urgently needed treatment. Ardent shah supporters, including David Rockefeller, a New York banker and philanthropist, and Henry Kissinger, pressured the president to allow the shah to fly to New York for specialized care.

The president broached the issue during his weekly foreign affairs breakfast in the White House Cabinet Room on October 19. Vance, in view of the shah's grave condition, changed his position, leaving Carter alone in opposition of the shah's visit. Hamilton Jordan, Carter's longtime aide who had recently assumed the job of White House chief of staff, raised a subject that always underlies presidential decision making—domestic politics. "Mr. President, if the shah dies in Mexico, can you imagine the field day Kissinger will have with that?" Jordan asked. "He'll say that first you caused the shah's downfall and now you've killed him."

"To hell with Henry Kissinger," Carter snapped. "I am the president of this country."

Vance and Brzezinski, finding themselves oddly in agreement on a foreign policy issue, urged Carter to consider the point on humanitarian principles. The president, a Sunday-school-teaching fundamentalist, eventually relented. Carter then ended the meeting with a haunting question. "What are you guys going to advise me to do if they overrun our embassy and take our people hostage?" When no one answered, Carter continued, "On that day we will all sit here with long drawn white faces and realize we've been had."

The following day in Tehran, the US chargé d'affaires, Bruce Laingen, advised Prime Minister Mehdi Bazargan and Foreign Minister Ibrahim Yazdi of Carter's planned invitation to the shah. The Iranians said that there "would be a sharp reaction in the country, but they could guarantee the protection" of embassy personnel. Nevertheless, Yazdi informally warned Laingen, the senior US diplomat in Iran, "You're opening Pandora's Box with this."

From Coup to "Set-in"

Mohammed Reza emerged as a staunch American ally through the good offices of the CIA. He had become the constitutional monarch of Iran in 1941 when his father abdicated as shah. (Shah is short for *shahanshah*, or king of kings.) Ten years later, leftist prime minister Mohammad Mossadeq persuaded the parliament, the Majlis, to nationalize the oil industry. Soon, Washington began to fret that Iran might fall to Soviet hegemony. In 1953, President Eisenhower authorized the CIA to engineer a coup against Mossadeq that was directed by CIA officer Kermit Roosevelt, Jr., Teddy's grandson.

After the successful takeover, the United States got a strong, anticommunist Iran to help guard against Soviet expansionism in the Middle East. Further, the US military-industrial complex got a free-spending consumer of US weapons systems. And the CIA got a chance to help create the SAVAK, the shah's intelligence and security service. Soon the shah relied heavily on 6,000 SAVAK agents and 100,000 informants to maintain order through intimidation, torture, and murder. William Sullivan, the US ambassador to Tehran from 1977 to 1979, described the period from the late 1960s through the early 1970s as "a reign of terror in Iran. . . . All political activity was suspect."

Resistance to the shah's governance arose from influential Islamic clerics, especially Grand Ayatollah Ruhollah Khomeini, whom the shah had exiled in 1964. The Ayatollah encouraged young men dissatisfied by the shah's modernization of Iran to resist the monarch. More than a decade of dissent and demonstration resulted in widespread protest and numerous strikes in Iran by the late summer of 1978. On September 8, the shah declared martial law, but twenty thousand Iranians surged through the streets of Tehran. The army fired into the crowd, killing hundreds that day, Black Friday. The tumult continued through the end of the year.

The shah appointed Shahpur Bakhtiar, a moderate reformer, as prime minister on January 2, 1979. That attempt at appeasement had little influence on the crowds in the street, and the shah decided to take a long vacation in Palms Springs, California. He and his family flew to Cairo on January 16, reportedly an interim stop en route to the States. With that opening, Khomeini made a triumphant return to Iran. The mullah immediately established a government parallel to that of Bakhtiar's and appointed Mehdi Bazargan as his provisional prime minister. As the clerics jockeyed for control of Iran in the ensuing months, the Carter administration was split on how to counter Soviet influence and foster a pro-Western Iranian government. The Iranian environment was ripe for a spark to set off another civil explosion.

In late October 1979, as Carter allowed the dreadfully ill shah to seek medical treatment in New York, Ibrahim Asgarzadeh broached a startling idea to his university friends in Tehran. He wanted to stage a sit-in at the American embassy to demonstrate against American support for the exiled shah. He began to talk with students from four Iranian universities about how they might accomplish the brazen plot. Asgarzadeh's planning sharpened on November 2 when he saw a news photo of Bazargan and Yazdi shaking hands with Brzezinski at a ceremony in Algeria marking the anniversary of that country's independence.

On a cold and damp Sunday, November 4, Asgarzadeh led three hundred coed college students, all unarmed, to the US embassy on Talaghani Avenue in central Tehran. They convinced compliant Iranian policemen guarding the main gate to take a break. Several students climbed over the gate and, with bolt cutters, sheared the locks and chains. One of the young women carried a sign in poorly spelled English: DON'T BE AFRAID. WE JUST WANT TO SET IN.

The Marines guarding the compound withdrew inside behind heavy locked doors. Chargé Laingen, who was at the Iranian foreign ministry at the time, ordered the Marines by radio to hold their fire.

The students cut the locks on the barred windows of the chancery and were soon inside. By 2:00 p.m., the students controlled the embassy compound and held sixty-three hostages. Nearby, Iranian officials offered Laingen and two others refuge at the foreign ministry as thousands of militants roamed the city. The diplomats later became hostages as well. Six embassy staffers were outside the compound that morning and successfully sought safety at the Canadian embassy. Jimmy Carter's premonition had come true.

No Good Options

As news of the embassy takeover flashed to Washington, the various operations and intelligence centers in town notified their respective principals. Secretary Vance notified Carter at Camp David, the Maryland presidential retreat, before Brzezinski called, thus rankling the national security adviser. The Situation Room called Jordan, who reacted like any presidential political adviser. He considered how the incident might affect the aspirations of Massachusetts senator Edward "Ted" Kennedy for challenging Carter for the 1980 Democratic presidential nomination. As Jordan talked about the potentially dangerous situation with another top Carter aide, Phil Wise, he said, "Don't forget, the press will be looking at this in the context of the campaign. It'll be over in a few hours, but it could provide a nice contrast between Carter and our friend from Massachusetts in how to handle a crisis."

On Monday morning November 5, Brzezinski chaired a session of the Special Coordinating Committee, a standing group established by Carter and Brzezinski to handle time-sensitive policy matters and crisis management at a cabinet level. The attendees generally included Vance, Secretary of Defense Harold Brown, JCS chairman General David Jones, Director of Central Intelligence Stansfield Turner, Press Secretary Jody Powell, presidential counsel Lloyd Cutler, and Jordan. Others, such as the attorney general and the treasury secretary, would attend some of the many meetings that followed. NSC Mideast staffer Gary Sick took the only set of notes, which Brzezinski later gave to Carter.

The SCC immediately sought a means of talking with Khomeini and his Revolutionary Council government. They settled on using two intermediaries—former attorney general Ramsey Clark and Senate staff member William Miller, both with useful contacts in Iran; also, Miller spoke Farsi, the Persian language of Iran. The only other major agenda item was contingency planning. The team decided to form a subgroup to examine possible military action to free the hostages.

Unknown to the SCC at the time were the intentions of the students once they occupied the embassy. Subsequent reporting confirmed Asgarzadeh's plan for a three-to-five-day sit-in. Khomeini likely knew about the plan beforehand, but regardless, he quickly used the crisis to help consolidate his remaking of the Iranian government. Within hours, the students had galvanized thousands of Iranians to join the Ayatollah's crusade. Khomeini's son clambered over the embassy fence to praise and exhort the students.

Khomeini and the other clerics soon announced their support of the students' action. That swept aside the students' plan for a brief event. Also, Prime Minister Bazargan resigned, leaving Khomeini's Revolutionary Council in charge of the government. On November 6, Carter met with his senior national security advisers at 8:00 a.m. in the Oval Office. He established the mood early on: "They have us by the balls."

Brzezinski suggested reacting with an undefined but credible threat of force. Vance opposed any direct threat in order to allow the Iranians a path of retreat. Given the difference of opinion, Carter elected not to choose a course of action immediately, but asked his advisers for a range of options, including retaliatory measures if the hostages were killed. Concerned about leaks, Carter directed that only small groups address the problem and that they avoid written minutes of the discussions. His exasperation showed when he addressed the end game: "Get our people out of Iran and break relations. Fuck 'em."

As Carter left the Oval Office for his weekly meeting with congressional leaders, he turned to Vance and Powell. "By the way, Cy and Jody," he said curtly, "I'm tired of seeing those bastards holding our people referred to as 'students.' . . . Get together and figure out what to call them. . . . They should be referred to as 'terrorists' or 'captors.'"

All of the president's advisers then moved to the Situation Room for what became their daily SCC meeting. During the ensuing months, cabinet heads and their most senior deputies would devote several

hours every day to the SCC meetings. They considered multiple crisis termination options—diplomatic, economic, and financial—except
for military contingency planning. Overall, the SCC served to discuss,
refine, and tee up proposals for Carter's consideration.

Carter met with the full National Security Council in the Cabinet Room later in the day. The president immediately laid down his
personal markers. First, get the hostages out alive. Second, start planning punitive actions. Third, no military operations on the ground in
Iran. Vance briefed the group on diplomatic initiatives during the past
forty-eight hours, and Turner said that chances for negotiating with the
students were poor. The militants had stated they would kill the hostages if the US attempted any rescue. Brown followed with his assessment that any rescue attempt would likely fail anyway. The meeting
soon ended with the establishment of two parallel crisis management
strategies—integrated economic and diplomatic initiatives, and close-
hold military planning. Those barred from the latter track, according
to Sick, "resented their exclusion." Adding to that tension was the fact
that NBC News planned to run a television story that evening about
the Clark-Miller mission to Tehran. The leak infuriated Carter and
led to his hearing even fewer voices during the crisis. That restriction,
coupled with the separate military planning track created a fertile environment for groupthink and excluded potentially skeptical experts.

On November 8, Carter canceled a planned trip to Canada in order
to remain engaged in the crisis management. Jordan had convinced him
that traveling at the time would send the wrong political message. Also
that day, the president learned that the Iranian Revolutionary Council
had prohibited Clark and Miller from entering the country. The next
day, at his Friday foreign policy breakfast, Carter asked Brzezinski for
his thoughts.

"Mr. President, you can't allow this thing to settle into a state of
normalcy," Brzezinski said. "If you do, it will paralyze your presidency."
He argued that the honor and dignity of the United States might eventually outweigh the hostages' lives, and the president should prepare
himself for a tough choice. Carter automatically turned to Vance for
his view.

"The hostages have been held only five days," the secretary said
with his usual even and lawyerly tone. "We're dealing with a volatile,

chaotic situation in Iran, and negotiation is the only way to free them." Vance then added, "The president and this nation will ultimately be judged by our restraint in the face of provocation, and on the safe return of our hostages." He reminded all that President Johnson had similarly resolved the USS *Pueblo* hostage situation.

"But that went on for a year!" retorted the action-minded Brzezinski.

"And Johnson," Jordan interjected, "wasn't in the middle of a re-election campaign."

As Carter groped for near-term options to free the hostages, State's Bureau of Intelligence and Research issued a gloomy judgment. Analysts concluded that no diplomatic, economic, or military pressure could free the hostages in the coming months. Experts polled by *Time* magazine agreed, calling any military rescue attempt suicidal. Further, Carter's frustration grew in parallel with the disparity of thought among his advisers. To CIA director Turner, it seemed "that almost every recommendation that came to him was countered by strong reservations on the part of one member of the national security team or another."

On November 14, Carter announced economic sanctions against Iran, including freezing Iranian accounts in US banks and banning US purchases of Iranian oil. Additionally, the administration appealed to the International Court of Justice for an order to release the hostages, ordered a reduction in Iran's Washington embassy staff, and sought to deport Iranians who were in the United States illegally. These actions were largely invisible to the American people, who watched the growing crisis on television. Public attention to the hostages' plight grew dramatically as the Iranian students exploited the American news media's lust for good visuals. Additionally, CBS anchor Walter Cronkite intoned the number of days the hostages had been in captivity at the close of every broadcast. ABC's Ted Koppel began a nightly show on the situation, *America Held Hostage*. The media attention helped Khomeini internally in Iran, and the event became one of the most extraordinary media phenomena in television history.

Carter canceled all of his campaign activities in order to remain at the White House. He invoked a "Rose Garden" strategy, one employed by other presidents near an election. But that position, coupled with the constant news hype, worried Bob Strauss. The veteran political operative would soon become Carter's campaign manager, and on November 17 warned Jordan, "The president has to do something. We can't stay in this posture much longer."

Mixed news reached the White House on November 18. The Iranians released thirteen of the hostages over a forty-eight-hour period. All were women or African-Americans. The Palestine Liberation Organization engineered their freedom but didn't take credit publicly. At the same time, though, the Ayatollah made an ominous public threat to the remaining hostages. He said that if Carter did not extradite the shah, Iran would put the hostages on trial. President Carter responded by gathering the NSC members at Camp David on November 23. The group reviewed the ongoing military planning, which by then included a series of escalatory steps ending with a total naval blockade and strikes on the oil industry. When the discussion turned to Khomeini's threatened trials, the group broke into two familiar factions. Vance, Mondale, and General Brown were against any direct threat of retaliation for trials. Brzezinski, Jordan, and Jody Powell favored drawing a line. "Ham whispered to me," Brzezinski wrote later, "that Carter simply would not be reelected president if he did not act firmly." Carter, saying, "I will not sit here as president and watch the trials," opted for a direct threat but one delivered discreetly. He authorized a message to Khomeini via the Swiss: Harm the hostages and we will mine or blockade all of your harbors. Subsequently, there was less rhetoric in Tehran about trials.

During the Thanksgiving holiday, the president asked Americans to pray for the hostages and ring church bells daily. He also promised not to light the National Christmas Tree until the hostages gained freedom. Beyond those gestures, Carter continued to pursue a two-track strategy of negotiation and sanctions pressure. Nothing else seemed likely to change the internal Iranian political equation that prevented the hostages' release. Meanwhile, the shah and his family left New York on December 2 for Lackland Air Force Base in Texas, and then flew to Panama on December 16. His departure had little effect on Ayatollah Khomeini's intransigence on the hostage matter.

The 1979 Christmas holiday season found Carter anything but joyous. In the view of political scientist Betty Glad, some of the president's woes were self-inflicted. "Carter had inflated the importance of the hostages to American foreign policy," Glad wrote in a 1989 analysis of Carter's crisis decision making. "Jimmy Carter helped create a feeling of emergency in the United States which suggested that the holding of hostages was a national security threat." According to Glad, Carter "suggested that the whole nation had been hurt by this assault on its integrity." Carter's suggestions that his critics were unpatriotic reinforced the president's message that America was in a dangerous conflict.

During the first seven weeks of the crisis, Carter focused on ideals—protect the country's interests and honor and the lives of the hostages. But presidential rhetoric expert Denise Bostdorff maintained the public expected Carter to take pragmatic and realistic steps to free the captives. So when he talked only of ideals, Bostdorff concluded, he "reinforced his public image as a passive leader." In her opinion, "Carter produced the most passive presidential crisis rhetoric of any chief executive from Truman through Reagan."

Two days after Christmas, Soviet military forces invaded Afghanistan, Iran's neighbor on the Soviet's southern flank. This "transformed the strategic environment in the region," Sick wrote later. Fearing that US military retaliatory strikes against Iran might precipitate a superpower confrontation involving the adjacent countries, Carter's team hoped for a negotiating breakthrough.

Do Something!

In early January 1980, Carter began to steel himself for conducting his Democratic primary campaign from his crisis management high ground in the Rose Garden. However, a sliver of hope for the hostages suddenly appeared. Iranian foreign minister Sadegh Ghotbzadeh, a Georgetown University graduate, reached out to establish a dialogue with the American government. He spoke with an aide to Panama's leader, General Omar Torrijos, and asked Panama to help him connect with Hamilton Jordan. Ghotbzadeh identified two men living in Paris as his intermediaries and picked Jordan because, as he said, "the State Department was controlled by Rockefeller and Kissinger."

Vance and Carter approved a response, and Jordan and Assistant Secretary of State Hal Saunders flew under assumed names to London on January 19. There they met French lawyer Christian Bourguet and Argentine businessman Hector Villalon. When Jordan questioned their bona fides, Bourguet called Ghotbzadeh and tried to get the Iranian to speak with Jordan on the phone. He refused because Khomeini had banned anyone from talking with Americans. Ghotbzadeh later sent a "To Whom It May Concern" letter identifying Bourguet and Villalon as his representatives.

On January 23, President Carter authorized Jordan and Saunders to continue with the initiative, which Carter's team called the French Connection. "What choice do we have?" Carter asked Jordan privately. "These bastards have held our people for two months now. Nothing we have tried diplomatically has worked." He said the time had come to take some risks. "You just pursue this thing aggressively and we'll see where it leads."

A few days later, on January 29, the CIA successfully whisked the six hostages hiding in the homes of Canadian and other Western diplomats to the airport for a flight out of Tehran. The 2012 film *Argo* told the story of their remarkable escape.

The French Connection operation added to the friction between Vance, whose team oversaw it, and Brzezinski. The latter, according to Sick, belittled the approach and felt the Iranians were merely "diddling along" the United States. Brzezinski's exclusion from the negotiations, Sick later wrote, "may also have influenced his views." But then Brzezinski, in a parallel move, had banned State from his secret military planning group.

As Jordan, Bourguet, and Villalon continued their clandestine meetings, a scenario for the hostages' freedom emerged. Iran would request a UN commission to travel to Tehran to hear the country's grievances and visit the hostages. The Iranians would respond by transferring the remaining fifty-three hostages from student control to the Iranian government. The secret negotiations continued toward that possible deal until February 23, when Khomeini halted talks until the Majlis elections were completed, perhaps in March. The UN Commission nevertheless traveled to Tehran, but Khomeini blocked their access to the hostages. The commission members gave up the task and departed on March 10.

Unwilling to talk publicly about these negotiations, Carter gave the appearance of dithering. Shortly before the UN mission failed, he sent Vice President Mondale to Capitol Hill to gauge feelings there about the hostage situation. "What the hell are you doing?" members asked the vice president. "This has been going on for months! It's time for action—punch them out, drop something on them—and we'll all feel better about it." Mondale said the atmosphere reminded him of the *Mayaguez* mindset: "You can't think of what to do, so just do anything."

The need for action gained urgency when on March 25 Carter lost the New York and Connecticut primaries to Kennedy. Carter responded by writing to Iranian prime minister Abolhassan Bani-Sadr. If the hostages were not handed over to the government immediately, he wrote, "we shall be taking additional non-belligerent measures that we have withheld until now." But a simultaneous development added to the president's woes. A purported letter from Carter to Khomeini surfaced in Iran, one in which the president apologized for American sins. It was a fabrication, but the news media seized on it as evidence that Carter's apparent do-nothing approach on the hostage situation included appeasement.

But then came some good news. Bani-Sadr promised to announce the hostage transfer on April 1. The Iranian also asked that Carter respond quickly and publicly in order to seal the deal. Buoyed, Carter asked Vance, Brzezinski, Saunders, Jordan, Vance's deputy Warren Christopher, David Aaron, and Sick to join him in the Oval Office at 5:00 a.m. on the 1st to await the text of Bani-Sadr's speech. Within thirty minutes, the Swiss embassy in Washington notified Saunders that Bani-Sadr had said all of the right things in Tehran. Christopher crafted a carefully worded statement for the US news media as the required response. Serendipitously, April 1 was the date of key primaries in Wisconsin and Kansas.

Carter read the statement to reporters at 7:20 a.m. in the Oval Office. The good news flashed across the country, including the Midwest where Carter won in Wisconsin and Kansas. Two days after April Fool's Day, Iran's Revolutionary Council approved the hostage transfer, but Khomeini vetoed the action. Upon hearing the news, Carter said to Jordan, "We look foolish. I go out and announce the plan, and forty-eight hours later it's falling apart. I'm not sure what to do now, but the options left aren't very attractive."

Carter's campaign pollster had predicted easy wins for the president in the Wisconsin and Kansas primaries. But the American press leaped upon what appeared to be Carter's manipulation of the crisis to his political advantage. The *New York Times* ran this headline on April 2—"Iran's Shadow on Primary: Timing of Speech by Carter Shows Interrelation of Presidential Campaign and the Hostage Crisis." *Washington Post* columnist David Broder also charged Carter with exploiting an illusionary bit of good hostage news and went further. "A look back over the past ten weeks of the 1980 political season shows something even more interesting: a clear pattern of pre-primary news created by the White House to shape a positive public perception of the president's handling of key matters of public concern." Jody Powell refutes the media claims in his memoir, and Jordan, Sick, and Saunders have written the same. But in the near real-time mashup of crisis reporting, political maneuvering, and newspaper sales, perceptions are critical.

Wag-the-dog accusations aside, Jimmy Carter had a real problem following the collapse of the French Connection and the apparent failure of his sanction-negotiate-hope crisis strategy. He found himself trapped by hostage safety concerns, national honor considerations, reelection demands, a devious opponent in Khomeini, and a critical domestic press. An April 6 *Washington Post* editorial said it all: "Iran: Enough."

Disaster at Desert I

By the time the French Connection began to loosen in mid-March, Brzezinski pushed an aggressive policy alternative—a hostage rescue operation. Carter agreed to listen to the results of Brzezinski's secret contingency planning. The president and his team convened for a day-long meeting at Camp David on March 22. They gathered in casual clothes in front of a comforting fire, and General Jones briefed the draft plan.

Eight US Navy RH-53D Sea Stallion helicopters flown by Marine pilots, staging from aircraft carrier USS *Nimitz* in the Arabian Sea, would fly nearly 600 miles inland at night to a landing strip called

Desert I. Six Air Force C-130 Hercules prop-driven transport aircraft would meet the helicopters there. The fixed-wing aircraft were to bring fuel in bladders and a team from the Army's Delta Force, the Pentagon's embryonic special operations unit. The C-130 aircraft would then leave Iran. The plan called for the refueled and empty choppers to fly to a mountainous hiding place until the second night.

The raiding force would drive into Tehran during the second night using local vehicles acquired by CIA officers on the ground. The team would rescue the hostages and then board the helicopters that were to swoop in and pick them up. They would fly to an Iranian airfield captured by special forces and meet inbound Air Force C-141 Starlifter jet transports. The Delta Force, hostages, and helicopter crews would depart, leaving the abandoned choppers for the Iranian Air Force.

General Jones noted that the plan for operation "Eagle Claw" was extraordinarily intricate, and the successful integration of the constituent parts worried him the most. Nevertheless, his bottom line, as described by Sick, was positive. "If the rescue team could get to the walls of the embassy compound without warning the students inside, and if the hostages were all inside the embassy, as it appeared they were, then he had high confidence that all the hostages could be rescued." President Carter made no decision on the rescue plan that day.

At an NSC meeting on April 7, Carter approved a series of sanctions against Iran. The United States would break diplomatic relations with Iran and expel all embassy and consular personnel; ban all exports to Iran, save food and medicine; survey all Iranian assets in the United States in preparation for confiscation; and invalidate visas held by Iranians in the United States, with careful scrutiny of renewals. Four days later, Carter hastily convened an NSC meeting despite Secretary Vance's vacation travel to Florida; his deputy, Warren Christopher, attended the meeting.

"Gentlemen," Carter said at the start, "I want you to know that I am seriously considering an attempt to rescue the hostages." Jordan thought to himself, *He's going to do it! He's had enough.* General Jones and Secretary Brown then laid out maps and briefed the whole mission. At the end, Carter said that he was deferring a decision until he talked to Vance, but he finished the meeting by saying that it was time to bring the hostages home. As the men filed out of the Cabinet Room,

Powell turned to Brown. "Mr. Secretary, the president is going to go with this thing, I can sense it. If we can bring our people out of there, it will do more good for this country than anything that has happened in twenty years."

"Yes," Brown replied, "and if we fail, that will be the end of the Carter presidency."

"But we really don't have much choice, do we?"

A stunned and angry Vance later wrote about hearing of Carter's decision, "I went to see the president . . . and spelled out my strong objections to the rescue mission." The president politely listed to Vance and offered to reassemble the crisis team to hear Vance's views. That gesture was sensible but opened the door for the secretary's humiliation in front of his peers. On the early afternoon of April 15, a few hours after Vance and Carter had met, the president and his team gathered for a secret meeting to hear Vance's position. The secretary of state detailed his objections and concluded, "I feel strongly that now is not the time to consider this option."

The president then asked, "Are there any reactions to Cy's comments?"

"There was an awkward silence," Jordan wrote later of the moment, "as Vance scanned the room, looking from Zbig, to Mondale, to Harold Brown, to Jody, and finally to me, his eyes begging for support. I fidgeted, feeling sorry for Cy, who sat there all alone." Vance resigned within days, but promised Carter he would not announce his decision until after the rescue attempt.

The hostage rescue mission began on Thursday, April 24. Carter and his crisis team went about their scheduled business but nervously waited for updates from the Pentagon. At 4:45 p.m., Brown called Brzezinski and said, "I think we have an abort situation." The secretary explained that the entire team had reached Desert I, but two of the eight helicopters were disabled and a third had turned back to *Nimitz*. Six choppers were the minimum needed for the mission, and the on-scene commander recommended mission termination.

Brzezinski ran to the Oval Office, interrupted Carter, and the two retreated to the president's study. The president called Brown at the Pentagon, got the details, and consented to aborting the operation. He hung up, then leaned over and put his arms and head down on

President Truman and General Douglas MacArthur on Wake Island in the middle of the Pacific Ocean during the early days of the Korean War.

President Truman at a press conference two days after Chinese communists had counterattacked UN forces in Korea.

President Eisenhower and Secretary Dulles addressed the nation on television shortly before the outbreak of the 1956 Suez War.

Dwight D. Eisenhower Presidential Library and Museum.

In a national TV address, Eisenhower used an aerial photograph of San Diego to demonstrate the U–2's aerial photo capabilities.

Dwight D. Eisenhower Presidential Library and Museum.

Soviet premier Nikita Khrushchev and President Eisenhower at Camp David in 1959.

Dwight D. Eisenhower Presidential Library and Museum.

This aerial image from a low-level Navy reconnaissance flight shows the construction of a Soviet warhead storage bunker in San Cristobal, Cuba.

(Left) A launch site for a Soviet SS-4 medium-range ballistic missile in Cuba.

(Below) President Kennedy met frequently with his Cuban Missile Crisis advisory group.

President Johnson and his advisers in the White House Situation Room during the 1967 Arab–Israeli War.

President Johnson meeting with his staff after North Korea seized the intelligence-gathering ship, USS *Pueblo*.

USS *Pueblo* gathered signals intelligence (SIGINT) by loitering offshore of communist countries in the Far East.

President Nixon, Secretary of State Henry Kissinger, and Chief of Staff Alexander Haig at Camp David during the 1973 Arab-Israeli War.

President Nixon met with Congressional leaders in the Cabinet Room on October 10, 1973, four days after the start of the war.

Gerald R. Ford Library, photograph by David Hume Kennerly.

President Ford and his crisis team in the Cabinet Room during the *Mayaguez* incident.

Associated Press.

Cambodian Khmer Rouge military personal aboard a former US Navy Swift boat alongside the cargo ship SS *Mayaguez*, which they had seized.

President Ford on the phone during a break from a White House dinner, speaking with Secretary of Defense Schlesinger about ongoing military operations during the crisis.

President Carter and his crisis advisers in the Cabinet Room during the Iranian hostage crisis.

Members of Carter's National Security Council joined the president at Camp David to discuss the threatened trial of American hostages in Tehran.

President Carter addressed the nation after the aborted hostage rescue mission. His face reflected the immense pressures of the prolonged crisis.

Notified of the bombing of the Marine barracks in Beirut, Lebanon, President Reagan immediately returned from a golf weekend in Georgia and met with his crisis team in the conference room in the Situation Room complex.

Ronald Regan Library.

President Reagan considered a military response to a Libyan-backed terrorist attack in West Berlin.

Ronald Regan Library.

Reagan briefing Congressional leaders on the impending military strikes on Libya.

Ronald Regan Library.

President George H. W. Bush preferred meeting with a small group of advisers during the 1990–91 Persian Gulf crisis.

President Bush decided unilaterally to end the Persian Gulf War at this meeting after only 100 hours of ground combat.

William J. Clinton Presidential Library.

Meeting in the Oval Office, President Clinton considered responses to al-Qaeda's bombing of US embassies in East Africa.

Shortly after Tomahawk cruise missiles struck targets in Afghanistan and Sudan, President Clinton addressed the news media on Martha's Vineyard, where he was vacationing.

William J. Clinton Presidential Library.

President George W. Bush at a Florida elementary school after a second plane hit the World Trade Center.

Before returning to Washington on 9/11, President Bush held a videoconference with key advisers in the Strategic Command's underground bunker in Nebraska.

Bush in the White House bomb shelter, the President's Emergency Operations Center, after addressing the nation on television in the evening of 9/11.

President Obama and his team in the Situation Room's conference room. Note the décor changes from Johnson to Reagan to Obama.

Early in the Arab Spring of 2011, President Obama called Egyptian president Hosni Mubarak from the Oval Office.

Official White House Photo by Pete Souza.

President Obama briefed congressional leaders in the Cabinet Room after a Syrian chemical weapons attack.

Official White House Photo by Pete Souza.

White House Photograph.

The author with his wife, Elin, sons, Erik (left) and Carter, and President Reagan.

White House Photograph.

The author as a White House social aide to President Nixon.

The author and George H. W. Bush.

The White House Situation Room is not just a room; it is the president's 24/7 intelligence center. And it is not underground, as the windows behind the duty officers attest in this mid–1980s image.

his desk. . . . Neither he nor Brzezinski said anything for several moments.

At Desert I, while crews repositioned the operational helicopters for refueling, one collided with a C-130 tanker. The explosion and fire killed eight men. At 5:58 p.m., General Jones called Carter, who was still in his study with Vance, Jordan, Mondale, and others. "Yes, Dave." Carter's face turned ashen as he listened to Jones.

"Are there any dead?" Carter asked. Those around the president stood silently.

"I understand," Carter said and placed the phone in the cradle.

Vance said, "Mr. President, I'm very, very sorry." Jordan bolted into the restroom and vomited.

Mixed reaction followed the public announcement of the desert debacle. The Republicans tempered immediate comments out of respect for the dead. However, some accused Carter of meddling in military operations as the Democrats had faulted Gerald Ford in the *Mayaguez* incident five years earlier. But the Pentagon paraded on-scene commander Colonel Charles Beckwith at a press conference, and he squelched all rumors of Carter's interference.

Vance's resignation quickly leaked, and Carter immediately countered with the nomination of Maine senator Edmund Muskie. Unnamed White House advisers claimed that although the rescue raid had failed, the mission was meant to "lance the boil" of the festering hostage crisis. Brzezinski had used that metaphor in the critical April 15 meeting in which Carter ordered the rescue mission. Carter decided to start campaigning again but badly handled his announcement of his intention on April 30. He mentioned in front of a reporter that the problems facing the country were "manageable enough" for him to exit the Rose Garden. One of the hostage's wives choked on the word "manageable" and said so to the media. Carter later said to Jordan, "Poor choice of words, huh?"

Other than dispersing the hostages in Tehran, the Iranians reacted passively to the failed rescue attempt. Khomeini was facing some counterrevolutionary forces during the spring and summer, and healthy hostages were still useful in focusing dissidents on the American Satan. However, Khomeini did allow the July 11 release of hostage Richard Queen, who was suffering from multiple sclerosis. The shah's death on July 27 caused no change in the situation. But just as the fall presidential campaign kicked off after Labor Day, a break in the impasse appeared.

Breakthrough

On September 10, the Iranian Majlis endorsed the country's first elected, albeit cleric-influenced government. Khomeini quickly authorized a trusted associate, Sadegh Tabatabai, to contact the West German ambassador in Tehran to start hostage-release negotiations. Tabatabai asked Gerhard Ritzel to pass to the Americans three conditions for the hostages' release: Return of frozen Iranian government assets, a US promise of no military or political intervention in Iran, and positive US steps toward facilitating the return of the former shah's personal assets. Two days later, Khomeini publicly signaled his support for negotiations. Carter and Muskie responded with alacrity, hoping that a deal might be done before the election. They appointed Christopher to lead a task force to begin negotiations with Tabatabai. Coincidently, Iraq invaded Iran on September 22, and the military parts and weapons that Iran had ordered before the embassy sit-in became a leverage point for the United States.

The potential for a last minute hostage deal worried the campaign team of the Republican challenger Ronald Reagan. Campaign manager Bill Casey fretted about what he called an "October Surprise" by Carter, a development that would dash any hopes for a Reagan victory. Casey set up a team of retired military and intelligence officers to monitor the negotiating process. The group, it was learned later, gave the media a series of false reports of imminent deals designed to be uncovered as distracting "little-boy-cries-wolf" stories.

Sick wrote in *All Fall Down* that the Iranians "made a concerted effort to end the crisis in September and October," but the Iraq war and internal squabbles wrecked their timeline. Most analyses of the hostage crisis endgame hold that the Khomeini government viewed Reagan as a much less willing negotiator and compromiser than Carter. It was thus in Iran's interest to make a deal with Carter. Conversely, Sick has since offered a circumstantial case that Casey had made a deal with the Iranians to keep the hostages until after the election. He details his case in a 1992 book, *October Surprise*.

The Iranians asked the Algerian government to mediate outstanding issues when negotiations bogged down in mid-October. Their successful efforts yielded approval by the Majlis on a key point on Sunday November 2, two days before both the one-year anniversary of the embassy takeover and the presidential election. Carter faced another decision on what to tell the American public at a critical campaign moment.

"We had to play it down the middle to avoid the press charge we were using the crisis for election purposes," Jordan recalled later. Carter tried to be even-handed when he made a statement later in the day regarding the Majlis action. "We are within two days of an important national election," he said. "Let me assure you that my decisions on this crucial matter will not be affected by the calendar." The president's good news had no effect. Ronald Reagan won the election with a landslide Electoral College tally of 489 to 49.

The final agreement took shape during the final two days of Carter's presidency. The president slept on the Oval Office couch as he desperately hoped for the hostages' release on his watch. While the hostages had boarded an Algerian aircraft on Reagan's inauguration day, January 20, 1981, communications between the plane's cockpit and the tower indicated nothing would happen until Reagan finished his oath. Aides told Carter of the hostages' departure from Tehran when he arrived at Andrews Air Force Base to board a flight home to Georgia.

During a post-inauguration luncheon in the Capitol, Reagan hoisted a champagne toast and announced to the world that the hostages had left Iranian airspace. Sadly, Carter made the same statement in front of a few folks in Plains, Georgia.

Assessment

With the exception of the wag-the-dog moment when he tried to rescue the hostages, President Carter patiently worked his way through the crisis. Nevertheless, the 444-day hostage ordeal allowed Jimmy Carter's critics to fashion a damaging caricature of a president in crisis. He was a weak-willed leader, they said, who was afraid to take bold action to free those people. When he had a little good news, he shamelessly used it to win a primary election over Ted Kennedy. When he had bad news, he wrapped himself in the American flag and from the Rose Garden called critics un-American. But when he finally did act, his penchant for involving himself in the military details doomed the rescue attempt to failure. The rest of the time, his critics argued, he just dithered and turned off the Christmas tree lights.

On the other hand, multiple real-life forces—issues largely unseen or ignored by the critics—inhibited bold action and thus unfortunately contributed to the caricature. Among the factors that forced cautious, incremental crisis management steps—muddling through—was Carter's dedication to keeping the hostages alive. Harbor mining and the destruction of oil refineries would bring hostages home in boxes. Moreover, air strikes could enflame the Muslim world with anti-American hatred, trigger an oil-supply emergency, strain relations with allies, and invite Soviet adventurism.

Another underappreciated influence on decision making was the policy chasm between Secretary Vance and National Security Adviser Brzezinski. Carter, who had dispensed with a chief of staff until his term's last year, wanted disparate opinions to reach him. On one hand, that friction between his two primary foreign policy advisers forced cautious decision making save for the rescue attempt. Regrettably, though, leaks from people in each camp of the Vance-Brzezinski competition forced Carter to reduce the number of crisis advisers and thus increased groupthink decisions such as the hostage rescue attempt.

Carter created high public expectations for decisive action by inflating the hostage situation into a veritable national emergency. His calls for prayer and church bells, coupled with his cancelation of campaign events increased attention to what he did or didn't do. The insatiable TV coverage made the situation seem even more dire by bringing the suffering of the hostages and their families into American living rooms and dens.

Carter's rhetoric about ideals, such as national honor, and his apparent inaction bewildered the public and created a contradiction that was difficult for him to solve. On the one hand, they wanted pragmatic actions to accompany the talk of national honor. Conversely, if he put the country's standing and credibility ahead of sixty-six lives in order to retaliate against Iran, Democratic voters would desert him in the primary elections, as would independents in the fall.

Carter and his advisers knew that the hostage situation would make or break his reelection bid. His bump upward in the polls early in the crisis demonstrated the situation's positive impact. However, touting the purported good news on the day of the Wisconsin and Kansas primaries backfired in the end. And then there is the rescue attempt. Amid cries of "Do something," Operation Eagle Claw seemed to many a wag-the-dog gambit, despite the protestations afterward from Carter's advisers. Other reasons for demonstrable action—including the collapse of the French Connection, dim short-term prospects for hostage release, and Vance's isolation—led to Carter's reversal on taking bold action.

On the plus side, Carter realized the limits of American power and understood, despite his evangelical bent, that other cultures will not always subscribe to democratic and Christian values. Putting aside his early idealistic rhetoric and the rescue gambit, he generally exercised caution and exhibited pragmatism in the face of unrealistic rants from the sidelines calling for action for the sake of action. Professor Betty Glad characterized his decision making this way: "Carter . . . provided somewhat better management of the Iranian hostage crisis than he is usually given credit for. He did make mistakes in admitting the shah into the United States, hyping the issue for almost six months, and launching an ill-fated rescue mission. But he avoided the temptation for military action, and skillfully used the Iranian assets he froze in the United States as a bargaining chip to secure the hostages' release."

Carter admitted in a 1981 *New York Times* interview that the crisis taught him that America couldn't influence every international crisis, and "there are limits even on our nation's great strength. It's the same kind of impotence that a powerful person feels when his child is kidnapped."

CHAPTER 8

RONALD REAGAN

Part I. Beirut Barracks Bombing, 1983

Bickering Advisers

"Let terrorists be aware that when the rules of international behavior are violated, our policy will be one of swift and effective retribution."
—*Ronald Reagan, January 27, 1981*

The driver of the yellow Mercedes Benz truck stomped on the gas pedal and headed for the concertina wire. The heavily loaded truck rammed through the coils and sped toward a four-story building housing 350 Marines and Navy personnel on the grounds of Beirut International Airport in Lebanon. As the driver passed by Lance Corporal Eddie DiFranco, he smiled at the Marine. DiFranco had been prohibited from having a round in the chamber of his M-16, so he grabbed his field telephone to alert the sergeant of the guard. The time was 6:22 a.m. on Sunday, October 23, 1983, and the Marines were sleeping in.

Sergeant Steve Russell, manning a guard post in front of the building, saw the oncoming truck and raced into the building yelling, "Hit the deck! Hit the deck!" The truck sped through an open gate in the surrounding chain link fence and crashed in the building lobby. The driver then detonated 12,000 pounds of explosives, and the blast sheared off all of the support columns, causing the entire structure to collapse. For a few moments after the explosion, dust and smoke accompanied a deathly silence. But then moans and cries for help shattered the scene. Two hundred and twenty-one Marines and twenty-one naval officers and men died either immediately or from their mortal injuries. One hundred others survived their wounds. The casualties were from a 1,200-man Navy and Marine force that had been deployed in Lebanon as part of a peacekeeping effort. The Multinational Force, or MNF, consisted of US, British, French, and Italian troops. A simultaneous truck bombing killed fifty-eight French soldiers at their Beirut encampment.

President Ronald Reagan was at Augusta National Golf Club in Georgia for a weekend of golf with Secretary of State George Shultz, Secretary of Treasury Donald Regan, and investment banker Nicholas Brady. Accompanying the men was Robert "Bud" McFarlane, whom Reagan had appointed his national security adviser six days earlier. The duty officer in the White House Situation Room called McFarlane at 2:00 a.m. to report the Beirut bombing. McFarlane gathered Shultz and awakened Reagan, who was staying in the club's Eisenhower Cabin. Dressed in his pajamas and robe, the president took the news badly. "He looked like a man, a seventy-two-year-old man," McFarlane wrote later, "who had just received a blow to the chest."

"How could this happen?" Reagan asked. "How bad is it?" McFarlane passed on the sparse information, and Reagan's anger replaced his grief. Those sons of bitches, Reagan said. Let's find a way to get them.

Reagan's Leadership Style

The bombing in Beirut arose from generations of conflict in the Levant and from events in the spring of 1982. Palestine Liberation Organization guerillas, staging from sanctuaries in Lebanon, had increased their attacks on Israel in May of that year to the point where the Israeli government decided to take radical action. Defense minister Ariel Sharon came to Washington that month to seek US support for Israeli military operations in Lebanon to chase both the PLO and Syrian military forces from that country. Several US officials strongly warned against such action, but Secretary of State Alexander Haig acknowledged Israel's right to her own decisions about self-defense. Sharon viewed that statement as an implicit green light. Israel Defense Force troops heeded that signal on June 6 when they invaded southern Lebanon. The immediate provocation for hostilities had been the assassination attempt on Israel's ambassador to London by members of Palestinian Abu Nidal's terrorist group three days previously. Soon Lebanon was inflamed with fighting among Israel, the PLO, Syria, the Lebanese army, and the militias of conflicting Lebanese political factions.

Israeli prime minister Menachem Begin was scheduled to meet with Reagan in Washington on June 21 to discuss the incursion. But the president's senior advisers had become rancorously split on what Reagan should say to Begin. Vice President George H. W. Bush, Secretary of Defense Casper "Cap" Weinberger, National Security Adviser William Clark, and political aide Michael Deaver favored sanctions against Israel and urged Reagan to cancel the Begin meeting. Secretary Haig, UN ambassador Jeane Kirkpatrick, and Director of Central Intelligence William Casey supported Israel's attempt to eliminate the PLO. At a meeting Reagan had with his senior advisers, Weinberger and Kirkpatrick bickered openly in front of the president. Reagan ultimately ruled against Haig, Kirkpatrick, and Casey, and the situation marked the end of a long line of squabbles between the secretary of state and most everyone else in the administration. Reagan accepted Haig's letter of resignation on June 25, although none had been offered.

By late summer, Israel had decisively defeated Syrian forces and had encircled Beirut. With savage intensity, the IDF attacked PLO hideouts and tragically killed hundreds of innocent Lebanese civilians in the process. The US television networks broadcast video of the carnage, and on August 12, Deaver had seen enough. He walked unannounced into the Oval Office and said to Reagan, "Mr. President, I have to leave."

"What do you mean?" ask Reagan.

"I can't be a part of this anymore, the bombings, the killing of children. It's wrong. And you're the one person on the face of the earth right now who can stop it. All you have to do is tell Begin you want it stopped." About that time, George Shultz, who had replaced Haig as secretary of state, joined them and arranged a call to Begin. After thirty minutes and two conversations with Begin, the IDF ceased fire.

Reagan turned to Deaver and Shultz and said, "I didn't know I had that kind of power."

When the PLO agreed to withdraw from Lebanon, that country's government asked the United States for a multinational force outside of UN auspices to guarantee Lebanese security. Reagan agreed to add Marines to a joint French and Italian MNF over vigorous objections by Weinberger. A Marine amphibious unit went ashore on August 24 for a thirty-day peacekeeping mission. The violence subsided, and after only seventeen days into the operation, Weinberger ordered the Marines to withdraw to their host Navy ships; Italy and France did the same. He did not coordinate with State or the NSC staff before issuing his orders.

Four days later, on September 14, Lebanese president-elect Bashir Gemayel was assassinated. In retaliation, the Phalange, a Lebanese Christian militia aligned with the Gemayel family, entered the Sabra and Shatila refugee camps. They killed at least 700 to 800, and perhaps thousands, of Lebanese and Palestinian Shiites, including women and children. An Israeli investigation later found the IDF had enabled the attack, and Sharon lost his job.

Reagan's advisers considered reinserting the MNF into Lebanon, but they remained divided over the question. Shultz, Casey, Clark, and presidential counselor Ed Meese supported the idea, while Weinberger and JCS chairman General John Vessey steadfastly opposed the proposal, citing the lack of a defined objective. Reagan nevertheless approved the redeployment, and on September 29, 1982, the Marines took up a static position at the Beirut airport. The Marines operated with peacetime rules of engagement to avoid violating the US War Powers Resolution that Congress passed in 1973. As a result, DiFranco and Russell carried arms without chambered rounds. (Their weapons had ammunition magazines, but each Marine would have to cock his rifle to inject the first bullet into the firing chamber before shooting.)

A quasi stalemate in Lebanon continued until April 18, when an Iranian-sponsored group later known as Hezbollah detonated a truck bomb at the US embassy in Beirut. Sixty-three people died, included seventeen Americans. The bombing killed eight CIA operations officers and thus eliminated the best source of local intelligence in Lebanon. Reagan resolved to press forward with peacekeeping operations, but nothing was done down the line to improve the safety of the exposed Marine position at the airport.

In July, the Marines began taking fire from several Lebanese militias and run-of-the-mill snipers. On August 29, the Druze militia, an ally of Syria, fired mortar rounds that killed two Marines, and the Americans returned fire for the first time. The Muslim militias viewed the Marines as foreign support for the minority Christian government, now led by Amin Gemayel, Bashir's son. The Marines were frustrated by their "presence" mission, a far cry from their aggressive Leatherneck heritage.

Back in Washington, Bud McFarlane replaced William Clark as national security adviser on October 17. Reagan expected McFarlane to stop, or at least mediate, a damaging internecine war among Reagan's senior advisers that would trouble the administration for years to come. It started with Secretary Haig's frequent quarrels with White House staffers, and reached full bloom between Weinberger and Shultz. Secretary of State Schulz more often favored the use of force. His defense counterpart, however, argued against any operation short of using overwhelming force in pursuit of a clear objective, and having the support of the public and Congress.

The president's biographer, Lou Cannon, described Reagan as a "cautious and uncertain leader who was tugged first one way and then another" by his advisers. According to Cannon, a reporter who had covered Reagan during both his California governorship and the presidency, Reagan disliked choosing between contradictory options proposed by key cabinet members. This was especially true when Weinberger and Shultz, both old Washington hands, sharply disagreed. Further, Reagan disliked arguments between advisers in his presence. He wanted his national security adviser to seek a compromise to end the argument. "This trait invited middle-ground solutions aimed at mending differences, even in circumstances such as Lebanon where the middle ground courted catastrophe," Cannon wrote. "Keeping George happy," or "finding a formula that Cap could accept" became the criterion for action.

Reagan's national security advisers from 1981 to 1986—Richard Allen, Judge William Clark, Bud McFarlane, and Vice Admiral John Poindexter—struggled to reconcile differences between senior

Reagan officials, especially those between George and Cap after July 1982. They had a tough job given Reagan's aversion to details and his acceptance of dissention among his national security principals. In response, McFarlane, and later Poindexter, acted with their NSC staff in accordance with Reagan's broad objectives. That initiative and activism fostered the sale of arms to Iran in return for the release of American hostages in Lebanon, and the covert aid to anticommunist rebels—the Contras—in Nicaragua. Those two NSC staff-run operations resulted in the Iran-Contra scandal that damaged his presidency.

A Canceled Retaliation

Immediately after the Beirut barracks bombing, Reagan and his golf group returned to Washington on the morning of October 23. The president met at 9:00 a.m. with his National Security Planning Group (NSPG), a rump assembly of the National Security Council. The fog of war obscured early information on the perpetrators of the bombing. Reagan, however, quickly announced his intent to follow the "swift and effective retribution" policy that he established at the start of his term. "The first thing I want to do is find out who did it and go after them with everything we've got."

The group met again at 4:00 p.m. and they discussed retaliatory strikes against known Hezbollah sites in Baalbek, a town in the Beqaa Valley of Lebanon. Weinberger disagreed. "I'm not an eye-for-an-eye man," he said, but then added, "I have no objection to bombing if you're going to accomplish something with it." The secretary argued, however, that there was insufficient targeting information. Most of the Joint Chiefs rejected retaliation. Chairman Vessey opposed action for moral reasons, saying such action is "beneath our dignity to retaliate against terrorists." He also suggested that retribution would bring more attacks on the Marines.

However, in the Situation Room that day Reagan wanted action. "Well, let's go after it," Reagan said. "Let's plan the mission, get ready and quick, and if possible, do it with the French. But do it." At the end of the meeting, Reagan's national security adviser Bud McFarlane repeated the president's decision. "As I understand it, Mr. President, you want the Pentagon to commence planning a retaliatory mission." Reagan agreed.

Members of Congress reacted sharply to the bombing. Senator Ernest Hollings (D-SC), for example, eloquently criticized the Marine mission: "If they were put there to fight, there are too few. If they were put there to die, there are too many."

Meanwhile, in what some critics later called a wag-the-dog moment, Reagan and his team authorized the US military invasion of the Caribbean nation of Grenada. Soviet and Cuban militarization of the island hit Reagan's anticommunist nerve, especially when a communist coup toppled the government. The ensuing violence and martial law threatened eight hundred American medical students enrolled in St. George's School of Medicine. US units swarmed ashore on October 25, two days after the Beirut bombing. The operation had been in the works before the Marines' disaster, but skeptics still hollered. Reagan responded when he addressed both Grenada and Lebanon in a televised speech on Thursday, October 27. The president and his speechwriters skillfully interwove the successful, but costly— nineteen Americans KIA—Grenada operation with the Beirut bombing. According to Reagan biographer Richard Reeves, Reagan tied the Marines in Lebanon to the "lovely little war" in Grenada through his anticommunist rhetoric. "The events in Lebanon and Grenada," Reagan said, "though oceans apart, are closely related."

Polls showed a quick drop in public support for Reagan, despite a chorus of "well dones" from the media and Congress. A *New York Times*–CBS News survey showed that only 34 percent of respondents considered that he handled both situations wisely, and 52 percent said he was too quick to use military force.

On November 10, Syrian forces fired a surface-to-air missile at a US Navy F-14 Tomcat fighter flying over Lebanon. It missed, and Weinberger, who wanted no further military involvement in Lebanon, downplayed the incident. That added to the rift with Shultz. "Not only was Weinberger against the State Department's Middle East policy," McFarlane wrote later, "he was against George Shultz personally, and that made winning him over virtually impossible."

Planning commenced for air strikes launched from a Navy carrier, a process that gained firmness on November 12 when the US and French intelligences services identified the October 23 airport bombers as Hezbollah. Reagan gave the final go-ahead for a retaliatory strike two days later. US actions would be coordinated with French retaliatory operations. However, during the early hours of November 16, Washington time, it became apparent to McFarlane and his deputy, John Poindexter, that someone down the line from the White House had aborted the planned attack. At 6:30 a.m., Weinberger called McFarlane.

"Well, I have decided that we really ought not to go ahead with this," the secretary said. "There are complications."

"Cap, what has gone wrong?" McFarlane asked.

"No, Bud, there are just too many factors here that are uncertain, and I do not believe it is prudent to go. We just weren't ready. We needed more time."

"The president isn't going to be able to understand this, Cap. You were there. You saw how strongly he felt about this."

"I'll be glad to talk with him. But I thought it was the wrong thing to do."

McFarlane spoke with Reagan a couple hours later and advised him of Weinberger's actions. "I don't understand," Reagan said. "Why didn't they do it?"

"There's no excuse for it, Mr. President," McFarlane replied. "You approved this operation, and Cap decided not to carry it out. The credibility of the United States in Damascus just went to zero. There's no justification."

"Gosh, that's really disappointing," Reagan said. "That's terrible. We should have blown the daylights out of them. I just don't understand."

Reagan offered his explanation of the reversal of the strike orders in his memoir: "I canceled them because our experts said they were not absolutely sure they were the right targets. I didn't want to kill innocent people." Weinberger, in his memoir, *Fighting for Peace*, called McFarlane's version of the episode "absurd."

On December 3, Syrian forces fired shoulder-mounted, surface-to-air missiles at US aircraft over Lebanon, and Reagan authorized strikes on fixed SAM batteries. The military executed the mission poorly, and two aircraft were lost and one pilot killed. Damage on the ground was skimpy—two gun emplacements destroyed and a radar temporarily knocked off line. That engagement solved nothing, so throughout December and January, Reagan's team debated a proposal to withdraw the Marines. Pressure came from Congress to remove them, and White House political operatives looked at the coming election year. Chief of Staff James Baker asked McFarlane, "Bud, what is the light at the end of the tunnel here?"

"There really isn't any."

By the end of January, Shultz was the lone advocate for keeping an armed presence in Lebanon. Seeing McFarlane side with Weinberger, Shultz called the White House and asked McFarlane, "What are you trying to do?"

"I'm trying to serve the country and the president," McFarlane said. "I don't believe . . . we're going to be able to forge an effective policy with you and Cap as much in disagreement as you are. I'm not going to leave the Marines vulnerable to the vicissitudes of cabinet warfare in Washington."

After an NSPG meeting on February 7, while Reagan was giving a speech in Las Vegas, Vice President Bush called the president and notified him of the general agreement on the Marines' redeployment; Reagan assented. Journalists David Martin and John Walcott wrote in their 1988 book, *Best Laid Plans*, of the president's decision: "It was probably the closest Ronald Reagan had come to being decisive during the entire eighteen-month agony of the American crusade in Lebanon." Lou Cannon offered this assessment, reflecting Reagan's actions during the Beirut crisis: "Often he held the reins of power so lightly that he did not appear to hold them at all."

Assessment

Little consensus on the quality of the president's management of the Beirut bombing disaster emerges from either experts or Reagan's senior advisers. The disparity of views presented me with an analytic problem that I faced in every chapter of this book—whom to believe. In this case, however, I held a position in the cheap seats of the West Wing at the time and was able to judge most of the participants with my own eyes. In the years since, I drew upon that experience to decide which interview, memoir, or biography to trust regarding crucial points in the crisis. I chose Lou Cannon's accounts because he was a good reporter, and Bud McFarlane's version because he's an honorable man with whom I spoke regularly. I also consulted with my former NSC colleagues, who all counseled setting aside some parts of Reagan's and Weinberger's memoirs. These factors led to my conclusion: President Reagan handled the Beirut bombing incident poorly. The administration had placed the Marines in a vulnerable position and then after the attack failed to carry out Reagan's order to retaliate.

President Reagan's opportunities for decisive crisis action were minimal given his disinclination to resolve fundamental disagreements between Weinberger other advisers regarding the Marines deployment and rules of engagement. Other presidents have suffered the opposite problem—too much harmony in Truman's crisis group, for example. And others excluded potentially useful devil's advocates and pursued faulty courses of action. In this case, however, the "team of rivals" atmosphere empowered Secretary Weinberger to stop the Reagan-ordered strike on Hezbollah targets in retaliation for the bombing. On the other hand, White House advisers twice ignored the objections of the uniformed military leadership. Chairman Vessey protested both deployments of the MNF, especially the second, which placed the Marines in an exposed position and pursuing a soft, noncombat mission. Reconciling policy and strategy differences between White House civilians and Pentagon generals is a challenge common to most presidential crises.

As a consequence of his advisers' differences, Reagan stumbled through the deployment of the MNF, the bombing, and the MNF's ultimate retreat. Critics who are unknowing of the science of muddling through and inclined to equate it to dithering could have accused Reagan of following a muddled approach to the crisis. Just as Eisenhower floundered through the 1960 U-2 incident, Reagan oversaw a tragedy in Lebanon. In sharp distinction to these failures, two examples of a president successfully using a reasoned and incremental muddling-through process are Kennedy during the Cuban Missile Crisis, and Reagan himself during the TWA-847 hijacking described in the next segment.

Biographer Cannon offered a sharp critique of Reagan's handling of the Beirut situation: "Lebanon . . . became an arena for trial-and-error

US foreign policy initiatives that ended in debacle. If measured in loss of American lives abroad, Lebanon was the greatest disaster of the Reagan presidency." Cannon went on to offer a broader assessment of Reagan's skills: "He was better suited to leading the nation than commanding its government."

Part II. Terrorism, 1985–86

Searching for Swift and Effective Action

As President Reagan's helicopter began its final approach to the South Lawn, the news media hastily arranged a bank of microphones outside the Diplomatic Reception Room entrance to the White House. It was 11:15 a.m. on June 16, 1985, and the blossoms on the adjacent Andrew Jackson magnolia were fading. But the photographers were focused on Marine One as Reagan returned from Camp David. On the previous Friday, Shiite terrorists had hijacked an American airliner, TWA Flight 847, while en route to Rome from Athens. The hijackers had forced the cockpit crew at gunpoint to make a bizarre series of flights between Algiers and Beirut on Friday, Saturday, and Sunday. In the plane's second of three landings in Beirut on Saturday, the hijackers had shot a passenger, US Navy petty officer Robert Stethem, and dumped his body on the runway.

Reagan's advisers had decided early on in the unfolding drama to keep the president on a "business-as-usual" path. Everyone had the "Carter syndrome" in mind, recalling how in 1979, President Carter dropped everything to concentrate on the Iran hostage incident. When that dragged on, Carter appeared helpless.

When the helicopter pilot cut the engines after landing, the press knew that was a sign that Reagan would make remarks before entering the White House. Wearing an informal plaid shirt in the early summer sunshine, Reagan reaffirmed his policy of not negotiating with terrorists and warned the hijackers: "For their own safety, they better turn these people loose." Afterward, spokesman Larry Speakes reiterated administration policy: "We do not make concessions. We do not give in to demands. We do not encourage other nations to do this." Yet over the next thirteen days, that's essentially what Reagan did, although with a bit of saber rattling.

After seizing the plane at 10:20 a.m. local time on Friday, the two Hezbollah hijackers, Mohammed Ali Hamadi and Hasan 'Izz-al-Din, forced Captain John Testrake to fly his Boeing 727 to Beirut International Airport. The hijackers collected passports and military IDs and identified those with Jewish-sounding names.

Testrake landed over objections from the tower, and the hijackers insisted on fuel; the Lebanese complied. The terrorists also released nineteen passengers and made their demands known over the radio. They wanted the release of 766 Arab prisoners in Israeli prisons and seventeen convicted terrorists held in Kuwait. Those imprisoned in Israel had been detained in Lebanon during the 1982–83 Israeli invasion and later transferred from the El Ansar camp in Lebanon to Atlit prison in Israel. The two hijackers repeatedly shouted in broken English, "Marines" and "New Jersey," references to the US Marine peacekeeping force in Lebanon during 1982 and 1983 and the accompanying ferocious shelling by battleship USS *New Jersey* in 1983.

Flight 847 then flew to Algiers, where the hijackers released twenty-one passengers, mostly women and children. They also demanded more fuel and beat passengers until the Algerian authorities complied. TWA lacked a fuel account in Algiers, so the head cabin attendant, Uli Derickson, fetched her Shell Oil credit card. Copilot Phil Maresca reached out his cockpit window and handed the card to the fuel technician. The charge was $6,000.

The airliner then flew back to Beirut and found the tower had turned off the landing aids and runway lights. At the last second, the runway lights came on, and Testrake landed hard at 2:30 a.m., with the passengers in a crash-landing position. The hijackers then killed Stethem to show their seriousness and let ten or twelve armed colleagues aboard. Before the plane departed for Algiers again, employees of Middle East Airlines brought food and water to the 727.

At dawn, the hijackers had Testrake fly again to Algiers. There, while not looting valuables from the remaining passengers, the hijackers made their demands known to Algerian officials. An Algerian doctor came aboard, checked on the passengers, and took three away with him. At this point, Testrake explained later, only men remained on the plane. The aircraft stayed in Algiers overnight, and the flight crew lay on rows of seats and fell asleep. After refueling the next morning—no credit card needed—Testrake took off shortly after 8:00 a.m. and flew back to Beirut. He and his copilot and flight engineer faked the failure of two of the three engines as they rolled to a stop on the runway. They didn't want to enable the hijackers any further, but that led to a dangerous situation.

Nabih Berri, the head of the Shiite Amal militia and the Lebanese government justice minister, appointed himself the negotiator between the hijackers and the Western governments whose citizens were involved. At about 2:00 a.m. on Monday, June 17, Berri removed the thirty-six remaining passengers and sent most of them to secret locations controlled by Amal. However, Hezbollah retained separate control of four passengers—those with apparent Jewish names. The three cockpit crew members stayed on the plane.

Starting on Sunday afternoon, June 16, Reagan began regular meetings with his National Security Planning Group that lasted until the crisis resolution. Ideas about rescuing the hostages surfaced immediately, but several factors limited the use of force. The removal of the passengers from the 727 ended any military option except for a potentially calamitous and bloody firefight in Beirut. The hostages wrote a letter to Reagan pleading against such action, which he received that day. It read: "We implore you not to take any direct military action on our behalf." Arrange the release of the Israeli prisoners, they asked. "*Now.*"

Another reason for discarding forceful solutions was that a negotiated settlement was available—through Israel's release of the Lebanese prisoners. However, Reagan's repeated statements about refusing concessions meant that no publicly discernable deal could be made without a loss of credibility at home and abroad. Further complicating the issue, Israel's position was that it wouldn't release the detainees *unless* the United States requested the action. Given this conundrum, Shultz and McFarlane urged the president to be patient while his team sought third parties to intervene, including Syria's Hafez al-Assad. McFarlane, who had met Berri during the Israeli occupation of Lebanon, talked directly with him.

Meanwhile, the hijackers eagerly exploited a relentless news media in Beirut, arranging interviews for themselves and the hostages. In what became a circus, the media dramatically publicized the hijackers' motives and highlighted President Reagan's apparent inability to do anything about the hijacking. Following the Iranian hostage-taking of 1979–81 and the non-response to the 1983 Marine barracks bombing, they seemed to suggest that terrorists had America's number.

Reagan held a press conference on Tuesday, June 18, and acknowledged the limits of his power and the need to safeguard the hostages' lives. "Retaliation . . . might just entail striking a blow in a general direction," he said, "and the result would be a terrorist act in itself and the killing and victimizing of innocent people." His comments echoed those of President Carter's during his hostage crisis. Reagan, who had repeatedly criticized Carter's passivity then, suddenly found himself sitting in his predecessor's chair, figuratively as well as literally.

Eventually, a plan for a "no-deal deal" with Israel evolved. On June 20, Shultz offered to determine Israel's intentions on the prisoner release in a "precise" way. Israel had planned to set free the Atlit prison detainees but stopped when the hijackers demanded the same action. Shultz went through a back channel to Israeli UN ambassador Benjamin Netanyahu and asked, "What can we expect Israel to do about all the Atlit prisoners on the assumption that there are no TWA 847 hostages being held?" Shultz stressed that the question was merely a request for clarification, not a change in US policy.

Israel's reply on June 21 was just as precise, but it allowed Robert Oakley, then State's counterterrorism coordinator, to later characterize the Israeli position. "Once the TWA hostages are released," Oakley mimicked the Israeli logic to PBS in 2001, "we will resume the release of prisoners which has been temporarily interrupted—we're not producing a quid pro quo, we're just doing something that we intended to do anyway, but we're not going to do it until the hostages are released."

The business-as-usual plan during the crisis foundered on June 24 when Reagan canceled his pending vacation in California. At an NSPG meeting that day, Casey and Shultz proposed more aggressive actions, including port blockades and airport closures in Lebanon. McFarlane argued for another two days of diplomacy. Don Regan, now chief of staff, worried about time slipping away and mentioned the Carter syndrome. "We don't have the luxury of waiting," he said. "Public opinion will desert the president."

The next day, June 25, McFarlane offered a timeline, or escalation ladder, that would lead to serious military operations against Lebanon and Syria if the hostages weren't released. Reagan approved the concept in principle but did not immediately order any direct action. He told McFarlane to tell Berri that forceful actions were on the table. Later in the day, Speakes told reporters that Reagan was rethinking his statement a week before—"I have to wait it out"—and was now considering "whatever actions are necessary." Further, administration sources told the *Washington Post* about options to blockade ports and close airports.

This mention of force got to Berri. He responded on June 26 by releasing an ill hostage and proposed that the remaining hostages be held in "escrow" in either the French or Swiss embassy, or transferred to Syria. At the same time, the back-channel communications with Israel paid off. Israeli prime minister Shimon Peres wrote Reagan, offering to drop the need for a public US request for the detainee release. Reagan responded and ratified the no-deal deal.

Also during this phase of the crisis, Assad reportedly asked Hashemi Rafsanjani, speaker of the Iranian parliament, to intercede with those Hezbollah members who held four of the hostages. That action, along with Israel's no-deal deal and Reagan's assurance to Assad that the Atlit prisoners would be released, formed the foundation for the TWA hostages' freedom. However, two late developments caused problems. On Thursday, June 27, the administration overreached and publicly insisted that seven American hostages previously kidnapped individually in Beirut be included in the TWA hostage release. On the following day, Reagan publicly called the hijackers "thugs, murderers, and barbarians."

On Saturday, Amal members gathered thirty-five hostages for transfer to Syria, but the four Hezbollah captives were absent. Reportedly, the hostage-takers considered themselves freedom fighters, not thugs or barbarians. Assad, hearing of the glitch, asked for and received assurances from the Reagan administration that the US would not retaliate against Hezbollah targets in Lebanon. Assad then leaned heavily on the Iranian facilitators of Hezbollah in Baalbek to release the missing four passengers. They were soon reunited with the others.

All thirty-nine hostages traveled with Syrian escort to Damascus on Sunday, June 30, and then on to Germany on US Air Force planes for physical examinations, counseling, and freedom. Reagan honored his promise to Assad and ordered no retaliatory actions after the hostage release.

A week later, on July 7, the headline for a *Washington Post* op-ed piece by then *Post* reporter Lou Cannon read, "What Happened to Reagan the Gunslinger?" The subhead added to the point: "Now His Problem Is Convincing Skeptics He Isn't a Pussycat." Cannon reminded readers of Reagan's "swift and effective retribution" pledge in 1981, and noted that Reagan's conservative supporters "would prefer a president who has more than talk in his antiterrorist arsenal." Norman Podhoretz, one of Reagan's conservative supporters, accused Reagan of caving in and paying for the hostages' return "with a ransom of shame." Further, the *Wall Street Journal* editorial page called the president "Jimmy Reagan."

Tit for Tat with Libya

The Friday night crowd was jumping at the La Belle discothèque in West Berlin on April 4, 1986. Among the hundreds dancing and drinking that night were off-duty US military personnel stationed in the US sector of the divided Cold War city. But at 1:49 a.m. Saturday morning, a terrorist bomb brought death and pain to the disco.

The explosion killed three, including Army sergeants Kenneth Ford and James Goins, and injured 230, dozens of whom were US military personnel. I was the director of the White House Situation Room at the time, and one of the White House phones in my home started ringing, the first of a cascade of calls to and from the Situation Room that evening. John Poindexter, who had succeeded McFarlane the previous December, was traveling with Reagan in California and notified the president.

Solid intelligence from NSA quickly identified Libya as the sponsor of the bombing. Reagan's crisis team unified rapidly on the need to take swift and effective retribution against Libyan leader Muammar Qadhafi's terrorist-support infrastructure. Reagan finally had a clear shot at retaliation, or so it seemed to a casual observer. Actually, the matter was far more complex, and the Reagan administration was partially responsible for the La Belle bombing and a flurry of simultaneous Libyan-backed terrorist incidents. The bombing was a Libyan move in a series of tit-for-tats with the United States that began in 1981.

Qadhafi had seized power in Libya, a former Italian colony, in 1969 and used the country's oil wealth to support his capricious international activities. As Reagan started his first term, his advisers saw Libya as a surrogate for Soviet expansionism in Africa and the Middle East. To test whether Qadhafi was ready to pick a fight with Uncle Sam, the US Navy began to challenge his territorial claims of the international waters of the Gulf of Sidra on the Libyan coast. The first maneuvers occurred in March 1981, with a more serious thrust in August. Two Soviet-made jets challenged carrier-based F-14s flying above the gulf and were shot down by the US aircraft. America had demonstrated its resolve, but Qadhafi redoubled his subversive activities.

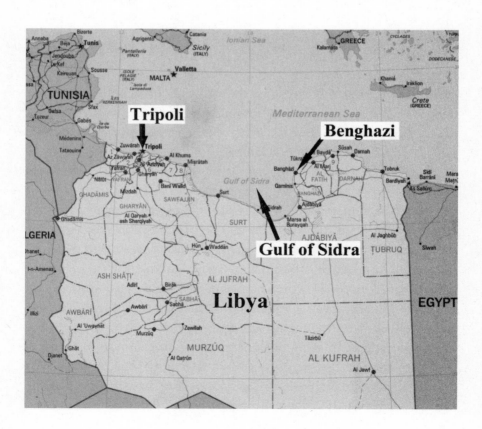

In the fall of 1981, Qadhafi threatened to kill Reagan and members of his cabinet, and evidence of the plan filtered into the White House. In November, the president approved a package of sanctions against Libya and ordered the preparation of military options designed to change Qadhafi's behavior, but not directly effect a "regime change," as such actions are called today. The administration also branded Qadhafi the "most dangerous man in the world." The sanctions appeared to force an observable diminution of Libyan-sponsored subversion and terrorism sponsorship.

Hostile actions by Libya picked up in 1984, when a Libyan freighter deployed anti-ship mines in the Red Sea; eighteen vessels were damaged. There was no evidence that Libya played a role the following year in the TWA 847 incident, but Qadhafi did provide training camps for the Palestinians who hijacked the Italian cruise ship *Achille Lauro*. However, in late August 1985, Reagan approved an aggressive program to thwart Qadhafi's adventurism, which included an appeal to Egyptian president Hosni Mubarak for a joint Egyptian-American invasion of Libya; Mubarak declined.

The Qadhafi-supported Abu Nidal Organization struck hard, though, on November 23, 1985, by hijacking an Egypt Air 737 en route from Athens to Cairo. A combined sixty people died in a gunfight aloft and in a shoot-out after an emergency landing in Malta. A month later, on December 27, ANO gunmen simultaneously attacked airports in Rome and Vienna, killing a total of eighteen people. Five of them were Americans, including an eleven-year-old girl. The ANO had used Libyan passports and weapons traced to Libya.

In an NSPG meeting on January 6, Shultz urged Reagan to approve a military strike on Libya and argued that such action was justifiable self-defense. Typically, Weinberger dissented and questioned the accuracy of the evidence of Libyan involvement and the deterrence effects on Qadhafi. He also said an assault might trigger retaliation against US citizens working in Libya; he didn't want another Iran-Carter situation. Reagan decided against a military option.

Nevertheless, Reagan did approve the preparation of contingency military targets in Libya, diplomatic initiatives, and the severance of almost all remaining economic ties with Libya. On the NSC staff, Howard Teicher, Jim Stark, Ollie North, and two others began developing a Libya strategy, one, according to Teicher, involving "steadily increasing pressures and disproportionate responses" to Libyan provocations.

One of the staff's initiatives was to again challenge Libya's claim to the Gulf of Sidra. Qadhafi had drawn a "line of death" across the gulf from the eastern headland near Benghazi to the western side near Misrata. He threatened to savage anyone that crossed the line. The Pentagon scheduled two "freedom of navigation" exercises north of the line in March, followed by a third into Qadhafi's death zone. The US Navy's Sixth Fleet would poke Qadhafi in the eye and force him to fight or back down.

The State Department contacted European allies before the start of the Gulf of Sidra operations. Although many had joined America on some sanctions, France, Italy, and West Germany didn't want to seriously disrupt their international trade with Libya. Further, they perceived the terrorism in 1986 as arising from political problems—the issues of Palestinian statehood and redress of the 1982 Israeli invasion of Lebanon, for example—which could not be solved with military attacks on Libya. British prime minister Margaret Thatcher, for one, warned against responding to the Rome and Vienna incidents with retaliatory strikes, which she considered "against international law."

Prior to the March naval operations, there was considerable discussion, debate, and argument among Reagan's advisers from State, Defense, and the NSC staff. They had to decide on how to retaliate if Qadhafi rose to the bait—what weapons systems and targets, and proportionality. At a March 14 NSPG meeting, Reagan approved targets, which were generally terrorist training and support sites, plus aircraft bases. However, at one point the president asked, "Could this lead into trouble? Could we end up with a less palatable situation than we have now?" His team assured him that untoward consequences, especially a Soviet intervention, were unlikely.

The first two operations failed to elicit a Libyan response, but on March 23, the Navy crossed the line of death. Libyan forces in Sirte fired two SA-5 SAMs at two F-14s and both missed. But the Navy did not retaliate immediately, and Poindexter and his staff feared Weinberger had again dragged his feet. Poindexter called JCS chairman Admiral William Crowe and said, "You and Cap better come over here and talk to the president. He's pretty hot." Poindexter later discovered that the commander of the Sixth Fleet had decided to wait until after dark before shooting back. Navy aircraft destroyed the SAM site and sank two patrol boats. It was now Qadhafi's turn for more tit-for-tat.

Two days later, Qadhafi's intelligence service sent instructions to more than thirty Libyan Peoples' Bureaus in Europe and Africa directing them to assault US targets. Authorities discovered some planned attacks early, but on April 2, a bomb exploded on TWA Flight 840 from Rome to Athens. It blew four Americans, including a nine-month-old child, through a hole in the fuselage. The plane later landed safely. Additionally, the East Berlin PLB wired home on April 4, with the message, "Tripoli will be happy when you see the headlines tomorrow." Their bomb exploded in the La Belle disco the following day.

Reagan's team reacted immediately with a debate on what to bomb in Libya. Poindexter proposed using the secret F-177 stealth aircraft and Tomahawk cruise missiles to limit collateral damage, a point important to Reagan. Crowe strongly disagreed, not wanting to risk losing that technology through some mishap to the Soviets via Qadhafi. Reagan finally approved five targets, which included the Aziziyah Barracks, Qadhafi's headquarters where he often slept, and utilized the Pentagon's preferred weapon systems—a mix of Air Force and carrier-based aircraft.

Thatcher grudgingly approved the use of UK-based Air Force F-111 Aardvarks, but France, Spain, and Italy declined permission for them to overfly en route to Libya. Teicher believed that France was still smarting from Weinberger's retreat from the planned French and American retaliation for the 1983 Beirut barracks bombing. As a result, the F-111s flew a debilitating fourteen-hour mission through the Strait of Gibraltar and back.

The US military struck Libya at 2:00 a.m. local time on April 15. Of the nine F-111s assigned to Tripoli targets, the rules of engagement on minimum ordnance accuracy prevented seven from releasing their bombs. Despite this, forty-one civilians died in the raid, and the Libyans claimed Qadhafi's adopted daughter was among those killed. While the physical damage to Libya was slight, Reagan appeared to have achieved some international political goals. Shultz wrote later: "We had emphatically put down a marker that the United States was ready and able to take military action against states that perpetrated terrorism." A *Washington Post*–ABC poll found that 76 percent of respondents approved of the bombing; Reagan's overall approval rating jumped to 70 percent.

Regrettably, Qadhafi responded immediately. On April 17, his operatives purchased three Beirut hostages, included American Peter Kilburn, and executed them in retaliation. The following September, the ANO hijacked Pan Am Flight 73 on the ground in Karachi, Pakistan. Twenty passengers died when Pakistani forces stormed the aircraft. Later reporting suggested Abu Nidal had recommended the operation to Tripoli in response to the US attack on Libya in April 1986. And in December 1988, Libyan agents, one of whom was later arrested, placed a bomb on Pan Am Flight 103, which was bound for Detroit from Frankfurt. The device detonated over Lockerbie, Scotland, killing all 259 aboard and eleven on the ground.

The families of those killed in the 1986 Tripoli attack and those who died in the Pan Am 103 bombing came together in 2008, at least in a legal sense. Both groups had sued, seeking restitution from the respective offending countries. The United States and Libya settled the lawsuits to the satisfaction of each group of plaintiffs.

Assessment

During the TWA 847 hijacking, Reagan faced the hard reality that it was difficult to find swift and effective options that would not backfire and kill helpless Americans. Reagan pursued a prudent, negotiated settlement of the TWA incident largely because that made sense in those circumstances. His change of tone grew out of the hard-knocks transformation from a candidate to a sitting president. Rhetoric is cheap on the sidelines, but in the middle of a life-or-death crisis, bold action is often enormously expensive, especially in human lives.

Early in the airliner crisis, however, Reagan had unsuccessfully looked for a big stick to swing to keep from falling prey to the "Carter syndrome." His aides portrayed him as conducting business as usual, but this approach didn't last too long, especially when the television sideshow started in Lebanon and Reagan's chief of staff worried that the American public might desert the president. At that point, making a deal, however removed that was from his anti-terrorism rhetoric, seemed to be the best solution. Reagan's cautious, incremental approach worked, and his Teflon coating didn't allow criticism to stick.

The 1986 La Belle disco bombing is more complicated. Reagan's bold and decisive response—air strikes on Libyan targets—should not be evaluated in isolation, but rather within the series of back-and-forth US and Libyan attacks. Qadhafi directed the La Belle disco bombing in retaliation for provocative US naval operations. Reagan's response, the April 1986 bombing of terrorist-related facilities in Libya, did not forestall further terrorism. Instead, Qadhafi responded with several more tit-for-tat terrorist incidents that culminated with the destruction of Pan Am Flight 103. In light of the consequences, Reagan's response to the La Belle bombing was bold but ineffective in achieving its deterrence goal. Indeed, it did the opposite. In 2008 the US government acknowledged its role in the cycle of retribution by paying a legal settlement to the families of the innocent Libyan victims of the retaliatory air strikes. Yet, from a domestic political perspective, Reagan did gain from his actions, and his standing rose in the polls.

As Reagan passively allowed the friction between George Shultz and Cap Weinberger to continue, the NSC staff became more operational and aggressive. Martin and Walcott offered this view of the White House staff's added initiative: "The president's involvement in foreign affairs was episodic, anecdotal, impulsive, and rarely decisive. It was no wonder that the staff of the National Security Council later concluded that the best way to serve Reagan was to do his job for him."

Finally, the state of Reagan's mind—his mental acuity—may have affected decision making during his second term. His son Ron wrote in 2011 that he thought something was amiss as early as 1984. Others have speculated as much, and in retrospect, I recall an instance in the afternoon of November 18, 1986, when I was shaken by the president's apparent uncertainty and even confusion. Admiral Poindexter, Ollie North, and others were preparing Reagan for his news conference the next day to discuss the revelation of the arms sales to Iran. The president was at a podium in the East Wing family theater rehearsing likely questions and answers, and staff members were scattered about in the theater seats. I quietly watched from the back row. I was embarrassed for him as he struggled with weapons terms, dates, and technical issues. But then, so were the reporters who covered the real press conference the next day and wrote of the president's "embarrassing bumbles" and "flustered" demeanor.

CHAPTER 9

GEORGE H. W. BUSH

Persian Gulf War, 1990–91

Triumph without Victory

The black Cadillac passed through the southwest gate of the White House and came to a stop outside the ground floor entrance to the West Wing. General Colin Powell stepped out and, carrying a black leather map case, walked past the uniformed Secret Service officer outside the Situation Room. The chairman of the Joint Chiefs ascended the stairs, and then walked around the corner and down the hall to the entry alcove outside the Oval Office. Powell was on time, as expected, for a scheduled 2:00 p.m. meeting with President George H. W. Bush.

Powell joined six other members of the "Gang of Eight" as they entered Bush's office—Vice President Dan Quayle, Secretary of State James Baker, Secretary of Defense Richard Cheney, White House chief of staff John Sununu, National Security Adviser Brent Scowcroft, and Scowcroft's deputy, Robert Gates. Bush welcomed his crisis team for their daily meeting. It was Wednesday, February 27, 1991, and the advisers gathered to update the president on the ground offensive in the Persian Gulf War. After thirty-eight days of aerial assaults on targets in both Iraqi-occupied Kuwait and Iraq itself, coalition soldiers and Marines had gone on the offensive four days earlier. Bush and Quayle sat in armchairs with their backs to the fireplace, and the others sat on two facing sofas. At the end of the U-shaped sitting area, Powell set his charts and maps on an easel and presented good news from battlefield.

"Mr. President," Powell said at the end of his briefing, "it's going much better that we expected. The Iraqi army is broken. All they're trying to do now is get out." Powell had described the slaughter of Iraqi troops bent on a hasty retreat from Kuwait on what became known as the "highway of death." The scenes made Powell uneasy.

"We don't want to be seen as killing for the sake of killing, Mr. President. I've talked to General Schwarzkopf," referring to the US and coalition commander. "I expect sometime tomorrow the job will be done, and I'll probably be bringing you a recommendation to stop the fighting."

"If that's the case," Bush said, "why not end it today?" The president caught everyone off guard with his question, but continued. "We're starting to pick up some undesirable public and political baggage with all those scenes of carnage. You say we've accomplished the mission. Why not end it?"

As the others talked about a cease-fire, Powell slipped into the president's private study off the Oval Office and called Norman Schwarzkopf, the commander in chief of the US Central Command who had his wartime headquarters in Riyadh, Saudi Arabia. "Norm, the president wants to know if we can end it now?"

"When is now?" Schwarzkopf asked.

"We're looking at this evening."

"I don't have any problem. Our objective is to drive 'em out, and we've done it." Schwarzkopf asked for time to consult with his subordinate commanders and promised to call Powell back.

The Gang of Eight reconvened at 5:30 p.m. in Bush's private office. Powell reported that Schwarzkopf had signed off on the cessation of fighting. Accordingly, Bush immediately ordered the suspension of hostilities. "In what was probably too cute by half," Scowcroft wrote later, "we agreed to end hostilities at midnight Washington time, for a ground war of exactly 100 hours." Powell called Schwarzkopf on a secure line and ordered a cease-fire in six hours. Schwarzkopf, in turn, called in his deputy, Lieutenant General Calvin Waller, and explained the timing.

"You have got to be shitting me," Waller said. "Why a cease-fire now?"

"One hundred hours has a nice ring," Schwarzkopf said.

"That's bullshit."

"Then you go argue with them."

And thus ended the 1990–1991 Persian Gulf War, the bold and decisive action that Bush undertook to resolve an international crisis caused by the August 2, 1990, invasion of Kuwait by neighboring Iraq.

Members of the Gang of Eight have offered reasons for the war's abrupt termination, and all are variations of a phrase made famous by Bush 43 in 2003—mission accomplished. On the other hand, Prince Bandar bin Sultan, the Saudi ambassador to the United States, said in late 1991, "We have a lot to do to finish with Iraq." Additionally, Richard Haass, the NSC staff point man for the war, thought the fighting should have continued in order to keep the surviving units of Iraq's elite Republican Guard and their modern tanks from escaping. The fact that coalition forces had not fully encircled this well-trained and equipped force by the February 28 cease-fire had not made it to Washington in time for Bush's decision.

On the battlefield, the Army's 24th Infantry Division commander, Major General Barry McCaffrey, later said they stopped too soon. A few days after the cease-fire, Schwarzkopf told a journalist that he should have fought two more days and immediately drew a sharp telephone rebuke from Bush. In 1992, *Newsweek* magazine cited military analyst Dr. Jeffrey Record on the war's termination: "I can't think of another case where a victorious army has declared a unilateral cessation of hostilities. From a purely military point of view it was a mistake, no question." The American public agreed. In a poll shortly after the cease-fire, 69 percent of those polled believed that the United States should have continued hostilities in order to remove Saddam Hussein from power. Lawrence Freedman, professor of War Studies at King's College, London, suggested that had the fight been brutal, "This restraint would have seemed prudent . . . However, the abrupt conclusion of the war suggested faint-heartedness."

The following views of just one of Bush's crisis decisions exemplify the range of opinions about the president's overall handling of the crisis:

"A triumph for American diplomacy and military might." —James Baker

"A triumph without victory." —*U.S. News & World Report*

"An incomplete success." —Michael Gordon and Lieutenant General Bernard Trainor

"Strategically inconclusive." —Zbigniew Brzezinski.

"Politically, it was a botched war." —American historian Theodore Draper

"A 'nothing war'; it resolved nothing and settled nothing." —Brown University professor emeritus Stephen Graubard

A Stunning Failure

Several factors had prompted Saddam Hussein to invade Kuwait, primary of which was seizing Kuwait's oil fields to ease his economic and geopolitical problems. The lengthy Iran-Iraq War, from 1980 to 1988, coupled with the decline in the price of crude oil, had undercut Iraqi finances. Saddam Hussein needed money to rebuild and rearm after the costly war. While the Saudis forgave the Iraqi debts incurred financing the war against Iran, Kuwait's ruling emir, Sheik Jabir al-Ahmed al-Sabah, did not. The disintegration of the Soviet Union robbed Saddam Hussein of a helpful benefactor, and he needed funds to continue his development of chemical and nuclear weapons programs. Luckily for Saddam Hussein, the American government was there to help, if he chose to trust it.

Reagan tilted toward Iraq during the 1980s war, largely because of anti-Iran biases generated by the 1979–81 Iran hostage crisis and a desire to ensure that neither side prevailed. Bush continued support to Iraq, and between 1985 and 1990, sales of US military systems and dual-use technology increased to $1 billion annually; overall trade rose to $3.5 billion in 1990. Bush formalized his outreach to Saddam Hussein in October 1989 with National Security Directive 26. That order allowed the US Commodity Credit Corporation, an arm of the Agriculture Department, to approve a $1 billion loan credit package for Iraq in November 1989. The credits went to private banks that advanced Iraq money to buy American agriculture products. In January 1990, Bush put aside congressional objections and authorized

a $200 million export-import loan to Iraq for buying grain. Baker later called the actions "the high-water mark of our efforts to moderate Iraqi behavior."

Regardless of the America overtures, Saddam Hussein, according to Southern Methodist University professor Jeffrey Engel, "perceived himself within Washington's crosshairs." Some of his wariness of better American relations arose from revelations in 1986 that the Reagan administration had sold arms to Iran to secure the release of American hostages in Beirut. And the state of affairs in the former Soviet Union deprived Iraq of protection from what Saddam Hussein saw as American post–Cold War muscle flexing and democracy building. Further, according to Engel, "Saddam Hussein believed the time was ripe for his nation to assume its rightful place as the leading Arab state." He attempted to reinforce his self-perceived Arab leadership by threatening Israel with chemical weapons in April 1990: "By God, we will make the fire eat up half of Israel, if it tries to do anything against Iraq."

Kuwait appeared to Saddam Hussein as a good target for adventurism—the country was weak militarily, had no mutual defense treaties, and was conveniently nearby. The Kuwait/Iraq border, a colonial artifact and long a source of tensions between the countries, inhibited Iraq's easy access to the Persian Gulf. Annexing Kuwait would fix that, plus give Saddam Hussein control of 20 percent of the world's oil reserves. His economic woes would be decreased.

The Iraqi foreign minister wrote to the Arab League, a group of cooperative Arab countries, on July 16, 1990, accusing Kuwait and the United Arab Emirates of "direct aggression." He claimed the countries had conspired against Iraq by exceeding oil production quotas set by the Organization of the Petroleum Exporting Countries. The State Department reacted by cabling US Middle East embassies on July 19 with two guidance points: "Disputes should be settled by peaceful means, not intimidation and threats of the use of force. Second, the United States takes no position on the substance of bilateral issues concerning Iraq and Kuwait." However, across town on the same day, Secretary Cheney sent another signal by telling reporters that US commitments made during the Iran-Iraq War to defend Kuwait had not changed.

Two days later, Iraqi military forces began massing at the Kuwait border. The UAE, a neighboring Persian Gulf nation, immediately requested that the United States join them in a military exercise in response. Bush approved the participation of three Air Force aircraft and six Navy ships on July 23. The next day, a senior administration official told the *New York Times* the actions were meant to "bolster a friend and lay down a marker for Saddam Hussein."

Multiple signals continued from Washington on July 24. State Department spokeswoman Margaret Tutwiler told reporters, "There is no place for coercion and intimidation in a civilized world," referring to Saddam Hussein's threats. On the other hand, she declared that the United States had no security commitments to Kuwait. On the same day, the *Washington Post* cited an unnamed "military official" as saying, "If Iraq seizes a small amount of Kuwaiti territory as a means of gaining additional leverage over Kuwait in OPEC, the United States probably would not directly challenge the move." NSC staffer Haass and others in Washington viewed the development as "a modern-day version of gunboat diplomacy," in which Saddam Hussein was attempting to bully Kuwait. They considered the maneuvering as a bluff.

On July 25, and with only an hour's notice, Saddam Hussein summoned US ambassador April Glaspie to his office. She had not talked with him privately before. Saddam Hussein spoke uninterrupted for thirty minutes about his country's economic troubles, US-Iraqi relations, American arms sales to Iran, the joint US-UAE maneuvers, and US subversive efforts against Iraq. "Repeated American statements last year," he said, "made it apparent that America did not regard us as friends."

When Glaspie had the chance, she encapsulated Bush's rapprochement policy for Iraq: "I have a direct instruction from the president to seek better relations with Iraq."

"But how?" Saddam Hussein asked. "We too have this desire. But matters are running contrary to this desire." Regarding his dispute with Kuwait, Saddam Hussein declared, "The solution must be found within an Arab framework and through direct bilateral relations."

Glaspie repeated the intent of the instructions from State the previous week: "I know you need funds. We understand that and our opinion is that you should have the opportunity to rebuild your country. But we have no opinion on the Arab-Arab conflicts, like your border disagreement with Kuwait." Saddam Hussein responded with an encouraging word when he said that Egyptian president Hosni Mubarak had just offered to mediate Iraq-Kuwait differences in immediate negotiations. Saddam Hussein pledged that nothing would happen until that session. Glaspie reflected that optimistic note in her cable to Washington after the meeting. "I believe we would be well-advised to ease off on public criticism of Iraq until we see how the negotiations develop."

The Kuwait-Iraq meeting with Mubarak failed to solve anything, and the Iraqi preparations for military action increased. Both the Defense Intelligence Agency and CIA warned of impending war. At 1:00 a.m. local time on Wednesday, August 2, Iraqi forces moved into Kuwait. Within twelve hours, Iraqi forces controlled the entire country. The emir and his family fled to Saudi Arabia.

Many have viewed Glaspie's statements to Saddam Hussein as a green light for the invasion, despite her following of State's instructions. In their book *The General's War*, *New York Times* correspondent Michael Gordon and retired Lieutenant General Bernard Trainor offered their assessment of the pre-crisis period: "The war was a stunning failure of America's policy of trying to deter war."

This Will Not Stand

Scowcroft briefed Bush on the invasion at 8:20 p.m. on August 1. They agreed to have an NSC meeting early the next morning before Bush left for an international conference in Aspen, Colorado. But across the Potomac River, the tone of the administration in the face of the Iraqi aggression was rather low-key. A Pentagon spokesman said that evening, "This ain't our show."

Overnight, the UN Security Council voted 14-0 to condemn Iraq's aggression and demand its withdrawal. At 5:00 a.m., August 2, Bush signed an order freezing Iraqi financial assets in the United States. Minutes before the eight o'clock National Security Council meeting in the Cabinet Room, Bush held a mini–photo op for the media pool. One reporter asked if he intended to intervene or send troops. Bush responded, "I'm not contemplating such action."

The group talked about broad strategic issues and the impact of the invasion on the flow of oil from the Gulf area. Defending Saudi Arabia got more attention than ejecting Saddam Hussein from Kuwait. Schwarzkopf, who flew in from Tampa, Florida, for the meeting, described existing war plans for protecting the Saudi peninsula, a huge undertaking involving 140,000 troops. The discussion remained unfocused and drifted among the many issues. According to someone in the room, the attitude about Kuwait's fate could have been summed up as, "Hey too bad about Kuwait, but it's just a gas station, and who cares whether the sign says Sinclair or Exxon." Scowcroft later described his reaction: "I was frankly appalled at the undertone of the discussion, which suggested resignation to the invasion and even adaptation to a fait accompli."

Bush soon left for Aspen and worked his habitual "telephone diplomacy" with other heads of state as he flew west. Jordan's King

Hussein, for one, promised an Arab attempt at mediation within forty-eight hours. As soon as practicable, Bush met with fellow conference attendee British prime minister Margaret Thatcher. She insisted on firm action: "If Iraq wins, no small state is safe. They won't stop here. . . . We must do everything possible."

Many accounts of the Bush-Thatcher conversations in Aspen incorrectly recount the Brit's attempt to stiffen the president's spine. "Remember, George," Thatcher reportedly said, "this is no time to go wobbly." Cheney called the incident a wives' tale in 2013, but Thatcher actually said it later in August in a separate conversation about Iraq sanctions. What Thatcher did say to Bush in Aspen were frank words on the domestic political value of a short and successful war, such as hers when the UK prevailed over Argentina in the 1982 Falklands War. "I was about to be defeated when the Falklands conflict happened," she said. "I stayed in office for eight years after that."

Bush returned a day early from Aspen and met with his advisers Friday morning in the Cabinet Room. With Scowcroft's support, Larry Eagleburger, who sat in, as Secretary Baker was traveling in Russia, urged a forceful reaction. "Under these circumstances, it is absolutely essential that the United States—collectively if possible, but individually if necessary—not only put a stop to this aggression but roll it back," Eagleburger said. After Cheney supported Scowcroft and Eagleburger, the talk turned to defending Saudi Arabia, and Bush committed to planning for that action.

During a twenty-four-hour period, Bush had started thinking about intervention. Thatcher had urged him to take a Churchillian stance against the Hitler-like Saddam Hussein, and Scowcroft had pestered him to take a firm position on the plane from Aspen. By the end of the meeting, Bush ordered CIA to create a covert plan to destabilize Saddam Hussein's regime and, hopefully unseat him. Bush then set about to thwart any efforts by the Saudi King Fahd, King Hussein, and Mubarak to broker a weak compromise with Saddam Hussein. Last, the president asked everyone to meet again at Camp David on Saturday and brief him on military options.

Both the *Washington Post* and the *New York Times* carried major stories Saturday morning, August 4, about Iraqi forces on the Saudi border. The Bush administration was skilled at leaking and spinning the media, and "sources" and "officials" had offered plenty of insider details about the threat to Saudi Arabia and its immense oil reserves.

At Camp David, Bush welcomed his team to the conference room at Aspen Lodge. Present were Vice President Quayle, the recently returned Baker, Sununu, Cheney, Powell, Schwarzkopf, Scowcroft, Haass, Director of Central Intelligence William Webster, and several others. Powell introduced the available military options: "There's a deterrence piece and a war-fighting piece." He asked Schwarzkopf to brief the overall Iraqi order-of-battle before getting into the options. Saddam Hussein had 900,000 ground troops in 63 divisions, of which eight were capable Republican Guard units; 5,646 tanks, including 1,072 modern Soviet-built T-72s; 10,000 armored vehicles; 3,500 pieces of artillery, but only 330 being self-propelled. "We should not have to worry about the air force after a fairly short period," Schwarzkopf said. "The navy's not a problem." Chemical weapons, however, were another matter altogether.

Schwarzkopf advised that he needed seventeen weeks to get the deterrence force in place—up to 250,000 soldiers, airmen, sailors, and Marines, plus weapons, aircraft, and ships. Logistics would be an enormous challenge given the distance to the gulf from the United States. Since the National Guard and reserves handled many logistic operations, call-ups would be required. Deploying active duty aircraft and crews would be quicker. On the other hand, if Bush wanted to eject Saddam Hussein from Kuwait, a war-fighting option needed a far larger force. Using traditional attack-to-defense force ratios of 3 or 4 to 1, and an Iraqi force of 100,000, the math was easy. Schwarzkopf needed eight to twelve months to deploy 400,000 US troops.

Several participants asked about airpower-only operations, but Cheney and Powell strongly discouraged that option. If the president ordered a deployment, both generals urged a hefty response. No more graduated, Vietnam-style operations; get back to the World War II model of brute force. Powell summarized his position, one that echoed the Weinberger Doctrine that he helped shape, of responding only with overwhelming force. "If you want to deter, don't put up a phony defense, don't create a phony deterrence. If you do it, do it real and do it right." After more discussion, Bush approved the deterrence plan, pending King Fahd's approval. "Our defense of Saudi Arabia has to be our focus," he said at meeting's end. Afterward, the president called King Fahd, and again on Sunday, and eventually the Saudi monarch agreed to receive a high-level US briefing team. Cheney, Schwarzkopf, and others departed immediately for Jiddah, Saudi Arabia, to consult with Fahd and attempt to gain his approval for deploying American troops to his country.

President Bush returned to the White House from Camp David on Sunday afternoon and made a few remarks to the assembled media. He mentioned the many calls that he had made to other leaders, and offered this summary of international reactions in his extemporaneous Bush-speak: "What's emerging is nobody is, seems to be showing up as willing to accept anything less than total withdrawal from Iraq . . . from Kuwait of the Iraqi forces, and no puppet regime." However, buried in his next disjointed sentence was a fragment that reflected his firmness: "there seems to be a united front out there that says Iraq, having committed brutal, naked aggression, ought to get out."

Bush then took questions but answered most with generalities or "I'm not going to comment on that." Two of his statements, though, showed an intense focus that his daughter, Dorothy Bush Koch, who was with him, considered quite a departure for her father. When asked how he and other world leaders would prevent a puppet regime in Kuwait, Bush tersely answered, "Just wait. Watch and learn." At the end, Bush put an edge on his voice and face, saying, "Please believe me, there are an awful lot of countries that are in total accord with what I've just said, and I salute them. This will not stand. This will not stand, this aggression against Kuwait."

This declaration startled some in the administration. Margaret Tutwiler at State, for example, wondered what had gotten into Bush. Powell, watching the president on television in his government quarters, noted a marked change in Bush's attitude since his first public comments on the previous Thursday. As he recalled later, Powell believed that Bush had just committed to liberating Kuwait. "He had listened quietly to his advisers," Powell wrote in his 1995 memoir. "He had consulted by phone with world leaders. And then, taking his own counsel, he had come to this momentous decision and revealed it at the first opportunity."

Bush biographer, Tim Naftali, remarked years later on the moment and Bush's style. "He led with his gut, with his instincts. George Bush was an emotive, emotional, intuitive, and instinctive leader." Further, several authors have noted that Bush had felt betrayed by Saddam Hussein after the administration had attempted to entice Iraq back into the mainstream international community.

Bush also personalized the crisis that day, an approach that would drive his rhetoric and decision making until war's end. During the brief news conference, he said "I" forty-four times. That was a radical change for him. He previously had chastised speechwriter Peggy Noonan for using the first person singular in his speeches. This would become George Bush's war.

A Politically Expedient Strategy

On Monday, August 6, King Fahd approved a massive US deployment to his kingdom. On Wednesday, President Bush addressed the nation in the morning and held a news conference in the afternoon. He declared that US military operations, with troops possibly exceeding 50,000, were for defensive purposes only. He hoped that UN-ordered economic sanctions, approved two days earlier, would force Saddam Hussein out of Kuwait. In a clear reference to Hitler, he mentioned Iraq's blitzkrieg into Kuwait, and saying that "appeasement does not work," cited the acquiescence by Great Britain and France to Hitler's 1938 annexation of Austria and part of Czechoslovakia. At the news conference, an early, multipart question began, "Are we at war?" Bush said no, the United States was merely sending forces to defend Saudi Arabia at that country's request. By the end of the news conference, Bush had cited four policy goals: Withdrawal of Iraqi troops from Kuwait, restoration of the Kuwaiti government, US security in the region, and protection of American lives. The American public quickly approved of Bush's actions. A *Washington Post*–ABC News poll revealed that 74 percent of respondents supported the president's decision, but only 27 percent favored using force to eject Iraq from Kuwait. Reaction on Capitol Hill was generally positive.

Also on the 8th, chief of staff Sununu reiterated the force size as 50,000 while talking to the media. That rankled Army chief of staff

General Carl Vuono. He thought the White House was minimizing the number in order to lessen adverse reactions. Vuono leaked the true size of the operation to the Associated Press—250,000. Unnamed administration sources then called that figure preposterous, but the Pentagon quickly released Vuono's total.

Bush kept the rhetoric flowing on August 15 in a speech at the Pentagon. At stake in Kuwait, he said, were "our jobs, our way of life, our own freedom, and freedom of friendly countries around the world." He didn't mention Hitler by name, but pointed to an instance fifty-two years ago when appeasing an aggressor backfired. With carefully chosen descriptors, Bush attempted to shape public opinion by painting a portrait of an evil Saddam Hussein. And he used rhetoric to evoke Americans' collective memory of the "good" war against Hitler. Likely in retaliation for Bush's harsh words, Saddam Hussein sent a public letter to the president with his own venom. He then detained 10,000 citizens from the UN coalition countries for use as human shields in defense of targets that he expected to attract air strikes. That resulted in a PR failure for Saddam Hussein, and the UN Security Council called for their release, with even Iraqi backers Cuba and Yemen supporting the measure.

On his way to Maine for vacation on August 10, Bush told reporters on Air Force One that he wanted to tighten enforcement of UN sanctions on Iraqi oil shipments. "I would advise Iraqi ships not to go out with oil," he said. Two days later, the exiled Kuwaiti emir asked Bush to enforce UN sanctions by interdicting Iraqi seaborne oil exports. On August 12, without consultation with his advisers or allies, Bush unilaterally ordered the US Navy to interdict Iraqi tankers. His spokesman said that the basis for the president's action was the right of individual and collective self-defense allowed by Article 51 of the UN charter. However, France, Canada, and Russia squawked, especially after a US Naval combatant fired across the bow of an Iraqi tanker on August 20 before letting it proceed. Baker convinced Bush to hold fire until State could get key coalition members to support an applicable UN Security Council resolution. Thatcher, who supported Bush's aggressive position, relented on seeking a UN endorsement, saying, "Well, all right George, but this is no time to go wobbly." The UN approved naval enforcement of sanctions on August 25.

Virtually everyone lauds Bush's skillful building of an international coalition against Iraq. At an August 22 news conference with Cheney and Powell in Kennebunkport, Maine, the president announced that twenty-two other nations had committed military forces to the coalition (thirty-four ultimately joined). Cheney said that the president had the existing authority to call up a maximum of 200,000 reservists, but far fewer would be needed. The next day, Cheney announced that 49,703 would be activated.

Bush resisted overtures from his staff about cutting short his August vacation. Adverse reaction to images of golf and fishing added to the domestic pressures on Bush that summer. The major difficulties included the brewing budget battle, GOP grumbling about the president breaking his 1988 campaign pledge on no new taxes, the savings and loan scandal, a looming recession, and rising gasoline prices. Bush's domestic polling lagged his crisis approval numbers.

On his last day in Maine, Bush cast doubt on any diplomatic solutions to the crisis. "I don't yet see fruitful negotiations," he told reporters. Bush briefed congressional leaders in Washington the following day, and they were generally supportive. Some, however, were concerned about the costs of Operation Desert Shield, the Saudi defense operation. Bush explained that multiple nations had pledged funds for the undertaking. Outside of the federal government, though, some conservatives criticized Bush for his handling of the Iraq situation. Pat Buchanan, a Bush colleague in the Reagan White House, led the charge. He said the president had "gone too far in terms of his rhetoric and too far in terms of commitment." Edward Luttwak, a foreign policy analyst at Washington's Center for Strategic and International Studies, railed against defending the Saudi kingdom, which he termed "oppressive and reactionary, and absolutist."

On September 9, Bush and Soviet president Mikhail Gorbachev met in Helsinki, Finland, and emerged on the same page after seven hours of discussion. Despite growing pressures from conservative factions in Russian politics, Gorbachev's alignment with the West was critical to Bush's crisis policies.

However, less harmony prevailed within the Pentagon. Air Force chief of staff General Michael Dugan was off the reservation when he talked with reporters from the *Los Angeles Times* and other papers in mid-September about the advantages of aerial bombing. "Air power is the only answer available to our country to avoid a bloody ground war." Further, Dugan spoke of advice from Israel about the targeting of air strikes, especially against Saddam Hussein and his family. Scowcroft immediately disowned Dugan on a Sunday television news show, and Cheney quickly fired him. The secretary then explained to the media: "Given the extreme delicacy and sensitivity of the current situation, it's incumbent upon senior officials to be discreet and tactful in their public statements, and I found those qualities lacking." Also, in view of the administration's concerted efforts to recruit Arab countries to act against Iraq, mention of Israel was a big mistake by Dugan.

Los Angeles Times reporter John Broder addressed another, more subtle facet of the matter—message control. "But perhaps his greatest transgression," Broder wrote, "was saying what he thought and letting himself be quoted saying it—a mortal sin in this administration, which jealously guards policy-making power and tightly controls the flow of information to the public." The Dugan situation paralleled the incident the previous month when John Sununu's spin on the number of US troops expected to be involved in the defense of Saudi Arabia angered Army chief of staff Carl Vuono, who leaked the accurate number.

President Bush had his hands full in late September. He talked seemingly nonstop with foreign leaders as the coalition continued to muster forces in the Gulf area. Also, he continued his harsh rhetoric, which sounded more and more like beating the drums of war. On the domestic front, a budget deal containing Bush's retreat from his "no new taxes" pledge failed in Congress. In the middle of a bitter tug-of-war with GOP hardliners and the Democrats, Bush spoke to the nation from the Oval Office on October 2. The *New York Times'* Andrew Rosenthal characterized the president's message as: "Prepare for economic pain at home and the possibility of war abroad." Within a week, polls had Bush's approval rating at 55 percent, down from the mid-70s in the first week of August. On October 1, both houses of Congress passed nonbinding resolutions supporting Bush's actions. However, both urged the administration to continue seeking diplomatic solutions, and neither authorized military action.

The uniformed military leadership's influence on Bush's decision making approached a low point about this time. Powell, for example, had favored sanctions to drive Saddam Hussein from Kuwait from the start. Sensing a turning point in Bush's mind from a combination of diplomacy and sanctions to war, Powell made a case for containment of Iraq to Cheney. The secretary didn't think Bush would buy that option. Powell then met one-on-one with Baker and then Scowcroft with the same pitch. Baker seemed amenable, but Scowcroft leaned toward military force. On Friday, October 5, Powell had a chance to speak directly to the president. "There is a case here for containment or strangulation policy," Powell said to Bush. With the 230,000 troops expected in place on December 1, Powell argued that the force would stalemate Saddam Hussein. "It may take a year, it may take two years, but it will work someday." Although Cheney and Scowcroft asked several questions, Bush seemed detached. Powell continued to press for a containment approach until the president halted the discussion by saying, "I don't think there's time politically for that strategy."

The next day Bush vetoed a continuing resolution to keep the government operating while he and Congress tried to resolve the budget standoff. A brief shutdown ensued until Bush signed another CR so he and Hill leaders could continue negotiations. That same weekend, Scowcroft asked Cheney to prepare a briefing for Bush on a military operation to force Saddam Hussein out of Kuwait. It was time to do something.

Checking Boxes, Spinning Messages

Powell hurriedly summoned members of Schwarzkopf's headquarters staff to Washington to brief their plan for offensive operations. On October 10 in the Pentagon's "Tank," a highly restricted conference room, the Joint Chiefs, Cheney, and their assistants gathered for the presentation. The briefers, led by Schwarzkopf's chief of staff, presented a combined air and ground plan, based on the limited forces the coalition had available in theater, which were deployed for strictly defensive operations. The air plan was solid, but his current force structure limited Schwarzkopf to a ground assault consisting of three feints and a risky straight-ahead attack into the Iraqi strength. It was a weak plan, and most everyone in the room said so. Powell told Cheney afterward, "We've just seen a first cut. . . . We'll get something better."

Schwarzkopf's briefing team presented the plan to the Gang of Eight the next day in the White House Situation Room. Scowcroft voiced his skepticism, as Cheney had the previous day. After two hours of discussion, Powell and the briefers got to the bottom line with the president—they needed a larger force. It would take at least until January 1 to transport more units to the Gulf. "The briefing made me realize," Bush wrote later, "we had a long way to go before the military was 'gung ho' and felt we had the means to accomplish our mission expeditiously, without impossible loss of life."

While Schwarzkopf began retooling his plan and identifying the additional forces required, Bush spoke in Texas on October 15 and continued the demonizing of Saddam Hussein. He spoke of "Hitler revisited," "war crimes," "ghastly atrocities," and the "systematic assault on the soul of a nation." He spoke at a rally in Vermont a week later and restated his message: "There's a parallel between what Hitler did to Poland and what Saddam Hussein has done to Kuwait."

At a hearing on the Hill, members of both parties on the Senate Foreign Relations Committee warned Secretary Baker not to take military action without a declaration of war or other congressional authority. Baker declared that the president must be free to attack Iraq but promised consultations.

Mid-October marked a sea change for Bush and his closest advisers in their Iraqi policy, according to Elizabeth Drew, then the Washington correspondent for *The New Yorker* magazine. Her sources reported that sanctions and an implied military threat were insufficient to eject Saddam Hussein from Kuwait. "Our original strategy wasn't working," a senior administration official told Drew later in the fall. "We were in a totally reactive mode." Other conversations with unnamed sources led Drew to conclude in December that the administration pushed sanctions early on as a gambit to gain time to get the military forces organized. Sanctions, a senior official told Drew, "were a box to check—if we had gone to military force soon, people would have said, 'Why didn't you try sanctions?'"

Regardless of Drew's conclusions, which are widely quoted in Gulf War accounts, the Bush chronicle of events as told to author Bob

Woodward details Bush's next step—the president's call for action. He summoned Cheney to the White House on October 24 and said he was ready to get going on an offensive military plan. However, nothing could be said officially until after the November 6 mid-term elections. Cheney, though, was free to release a trial balloon on the October 25 Sunday TV shows. Appearing on each of the three broadcast networks, he mentioned adding more forces. It was an adroit move to sensitize the media and the public for later announcements.

A group of congressional leaders met with Bush at the White House on October 30 to hear a Gulf status report. The president talked about hostage maltreatment in Kuwait, a theme that even the sanction-minded Baker had jumped on the previous day in California. According to Woodward, several Democrats believed Bush would use the hostage situation as a casus belli for war. Reportedly, the meeting became heated and highly emotional.

That afternoon, Powell briefed Bush on a profoundly improved plan to attack Iraq and force its troops from Kuwait. To implement the operation, he needed three armored divisions from Europe to execute high-speed flanking attacks on the Iraqis. Additionally, Schwarzkopf wanted to double the Air Force aircraft and Marine units already in theater and add three more aircraft carriers. Cheney endorsed the proposal, and with little fuss, the president said, "If that's what you need, we'll do it."

Bush committed the United States to a huge and costly war outside his normal policy and crisis management structures. Once briefed by Powell or Schwarzkopf, Bush largely held the uniformed military leaders beyond Powell at arm's length from the Bush-Baker-Cheney-Scowcroft decision-making process. At the time of Cheney's TV appearances to sneak preview force increases, Powell was returning from consultations with Schwarzkopf. The chairman was flabbergasted. "What's going on?" he asked rhetorically. "Goddamnit, I'll never travel again. I haven't seen the president on this." Preventing leaks by employing a small group of decision-makers is a common crisis management technique. But Bush may have denied himself of valuable counsel by his highly personalized, close-to-the-vest style. In any event, the politically savvy President Bush withheld his decision from the public until after the November 6 election. By then, a quarter of a million men and women had started deployments to the Persian Gulf.

Reaction from Capitol Hill to the massive deployment was immediate and loud. Committee chairmen scheduled hearings for late November, and individual members sounded off about letting sanctions have a chance to work. The added attention and resultant public awareness led to disconcerting numbers for Bush in a *New York Times* poll released on November 16. A three-to-one majority of respondents favored both a full congressional debate on the prospective war and a congressional declaration of war. Approval of his handling of the crisis fell to 54 percent.

The outcry led to a tactical decision by Bush to seek a UN resolution on the use of force in order to better manage a possible congressional vote on war. The timing of the initiative was perfect in that the United States held the rotating Security Council chair for the month of November. Bush told Senator Richard Lugar (R-IN) on November 15 that a UN vote "would focus the issue for Congress."

Bush and his team also created a buzzword campaign using symbolic language to manipulate public opinion. Baker and Bush suddenly mentioned that jobs would be at stake if oil imports were cut. Bush sounded other effective PR notes on his image-shaping horn—"rape, pillage, and plunder," "naked aggression," and hostages and brutality. He even called attention to the biggest wolf in the Persian Gulf forest—Saddam Hussein's chemical and biological weapons and his pursuit of nuclear weapons. According to *Newsweek* magazine, many thought the effort was too glib. "It was an embarrassing display," a former Bush adviser told the magazine. "Very few people were fooled." Additionally, the administration fared poorly in trying to send signals simultaneously to a rash Saddam Hussein and a wary American public uninterested in war. "Every time we score with one," a Baker aide told the media, "we set ourselves back with the other."

On November 29, with help from the Russians and several Arab states, the United States successfully negotiated the passage of UN Security Council Resolution 678. It authorized the use of military force to drive Iraq out of Kuwait if Saddam Hussein's troops had not left by January 15, 1991. Gorbachev had insisted on the deadline. This development helped strengthen Bush's hand domestically and internationally. But a congressional vote was pending, so he needed another skillful neutralization of critics. Baker proposed a gambit, and Bush immediately accepted it after brief discussion with just two of his closest advisers, according to Drew and Woodward. At 11:00 a.m. November 30, Bush made a surprise announcement to the media in the White House.

> To go the extra mile for peace, I will issue an invitation to [Iraqi] Foreign Minister Tarik Aziz to come to Washington at a mutually convenient time during the latter part of the week of Dec. 10 to meet with me. And I'll invite ambassadors of several of our coalition partners in the gulf to join me at that meeting.
>
> In addition, I am asking Secretary Jim Baker to go to Baghdad to see Saddam Hussein, and I will suggest to Iraq's president that he receive the secretary of state at a mutually convenient time between December 15 and January 15 of next year.

This immediately quieted critics. But it also sent a terrible signal to Saddam Hussein, which Prince Bandar viewed as a sign of weakness on Bush's part. Bandar also criticized Bush for inviting allies to the discussions because it implied the other countries were US "patsies." Scowcroft told Bandar that the diplomatic maneuvers were just "exercises." Also, an anonymous administration source said Bush had made the offer for "domestic reasons." Nevertheless, the ensuing farce of publicly negotiating dates and intransigent conditions for the meetings scuttled any chance for engagement. On the other hand, Saddam Hussein released the hostages as a response to the offer.

Bush allowed his Texas cowboy side to override his East Coast Andover-Yale mien at a December 20 meeting with congressmen. When remarking about Saddam Hussein and the chance of war, he said, "If we get into an armed situation, he's going to get his ass kicked." This paralleled Bush's habit of referring to the Iraqi ruler by the first part of his name and mispronouncing it as "SAD-dam." Several writers have noted that pronunciation means "little boy who shines shoes." Additionally, a former Pentagon Mideast official told journalist Elizabeth Drew, "You don't talk to Arabs like they are dogs in the street. You don't say you're going to kick their ass."

The tough guy image Bush projected during the five-month run-up to the war caused Washington observers to theorize that he was trying to shake the "wimp" characterization he acquired as vice president. *Newsweek* ran a cover story in its October 11, 1987, issue titled, "Bush Battles the Wimp Factor." Former *Newsweek* Washington bureau chief Evan Thomas said the term grew out of Bush's WASP habits and dress, notwithstanding Bush's heroic service as a Navy combat pilot in World War II. *Washington Post* columnist George Will added to the wimp image when he called the vice president Reagan's "lapdog."

Several members of Congress talked about the wimp issue with Drew in January 1991. A senator said to her, "We all know instinctively that this is not a strong man. . . . I don't know anyone who's honest with himself who doesn't think this." Another member described Bush's "obsession" with Iraq, "to the exclusion of everything else." This certainly could have been normal Washington backbiting, but Drew added her own thoughts: "A lot of people here think that the president, by his terms for a settlement and by his rhetoric, pushed Saddam Hussein—as well as himself—into a corner." But then, as Drew concluded, that was the plan all along.

On January 3, minutes before Bush was to meet with congressional leaders, White House spokesman Marlin Fitzwater told the media that Baker would meet with Iraqi foreign minister Aziz in Geneva on January 9. That nimble move gathered goodwill for Bush in the pending vote on the Hill for authorizing war. Clearly another box checked, and the Aziz-Baker meeting solved nothing.

President Bush essentially gave Congress a fait accompli when the House and Senate began debate on January 10 on a use-of-force authorization. It was a tough call for many members, and the administration enlisted the American-Israeli Political Action Committee, the powerful Israel lobby, to influence voting. Cheney reportedly told members who may have doubted Bush's use of force, "Don't vote for this if you think we're not going." On January 12, both houses of Congress authorized the president to start a war with Iraq. The senate voted 52 to 47 in favor, and the house, 250 to 183.

At 1:00 a.m. local on January 17, US Air Force and Army helicopters took off from a Saudi base and flew at low altitude toward Iraqi early warning radars on the border. Thirty minutes later, US Navy combatants in the Red Sea and Persian Gulf fired Tomahawk cruise missiles at Baghdad targets. Operation Desert Storm had started, and President Bush stopped it forty-two days later.

Yet, when the war ended, Saddam Hussein remained in power, and for that critics blame Bush's limited war goals. Two authors, however, have offered a nuanced view of the matter. Lawrence Freedman and Efraim Karsh, in their book *The Gulf Conflict, 1990–1991*, wrote of the continuation of Saddam Hussein's reign: "Perhaps if, in President Bush's rhetoric, he had not been built up into such a monster all this would have sufficed, but for a monster it was not good enough."

That monster reared up a few days after the coalition's unilateral cease-fire on February 28. Heeding a call from President Bush in mid-February to overthrow Saddam Hussein, two oppressed groups in Iraq—the Kurds in the north, and Shiites in the south—started an intifada, Arabic for "casting off." Saddam Hussein used the forces that survived the incomplete encirclement at war's end to crush the insurrections and kill tens of thousands. Bush decided against intervention for fear of entering the quagmire of an Iraqi civil war, which would become the consequence of his son's invasion of Iraq in 2003. Conflicting forces battered the administration during this time, and Richard Haass captured the situation when he wrote: "It must be said that US policymaking during this period was ragged. There is simply no other word for it."

By the end of hostilities, the 800,000-man coalition force, which included 540,000 Americans, had lost only 240 killed in action by hostile fire; of them, 148 were Americans. The total number of Americans who died in theater was 383, which included deaths by accident and non-hostile incidents. Their sacrifices helped force Iraq from Kuwait. On the other hand, the Iraqi people certainly didn't fare as well. In late 1991, US Census Bureau analyst Beth Daponte calculated Iraqi deaths during the Gulf War and immediately afterward. Using only unclassified reports, she concluded that the war, the Kurdish and Shiite rebellions, and postwar deprivation had killed 158,001 Iraqis—86,194 men, 39,612 women, and 32,195 children. Her superiors fired Daponte in April 1992 for reporting what they called false information, but subsequently reinstated her after the censorship accusations hit the fan.

Assessment

Within three days of Iraq's invasion of Kuwait, President George H. W. Bush decided to take decisive action to resolve the crisis. His assembly of an international coalition to oppose Iraq was masterfully done and a model for future presidents. Secretary Baker, who favored sanctions instead, and General Powell, who insisted that military operations match political goals, restrained Bush from forceful action until the military was ready. Bush drew a red line in the sand and doggedly stood by it, despite the dangers of drawing it early in the crisis.

Other measures of success in Bush's handling of the crisis include what he prevented from happening. The short war precluded Iraqi control of 20 percent of the world's oil reserves. The action averted the Iraqi "Finlandization" of Saudi Arabia in the manner that the Soviets forced neighboring Finland to act as a client state during the Cold War. Bush thwarted the emergence of Iraq as the dominant Arab state, and slowed Saddam Hussein's pursuit of nuclear weapons. Plus, the hasty termination avoided a costly and divisive land war in the Middle East and lasting Arab hostility against the United States. But then, that happened during and after the next war with Iraq.

Not all of Bush's actions and decisions, however, were unqualified successes. Bush and his team marshaled public support at key points with tactically adroit announcements and PR moves, but some were ham-handed and looked like PR moves and spin. Bush's tight control of his planning details and lack of candor with the Hill and the news media kept Saddam Hussein off guard and unknowing of the next step, but had similar effects on the American people. Casting Saddam Hussein as an evil, Hitler-like figure helped win public support but also oversimplified a complex Mideast problem set in an emerging post–Cold War environment that involved huge crude oil stakes.

The president allowed the military to develop war plans in the generals' comfort zone, but he kept all but Powell out of the strategic meetings. Bush also generally excluded Middle East experts and devil's advocates from his critical decision-making sessions. His withholding of support for the Kurds and Shiites after calling for their uprising was a tough decision, but one that magnified criticism of his early termination of the war. Last, and probably most damning, his policy toward

Saddam Hussein prior to the Kuwait invasion created, at best, a benign environment for the invasion, and at worst, invited it. This "stunning failure," as Gordon and Trainor called it, coupled with the untoward ramifications of the war's abrupt end, precludes a clean, straightforward assessment of President Bush's handling of the crisis.

In all of these situations, whether handled well or poorly, Bush demonstrated his understanding of the American public's primary expectation of a president during a crisis—take charge and do something. Previously a conciliatory and pragmatic politician who had been called a wimp, he seemingly morphed into a kick-ass tough guy in the days immediately following Iraq's invasion of Kuwait. That apparently self-induced personality shift was reminiscent in part of Ford's overreaction during the *Mayaguez* incident, and Carter's bold rescue attempt in the middle of his fifteen-month pursuit of the hostages' freedom through diplomacy and negotiation.

Every side claimed victory after the Persian Gulf War. Kuwait reappeared as a country, and Saudi Arabia was still free. Saddam Hussein remained in power after raping and pillaging. The United States and its coalition partners won the war. The American military chipped away at the damaging legacy of the unpopular Vietnam War, eased the wounds left from the 1983 Beirut barracks bombing fiasco, and held a victory parade in the nation's capital.

CHAPTER 10

BILL CLINTON

East Africa Embassy Bombings, 1998

Two Crises

"Gayle, Sit Room calling. Are you awake?"

Gayle Smith, the senior director for African affairs on the NSC staff, shook away the cobwebs and glanced at her bedside clock: 3:45 a.m. "Yes. What's up?"

"There have been explosions at our embassies in Kenya and Tanzania," the duty officer reported. "State has no direct communications with the embassies, but they are talking on cell phones to people onsite in capitals, Nairobi and Dar es Salaam. We have nothing on casualties, but CNN is trying to get cameras on the scene ASAP. We've called Sandy, Jim, Dick, and Leon. Anyone else?"

"No, that's the right list. I'll be there in an hour."

As Smith dressed and drove to the White House in the muggy pre-dawn hours of August 7, 1998, Sandy Berger, national security adviser to President Bill Clinton, called the boss. Leon Furth called Vice President Al Gore, and Berger's deputy, Jim Steinberg, also quickly headed for his West Wing office. Richard "Dick" Clarke, the NSC point man for terrorism raced across town to the Situation Room and its Secure Video Teleconference Room.

By 5:00 a.m., Clarke and Smith saw on the teleconference monitors the faces of Assistant Secretary of State for African Affairs Susan

Rice and representatives from the CIA, FBI, Pentagon, Federal Emergency Management Agency, Justice Department, and others. They constituted the Counterterrorism Security Group, an action committee chaired by Clarke, who also acted as the federal government's counterterrorism coordinator.

"First, rescue," Clarke announced to start the session. "We need to get teams there fast." After a rapid-fire discussion, Clarke moved to the next topic on his triage list. "Second, security. DoD, what have you got nearby that can secure the two sites?" The group continued stepping through Clarke's checklist—evidence gathering, coordination, airlift, security at other embassies, and finally, attribution and response. "CIA, let's meet in my office at 7:30 to go over the evidence," Clarke said, already thinking of Osama bin Laden and al-Qaeda. "The senior officer from each CSG agency is invited. I suspect we all know what the evidence will show. We will need to give the president options."

Clinton didn't wait for all of the CSG recommendations to bubble up the chain, according to Sit Room senior duty officer Tony Campanella. "The president wanted to talk with our ambassador in Nairobi and the chief of mission in Dar es Salaam, as well as the presidents of Kenya and Tanzania," Campanella told me later. "We lined everybody up in a row—Ambassador Prudence Bushnell in Nairobi, John Lange in Dar es Salaam, Kenyan president Daniel arap Moi, and Tanzanian leader Benjamin Mkapa. President Clinton just stayed on the phone, talking to each in turn."

Over the next few days, the CSG and more senior national security coordinating groups met in the Situation Room's conference room to consider America's response. The Deputies Committee, headed by Jim Steinberg, met to discuss which policy and action options to recommend to Clinton's cabinet-level advisers—the Principals Committee. But by this time in his second term, Clinton favored discussing many crises and major policy matters with his "Small Group." Members included Secretary of State Madeleine Albright, Secretary of Defense William Cohen, Joint Chiefs chairman General Hugh Shelton, Attorney General Janet Reno, Director of Central Intelligence George Tenet, and Berger. The restricted number of participants reflected their intent, which they made public later, to prevent leaks about their deliberations. Clinton fostered a relaxed atmosphere in their meetings, but according to author Steve Coll, there were "chronic disagreements and tensions." For example, Berger considered Reno "defensive and uncooperative," and Albright and Cohen quarreled over institutional policy biases.

In 1998, the Clinton administration had begun to consider terrorism to be both a law enforcement and a national security problem. The FBI handled domestic incidents—the 1995 Oklahoma City bombing, for example—and collected physical evidence overseas. CIA sought information on international terrorist incidents, either in planning or afterward, such as the 1996 Saudi Khobar Towers bombing executed by Hezbollah. The vast chasm between the gathering of evidence for legal proceedings and sensitive intelligence operations contributed to the oft-noted connecting-the-dots failures before the 9/11 attacks.

The administration's early embassy-bombing crisis meetings focused on attribution—who had perpetrated the attacks, and many people saw the hand of al-Qaeda and its wealthy patron, a Saudi named Osama bin Laden. Al-Qaeda—meaning "the base" or "foundation"—arose from the mujahidin resistance against the Soviet Army in Afghanistan in the 1980s. The organization's antecedent was the Maktab al-Khidmat (Services Bureau) network founded in 1984 by Sheikh Abdullah Azzam. He had established the bureau to manage an international network of recruiting centers to attract Muslim men to join the Afghani war. One of Azzam's protégés, bin Laden, the seventeenth of fifty-seven children of a Saudi construction executive (and multiple wives), helped fund the Maktab al-Khidmat. By the spring of 1988 when the Soviets announced their intention to leave Afghanistan, the mujahidin looked for other targets for "jihad"—a struggle against the enemies of Islam.

In late 1989, a car bomb killed Azzam, leaving bin Laden in full control of the bureau and al-Qaeda. When US and Western military forces deployed to Saudi Arabia during the Persian Gulf War, bin Laden angrily viewed their presence as an affront to Islam. The Saudi government forced bin Laden to flee to Sudan, where, in the words of the 9/11 Commission, he "set up a large and complex set of intertwined business and terrorist enterprises." Bin Laden viewed himself as the leader of an international jihadist confederation.

Al-Qaeda affiliates led the resistance against US forces in Somalia, including the gruesome 1993 downing of two Black Hawk helicopters during the Battle of Mogadishu. While a few believe bin Laden engineered the 1993 World Trade Center bombing, others, including the 9/11 Commission, did not see a firm and enduring connection between bin Laden and that event. Also, bin Laden told CNN's Peter Arnett in 1997 that he had "no connection" to WTC-93. Retired CIA official Paul Pillar agreed: "A decade's worth of research was unable to conclude that Mr. bin Laden had instigated the attack."

In 1996, bin Laden moved his base from Sudan to Afghanistan, where he established a chain of training camps for aspiring jihadists. That activity culminated in February 1998, when bin Laden issued a public "fatwa"—a ruling—that the United States had declared war against God, and that every Muslim should kill Americans and Jews. Additionally, in May 1998, bin Laden held a press conference in Afghanistan to announce his jihad against the "Crusaders and Jews." The operations that followed the bin Laden declarations included the bombings in Nairobi and in Dar es Salaam. Al-Qaeda cell members in Africa planned and executed the attacks, which killed 220 people, including twelve Americans and forty local citizens employed at the embassies. Nearly 5,000 Africans and Americans were injured. During the seven days that followed the bombings, FBI agents abroad detained and questioned suspects in the bombings and sifted through the devastated embassies for evidence. CIA and the other national intelligence agencies looked for confirmation of the al-Qaeda connection.

"Then Fucking Do It!"

President Bill Clinton walked along the Rose Garden Colonnade from the residence to the West Wing and directly into the Oval Office. Washington's heat and humidity were oppressive that Friday morning, August 14, 1998, so he didn't linger outside. Already running late at 9:15 a.m., as he chronically was prone to do, he faced a full schedule of meetings and briefings until a 12:10 p.m. political luncheon at the Hay-Adams Hotel across Lafayette Park from the White House.

Clinton's route to the Oval Office spared him from seeing the many morning newspapers that appeared daily atop tables throughout the West Wing. Each had front-page headlines about the day's two biggest stories. The first, the continuing soap opera about Clinton's sexual relations with Monica Lewinsky, dominated above the fold. The second, the continuing repercussions of the US embassy bombings in Africa the previous week, reflected a more routine presidential crisis. A sidebar to one of the main Lewinsky articles speculated on Clinton's strategy for his upcoming appearance before a grand jury investigating his indiscretions and alleged perjury about them. The president was scheduled to make sworn testimony to the grand jury via closed circuit television the following Monday.

Upon Clinton's return from the Hay-Adams at 1:30 p.m., his wife Hillary and the White House staff surprised the president with a small party to celebrate a few days early his fifty-second birthday. They gathered in the shade of a tree on the South Lawn just outside the Oval Office. The Marine Band played, and in the words of Press Secretary Mike McCurry, "We ate cake, we drank iced tea, and we had a jolly good time."

Inside the Oval Office, waiting for Clinton to finish his piece of cake, was the Principals Committee, plus a few other aides. Once Clinton took a seat in a chair by the fireplace, Tenet opened the discussion by confirming that bombings were the work of al-Qaeda. "This one is a slam dunk, Mr. President," a phrase that Tenet would use again in 2003 regarding Iraqi weapons of mass destruction. "There is no doubt that this was an al-Qaeda operation. Both we and the bureau have plenty of evidence." He went on to detail the arrest of two of the attack plotters, Mohammed Odeh and Rashed Daoud al-Owhali. But Tenet's biggest intelligence nugget sharpened the issue of retaliation.

Frustrated by NSA's refusal to share raw intercept data from al-Qaeda's satellite phones, CIA had devised their own signals-gathering capability. From that, CIA had intercepted one side of a satellite phone conversation that indicated that Osama bin Laden and others planned to meet on August 20 at the Zawhar Kili training camp, one of six al-Qaeda bases near Khost, Afghanistan. It was there the previous May that bin Laden had announced his intentions to reporters. Everyone immediately acknowledged the value of hitting that camp and others nearby. Dick Clarke slipped a note to Tenet—"You thinking what I'm thinking?"

The group knew that any response to the bombings had to be proportional, which ruled out an invasion of Afghanistan to disrupt al-Qaeda infrastructure and leadership. America's allies would not support a ground attack. A special forces raid was an option, but it would take too long to organize the large force that the Pentagon envisioned. Cruise missile strikes on targets that General Shelton had been assembling seemed a better option, and safer, considering the risks of losing aircraft pilots. Although unstated, the participants also knew that the media and Clinton's political foes would mock any bold action as an attempt to draw attention away from his sex scandal.

Since US law prohibited assassinations, the target ostensibly would be al-Qaeda facilities. Reagan had done the same in a 1986 strike against five Libyan targets that included Muammar Qadhafi's compound, the Aziziyah Barracks. Clinton instructed the team to plan a cruise missile strike on August 20 against the Khost camps and propose other al-Qaeda targets to hit simultaneously. As Albright wrote later, the group wanted to duplicate the simultaneity of the embassy bombings.

As the meeting broke up, Clarke and a couple of others hesitantly approached Clinton. They talked about the expected backlash from those who would construe his missile strikes to be a diversion from the Lewinsky scandal. They referred to the popular movie *Wag the Dog*, which has a fictional president doing the same thing. Clinton lost his temper.

"Don't you fucking tell me about my political problems, or my personal problems," Clinton said. "You tell me about national security. Is it the right thing to do?" referring to the planned cruise attacks. Clarke assented. "Then fucking do it."

The White House staff, probably Berger, told Shelton and Cohen to exclude the service chiefs and the Defense Intelligence Agency from the decision to mount a cruise missile strike. Minimizing leaks was the basis for that decision. They didn't want to spook bin Laden into skipping the reported August 20 meeting at Zawhar Kili. But Berger's approach excluded experienced military targeteers and their expertise in matching weapons to targets. For example, as Paul Pillar noted in 2011, the facilities in Khost were "simple housing, firing ranges, and assembly areas, with few substantial structures that could not be easily replaced or repaired." Pillar wrote that objectives beyond demolition would have better benefits in a military retaliation for a terrorist incident sponsored by non-state actors—and would both send a message and act as deterrence of future attacks. Conversely, a military strike also yields untoward effects, proving terrorist claims of Western aggression and producing counter-retaliation rather than a cessation of terrorism. An example is Reagan's 1986–1988 sequence of actions involving the US challenge to Libyan-claimed international waters, the La Belle disco bombing, the US retaliatory attack on Libya, and the Pan Am 103 bombing.

While the secret mission–planning wheels turned in the Pentagon, Reno urged delay. She wanted more time for the FBI to build a legal case against al-Qaeda. Her position reflected the administration's struggle with integrating the conflicting interests among three of the major tenets of counterterrorism policies during Clinton's second term: conducting legal investigations, protecting sensitive intelligence sources, and limiting access to secret military operations. Further evidence of those unreconciled pressures was the exclusion of FBI director Louis Freeh from the retaliation planning. "The FBI has left a bad taste in other departments," a White House official involved in the missile attacks said afterward, "because it leaks like a sieve."

Selection of the second cruise-missile target arose from CIA suspicions that bin Laden was developing chemical weapons at al-Shifa, ostensibly a pharmaceutical factory in Khartoum, Sudan. CIA acquired a soil sample that an Egyptian intelligence service asset had collected across the street on property not connected with the factory. A test in the United States purportedly revealed the presence of EMPTA, O-ethyl methylphosphonothioic acid, a precursor chemical to the deadly nerve gas, VX.

A third target also made the list, a Sudanese storage facility thought to be linked to bin Laden. At the last minute, on August 20, Clinton rejected that target when senior military officers became concerned about potential civilian casualties. Anonymous administration officials told the *New York Times* a year later that Shelton and other Pentagon generals objected to the advice Clinton's civilian advisers had given them on the site.

In the early afternoon of August 17, Clinton acknowledged an improper relationship with Lewinsky to the special prosecutor and grand jury. At 10:02 p.m. that evening, he repeated that statement in a four-minute television address to the nation. The next morning, Berger briefed Clinton that the cruise missile attacks were on schedule for the August 20 launch. The Clinton family then left for what must have been a tumultuous vacation on Martha's Vineyard.

Clinton gave Berger the "Go" order for the strikes at 3:00 a.m. EDT on the 20th. Early that afternoon, seventy-five conventional-warhead Tomahawks began hitting the Khost camps, and thirteen exploded at al-Sharif. Clinton announced the attacks to pool reporters on Martha's Vineyard at two in the afternoon. Afterward, he flew to Washington and delivered a formal television speech from the Oval Office. He began with, "Today I ordered our armed forces to strike at terrorist-related facilities in Afghanistan and Sudan because of the imminent threat they presented to our national security."

The next afternoon, Berger spoke to reporters in the White House Press Briefing Room. He talked about the evidence of al-Qaeda's involvement, the concern about a continuing threat from the group, and the estimated damage to the targets. Regarding the timing, he said, "We also had received at that point some information indicating that there may be a gathering of bin Laden's terrorist network at the Khost camp on August 20th. That became a date that influenced our planning."

When asked about the Sudanese pharmaceutical plant, Berger responded. "Let me be very clear about this. There is no question in my mind that the Sudanese factory was producing chemicals that are used, can be used, in VX gas. This was a plant that was producing chemical warfare related weapons and we have physical evidence of that fact." That same day, Sudanese officials called the plant's destruction "a criminal act," a condemnation repeated by Middle Eastern militants who threatened retribution.

Reaction to the attacks by the media and politicians took two paths. There was general bipartisan support on the Hill, an expected reaction following US military operations. House Speaker Newt Gingrich (R-GA) spoke for many: "I think the president did exactly the right thing." Conversely, a whirlwind of "wagging-the-dog" criticism arose from some of Clinton's political opponents and right-wing commentators. Since the attacks came on the heels of his admission that he had misled the public about Lewinsky, some on the Hill accused the president of changing the subject. Senator Dan Coats (R-IN) said that Clinton had lost credibility on the Hill. "I just hope and pray the decision . . . was made on the basis of sound judgment and made for the right reasons," Coats said to reporters, "and not made because it was necessary to save the president's job." A *Los Angeles Times* poll immediately after the strikes revealed that three-quarters of respondents approved of Clinton's action. However, 40 percent thought his personal woes at least partially influenced his decision.

Missile Strike Results

Bobby May of Marianna, Arkansas, a longtime Clinton friend, watched the post-strike hubbub on CNN while staying in a Khartoum hotel. The businessman was traveling in Africa in search of oil and gas investments. "I couldn't believe my ears," he said later. "I spent a total of two months in Khartoum. One of the places where the Sudanese like to take you is the pharmaceutical plant. It was a showplace for them." May said that schoolchildren routinely toured the plant, and he had visited the plant shortly before the attacks with another Clinton friend, Bishop H. H. Brookins of the African Methodist Episcopal Church in Nashville, Tennessee. They walked through the facility without restrictions on their movements and watched employees package medicines.

A month later, "senior national security advisers" admitted to the *New York Times* "they had no evidence directly linking Mr. bin Laden to the factory at the time the president ordered the strike." Soon, leaks suggested that all other intelligence reporting that tied the plant to chemical weapons had been discredited save for the soil sample. Moreover, the *Los Angeles Times* reported that EMPTA is also found in everyday products. "It's fairly commonly known that these [substances] are used in pesticides and herbicides," Mike Hiskey told the *Times*; Hiskey was then a chemist and explosives expert at Los Alamos National Laboratory in New Mexico. Further, an inspector with the Organization for the Prohibition of Chemical Weapons told a reporter that EMPTA is highly reactive. Once it touched the ground, it would begin to break down. He said that someone would have to empty a flask and immediately take a sample to capture the chemical intact.

A year later, according to the *New York Times*, second-guessing from the participants surfaced about the al-Shifa targeting. "Officials," wrote reporter James Risen, "are still troubled by the lack of a full airing of what they view as gaps in the evidence linking the plant. . . . And they complain that the decision-making process was so secretive that al-Shifa was not vetted by many government experts on chemical weapons sites or terrorism." Further, Tenet said bin Laden's connection to the plant could be "drawn only indirectly and by inference." Nonetheless, Berger told Risen, that Tenet firmly supported al-Shifa as a target. "I would say the director was very clear in his judgment that the plant was associated with chemical weapons," Berger said. "No one in the discussion questioned whether al-Shifa was an appropriate target."

Bin Laden was not at the training camp complex near Khost when the missiles struck. Clarke said later, "The best post-facto intelligence we had was that bin Laden had left the training camp within an hour of the attack." Lawrence Wright wrote in *The Looming Tower* that bin Laden had decided en route to skip the meeting. Authors Peter Bergen—*Holy War, Inc.*—and Steve Coll—*Ghost Wars*—offer several reasons that should have alerted bin Laden to stay away. First, the American diplomats evacuated from nearby Pakistan before the strikes. Second, an al-Qaeda defector said that bin Laden's followers had left the camps before the Africa embassy bombings in anticipation of US retaliation. Third, Zawhar Kili was the site where bin Laden issued his February fatwa and held his May press conference, and he expected it to be targeted. Last, Pakistani intelligence and cabinet officials knew the strike was coming and assumed bin Laden would also know. Bin Laden's second in command, Ayman al-Zawahiri, called Pakistani journalist Rahimullah Yusufzai the following day to announce that he and bin Laden were alive. "Tell the Americans that we aren't afraid of bombardment."

Most of the missiles destroyed most of the camps' structures. However, Yusufzai visited the complex two weeks later and wrote: "Life is back to normal at the simply-built camps." Estimates of the deaths at the training camps vary widely. Wright quotes Berger claiming that "twenty or thirty al-Qaeda operatives were killed," and the Afghani Taliban reported twenty-two Afghans died. Wright interviewed a survivor, Abdul Rahman Khadr, who had been at the Farouk camp in the complex. He said that a total of six men had died. That number matched the total a former Pakistani intelligence chief gave to Wright. But the attack also hurt the United States. Both Wright and Bergen reported that one or more Tomahawks failed to explode at the Khost complex, and bin Laden sold them to China for $10 million.

Assessment

Once the CIA identified al-Qaeda as the perpetrator of the bombings, Clinton moved quickly and decisively to retaliate. He conferred with a limited group of advisers, pushed aside suggestions that his actions would look contrived in light of the Lewinsky scandal, and took public credit for bold and resolute action. Nevertheless, the strike in Afghanistan was ineffective, and the Sudan attack proved to be an egregious error. Clinton mishandled the crisis.

President Clinton's decision-making process during this incident markedly deviated from his normally hesitant approach to pressing foreign policy decisions. There are six publicly known instances both before and after August 1998 in which Clinton and his team attempted to kidnap or kill bin Laden or degrade his operations. On the other occasions, they used experts to game out all facets of a possible attack but ultimately backed away as they worried about faulty intelligence and the loss of innocent life. During the period August 7–20, President Clinton abandoned his normal decision-making process and caution. He acted almost impulsively. He was near the nadir of his presidency, and it appears that the severely damaged president looked for a tail to wag the dog.

Several Clinton biographers have described his indecisiveness in the face of tough decisions. Foremost is Dick Morris, who had been both a highly influential consultant to Clinton, and later, a harsh critic. Morris accuses him of "timidity, hypersensitivity to public reaction, and fearing failure." He points to a pattern among Clinton's responses to terrorism that arose from Clinton's political caution. "Paralyzed by political risk," Morris wrote in 2005, "he was always hesitant to take direct action."

Biographer Nigel Hamilton described Clinton as a "wholly new kind of president—one who rules not by decisiveness but by a procedure unique in the annals of the White House: 'swirl.'" Clinton wanted multiple advisers swirling around him constantly, a decision-making process that fed his indecisiveness. Hamilton quotes one of Clinton's chiefs of staff, Leon Panetta, on Clinton's methods: "The way Clinton arrived at decisions was he opened the door to every approach."

Clinton's use of the six advisers in the Small Group was a radical departure from his swirl approach. Team members have said they wanted to limit leaks, but the pre-strike evacuation of Americans from Pakistan proved that tactic ineffective. This approach narrowed the range of opinions reaching Clinton. For example, the president excluded all of the uniformed military leadership except Shelton, as well as some voices at State. Surprisingly for a problem—terrorism—that Clinton previously had treated as a law enforcement issue, he kept Director Freeh out of the loop. This approach, which led to a lot of carping from Justice and the FBI after the strikes, may have deprived Clinton of a broader set of options.

Even if Clinton's intentions were more honorable, the broad reaction to the perception of wagging the dog undercut the don't-tread-on-me message that the strike should have sent to al-Qaeda. Worse, as Peter Bergen wrote, the missile attacks had an unintended consequence: "They turned bin Laden from a marginal figure in the Muslim world into a global celebrity."

Lawrence Wright agrees: "When bin Laden's exhilarated voice came crackling across a radio transmission—'By the grace of God, I am alive'—the forces of anti-Americanism had found their champion."

CHAPTER 11

GEORGE W. BUSH

Hijacked Airliner Attacks, 2001

The Wrong War

In the minutes that followed the 2001 attack on New York City's World Trade Center, horror and shock swept through America. In the White House Situation Room, the 24/7 nerve center of the presidency, the on-duty staff joined all Americans in disbelief as they watched the second of two airliners hit the Trade Center. Along with millions of others, they asked themselves, "What's next?"

Quickly, an answer. A third hijacked plane, American Flight 77, alarmed air traffic controllers. Victor Padgett, a supervisor at nearby Reagan National Airport, saw that the terrorists had aimed the aircraft at Washington, DC. At 9:33 a.m. on September 11, he called the Secret Service command center at the White House. He urged the agents to order an evacuation. He then punctuated the call, "What I'm telling you, buddy, if you've got people, you'd better get them out of there! And I mean right *goddamned* now."

With President George W. Bush out of town, Secret Service agents rushed to the West Wing office of Vice President Richard Cheney. Agent Jimmy Scott said urgently, "Sir, we have to leave now." From behind Cheney, Scott braced the vice president's shoulder with his left hand and with his right grabbed the back of Cheney's belt. He then half-carried and half-pushed Cheney down the stairs and through the hall near the Situation Room. Cheney and his escorts then entered a secret tunnel to a bomb shelter under the White House's East Wing. Built in the 1930s, the shelter's formal name is the President's Emergency Operations Center (PEOC). National Security Adviser Condoleezza Rice and other senior staff members later relocated to the PEOC.

A few nervous heartbeats later, at 9:37 a.m., American 77 crashed into the Pentagon. The Secret Service redoubled its evacuation efforts, fearing other planes might still threaten the White House. Assistant Press Secretary Jennifer Millerwise described the scene outside: "Someone from the Secret Service yelled, 'Women, drop your heels and run! Drop your heels and run!'"

The Situation Room staff refused the evacuation order and remained at their stations on the operations deck. Senior duty officer Rob Hargis argued that the Situation Room had to keep operating while President Bush was traveling in Florida and the vice president in the PEOC. The team decided to preserve the identities of those in the facility in the event an aircraft hit the White House. Hargis's communications assistant faxed a list of everyone's names to the CIA operations center. The duty officers called it the Dead List.

America Is Under Attack

President Bush had flown to Sarasota, Florida, on September 10 and prepared to spend the night at the Colony Beach and Tennis Resort on Longboat Key, across the John Ringling Causeway from downtown Sarasota. The president had a scheduled appearance the following morning at Emma E. Booker Elementary School where he planned to publicize his education initiative, No Child Left Behind. Shortly after 8:00 a.m. the next morning, the president met with CIA briefer Mike Morell for his daily intelligence update. With Morrell was the director of the White House Situation Room, Navy Captain Deborah Loewer, who represented Rice on this short, two-day trip. The Mideast peace process dominated the fifteen-minute session.

The president and his motorcade departed Longboat Key at 8:39 a.m. en route to Booker School, which was located nine miles away and in the general direction of the Sarasota-Bradenton International

Airport. Within minutes of American Flight 11's striking the north tower of the World Trade Center at 8:46 a.m., cell phones began to ring in the sport utility vehicles following Bush's limousine. One was Captain Loewer's.

"Rob Hargis called me at 8:50 a.m.," Loewer recalled later. She was in the fourth vehicle of the motorcade, and once it reached the school five minutes later, Loewer ran toward the presidential limousine. The diminutive naval officer, who wore civilian clothes on the job, approached Bush and Chief of Staff Andy Card as they walked to the school's entrance. "Mr. President, an aircraft has hit one of the World Trade Center towers in New York. Fire and smoke are coming from a point about four-fifths of the way up. We have no further information at this time."

"Thank you Captain," Bush said. "Keep me informed."

Rice, still in her West Wing office at this point, called the Florida site's holding room, a converted classroom at Booker that served as a combination communications center and staging point for the president. She told a staff aide that she had to talk to Bush, who was chatting with a welcoming committee in the school lobby. Once Bush picked up a secure handset, Rice repeated much of the information that Loewer already had given him. She first said the plane appeared to have been private aircraft, but when alerted by an aide, she changed that description to a commercial airliner before the conversation ended. Afterward, Bush calmly entered the classroom and began his photo op with sixteen second graders and their teacher, Sandra Kay Daniels. On every wall, the children's artwork competed for space with posters about handwriting, arithmetic, and spelling. Bush sat next to Daniels in the front of the room.

Loewer walked quickly to the holding room. She asked a technician to bring in a television and then called Hargis on a secure line for updates. At 9:03 a.m., Loewer and the others in the room saw United Flight 175 strike the south tower. She immediately entered the classroom and whispered to Card, "A second plane has hit the Trade Center. We're under attack." The children, each dressed in a white polo shirt and black shorts or skirt, had just finished a spelling and pronunciation drill and they were reaching for their reading books. Card took advantage of the lull and whispered in Bush's right ear, "A second plane hit the second tower. America is under attack."

The look on the president's face reflected his astonishment and, in the view of some, befuddlement. The children, unencumbered by the newsflash, began to read in unison *The Pet Goat*. Soon Bush joined them. "A . . . girl . . . got . . . a . . . pet . . . goat." Press Secretary Ari Fleischer maneuvered to the back of the room near the knot of reporters and cameramen, whose cell phones had been vibrating in unison. He caught Bush's eye and held up a legal pad on which he had written in large block letters, "DON'T SAY ANYTHING YET." Bush nodded slightly.

The president appeared unnerved but patiently continued with the group reading. He said later that he didn't want to alarm the children. Seven minutes after Card whispered the startling news, the president excused himself and retreated to the holding room. As he entered the room, Loewer asked him, "Who would you like to speak with first?" He chose Cheney, which surprised no one. During the 2000 campaign, Bush had praised his running mate: "Mark my words. There will be a crisis in my administration and Dick Cheney is exactly the man you want at your side in a crisis." Cheney had unshakable opinions about everything foreign and domestic, had strong political beliefs, and was quite willing to discreetly guide a new president. "Am I the evil genius in the corner that nobody ever sees come out of his hole?" Cheney asked rhetorically in 2004. "It's a nice way to operate, actually."

Fleischer and Communications Director Dan Bartlett drafted a short statement for Bush, and the president walked to the school library at 9:30 a.m. Clad in the usual presidential suit and tie, Bush stepped behind a modest podium adorned with the presidential seal. Arrayed behind him were dozens of people—school kids, teacher, parents, and politicians—all posed and staged for the originally planned photo op. What they experienced instead was Bush's declaration of war.

The president nervously shuffled his notes, fidgeted, and cleared his throat. Much of the nation, at least in the eastern and central time zones, watched him on live television. "Ladies and gentlemen," he began, "this is a . . . difficult moment for America." He spoke for less than two minutes and in a manner wholly unlike his usual self-assured demeanor. He ended with a statement hauntingly reminiscent of one his father used when Iraq's Saddam Hussein invaded Kuwait in 1990: "Terrorism against our nation *will not stand*."

Afterward, the entire presidential traveling party, including the media pool, rushed to the motorcade, and at 9:35 a.m., began a breakneck race to the airport. East on Martin Luther King, then north on Route 41 at 80 miles per hour. While they were en route, at 9:37 a.m., American Flight 77 slammed into the Pentagon, and Rice quickly called Bush with the news. The vehicles entered the airport grounds through a back gate and sped directly toward Air Force One. Loewer recalled the scene around the blue and white 747. "The tarmac was swarming with tense people as we arrived," Loewer said. "Security and bomb-sniffing dogs were everywhere, checking luggage and the aircraft itself. People scrambled on and off the plane."

At 9:45 a.m., Bush again connected with Cheney. "We're at war, Dick. And we're going to find out who did this, and we're going to kick their ass." Again, words his father used in 1990. Cheney urged Bush not to return to Washington. A fourth hijacked airliner, United Flight 93, appeared headed for Washington and most assumed it would target either the White House or the Capitol. Concerned about the federal government's ability to continue functioning, Cheney reverted to his participation in the long-standing but secret Continuity of Government program. In the event of a Soviet missile attack on Washington during the Cold War, COG procedures would enable the president and other key officials to evacuate the city and seek safety in "undisclosed" locations. "So I urged him," Cheney said later, "not to return until we could find out what the hell was going on."

Meanwhile, several of Bush's staff quickly made a decision. Card, Secret Service agent Edward Marinzel, the president's on-duty military aide, Lieutenant Colonel Thomas Gould, and Air Force One command pilot, Colonel Mark Tillman, decided to depart immediately and determine their destination afterward. At 9:54 a.m., Air Force One started its takeoff roll, and once airborne, Tillman put the huge aircraft into a steep, teeth-rattling ascent. His intent was to get quickly to an altitude above 40,000 feet, which would put the aircraft above the normal ceiling of commercial airliners. Once there, Tillman flew north, awaiting further orders.

Ground Stop

Lower Manhattan became a living hell for those who survived the initial impacts on the twin towers. People fled the Trade Center complex, seeking escape on waterfront ferries, the East River bridges, and every avenue headed north. The situation grew worse after the south tower collapsed at 9:59 a.m. and the north at 10:28 a.m. In Arlington, Virginia, thousands of people ran out of the Pentagon and onto the streets that radiate away from buildings. The bridges across the Potomac River offered no refuge as they swelled with people running from downtown Washington.

Several of Bush's key advisers were out of town. Secretary of State Colin Powell, a retired Army general, was in Lima, Peru. General Henry Shelton, chairman of the Joint Chiefs, was en route to Europe. Attorney General John Ashcroft was on a plane to Milwaukee, Wisconsin. FEMA director Joe Allbaugh was attending a conference in Montana. Secretary of Defense Donald Rumsfeld, however, had been in his Pentagon office when American 77 struck the building. He became unreachable when he abandoned his command center and joined others helping injured people near the impact site.

Richard Clarke, the longtime NSC staff director for counterterrorism, was in a meeting three blocks from the White House when the first airliner struck the World Trade Center. He ran to the Situation Room and quickly established a secure video teleconference with all of the critical department and agency contacts. He used a small conference room off the operations deck as his command post. Clarke's CSG interagency taskforce would serve as the focal point for the hands-on federal crisis management through the critical phases of September 11.

Among Clarke's most pressing needs was to determine the number of hijacked airliners. While he barked questions from the Situation Room, Federal Aviation Authority officials in the greater Washington area urgently worked the problem. Soon, air traffic control managers at the FAA's Command Center in Herndon, Virginia, became aware of American 11's suspicious flight activity thirty-three minutes before the airliner hit the north tower at 8:46 a.m. Once the second plane hit the south tower, FAA officials scrambled to identify other potential problems among the 4,452 planes in the air over the United States at that moment.

Transportation secretary Norman Mineta, whose department included the FAA, had entered the PEOC at about 9:25 a.m. He later said that at 9:45 he ordered a "national ground stop," an unprecedented order to planes in the air to land immediately and those on the ground to stay there. However, managers at the Herndon Command Center had already given that order without direction from above. Linda Schuessler, manager of tactical operations in Herndon that morning, described what really happened. "At 9:26 a.m., the command center verbally ordered a ground stop to all FAA facilities to prevent any take-offs," Schuessler told me. "At 9:45, we ordered all inflight aircraft to land immediately. About fifteen to twenty minutes later, Mineta verbally gave his orders to us via FAA headquarters." Schuessler said that the senior managers in the command center had recognized the need for a ground stop. "It was done collaboratively."

Vladimir Putin Calls

United Flight 93 had passed near Pittsburgh, Pennsylvania, about the time Air Force One roared into the Florida sky. Air traffic controllers had determined the plane, which was on a scheduled flight from Newark, New Jersey, to San Francisco, had departed its intended flight path. The terrorists had hijacked the airliner at 9:28 a.m. and turned east minutes later. After American 77 hit the Pentagon at 9:37 a.m., military commanders rushed to send fighter aircraft aloft to protect New York and Washington from further assault. But what were the Air Force and Air National Guard pilots supposed to do if confronted with a hijacked airliner full of innocent passengers? Shoot it down?

The president and Cheney spoke shortly after Bush's 9:54 a.m. takeoff about the rules of engagement for the fighter patrols. The vice president asked Bush to grant authority to the Pentagon to engage duly identified hijacked airliners. Bush replied, "You bet." The president said later that he fully understood the gravity of the matter, but he realized the necessity of saving greater numbers of lives. "We had a little discussion," Bush said of the conversation, "but not much." Communication difficulties, caution, and the incomplete understanding of these unprecedented circumstances delayed the engagement orders until well after United 93 had crashed. Gallant passengers forced the hijackers to fly the aircraft into the earth near Shanksville, Pennsylvania, at 10:03 a.m. Their courage prevented the need for an unthinkable air-to-air engagement.

Meanwhile, in the Situation Room, Rob Hargis and his team managed what Hargis later called "controlled chaos," a condition that lasted well into the night. He and his team focused on keeping their primary customers apprised of the evolving circumstances. They had a constant back-and-forth with Cheney and Rice, who struggled with limited communications in the underground PEOC. The staff maintained voice lines to Air Force One and Loewer, and everyone answered myriad incoming calls.

Some of the early calls reflected the fog of uncertainty that bedeviled Washington. False alarms had a car bomb exploding at the State Department, a fire on the Mall, and an unidentified inbound aircraft. Hargis fielded a call about a reported fire in the Eisenhower Executive Office Building, an aging granite edifice across a lane from the Situation Room's ground-level location in the West Wing. Hargis turned to John Sherman, one of his fellow duty officers. "John, can you confirm that the Executive Office Building is on fire?" Sherman, with a phone in one ear, calmly stood up and pulled aside the window curtains behind his workstation. Seeing no smoke, he dryly reported, "If it's on fire, it's not serious," and went back to his phone call.

Many governments called with messages of concern and solidarity—Germany, Belgium, Argentina, France, and Brazil, for example. Russian president Vladimir Putin placed a more substantive call. Shortly after American 77 crashed into the Pentagon, acting chairman of the Joint Chiefs, General Richard Myers, ordered the US military to assume DEFCON 3, a heightened state of readiness that had been implemented last during the 1973 October War. Within minutes, US ambassador to Moscow Alexander Vershbow, called the Situation Room and said that Putin wanted to speak with Bush. A duty officer then called Rice in the PEOC; she, in turn, asked to be connected to the Russian minister of defense Sergei Ivanov in Moscow. Ivanov arranged for Rice and Putin to talk at 11:50 a.m. Once connected, Rice advised the Russian that US forces had gone on alert.

"I know, I've seen them," Putin responded. He went on to say that he understood that the change in US military readiness status was not threatening to Russia. He offered his country's help and added, "You don't have to worry about us."

"For one moment, I had this moment of reflection," Rice said later. "I thought, *The Cold War is really over.*"

Barksdale Air Force Base

As Air Force One leveled off at 45,000 feet on a northerly heading, Andy Card continued discussing where the president should go next. He and Gould, Marinzel, and Loewer started with Cheney's recommendation that Bush stay away from Washington. The talk took an abrupt turn when Cheney called Bush at 10:32 a.m. to report disturbing news—a direct threat to "Angel," the classified Secret Service codename for Air Force One. Alarm rapidly echoed throughout the president's aircraft, the Pentagon's National Military Command Center, the Situation Room, and the PEOC. But then another development added even more urgency to Card's deliberations.

Three minutes after Cheney's warning, air traffic controllers advised Colonel Tillman that an unidentified aircraft was flying toward him. The plane was unresponsive to the controllers' radio calls and might be another hijacked airliner intent on ramming Air Force One. People on board the jet wondered, When will this end?

Card and the others quickly decided they had to get the president to a safe place. Their first choice was the underground bunker at Strategic Command's headquarters at Offutt Air Force base near Omaha, Nebraska. The facility was a critical node in the COG system, one designed to support a president who is forced to leave Washington. But it had a downside—its distance from Florida. Moreover, Bush wanted to address the nation on television, but Air Force One lacked a broadcast capability.

Colonel Tillman instead recommended Barksdale Air Force Base in Shreveport, Louisiana. "It was a B-52 base," Tillman said later. "Tremendous security. A kind of place you could definitely have the president hide out, address the nation, and still be completely secure." In Barksdale they could refuel, offload nonessential personnel and the news media, and allow the president to make a televised statement. The 747 quickly banked hard to the left toward Louisiana.

The FAA determined later that the pilot of the plane headed toward Air Force One had inadvertently failed to turn on his identification transponder. An extensive investigation during the weeks following September 11 revealed that the threat to Angel was unfounded. The 9/11 Commission Report concluded that the warning came from a misunderstanding by a Situation Room duty officer. Not true, Hargis told me. "We never received a threat to Air Force One and never used the word 'Angel.'"

Soon after 11:00 a.m., cable news anchors began talking about President Bush's disappearance. The Secret Service lived up to its name and refused to disclose Bush's whereabouts and actions. Additionally, Fleischer instructed the media aboard Air Force One to neither report their location nor use their cell phones once at Barksdale. That embargo wilted when Air Force One began its descent into Barksdale. "I was in the president's cabin and noticed a local news broadcast from a Shreveport station on the TV," Captain Loewer told me. "They had a camera near the base, and there we were, on the screen, on final approach to Barksdale." Air Force One landed at 11:45 a.m. Thousands of other aircraft also were landing all over the United States, and by 12:16 p.m., the FAA reported that all were on the ground.

Air Force drivers ferried Bush and his party to a headquarters building, with the president inelegantly riding in a Dodge Caravan. There, Bush phoned Cheney while Fleischer drafted brief remarks for the president to make in his television appearance. The base facilities had no means for broadcasting a live transmission, so Bush and the media filed into a conference room to tape his speech. Standing in front of two American flags and portraits of Air Force heroes, the president spoke for two minutes. His performance was not as smooth as he might have wished, considering a public hungry for reassurance. Nevertheless, he pressed his point: "Make no mistake, the United States will hunt down and punish those responsible for these cowardly acts."

Master Sargent Rich Del Haya escorted a CBS producer and reporter as they took the tape off the base and gave it to a satellite truck from the local CBS affiliate. The crew uplinked the speech at 1:09 p.m. Bush then demanded to return to the White House. "I want to go back home ASAP," he told Card. "I don't want whoever did this holding me outside of Washington."

"The right thing to do is let the dust settle," Card replied. He may have regretted that idiom later, considering the toxic dust that blanketed lower Manhattan after the towers' collapse. The president ultimately agreed to fly to Nebraska. With a skeleton staff and only five of the original thirteen media pool members, Air Force One took off at 1:37 p.m. en route to Offutt Air Force Base.

Kick Some Ass

At 3:30 p.m. in Strategic Command's underground vault, Bush began his first NSC meeting on September 11. Video teleconferencing had been available to presidents since the 1980s, and the ease of connectivity helped Bush that afternoon. Present on the president's split screen were Cheney, Rice, Secretary Rumsfeld, Director of Central Intelligence George Tenet, and FBI director Robert Mueller. Card and the head of Strategic Command, Admiral Richard Mies, sat beside the president. Tenet said that he was almost certain that al-Qaeda was responsible for the hijackings. Intelligence sources, he said, had intercepted conversations among bin Laden associates bragging about the assault.

"Get your ears up," the president told Tenet and the others. "The primary mission of this administration is to find them and catch them." At the meeting's close, Bush declared that he was returning to Washington. He signed off by saying: "We will find these people. They will pay. And I don't want you to have any doubt about it."

On the leg back to Washington, Bush visited with the reduced media pool. Jacketless, he joked a bit but soon turned serious. "We're gonna get those bastards," he said. "No thug is gonna bring our country down." When Associated Press reporter Sonya Ross began typing on her laptop, Bush withdrew into his presidential shell. "Hey," he warned, "that's off the record." Air Force One arrived at Andrews Air Force Base at 6:42 p.m. Loewer rode with the president in his helicopter to the White House, and the aircraft made a brief fly-by of the Pentagon. She later described the burning building: "It was a horrible sight."

Upon arrival at the White House at 6:54 p.m., the president reviewed a draft of his planned speech to the nation scheduled for at 8:30. He then reunited with the First Lady in the PEOC, and they chatted briefly with the vice president and his wife Lynne. After freshening up and practicing his speech, Bush sat at his Oval Office desk and readied himself for his address.

"Good evening. Today, our fellow citizens, our way of life, our very freedom came under attack in a series of deliberate and deadly terrorist acts." He continued to speak for seven minutes and tried to reassure the American people that the country could withstand the evil acts of the day. He spoke encouragingly about the continuing rescue operations in New York and Washington and declared that the federal government would bring those responsible for the attacks to justice. The president included a statement in the speech that foreshadowed his administration's next steps: "We will make no distinction between the terrorists who committed these acts and those who harbor them."

The president convened a formal NSC meeting at 9:00 p.m. in the PEOC's cramped, subterranean conference room, where the air had ripened during the long day. After a few remarks, Rice asked the deputies and assistants to depart the confined space, leaving only the principals: Bush; Cheney; Powell, who had returned from Peru; Rumsfeld; Tenet; Rice; Card; and General Myers, who was subbing for the absent chairman, General Hugh Shelton. The group became what Bush called his war cabinet, although others—Attorney General Ashcroft and Director Mueller, for example—would attend occasionally.

The war cabinet would not be a smoothly collaborative body. Powerful egos competed for the president's ear, hardly a phenomenon unique to the forty-third president. Rumsfeld could be a prickly debater who challenged Rice almost as frequently as he challenged his generals. The secretive Cheney often diverged sharply from Rice's positions as he created a huge center of power in the White House. Powell was less dogmatic than were Rumsfeld and Cheney, having honed his pragmatism as Reagan's national security adviser and as chairman of the Joint Chiefs. Card often acted as the referee.

Bush repeated a line of thought that he had expressed that morning in Sarasota: "I want you all to understand that we are at war and we will stay at war until this is done. Nothing else matters. Everything is available for the pursuit of this war. Any barriers in your way, they're gone." The group discussed rescue operations, the economic impacts of the terrorist attacks, the Taliban regime in Afghanistan and its sheltering of al-Qaeda, and many more questions for which they had few answers. One subject, though, drew a pointed response from a weary Bush. Rumsfeld mentioned that international law generally supported the application of armed force to prevent possible follow-on attacks but not for reprisal. "No!" Bush snapped, his voice filling the bunker. "I don't care what the international lawyers say, we are going to kick some ass."

I Can Hear You

During the morning of September 11, only a few people attempted to "manage" one of America's gravest crises. Among them were first responders in New York and Arlington, several air traffic control officials in the FAA commander center, and the gallant passengers of United 93. President Bush could only fight the fog of war. For the rest of that day and the weeks that followed, his main goal was to search for response options.

Prior to 9/11, political opponents and certain sectors of the news media doubted that the rookie president had the intellectual capacity and experience to manage an enormous crisis. His many critics saw him as an accidental president, thanks to Florida's voting procedures, and as a semi-successful scion of a powerful political family whose connections helped at every turn. Even Bush admitted seven years later, "I think I was unprepared for war." And of course, anyone who saw the look on Bush's face when Card whispered the news in his ear may have questioned the president's readiness. Nevertheless, the horrific nature of the terrorist attacks generally stifled most criticism of President Bush in the days following September 11. "Rally around the president" was the byword for nearly all Americans.

But Washington is a tough town for politicians, and opponents are loath to pass on opportunities to criticize regardless of the times. Bush's decision to remain at secure locations for the day sparked some carping and cynicism. Representative Martin Meehan (D-MA), for example, loudly doubted the threat to Air Force One. "That's just PR.

That's just spin," he said. Reporter Dan Balz of the *Washington Post* offered his take in a September 12 article. "Until his speech last night, Bush was largely invisible to a nervous public as he flew from Florida to Air Force bases in Louisiana and Nebraska before returning to Washington about 7 p.m.," Balz wrote. "Bush's decidedly low profile was jarring even to some of his allies and raised questions about whether he should have done more to reassure the country."

The president tamped down further possible criticism with two major actions during the following weeks. The first was his dramatic statement at Ground Zero on September 14: "I can hear you, the rest of the world hears you. And the people who knocked these buildings down will hear all of us soon." Second, he gave a forceful speech before Congress on September 20. "Fierce . . . eloquent . . . powerful," declared the network news anchors afterward. Bush's confident performance garnered praise in most corners. "I thought it was A-plus," pronounced historian Michal Beschloss. "Every word he said, you really knew he meant it." Bush appeared to have the nation behind him, and the public looked for bold and decisive action.

Unknown to the public, however, members of the Bush administration had already begun on September 11 to expand the crosshairs beyond al-Qaeda. Powerful voices argued immediately for the conflating of Saddam Hussein and Iraq with bin Laden and al-Qaeda. This secret campaign would succeed and prove to be Bush's undoing in managing the consequences of the 9/11 crisis.

Going to War

President Bush twice met with his war cabinet on September 12. In the morning session, they talked in generalities of how to respond and with what objectives and which allies. Rumsfeld, for example, said, "It is critical how we define goals at the start." He went on to discuss which targets that potential allies would want defined. "Do we focus on bin Laden and al-Qaeda or terrorism more broadly?" he asked.

"The goal is terrorism in its broadest sense," Powell replied, "focusing first on the organization that acted yesterday."

"To the extent we define our task broadly," Cheney offered, "including those who support terrorism, then we get at states. And it's easier to find them than it is to find bin Laden." Bush pressed Rumsfeld on what the military could do immediately.

"Very little, effectively," the secretary replied.

"I want to get moving," Bush emphasized.

Director Tenet responded the next day to Bush's request for action. In a meeting in the conference room of the Situation Room, he offered Bush a CIA war plan for Afghanistan. "We're prepared to launch in short order an aggressive covert action program that will carry the fight to the enemy, particularly al-Qaeda and its Taliban protectors in Afghanistan." He said that a CIA paramilitary team would link up with the main anti-Taliban force in country, the Northern Alliance, and then, with assistance from US special operations forces, oust the Islamic fundamentalist Taliban regime. He introduced his counterterrorist assistant, Cofer Black, an old-school CIA hand whose bona fides included the capture of the Venezuelan-born terrorist Carlos the Jackal.

As Black clicked through his Power Point slides, he said, "Mr. President, we can do this. . . . But you've got to understand, people are going to die. . . . Americans are going to die—my colleagues and my friends."

"That's war," Bush said evenly. Black continued with his pitch and kept piling on the theatrics, especially about the anticipated death of al-Qaeda terrorists. "When we're through with them, they will have flies walking across their eyeballs."

On the following day, September 14, Bush presided over a full cabinet meeting and became emotional as the attendees applauded when he entered the room. He then participated in a moving midday service honoring the attack victims at Washington National Cathedral. The president spoke of grief and healing, but focused at one point on war, an unlikely subject in a soaring cathedral dedicated to peaceful worship. "This conflict has begun on the timing and terms of others. It will end in a way, and an hour, of our choosing."

The president, his war cabinet, and a few others gathered at the presidential mountain retreat at Camp David on September 15. In the conference room of Laurel Lodge, the major subjects of discussion included Director Tenet's plan of action and General Shelton's military options. Tenet started his presentation by distributing a package labeled "Going to War." The first page carried the title "Initial Hook: Destroying al-Qaeda, Closing the Safe Haven." He urged using CIA covert operators and military special operations forces to help resistance militias overthrow the Taliban.

Chairman Shelton offered three military options in concert with Tenet's plans. The first solely consisted of a cruise missile strike, which must have elicited some pushback. Bill Clinton launched a similar strike against al-Qaeda in 1998, and it was wholly ineffective. The second added attack aircraft and bombers to the first option. The third was all of the above, plus special operations units and perhaps a few selected Army and Marine units.

Familiar themes surfaced immediately. They talked of quagmires, such as what the United States had faced in Vietnam and the Soviets in Afghanistan, and the matter of coalition building. Regarding the latter, Powell said that the growing international coalition would be primed for targeting al-Qaeda, but pursuing other groups and countries would rapidly thin the ranks, leaving the United States alone. Bush responded: "That's okay with me. We are America."

The president announced his decisions in a war cabinet meeting on September 17. "It starts today," he said, referring to his planned response to the terrorist attacks. "I want the CIA to be first on the ground," he said, speaking of Afghanistan, and then moved on to what he wanted from Ashcroft and the FBI. Additionally, Powell was to issue an ultimatum to the Taliban, demanding they turn over bin Laden or else. Bush said of the Taliban, "I want to have them quaking in their boots." The discussion turned to a suggestion that Iraq was involved in the 9/11 attacks, but almost all of Bush's advisers recommended against including that country in early military operations. The president agreed, but added, "I believe Iraq was involved, but I'm not going to strike them now." The president did say, however, that he wanted Rumsfeld to make plans for future military action in Iraq. At the end of the meeting, the president completed his directives by telling Rumsfeld to go with Shelton's third option in Afghanistan. "We're going to rain holy hell on them."

Bush enjoyed a helpful wind at his back from the international community and Congress at this point. On September 12, the UN Security Council had produced a firm resolution supporting broad means to combat terrorist acts. Two days later, the US Congress had authorized Bush's use of military force against those who committed or aided the 9/11 attacks. Even NATO had invoked its Article 5, which defined an attack against one member as an attack against all members.

The anthrax poison letters attacks of September and October 2001 further complicated President Bush's management of the post-9/11 environment. An unknown person had sent letters containing the anthrax-causing bacteria through the US mail to government officials and news media outlets. The episode added to the national tension and eventually boosted calls from within the administration to counter Saddam Hussein's supposed weapons of mass destruction. Five people died from anthrax, and seventeen others survived infection.

Bin Laden's Escape

A CIA team codenamed JAWBREAKER hit the ground first in Afghanistan on September 26. A massive air assault on Taliban targets began on October 7. Special ops teams, including the Army's Delta Force, arrived and used lasers to designate targets for the attack aircraft. Yet little of the early success in Afghanistan reached either the public or the news media, and criticism soon surfaced.

The *New York Times* on October 31 carried a story by R. W. Apple with the headline "A Military Quagmire Remembered: Afghanistan as Vietnam." Apple wrote about the discouraging progress of the Northern Alliance. He also reported that Senator John McCain (R-AZ) had urged the use of American ground troops and quoted two conservative writers who lamented Bush's use of half measures. The tone of the public discourse changed on November 9 when the key northern Afghanistan city of Mazar-e-Sharif fell to the Uzbek general leading the Northern Alliance, Abdul Rashid Dostum. When Kabul fell on the twelfth, the Northern Alliance controlled half of Afghanistan. The remaining Taliban either surrendered or deserted their last stronghold in Kandahar on December 7.

Four weeks before, however, bin Laden and his closest advisers had fled first to Jalalabad and then later to Tora Bora, a complex of natural caves in the White Mountains of eastern Afghanistan. CIA agents and special ops units gave chase and directed air strikes in the area. But they needed help, so Hank Crumpton, the chief of CIA operations in Afghanistan, sought assistance from the military. He contacted General Tommy Franks, the commander of US military forces there, and requested troops to block bin Laden's escape from Tora Bora. Franks declined for two reasons: First, he cited Rumsfeld's order to minimize the "footprint" of US forces in the area and, second, the long lead time needed to insert any new forces. Instead, CIA and Delta Force personnel would have to rely on Afghani militias to cut off bin Laden's escape routes.

Author Peter Bergen, a well-regarded expert on bin Laden and al-Qaeda, wrote of the small force pursuing bin Laden: "In the end there were probably more journalists at Tora Bora than there were Western soldiers, who totaled around seventy or so Delta operators, Green Berets, and British Special Boat Service troops." Al-Qaeda, in the meantime, paid local villagers to guide 600 people on mules into Pakistan. Bergen estimated that bin Laden escaped with them on or about December 13.

Bush succeeded in expelling the Taliban but failed to destroy al-Qaeda. He accomplished the former with air power, ten thousand resistance fighters, 110 CIA operatives, and 316 special operations forces troops. With the exception of a small, one-day operation, conventional US troops did not enter the fight until November 25. That economy of effort, however, allowed bin Laden and his senior leadership to fight on.

After this seemingly painless operation against the Taliban, President Bush turned his guns to the west and Iraq. He let Afghanistan slide into the quagmire that everyone had feared. In 2004, an experienced military consultant offered his assessment of Bush's de-emphasis of Afghanistan to *The New Yorker* magazine: "From January 2002 on, we were in the process of snatching defeat from the jaws of victory."

Pivot to Iraq

President Bush's first treasury secretary, Paul O'Neill, said that as soon as Bush took office in January 2001, the White House talked of preemptively ousting Saddam Hussein. "From the very beginning, there was a conviction that Saddam Hussein is a bad person and that he needed to go," O'Neill told the CBS TV show *60 Minutes* in 2004. "It was all about finding a way to do it. That was the tone of it. The president saying, 'Go find me a way to do this.'"

Secretary Rumsfeld first raised the issue of attacking Iraq during a meeting in the Pentagon a few hours after the plane had hit the building. Notes taken during the session by Stephen Cambone, a key Rumsfeld assistant, indicated that the secretary sought information that would permit the United States to strike Saddam Hussein at the same time as bin Laden. "Go massive," the notes quote Rumsfeld. "Sweep it all up. Things related and not."

Rumsfeld then broached the idea in both war cabinet meetings on September 12. His deputy, Paul Wolfowitz, a neoconservative hawk on Iraq, argued in the afternoon for including Iraq and its leader, Saddam Hussein, in the first round of military retaliation. Shelton and Powell urged waiting on Iraq. Powell said that the American public wanted action on al-Qaeda, a point that Bush tentatively seconded.

President Bush, however, revealed his true interest in Saddam Hussein that evening. When casually walking through the Situation Room complex, he started a conversation with Dick Clarke and several others. "I know you have a lot to do and all, but I want you, as soon as you can, to go back over everything, everything. See if Saddam did this."

"But Mr. President, al-Qaeda did this," Clarke replied.

"I know, I know, but . . . see if Saddam was involved." When Clarke gave Bush a few more "buts," the president grew testy.

"Look into Iraq, Saddam," he demanded and left.

One of Clarke's assistants captured the moment: "Wolfowitz got to him."

Deputy Secretary Wolfowitz spoke publicly during the week after 9/11 about including Iraq in Bush's war plans to counter al-Qaeda. That prompted a private exchange between Powell and Shelton about their concerns about the direction charted by Rumsfeld and Wolfowitz. "What the hell, what are these guys thinking about?" Powell asked Shelton. "Can't you get these guys back in the box?"

On November 21, two weeks before the Taliban fell, Bush started the wheels turning toward Iraq. "What kind of war plan do you have for Iraq?" he asked Rumsfeld in private. The secretary hemmed a bit about the military's slow pace on war plans. "Let's get started on this," Bush said. The president told Rumsfeld to keep the planning secret.

President Bush subtly introduced his pivot away from Afghanistan in his January 29, 2002, State of the Union address. Referring to Iraq, Iran, and North Korea, he said, "States like these and their terrorist allies constitute an axis of evil, arming to threaten the peace of the world. By seeking weapons of mass destruction, these regimes pose a grave and growing danger."

During the spring and summer of 2002, the Bush administration began to build the public case for war with Iraq. Initially, the casus belli was the purported operational link between al-Qaeda and Saddam Hussein. That connection, however tenuous, was an easy sell, and by early 2003, a Knight Ridder poll revealed that 44 percent of American respondents believed that most or some of the 9/11 hijackers were Iraqis. Rand Beers, who picked up Clarke's NSC counterterrorism job in 2002, said that 70 percent of Americans believed that Iraq attacked the World Trade Center and the Pentagon.

As the flawed intelligence that tied al-Qaeda to Iraq was discredited, Bush, Cheney, and the Pentagon began to cite Iraqi WMD programs as reason enough for war. The vice president led the campaign, and on August 29 he declared in a speech in Nashville, Tennessee, that there was no doubt that Saddam Hussein had WMD. Further, he added, "Many of us are convinced that Saddam Hussein will acquire nuclear weapons fairly soon." The selling of the WMD scenario climaxed in February 2003 when Secretary Powell staked his reputation at the UN by citing "solid intelligence" of Iraqi existing biological and chemical weapons. He further stated that Saddam Hussein "remains determined to acquire nuclear weapons."

The pivot to Iraq offended Rand Beers, and he soon quit in disgust. He told Clarke about how Bush's team set aside al-Qaeda in favor of Iraq. "They still don't get it. Insteada goin' all out against al-Qaeda and eliminating our vulnerabilities at home, they wanna fuckin' invade Iraq again." Beers lamented that the Afghan operation had not captured bin Laden and that the Taliban were regrouping because the token US military force there was ineffective. "They aren't going to send more troops. . . . They're holding back, waiting to invade Iraq." A senior Bush administration official explained to the *Washington Post* in January 2003 how the Iraq hawks had won the day. "The issue got away from the president. He wasn't controlling the tone or the direction." The official went on to say that those wearing Iraq like an albatross around their necks had influenced the president and "painted him into a corner."

US and coalition forces invaded Iraq on March 19, 2003. Eventually, the house of cards campaign alleging Saddam Hussein's WMD fully collapsed when US and coalition forces did not find them. President Bush's declaration on May 1, 2003, that the war's mission had been accomplished rang hollow. Worse, his jokes about the missing Iraq WMD at the Radio and Television Correspondents' Association dinner in March 2004 were disgraceful. He showed images of himself looking under the Oval Office furniture and said, "Those weapons of mass destruction must be somewhere!"

America's battle against al-Qaeda continues to the present, despite the killing of bin Laden in May 2011. US combat operations in Afghanistan were scheduled to end in December 2014, and President Obama withdrew American military forces from Iraq in 2011.

Assessment

After muddling through September 11, President Bush executed bold action twenty-six days later. His two-month initiative in Afghanistan had a limited objective—unseat the Taliban and deny a base for al-Qaeda—and he allocated a limited force to do so. The approach was a dramatic shift from the massive operation that Colin Powell demanded from Bush 41 in the Persian Gulf War. The aftermath, an unevenly resourced attempt at nation building and the resultant quagmire, still plagues America. Bush's larger action, the Global War on Terror, as he called it, had grander goals and resources and it prevented further major attacks on the United States. However, some of the president's harshest critics consider his decision to include the invasion of Iraq in that strategy to be the biggest foreign policy blunder in modern American history.

Bush's decision making was partially similar to the groupthink that affected Truman and his advisers. Richard Haass, the point man on the NSC staff during the Gulf War and a high-ranking State appointee on 9/11, saw too few countering opinions in Bush 43's deliberations. "Too many assumptions got accepted or built in," Haass said in 2004. However, when differences among Bush's advisers, especially between Defense and State, did arise, an imbalance resulted. A senior administration official said that when Wolfowitz and his fellow neocons began beating the Iraq war drum, "Defense had their thumb on the scale."

Haass agreed and attributed this advantage to several factors. Rumsfeld silenced voices from the Joint Chiefs, whose opinions the civilians had stifled in some previous crises. Rumsfeld's major ally, the vice president, exercised great influence, and, as Haass put it, got "three bites of the apple." Cheney had his large staff at every meeting, he sat in on the principals-only sessions, and he talked with Bush one-on-one. The NSC staff often tilted toward the Defense-Cheney bias, thus leaving State, in Haass's words, "behind two and a half to one" at the start of any discussion. These circumstances formed the major impetus for groupthink dynamics.

These and other influences at work—Bush's foreign policy inexperience, for example—produced a policy shift away from pursuing al-Qaeda to invading Iraq. But that change obscured the relative ineffectiveness of the coalition strike against the Taliban. In 2002, the Pentagon commissioned a study to assess the initial military response to the 9/11 attacks. The study's author, retired Army Colonel Hy Rothstein, found that operations in Afghanistan had failed to convert initial tactical gains into a strategic victory. Further, Rothstein said the campaign had been minimally successful "at being able to achieve the primary goal of ensuring that al-Qaeda could no longer operate in Afghanistan." His report, however, found very little traction in Washington at that time.

Books about Bush's war with Iraq reflect the opposing judgments across the political spectrum. Indictments include David Corn's *The Lies of George W. Bush*; Michael Isikoff and David Corn's *Hubris: The Inside Story of Spin, Scandal, and the Selling of the Iraq War*; and Thomas Ricks's *Fiasco: The American Military Venture into Iraq*. Bill Sammon leads the way on the other side with two books: *Fighting Back: The War on Terrorism from Inside the White House* and *Strategery: How George W. Bush Is Defeating Terrorists, Outwitting Democrats, and Confounding the Mainstream Media*.

Sympathetic observers of George W. Bush beyond Bill Sammon seem to have only a narrow hindsight argument in support of the Iraq War. When faced with the absence of Iraqi WMD and the invalidation of bogus claims of Iraqi complicity in the 9/11 attacks, they have only one benefit of the US invasion of Iraq to assert—America and its allies purged the world of a bad man. However, Zbigniew Brzezinski offered his take on eliminating malevolence. "Bush II was the vigilante, mobilizing domestic fears to pursue a self-declared existential struggle against the forces of evil."

Last, Peter Bergen has offered this critical assessment of the 9/11 crisis. "Just as bin Laden made a large strategic error in attacking the United States on 9/11, so too President Bush—having presided over the campaign in Afghanistan that came close to destroying al-Qaeda—would make his own deeply flawed decision to attack Iraq, which breathed new life into bin Laden's holy war."

CHAPTER 12

BARACK OBAMA

The Arab Spring, 2011–14

Selective Engagement

Press Secretary Jay Carney worked his way through a series of tough questions from reporters in the James Brady Press Briefing Room in the White House. In the early afternoon of March 7, 2011, the main subject in the cramped, camera-strewn space was the seemingly endless and bloody developments in the Arab Spring, a period of demonstrations, political upheavals, and death in the Middle East and North Africa. On that day, the revolt du jour was in Libya, where the ruthless dictator Muammar Qadhafi was intent on crushing protesters in the eastern part of the country near Egypt. A few days earlier, Qadhafi had announced to the rebels that he would "fight until the last man, the last woman, the last bullet." His son, Saif, echoed that threat and promised "thousands of deaths, and rivers of blood will run through Libya." ABC News correspondent Jake Tapper asked Carney what President Barack Obama planned to do about helping the Libyan rebels.

Carney danced around a bit, as all press secretaries do when asked simple questions about complex matters. "We're talking here a matter of days and weeks that all of this has transpired," Carney said. "We are monitoring the situation very closely, obviously, and aware of the ongoing violence." Carney also cited Obama's demand that Qadhafi step aside.

"I wasn't talking about it in terms of days," Tapper said, "so much as I was in terms of lives. And I'm wondering—more than a thousand people have died, according to the United Nations. How many more people have to die before the United States decides, okay, we're going to take this one step of a no-fly zone, for example, or we're going to arm the rebels, for example? What needs to happen? How many more people have to die?"

Tapper's questions reflected the debate running throughout the capitals of Europe and the Middle East, as well as at both ends of Pennsylvania Avenue in Washington. Moreover, sharp differences plagued Obama's national security team. UN ambassador Susan Rice and NSC staffer Samantha Power advocated humanitarian intervention. On the other hand, Secretary of Defense Robert Gates cited the dangers of starting a third simultaneous war. He had said publicly that any secretary of defense suggesting sending American military forces into the area should "have his head examined."

Despite Gates's view, Obama gathered his national security team to assess the impact of Qadhafi's violent repression of his people on US interests and what to do about it. They met in the primary conference room of the White House Situation Room complex at 4:10 p.m. on Tuesday, March 15. The eighteen attendees included Gates, Vice President Joe Biden, Chairman of the Joint Chiefs of Staff Admiral Mike Mullen, CIA Director Leon Panetta, National Security Adviser Tom Donilon, Chief of Staff Bill Daley, and others. Secretary of State Hillary Clinton joined the group from Egypt via secure telephone, and Susan Rice attended from New York through a secure video link. The subject was the Libyan uprising.

As all sessions of this sort, a "principals" meeting in White House decision-making terms, it started with an intelligence update on the Libyan situation. Tens of thousands of Qadhafi's troops were marching toward the insurgent center of power, Benghazi, in eastern Libya on the Mediterranean coast. UN sanctions and diplomatic moves had not stopped Qadhafi. Next, Admiral Mullen offered options for US action, but had only two. The first was a French and British proposal for a no-fly zone to blunt attempts by the Libyan air force to attack the retreating rebels. The United States and its allies had used this tactic in Iraq from 1991 to 2003 and in the Balkans from 1993 to 1995. Gates and the Joint Chiefs opposed the idea, and Gates had talked publicly about its risk of escalation. The second alternative was to do nothing. The narrowness of the options disturbed Obama.

"Will this no-fly zone stop the scenario we just heard about?" Obama asked Mullen, referring to the prospect of Qadhafi slaughtering Libyans.

"No, sir," Mullen replied. "It won't stop the advance of Qadhafi's forces."

"This notion that we're going to put some planes in the air to fly over a massacre just doesn't make a lot of sense," the president said. "We could feel really good about ourselves, on the right side of history, and the people would still get killed." Exasperated, Obama leaned forward in his chair and said, "I want more options."

"Obama structures meetings so that they're not debates," one meeting participant later told author Michael Lewis. "They're minispeeches. He likes to make decisions by having his mind occupying the various positions. He likes to imagine holding the view." Another principal added, "He seems very much to want to hear from people. Even when he's made up his mind he wants to cherry-pick the best arguments to justify what he wants to do."

"I want to hear from some other folks in the room," he said, pointing to the deputies and National Security Council staffers seated along the room's walls. The ensuing discussion highlighted the domestic political pitfalls of a Libyan intervention and the downsides of yet another war against a Muslim nation. The fundamental, brass-tack question they asked each other largely remained unanswered: Were the country's national interests at stake? A frustrated Obama spoke, "I don't know why we are even having this meeting."

With that, Obama adjourned the session and asked his team to reconvene later that evening after he and his wife finished entertaining guests for dinner. At 9:00 p.m., the advisers presented Obama with three military options: provide intelligence and logistics support to the British and French, execute a no-fly zone, or use US forces to attack the Libyan military and stop its advance toward Benghazi. Critical to the last choice was gaining a UN resolution authorizing "all necessary measures"—UN code words for military intervention. Further deliberations ensued, especially on how the American public viewed engaging Libya. "How are we going to explain to the American people why we're in Libya," asked Daley. "Who gives a shit about Libya?"

Obama ultimately chose to intervene and not sit by as Qadhafi killed his country's people. He declared, "That's not who we are." He instructed Rice to negotiate a UN resolution the next day at UN headquarters. "I want to call everyone's bluff up in New York," Obama said of allies pushing a no-fly zone. Instead of that option, he wanted UN authorization allowing all necessary measures. "That's the only thing we're going to support, because that's the only thing that's going to make a difference." He also insisted on two major limits on US participation: no ground troops and a finite duration of operations—days, not weeks. The March 15 principals meeting and Obama's decision marked a major shift in his approach to the tumult of the Arab Spring.

Arab Spring, Early Rounds

A foreign policy neophyte when he won the presidency in 2008, Obama quickly steered away from the unilateral application of American force that highlighted the wars in Afghanistan and Iraq. As *New Yorker* editor David Remnick described in January 2014, Obama advocated "a foreign policy sensibility that was wary of American overreach." Remnick added, "If George W. Bush's foreign policy was largely a reaction to 9/11, Obama's has been a reaction to the reaction."

Obama's initial foreign policy, besides the "anything but Bush" approach, included three central tenets: opposition to the Iraq war, pragmatic engagement with dictators, and enhanced diplomacy and multilateralism. Obama believed that America needed a new spirit of humility. More specifically in the Middle East, as Obama said in a June 2009 speech in Cairo, he pledged "to seek a new beginning between the United States and Muslims."

Early on, Obama pushed less forcefully than his predecessor to spread democracy throughout the world, especially the Middle East where some autocrats were valuable allies. He highlighted his less aggressive agenda in the Cairo speech. In a reference to the Iraq War, Obama drew a line: "No system of government can or should be imposed by one nation on any other." His watching from the sideline a week later when Iranians started their short-lived public protest movement, the Green Revolution, seconded his point. Obama formalized that approach in his May 2010 National Security Strategy in which a freedom agenda was not high in the priorities.

Nevertheless, he needed to have some idealism arrows in his quiver. In the summer of 2010, Obama presciently tasked his senior foreign policy advisers to devise strategies to deal with a potential conundrum. How could he reconcile democratic and human rights concerns in countries that are vital to US national interests? He needed an answer, because as a candidate in 2008, Obama had advocated a foreign policy "no longer driven by ideology and politics but one that is based on a realistic assessment of the sobering facts on the ground and our interests in the region."

Obama's foreign policy course changes and seemingly passive policies didn't sit well with his critics. Conservatives viewed him as America's chief apologizer, especially when Obama physically bowed to the Saudi king in early 2009. Bush 43 aide John Bolton called Obama the "ditherer in chief" in late 2009. Bolton considered indecision and weakness to be toxic in international affairs, and "that's all Obama has shown us so far."

The first round in the Arab Spring began on December 17, 2010, when Mohamed Bouazizi, a vegetable seller in Tunis, self-immolated. According to Mideast specialist Marc Lynch of George Washington University, "It was a calculated political act designed to provoke precisely the kind of popular response it achieved," Bouazizi's death mobilized protests against high unemployment, repressed political and religious freedoms, and a violent and authoritarian government. His death and the Jasmine Revolution that followed chased President Zine El Abidine Ben Ali from office on January 14. Round two would be a bit more dicey.

Egyptian citizens, responding to years of repression, began mass demonstrations on January 25. Unlike Tunisia, Egypt was a key US ally and a major Mideast country in which one in four Arabs lived. American presidents had tolerated autocratic Egyptian regimes for decades because of the country's strategic location, which bridged three continents; the Suez Canal; and Egypt's peace treaty with Israel. Egypt's stability was in the best national security interests of the United States, and the annual $1.5 billion in US aid to Egypt reflected major American interests.

The Obama administration initially reacted hesitantly to the Egyptian demonstrations. On January 26, Secretary Clinton urged the Egyptian authorities not to prevent peaceful protests or block communications, including on social media sites. But Press Secretary Robert Gibbs, Jay Carney's predecessor, declared, "Egypt is a strong ally." The next day, Biden appeared on the PBS *NewsHour* saying that it was not time for Egyptian president Hosni Mubarak to step aside. Rather, he said, "I hope Mubarak, President Mubarak, is going to respond to some of the legitimate concerns that are being raised."

On Friday, January 28, tens of thousands of protesters produced a "day of rage" in Cairo's Tahrir Square. The demonstrations gained coherence the following day when the Muslim Brotherhood, a long-standing Islamist social and political organization in Egypt, joined the protests. The Brotherhood, which had been banned by Nasser, had regained its influence under Sadat. During Mubarak's reign, the organization became the largest opposition force in Egypt. The Brotherhood had achieved legitimacy in 2005 by winning seats in the Egyptian parliament. Marc Lynch captured the significance of the Brotherhood's weighty presence in the nascent revolution when he wrote: "Mubarak's prospects for survival dimmed."

In the White House, the Principals Committee met in the afternoon without Obama and collectively felt that he should not comment on the bourgeoning revolution. Separately, though, Gibbs urged Obama to disregard his national security advisers and say something. Obama joined the principals in mid-meeting and convinced them that he had to make a statement. Obama also called Mubarak, urging that he move toward a transition government. Further, Obama approved sending an emissary, former US ambassador to Egypt Frank Wisner, to carry the same message to Mubarak.

A turning point in Egypt came on January 31, when the army announced that its soldiers wouldn't fire on the demonstrators. The next day, while Obama met with his team in the Situation Room, Mubarak appeared on Egyptian television and declared that he would not run for reelection. Obama feared that Mubarak would simply let his vice president form a new government while he remained in power. Defense and State continued to press for standing with an ally, but

Obama made his own decision. "I'm going upstairs to call Mubarak and tell him he should step down."

On the phone in the Oval Office, Obama told the Egyptian that it was time to leave the government. When Mubarak countered, Obama said, "With all due respect . . . we don't believe the protests are going to die down." Mubarak responded with reasons that prohibited his resignation.

"Mr. President," Obama said, "I always respect my elders. You've been in politics a long time. There are moments in history that, just because things have been the same way in the past, doesn't mean they will be the same way in the future." Mubarak nevertheless continued to resist until the call ended. Obama asked for a quickly written script and then stepped in front of live television cameras in the Grand Foyer of the White House. He repeated his message to Mubarak: "What is clear, and what I indicated tonight to President Mubarak, is my belief that an orderly transition must be meaningful, it must be peaceful, and it *must begin now*."

On that same day, National Security Adviser Tom Donilon created a matrix that assigned officials at State, Defense, and the White House to call targeted foreign leaders and counterparts. They were to lobby for Mubarak's resignation. Obama was in the spreadsheet and called the leaders of Israel, Saudi Arabia, and Turkey. Reaction to Obama's initiative varied from rage in Saudi Arabia, criticism from Israel, and nervous silence from Jordan, Kuwait, and other countries. Iran tried to enter the rhetorical fray, with little effect, and al-Qaeda remained silent.

The more experienced Obama advisers—Biden, Clinton, Gates, and Donilon—favored a cautious approach that might keep Mubarak associates in power after a transition. They also warned about possible intrigue from the Muslim Brotherhood. Those pushing for democratic change—the "Obamians" as James Mann called them in his book of the same name—included Deputy National Security Adviser for Strategic Communications Ben Rhodes and NSC staff member Samantha Power. However, as Mann notes, the latter group had the support of Donilon's principal deputy, Denis McDonough, and President Obama. This debate arose from the conflict between two motives:

the idealism of promoting the freedom agenda and the realistic need for geopolitical stability. The debate moved outside the West Wing when special envoy Wisner publicly suggested that Mubarak stay in office for a while. The administration gasped and quickly noted Wisner had been speaking as a private citizen. Obama pounded his desk and demanded better message control.

As the protests continued, Obama and his team continued to pursue two parallel strategies for Egypt. They publicly endorsed Egyptian negotiations on a new government while privately working to have Mubarak resign. The public and the media, unaware of the private track, accused Obama of wavering. Soon, administration sources reacted and began giving quotes on background to favored reporters about Obama's behind-the-scenes actions.

On Capitol Hill, House Republican leaders generally supported Obama's actions, but a few on the strident right mongered a few fears. Fox News' Glenn Beck, for example, saw a looming Muslim caliphate that would stretch from Morocco to the Philippines. Former Bush 43 team member Donald Rumsfeld worried that the Muslim Brotherhood would hijack a post-Mubarak regime: "Extremists, like the Muslim Brotherhood . . . are not there for democracy." John Bolton criticized the administration for changing its public stance. Nevertheless, the situation changed on February 10 when Mubarak ceded power to his vice president, Omar Suleiman, but chose not to resign. The next day, the Egyptian army quietly removed Mubarak from his office, and a council of military officers assumed control of the country. Perhaps it was a coup in the eyes of some, but hardly to the throng in Tahrir Square.

Mideast specialist Marc Lynch of George Washington University has rebutted any accusations of dithering from Obama critics. "Only *six days* after Egypt's protests began," Lynch wrote in 2012, "the United States had unequivocally and publicly called for the president of its closest Arab ally to step down." Regardless, instability in Egypt returned when Muslim Brotherhood member Mohammed Morsi won a presidential election in June 2012. After a turbulent year, the Egyptian Army threw him out, and the head of the army, Field Marshall Abdel Fattah al-Sisi, was elected president in June 2014.

Next up in the Arab Spring was Bahrain, a small Sunni kingdom on an island in the Persian Gulf connected by a causeway to the Saudi coast. Since 1995, it has been the home port of the headquarters staff of the US Navy's Fifth Fleet. On February 14, protesters, largely from the 60 percent Shiite majority in the country, began demonstrating for political reform. The demonstrations became violent and threatened the vitally important financial district in the capital of Manama on March 13. The next day, troops from Saudi Arabia and the United Arab Emirates crossed the causeway from the mainland and quickly put a deadly end to the Arab Spring in Bahrain. Obama neither could nor wanted to do much about the Bahrain uprising. Given critical American relations with Saudi Arabia, both geopolitical and oil in nature, national interests trumped idealism. Hillary Clinton summarized the Bahrain experience in her 2014 book, *Hard Choices*: "I wished we had better options in Bahrain and more leverage to produce a positive outcome."

Libyan Intervention

Qadhafi began seeking a normalization of his relations with other countries in the 1990s, and in 2003 agreed to shut down his weapons of mass destruction program. The United States reestablished diplomatic relations with Libya in 2006. As mentioned in chapter 8, the United States and Libya settled lawsuits that arose from both the 1988 bombing of Pan Am Flight 103 over Lockerbie, Scotland, and the 1986 US bombing of Libya. When Secretary of State Condoleezza Rice visited Tripoli in 2008, Qadhafi said his country "did not want to be friends with the United States, it just wanted to be left alone." The Obama administration hewed to Qadhafi's request, and Libya stayed off its radar screen until February 17, 2011. Demonstrators in Benghazi, just seven days after Mubarak's ouster, protested against the government's brutal suppression of human rights and public dissent. The following week, police killed twenty-four people.

On February 23, Obama addressed the media and spoke in bland terms about possible US actions. However, Obama mentioned a key point that governed his rhetoric during the first two weeks of the Libyan situation. "First, we are doing everything we can to protect American citizens," Obama said. "In Libya, we've urged our people to leave the country and the State Department is assisting those in need of support." The size of the Libyan protest movement, government violence, and the death toll increased to the point on February 25 that the Arab League suspended Libya's membership; the next day the UN Security Council imposed sanctions on Libya.

During the evacuation of American citizens, which largely ended on February 26, US government officials talked little about Qadhafi's ruthlessness to minimize retaliation aimed at Americans in the country. The president didn't want another hostage crisis on top of violent demonstrations. That relative silence prompted critics in Washington, especially those with no skin in the game, to voice a chorus of rants about what appeared to be an overly cautious Obama. As expected, opposing politicians said what they always say in presidential crises. Senator John McCain declared, "We can't risk allowing Qadhafi to massacre people from the air." McCain, who would run against Obama in 2012, looked to score political points and portrayed Obama as indecisive and weak. In a more unusual development, former national security advisers to Democratic presidents, Sandy Berger and Zbigniew Brzezinski, also called for action. Joining them was a former Obama State Department official, Anne-Marie Slaughter, who urged action in a *New York Times* op-ed titled, "Fiddling While Libya Burns." Bill Clinton called for a no-fly zone and arming the rebels. Obama suffered the heat in silence in order to safely evacuate Americans.

Internal divisions appeared in the administration about possible US responses to the growing Libyan violence. Proponents of intervention to save Libyan lives included UN ambassador Rice, communications adviser Rhodes, and Samantha Power. Those proposing caution about possible military intervention included Vice President Biden, National Security Adviser Donilon, Chief of Staff Daley, Chairman Mullen, Denis McDonough, Secretary Gates, and initially, Secretary Clinton. "I believed that what was happening in Libya," Gates wrote in his 2014 memoir, *Duty*, "was not a vital national interest of the United States." Further, Gates repeated a question that he raised at the time: "Can I just finish the two wars we're already in before you go looking for new ones?"

Gates became frustrated with the White House staff rattling the Pentagon's sabers without understanding the resources needed to implement military options, including a no-fly zone. "Don't give the

White House staff and National Security Council staff too much information on the military options," he instructed Mullen and others on February 28. "They don't understand it, and 'experts' like Samantha Power will decide when we should move militarily." Gates strengthened that restriction on March 2, telling Admiral Mullen to provide no information on military options to the White House without his approval, "especially any options to take out Qadhafi." Gates's apprehensions, at least in part, were well founded. Many civilians, whether on the sideline, in Congress, or within an administration, talk as if using military force was akin to a battleship board game. Send in the carriers! Further, it's easy for politicians to mismatch military means with political ends, just as many military officers haven't a clue about the intricacies of international politics.

Civilian-military relationships notwithstanding, conflicting positions among advisers have historically forced presidents to work through unanticipated crises cautiously. But there were other factors affecting Obama's decision making: his own hardening policy of selective engagement, concern about fighting even more Muslims, and the long-distance concerns associated with the 2012 election. As Bill Daley bluntly noted, many felt that Libya wasn't worth the costs and risks of intervention. Nevertheless, Obama beefed up his rhetoric and, on March 3, echoed his Mubarak line to Qadhafi: "The violence must stop; Muammar Qadhafi has lost the legitimacy to lead and he must leave."

Secretary Clinton, however, put limits on US action in testimony to a House subcommittee on March 10: "I'm one of those who believes that absent international authorization, the United States acting alone would be stepping into a situation whose consequences are unforeseeable." Several developments, however, forced Obama to consider taking assertive, although limited, action. First was the Arab League's endorsement of a no-fly zone on March 12. The decision gave considerable cover to a European and American intervention. Next was pressure from Britain and France to join in a military operation. Third, Qadhafi's forces began to steamroll the opposition.

But the tipping point for Obama was Hillary Clinton's decision to change her position on military intervention. Given the Arab League position and the threatened massacre of Libyan civilians, Clinton joined Power and Rice to urge Obama to unite with France and Britain in a military intervention. Her break from Gates on Libya was a departure from their previous agreement on most foreign policy matters. Obama, who knew that he had to act soon, used her decision as the reason for calling for the critical March 15 principals meeting in the Situation Room. "We knew we didn't have a lot of time," he said later, "somewhere between two days and two weeks."

Leading From Behind

After Obama decided to intervene during the March 15 principals meeting, Susan Rice went to work on a strong UN resolution. Clinton twisted Mideast arms and called Russian Foreign Minister Sergei Lavrov, arguing for a UN resolution authorizing all necessary measures. She said to Lavrov, "Our goal is to protect civilians from brutal and indiscriminate attacks. The no-fly zone is necessary, but insufficient. We need additional measures."

"We can't vote in favor," Lavrov said at the end of their call. "But we will abstain and it will pass."

Obama met with his advisers again on March 17. As before, Biden, Gates, Mullen, Donilon, Daley, and others opposed military action, with Clinton, Rice, Rhodes, and Power in favor. Obama sided with Clinton and the Obamians. On the same day, Rice saw Lavrov's prediction come true at the UN. With abstentions from Russia, China, Germany, and two others, the UN Security Council approved Resolution 1973, which authorized all necessary measures to protect Libyan civilians under attack.

At Obama's direction, the Pentagon refined a plan of attack that integrated US forces with strike aircraft from eight NATO members and units from the UAE, Jordan, and Qatar. The president wanted the US military to lead the intervention initially by taking out the Libyan air defense and command and control capabilities and then ease back to a supporting role. He didn't want to be seen attacking yet another Muslim country or interposing American solutions in the turmoil of the Arab Spring. These preparations, however, were not visible to critics, who assumed that Obama had done nothing during the period from March 8 to18. Newt Gingrich called him "the spectator-in-chief."

Rick Santorum referred to Obama "as indecisive as I've ever seen a president in dealing with a crisis."

The president defined his intentions for limiting direct US operations when he briefed a Congressional delegation on March 18. In talking with bipartisan House and Senate leaders, in a combined face-to-face meeting and telephone conference call, Obama stressed the limited objectives and promised no employment of ground troops. No one objected, and Obama declared he could act alone under the War Powers Resolution; the meeting served as his required notification. Afterward, Obama spoke to the nation and gave Qadhafi an ultimatum to cease hostilities or "consequences" would follow. Obama later left on a scheduled trip to South America.

The next day, while on a conference call with Washington from Brazil, Obama ordered the strikes to begin. At 3:00 p.m. Washington time, 110 cruise missiles slammed into Libyan air defense targets, followed by initial assaults by manned aircraft. While the initial assault went smoothly, there were kinks on the Pentagon–White House axis. At a principals meeting on the 19th without Obama, Gates lost his temper at what he viewed as interference by the White House staff in tactical military matters. To Donilon and Daley, Obama's top two White House staff members, Gates snapped, "You are the biggest micromanagers I have ever worked with. You can't use a screwdriver reaching from DC to Libya on our military operations. The president has given us his strategic direction. For God's sake, now let us run it."

Reaction to Obama's actions varied widely in Washington. David Rothkopf, who would become the CEO of *Foreign Policy* magazine in 2012, voiced his opinion in a March *Washington Post* op-ed. "For those of us who have decried for years the image of a John Wayne America, a bully with an itchy trigger finger, the more temperate attitude is welcome." But Rothkopf also argued that Obama's approach must also have an "or else" facet to be successful. On Capitol Hill, several Democratic House members, including Representatives Jerrold Nadler, Donna Edwards, Dennis Kucinich, Maxine Waters, and Barbara Lee, blasted Obama for acting without congressional approval. Kucinich even raised the issue of impeachment. In the Senate, Republican John Cornyn tweeted, "On Libya, is Congress going to assert its constitutional role or be a potted plant?"

With the 2012 presidential election looming, prospective GOP nominees jumped in. Mitt Romney supported the intervention but criticized Obama's leadership: "He's tentative, indecisive, timid and nuanced." (The latter trait was keyed to George W. "I-don't-do-nuance" Bush.) Tim Pawlenty accused Obama of passing the leader-of-the-free-world baton to French president Nicolas Sarkozy. Gingrich seemingly reversed himself and opportunistically told the news media that he would not have intervened. "It is impossible to make sense of the standard of intervention in Libya," the former speaker said, "except opportunism and news media publicity."

The US military led the way on the initial strikes in Libya. But as Obama promised, the Pentagon turned over the leadership of the campaign to NATO on March 30, eleven days into the operation. The United States continued to provide the majority of intelligence, surveillance, and reconnaissance capabilities and mid-air refueling aircraft. According to Gates, the NATO allies ran though their stores of precision-guided weapons after three months, and the Pentagon had to resupply them. Further, toward the end of the months-long mission, US aircraft returned to combat.

The unusual US role of supporting allied combat operations instead of leading them produced the most damning sound bite of the intervention. An unnamed Obama adviser in a late April interview with *New Yorker* writer Ryan Lizza described the president's actions in Libya as "leading from behind." The source then added, "It's so at odds with the John Wayne expectation for what America is in the world. But it's necessary for shepherding us through this phase." Lizza then noted that since "the US is reviled in many parts of the world, pursuing our interests and spreading our ideals thus requires stealth and modesty as well as military strength."

Regardless of the context, Obama critics feasted on the phrase. Lizza commented later that conservatives believed the remark "provided an Aha! moment that exposed Obama for the feckless and weak foreign policy president they believed him to be." Lizza also noted that Obama led from the front when he sent Navy SEALs to kill bin Laden on the same day that *The New Yorker* published his article.

President Obama faced a War Powers Resolution deadline as the hostilities continued into May. The law requires the president to cease military action if Congress has not approved of the operation within sixty days of the initiation. Although some administration lawyers recommended seeking authorization from the Hill for continued operations, those at State and in the White House told Obama that support to NATO didn't cross the resolution's threshold for a war. He picked that option, and reaction on the Hill was immediate.

"The president is not a king, and he shouldn't act like a king," declared Representative Dan Burton (R-IN). Even a House Democrat weighed in. "It's time for Congress to step forward," said Brad Sherman (D-CA). "It's time to stop shredding the US Constitution in a presumed effort to bring democracy and constitutional rule of law to Libya." When the House of Representatives did step forward on June 24, the War Powers debate fizzled when the members found themselves in muddied waters. The chamber first rejected a bill authorizing the Libyan operation, 295-123. Immediately afterward, the House shifted the football from one hand to the other, and defeated, 238-180, a proposal prohibiting funding of offensive military operations in Libya. The Senate did not schedule a vote.

Nineteen nations eventually joined the coalition that enforced the UN resolution, and combat sorties over Libya dragged on for seven months, hardly the in-and-out intervention that proponents expected. Nevertheless, the Libyan rebels captured Tripoli in August, and killed Qadhafi on October 20, 2011. The National Transitional Congress, formed early in the civil war, became an interim government until August 2012. Since then the General National Congress has governed Libya, with the head of the parliament serving as head of state.

Obama's thoughtful critics during the Tunisia-Bahrain-Libya portions of the Arab Spring called him timid, inconsistent, and lacking of a cohesive doctrine. (I'm disregarding GOP presidential hopefuls because most were simply spinning the issues to win support from Tea Party voters in the 2012 primary elections.) Those who appreciated Obama's cautious and pragmatic approach—one of selective engagement that didn't force the same solution on every situation—thought his backseat strategy in Libya did not equate to a failure of American leadership. In Bahrain, strategic national interest won out over human rights, but in Libya, humanitarian concerns were more important than

Libya's geopolitical insignificance. Syria is another story altogether and is addressed next in this chapter.

As with all presidential crises, outsiders are dependent on the insiders to recount what happened in the White House in each situation. Regarding Obama's decision making on the Libyan intervention, President Obama and his team provided the vetted version to writers, including Michael Lewis, David Corn, and James Mann. About the only significant exception is Bob Gates, who included a bit more of the unsanctioned and unsavory sausage-making details in his 2014 memoir.

One last point on Libya: The deadly attack by Libyan militia members in September 2012 on the diplomatic and covert CIA facilities in Benghazi reflected the continued chaos in Libya a year after Qadhafi's death. The death of four Americans, including American ambassador Christopher Stevens, was tragic and might have been prevented by greater attention to the outpost's security at mid-levels and below in the State Department. However, the incident was not a presidential crisis, and political grandstanding by Capitol Hill Republicans has blown the incident far out of proportion.

A Red Line on Syrian Chemical Weapons

The Syrian civil war, ongoing at the time of this writing, began during the Arab Spring of 2011 when the Syrian people heard cries for change in Tunisia, Libya, and Egypt. The movement started slowly because of the iron grip that the autocratic ruler, Bashar al-Assad, had on the populace. That control began when his father, Hafez al-Assad, came to power in 1970 and systematically crushed any opposition to his Ba'ath Party. A grisly example of this repression was his reaction to a 1982 uprising fomented by the Muslim Brotherhood in southern Syria. The Syrian Army killed between 10,000 and 40,000 people in and around the town of Hama. Tensions continued along sectarian lines, however. The senior al-Assad and his close associates were Alawites, a minority Shiite sect that dominated the 70 percent Sunni majority in the country.

Upon the father's death in 2000, his son Bashar became president. When serious protests arose in March 2011, the younger Assad responded with brutal violence, and by the end of the summer, 2,000 protestors had died. Despite widespread criticism of Assad by Syria's neighbors, none of those countries seemed interested in supporting his overthrow. Israel welcomed the stability on its Syrian border, and the nearby Arab countries didn't want a Syrian civil war that exported violence, refugees, and sectarian conflict into their populations. And that's what they have gotten, along with the emergence of the Islamic State of Iraq and Syria (or "wa al-Sham," "and Levant"), known by its initials as ISIS (or ISIL).

Additionally, Syria had vocal supporters—Russia and China from afar, and Iran and Turkey nearby. In the West, both the United States and NATO announced they had no intention of intervening militarily, pointing at the differences between Libya and Syria. Professor Marc Lynch described the major dissimilarities. "Syria's terrain was far less favorable to air power than Libya's. Urban fighting was far more likely than convoys of trucks in the desert. And absolutely nobody had an interest in invading and occupying Syria after the long years in next-door Iraq."

Hillary Clinton, in her 2014 memoir, *Hard Choices*, called Syria a "wicked problem." She described the Syria-related conundrums facing President Obama in the spring of 2012, a year into the Syrian civil war as follows: "Do nothing, and a humanitarian disaster envelops the region. Intervene militarily, and risk opening Pandora's box and wading into another quagmire, like Iraq. Send aid to the rebels, and watch it end up in the hands of the extremists." Clinton understood, as did Obama, that the United States had little leverage to stop the deaths and human suffering in Syria. Yet those nations with leverage—Russia, for example—had done nothing to stop the bloodshed.

In mid-August 2012, the Syria civil war took a dangerous turn. Sensitive intelligence sensors and sources revealed that Syrian military units were moving or mixing chemical weapon components, and their use might be imminent. That information caused President Obama and his closest national security advisers to meet over the weekend of August 18 and 19. They debated how the United States might deter Syrian president Bashar al-Assad from employing this weapon of mass destruction in the long-running insurrection against his government. The new crisis came at a bad time, as the fall election campaign for the

2012 presidential election was about to kick off. The presumed GOP candidate, Mitt Romney, was probing Obama's every move and statement for grist to use in the campaign spin mills.

Obama sent Assad a stern warning against chemical weapons use via intermediaries. Additionally, the president appeared unexpectedly in the Brady Press Briefing Room on Monday afternoon, August 20, to deliver a carefully worded public warning to Assad. "The idea was to put a chill into the Assad regime without actually trapping the president into any predetermined action," a senior official later told the *New York Times*. But the president ad-libbed.

"We have been very clear to the Assad regime," the president said, "but also to other players on the ground, that a red line for us is we start seeing a whole bunch of chemical weapons moving around or being utilized. That would change my calculus."

"What the president said in August was unscripted," an administration source said later. Another suggested that the "red line" phrase had lodged in his mind from the election-year debate on drawing a line in the sand over Iranian nuclear weapon aspirations. Regardless, Obama had rhetorically painted himself into a corner and restricted his future options if Assad actually attacked Syrian rebels with gas. The statement was reminiscent of John Kennedy's remarks at a press conference prior to the Cuban Missile Crisis in which he drew a red line around potential Soviet offensive missile bases in Cuba. He later regretted doing so.

Assad's potential use of chemical weapons reinvigorated discussion within the administration about how the United States might intervene. Two days after Obama's ad-lib remarks, he met with his senior advisers to hear former general David Petraeus, the new CIA director, pitch a plan to arm and train selected Syrian rebels. Secretary Clinton, Secretary of Defense Leon Panetta, and Joint Chiefs chairman General Martin Dempsey supported the proposal, while UN ambassador Rice argued that the effort would have little effect in the conflict. Obama, concerned about unintended consequences—he pointed to the US arming of the Afghani mujahidin that gave birth to al-Qaeda— decided not to arm or train Syrian rebels.

On December 3, 2012, administration sources told the *Washington Post* that Obama had again warned Assad that deploying chemical weapons was "totally unacceptable." At the same time, Secretary Clinton, while in Prague, declared, "This is a red line for the United States." But the administration also acknowledged that it was hampered by the red-line drawing. "We're kind of boxed in," an official told the *New York Times*. "There's an issue of presidential credibility here. But our options are quite limited."

Syrian forces allegedly used chemical weapons on March 19, 2013, against rebels in the city of Aleppo. By the following month, the UK, France, and Israel had concluded as such. But Obama said publicly, "We have to make sure that we know exactly what happened . . . what we can prove." To some, that was a lesson learned from Colin Powell's 2003 testimony at the UN on Saddam Hussein's WMD, in which he presented allegations that proved groundless. *Washington Post* reporter Jennifer Rubin saw it another way: "President Obama evaded, ducked and erased whatever line he had drawn. He has said that he 'doesn't bluff.' But that is precisely what he has done in Syria, and now with his bluff called, he has only double talk left." Susan Glasser, now editor of *Politico*, added a *Post* op-ed on May 5, writing, "When it comes to Syria, Obama needs an 'or else.' Better yet, he should give up red lines altogether; it's one presidential tool that should be tossed out with the trash." Regardless of media criticism, a Gallup poll later in May showed poor public support for intervention—68 percent of respondents were opposed to US military operations in Syria. While public discourse on the president's apparent inaction swirled about Washington, Obama reacted quietly to the reported Aleppo CW attack by authorizing a covert CIA program to arm and train Syrian rebels.

A June analysis by the State Department concluded that Assad had repeatedly employed chemical weapons on Syrians. State analysts added, if the administration didn't "impose consequences," Assad would interpret the inaction as a "green light for chemical weapons use." The administration acknowledged that red line crossing on June 13. "The president has said that the use of chemical weapons would change his calculus, and it has," Ben Rhodes told the media. He added that US intelligence agencies were now highly certain that the Syrian government had "used chemical weapons, including the nerve agent sarin, on a small scale against the opposition multiple times in the last year." This development prompted Obama to strengthen the secret

CIA-run arms and training program for the Syrian rebels that he had authorized two months before. The administration gained Congressional funding for the rebel support program, and by September 2014 the CIA had trained two to three thousand men of the Free Syrian Army at a Jordanian facility.

Two GOP senators joined the fray, adding America's possible loss of credibility to the many pressures affecting Obama's crisis decision making. John McCain and Lindsey Graham (R-SC), two longtime Obama critics, said in a statement, "US credibility is on the line. Now is not the time to merely take the next incremental step. Now is the time for more decisive actions." They advocated long-range missile attacks on Syrian military targets.

President Obama, however, didn't move quickly toward a bold reaction, largely because no good decisive options were available. Military options tended toward all-out war. In 2012, Joint Chiefs chairman General Martin Dempsey determined that imposing a no-fly zone, for example, would require 70,000 American servicemen to destroy Syria's air defense system and establish air superiority over the country. When the Pentagon proposed paramilitary operations in Syria, Obama advisers couldn't agree on the plan's expected effectiveness, with Susan Rice arguing the option would pull the country into a quagmire. Obama ultimately soured on the idea.

Among the more reasoned opponents of radical action was three-time Pulitzer Prize–winning columnist Thomas Friedman of the *New York Times*. "The Obama team has clearly struggled with its Syria policy, but, in fairness, this is a wickedly complex problem," Friedman wrote in September 2013. "We need a policy response that simultaneously deters another Syrian poison gas attack, doesn't embroil America in the Syrian civil war, and also doesn't lead to the sudden collapse of the Syrian state with all its chemical weapons, or, worse, a strengthening of the Syrian regime and its allies Hezbollah and Iran."

"Look, you wrestle with it," Obama said to *New Yorker* editor David Remnick months later. "The only time I get frustrated is when folks act like it's not complicated and there aren't some real tough decisions, and are sanctimonious, as if somehow these aren't complicated questions." The complexity of the Syrian situation fostered continued disagreement on the right course of action within the Obama team.

For example, Power kept pushing for humanitarian relief. In a conversation with McDonough, now chief of staff, she said, "Denis, if you had met the rebels as frequently as I have, you would be as passionate as I am."

"Samantha," McDonough replied, "we'll just have to agree to disagree."

On August 21, Syrian forces launched rockets carrying chemical weapons at the Damascus suburb of Ghouta, killing over 1,400 people, including hundreds of children. Obama's advisers shuddered, not only at the video of the carnage but also at their immediate challenge. In a Situation Room meeting on Saturday, August 24, Obama talked of shifting policy gears: "I haven't made a decision yet on military action. But when I raised the issue of chemical weapons last summer," the president said, referring to his August 2012 red-line statement, "this is what I was talking about."

Despite the August vacation period in Washington, the city was abuzz with Obama's options on military retaliation against Syria. The president, in a PBS interview on the 28th, talked of a limited "shot across the bow" for Assad. "We don't have good options, great options, for the region," he said, describing the probable untoward consequences of military strikes. Interestingly, military experts agreed on Obama's limited options, with retired Marine Lieutenant General Gregory Newbold leading the way. "There's a broad naiveté in the political class about America's obligations in foreign policy issues," Newbold told the *Washington Post*, "and scary simplicity about the effects that employing American military power can achieve." An anonymous active duty officer said, "I can't believe the president is even considering it." Experts also respected the decision not to target CW storage sites, for that would expose everyone around them to lethal gas and leave any surviving munitions available for salvage by terrorists. Some Republican and Democratic members of the House, however, remained sensitive about being out of the loop on the Libyan intervention and rejected military action in Syria. One hundred eighty-six members signed a letter to the president on August 29, demanding a vote on the use of force in Syria.

Obama's action alternatives shrunk further when the British parliament rejected Prime Minister David Cameron's proposal to attack Syria jointly with the United States. France, on the other hand, remained committed to participating in military strikes. Accordingly, five US Navy combatants, all loaded with Tomahawk cruise missiles, were on station in the eastern Mediterranean. In-theater military commanders expected a launch order late Saturday, Washington time, on August 30. About that time, President Obama asked McDonough, now his chief of staff, to walk with him in the stifling heat around the White House South Lawn. They talked about whether Obama should order the strike on Syria, and then decided to summon the senior White House staff for one last discussion at seven o'clock in the Oval Office. That group included the new national security adviser, Susan Rice, her deputies, congressional liaison chief Rob Nabors, and several communications and legal advisers.

"I have a big idea I want to run by you guys," Obama said at the start. He then followed with a question, How about if we ask Congress for authorization to intervene in Syria? That startled everybody save McDonough, and familiar divisions among Obama's team arose again. The ensuing sharp debate ranged from preserving a president's prerogative for military operations to the political consequences and the risk of a negative vote. Yet the president had to act, and with only France at his side, he looked for another partner—Congress. It was a gamble, but Obama wanted lawmakers to share accountability for US actions in Syria. Besides, if Congress withheld authorization, Obama could gain wiggle room in his red-line box. Luckily, Chairman Dempsey had told Obama that the cruise missile targets were not perishable and the military could accommodate a delay, allowing time for a vote.

Rice had reservations, and Obama's new secretary of defense, Chuck Hagel, voiced his concern on the phone. Nevertheless, Obama followed his instincts, and while Rhodes prepared a public statement for the next day, Obama called vacationing congressional leaders to request a vote as soon as possible. Alone in his red-line box, without the UK and the UN, he wanted more from Congress than the usual rants. An Obama aide said later of Congress, "We don't want them to have their cake and eat it, too."

Obama's reversal left French president François Hollande in the lurch. He had been more aggressive than Obama and Cameron about striking Syria prior to August 29. After Obama punted to Congress, French critics accused Hollande of timid deference to America, joining those who had faulted him earlier for proposing military action without a UN mandate.

As leaders on the Hill prepared for votes during the week of September 9, reaction to Obama's proposal by members and staff varied widely. On the Democratic side, a staffer said, "He knows we will vote it down. It's his way out." Representative Peter King (R-NY) demonstrated the ability of politicians to bend any development to their use. "President Obama is abdicating his responsibility as commander in chief," said King, who endorsed a strike, "and undermining the authority of future presidents." The situation on the Hill grew more complex on September 2 when John Kerry, Clinton's replacement as secretary of state, Hagel, and General Dempsey appeared at a Senate hearing. Many onlookers viewed Dempsey as a reluctant witness for military intervention. "He appeared to want to disappear behind his medals and ribbons," one reporter wrote. "He left little doubt that he was simply carrying out orders."

Savvy observers credited Obama with an attempt to pave the way on the Hill for looming funding votes in Congress. Stiffing Congress on Syria wouldn't help in anticipated votes on the budget and debt limits. *Washington Post* columnist Harold Myerson gave his view on Obama's move. "He's compelled Republicans to divert their attention from their concocted crises to an issue of actual substance." Further, Obama understood that the public had no interest in engaging Syria. A *Washington Post*–ABC News poll on September 2 showed that 59 percent of Americans opposed missile strikes. On other hand, though, only 36 percent approved of Obama's handling of the Syrian situation.

The administration launched a full court press, to use an Obama sports metaphor, to lobby Congress before the votes. The juggernaut American Israel Political Action Committee, AIPAC, lent its heft to the push for missile strikes. But on September 9, Kerry made an offhand remark in London when asked if Assad could avoid an attack. "Sure," Kerry said, "he could turn over every bit of his weapons to the international community within the next week, without delay. But, he isn't about to."

That *apparent* ad-lib resonated with the Russians, and Foreign Minister Lavrov quickly called Kerry with an offer to help broker a deal with Syria. On September 10, Obama spoke to the nation about the Russian offer, but said that he would not yet take military operations off the table. He did ask congressional leaders before the speech to postpone voting on a strike authorization. The Russians prevailed on Assad to accept the deal, and the Syrian president then blithely shrugged off the setback, describing the weapons as "obsolete." But the whole thing seemed a little too pat at the time, and cynics began to question the spontaneity of the Kerry-Lavrov connection.

Members of Congress didn't dwell excessively on the origins of the Kerry initiative because they were off the hook. Senator Rob Portman (R-OH) declared, "Everybody was sort of breathing a sigh of relief." That didn't stop his colleague, Jeff Sessions (R-AL), from spinning the moment by saying that Congress had forced Obama's retreat. "Congress," he said, "served its role in backing him off." The administration volleyed back with its own spin. Deputy national security adviser Tiny Blinken noted the deal arose from "the threat of US action and the pressure that the president is exerting."

On September 27, the UN Security Council unanimously approved a resolution requiring Syria to give up its chemical weapons. The Organization for the Prohibition of Chemical Weapons began collecting the munitions soon afterward, and in late June 2014 announced that all of Syria's declared chemical weapons, 1,300 tons of materials, had been removed from the country. However, news reports in September 2014 suggested that Syria might be hiding undeclared weapons and using chlorine in "barrel bombs" dropped by Syrian aircraft on civilians. Chlorine is not banned by the chemical weapons treaty, but weaponizing it constitutes a war crime.

There appears to have been more than met the eye in the "last minute" US-Russia deal on Syrian chemical weapons. Retired State department official, Ambassador Tom Pickering, whose extraordinary diplomatic career intersected with many of this book's crises, agrees. "I have reason to believe that we had been having significant talks with the Russians before Kerry's remarks," he told me during the March 2014 Russia-Crimea crisis. "I have to think that Russian president Vladimir Putin made the move to avoid a US attack, partly to save Assad in the immediate period, and partly it was like Crimea in reverse—there was nothing he could do against us to offset the effects of that attack."

Supporting Pickering's estimate was a *Washington Post* report in September 2013. According to correspondent Walter Pincus, Obama and Putin had discussed a possible solution to the Syrian chemical weapons issue in June 2012. In May of the following year, Kerry and Lavrov had begun a series of talks on Assad's relinquishing chemical weapon stockpiles. "The two agreed that Russian and US technical experts should begin quietly meeting on details," Pincus wrote, "though there was little expectation that a program would be immediately needed."

On the broader Syrian front, President Obama requested Congress in June 2014 to authorize additional resources to train and equip Syrian opposition forces. Three months later, Obama sought even more arms and training for Syrian rebels as part of his announced strategy to degrade and destroy the Islamic State. In a major speech to the nation on September 10, Obama announced his strategy to combat the radical organization. The central facet of the plan would be sustained airstrikes against Islamic State targets, both in Iraq and Syria. Additionally, the president began gathering European and Mideast countries to participate in either air-to-ground combat operations or supporting roles, such as Saudi Arabia's training of Syrian rebels. Obama's plan was a marked shift from his uninspiring statement a week earlier about confronting the Islamic State threat: "We don't have a strategy yet." There is great value in thinking through action alternatives and gathering allies before announcing crisis decisions, but the public expects a more confidence-inspiring way for a president to explain a delay in formulating a plan.

Assessment

Political opponents of President Obama, who were eager to exploit to their advantage the successive developments of the Arab Spring, leaped to immediate judgments of his handling of the crises. Simultaneously, the president's staff managed the administration's counter-message in real time. Thoughtful historians will likely wait a while to judge Obama's crisis decision making, especially because what was known through 2014 about Obama's deliberations was largely doled out by his spinmeisters. To be fair, though, that was the case in all of the White House crises addressed in this book.

But there are facets of Obama's crisis management that are observable and understandable. He seems to have reacted to unforeseen incidents with a pragmatic, case-by-case approach, in which he favored incremental actions. He eschewed a one-size-fits-all doctrine, knowing that the idealism of the zero-sum, bipolar Cold War era doesn't work well today. Bush 43's invasion of Iraq became the sine qua non in Obama's mind about the limits of idealism, to say nothing about his negative attitude toward starting another war. Obama must have prompted Ben Rhodes's pronouncement: "In the foreign policy establishment, to be an idealist you have to be for military intervention."

President Obama attempted to balance human rights idealism and national interests in the first three important Arab Spring uprisings. He did little as Tunisians ejected the corrupt Ben Ali regime, but tilted toward democracy in Egypt despite long-standing US ties to Mubarak. In Bahrain, Obama steered an opposite course by choosing continued strong relations with Saudi Arabia over Bahraini democracy.

In the Libyan civil war, Obama chose incremental actions as he attempted to thread the decision-making needle while buffeted by humanitarian demands, adviser disagreements, omnipresent domestic politics pressures, and conflicting national interests. In the short term, he succeeded, but as time passed, post-Qadhafi Libya has descended into chaos. In August 2014, President Obama said he regretted not implementing an on-the-ground operation to help the country establish a workable democracy. "So that's a lesson," he said on August 8, "that I now apply every time I ask the question, 'Should we intervene, militarily? Do we have an answer [for] the day after?'"

In the Syrian chemical weapons confrontation, Obama's actions during the thirteen months from his August 2012 drawing of the red line to the Kerry-Lavrov deal form a classic example of a president cautiously handling a crisis—muddling through in the best sense of the phrase. He faced every factor that had historically impeded bold and decisive action by his predecessors since 1950. The most significant forces acting on Obama included a lack of public support for starting another war on top of Iraq and Afghanistan, the military's skepticism of "surgical" or limited operations, division among his advisers on the least damaging alternatives, domestic political opponents' attempts to make him fail, and the enormous consequences of a miscalculation. On top of all this, Obama would have to enforce his red line or lose credibility in his effort to do the same if Iran were to produce weapons from its nuclear program. Last, President Obama rightly saw the Syrian civil war, and the chemical weapons facet of it, as a situation in which America had little influence. Bold US military action would likely have had little effect but could still set the Mideast afire, or, according to Zbigniew Brzezinski, at least risk "a large-scale disaster for the United States."

As Obama searched for doable options, he should have better explained how the Tomahawk missiles he had held at the ready would have changed Assad's behavior. Moreover, he gave the appearance of dithering, especially to his GOP opponents. But presidents don't dither; they just never get a win-win, free-lunch option. They appear to vacillate as they privately search for least-evil choices while armchair quarterbacks shout, "Do something!" from the sidelines.

Opportunistic critics may have exaggerated the "losing credibility" argument about the red line. Columnist Tom Friedman noted in September 2013 that Obama's credibility shouldn't have been an issue when the major accelerant in the Syrian civil war is the Sunni-Shiite fight that started in the seventh century AD. *The New Yorker's* Amy Davidson also downplayed the credibility angle. "The political price he'll pay," Davidson wrote at the time, "for backing away from something that a majority of the House and the Senate, his own party, the American people, and many of our allies never wanted may just be overstated."

Both President Obama and former Secretary Clinton reflected in August 2014 on the issue of supporting Syrian rebels since 2011. Obama had resisted supporting the Syrian rebels early in their insurrection, and authorized only a modest CIA training and arms supply effort in April 2013 in response to the growing chemical weapons problem. Obama restated the complexity of the matter on August 8, 2014, saying that arming secular Syrian rebels has "always been a fantasy." Non-jihadists armed with American weapons, he said, doing battle with "not only a well-armed state but also a well-armed state backed by Russia, backed by Iran, a battle-hardened Hezbollah, that was never in the cards."

Former secretary of state Clinton, on the other hand, intimated that the rise of Islamist State, or ISIS, might have been connected to US caution in supporting the Syrian rebels. At one point in an August 10 interview with Jeffrey Goldberg of the *Atlantic*, he asked her if ISIS might be a lesser threat now if the United States had aided moderate Syrian rebels. "Well, I don't know the answer to that," Clinton responded. "I know that the failure to help build up a credible fighting force of the people who were the originators of the protests against Assad—there were Islamists, there were secularists, there was everything in the middle—the failure to do that left a big vacuum, which the jihadists have now filled." That comment prompted the *Atlantic* to title the interview, "Hillary Clinton: 'Failure' to Help Syrian Rebels Led to the Rise of ISIS." That allowed second- and third-party media outlets to hype a Obama-Clinton rift.

Clinton hedged a bit later in the Goldberg interview, but that was lost in the resulting media buzz. She recounted how she and former US ambassador to Syria Robert Ford had argued for supporting selected Syrian opposition forces. But she then added, "I can't sit here today and say that if we had done what I recommended, and what Robert Ford recommended, that we'd be in a demonstrably different place." That statement places her closer to Obama's pessimistic conclusion. Regardless of these carefully phrased statements, Clinton is positioning herself for the 2016 presidential election. Portraying herself as a more assertive and muscular foreign policy practitioner is a wholly expected move in the face of Obama's declining approval ratings and his caution in the face of multiple international challenges in the late summer of 2014: the Russia-Ukraine confrontation; Hamas-Israel hostilities; continuing Syrian bloodshed; fighting among ISIS, Iraq, and the Kurds; and other crises.

One last point on the difficulties Obama faced in the Syrian situation. Rod McDaniel, a former Navy and White House colleague of mine, is an experienced director of political-military war games. In his participation in or observation of crisis simulations involving American or coalition military intervention in the Syria civil war, no sensible options made any difference in the conflict. McDaniel, a former NSC executive secretary, said that participants often used the phrase "needs to burn itself out." In these games, the United States had no capability to "fix" the Syrian chaos. Further, feasible options to contain or mitigate Syrian chaos were few in number and limited in their likely effect. Syria appears to be a defining case of no good options for the American president.

AFTERWORD

Unanticipated international crises have bedeviled American presidents since the nation's birth, and the seventeen crises surveyed in this book are but a few recent and illustrative examples. While the speed of communications, technology for gaining situational awareness, and nature of global relationships have changed since 1950, some common threads have remained. The threat of large-scale use of weapons of mass destruction still hovers over some confrontations, just as governments around the globe continue to advance their national interests by grabbing more land or resources, seeking military parity or dominance, or repressing a domestic population. American presidents continue trying to protect the country's citizens at home and abroad and to uphold the nation's honor and credibility in the face of the pragmatic need to *do something*.

I firmly believe that each president in this survey, when awakened by the 3:00 a.m. phone call, committed himself to do the right thing. Doing it decisively was an option that must have entered each of their minds, because all were aware of public expectations for such action from presidents in a crisis. Some indeed reacted boldly, but few succeeded either in the short or long term. Others took a cautious approach, a decision that has yielded more successes than failures. A third group simply botched the management of the crisis. And a few presidents attempted to use an international crisis to divert attention from another problem, usually domestic in nature.

The graph included in the introduction broadly compares the results in these seventeen case studies. As I mentioned there, I aggregated conclusions from foreign affairs experts on each situation and then used the relative degree of success or failure to pick a spot on the two axes for each crisis. As we've seen, George H. W. Bush's handling of the 1990 Iraqi invasion of Kuwait appears to be the only crisis resolved through bold action. However, critics believe that that case deserves an asterisk and have portrayed the outcome as a triumph without victory. Bold reactions that yielded disappointing results, deadly or messy consequences, or long-term troubles include Truman during the Korean War, Eisenhower's response to 1956 Suez War, Reagan's deadly, seven-year tit-for-tat sequence with Libya's Muammar Qadhafi, Clinton and the 1998 embassy bombings, George W. Bush's wars in Afghanistan and Iraq, and Obama's Libyan intervention. Ford's bold response to the *Mayaguez* incident was an overreaction.

The category of successful crisis resolution through cautious and incremental steps includes Kennedy during the Cuban Missile Crisis, Johnson in both the 1967 Arab-Israeli War and USS *Pueblo* seizure, Nixon/Kissinger in the October War, Carter during most of the Iran hostage ordeal, Reagan in response to the 1985 TWA hijacking, and the narrow matter of Obama drawing a line on Syrian chemical weapons. A third category, that of a stumbling response, includes Eisenhower's management of the U-2 shootdown and Reagan's missteps after the 1983 bombing of the Marine barracks in Beirut. In all three groups of crises can be found the wag-the-dog type of manipulation—used notably by Nixon, Clinton, and Carter in the hostage rescue attempt.

The value of examining crises over a sixty-five-year span, a study unprecedented for the period of time it covers, lies in the identification of patterns of presidential actions, common problems, and considerations for the future. Newly elected presidents have made rookie mistakes, either through inexperience or from the hubris that comes with winning the presidential election. Future White House staffs, as well as the attending news media, may benefit from the takeaways from this survey.

Domestic political issues, whether they spring from election pressures or special interest groups, are always present in the White House during international crises, *no matter what anybody says to the contrary*. The most insidious manifestation of this truism is the wag-the-dog behavior that has reappeared regularly.

Finding the least risky, yet most effective response to a crisis is hard work. Virtually every available option has an untoward side, and most sideline quarterbacks either are unaware of such dangers or ignore them. Reading gratuitous and ill-informed advice from a president's political opponents reminds me of a lesson on decision making that a professor gave my class at the US Naval War College. He offered the two most reliable rules of thumb when choosing among action alternatives: "There's no such thing as a free lunch," and "It all depends." Truman, Eisenhower, Kennedy, and a few other presidents often fell back on a more rigid rule during crises, confront communist expansionism, but humanitarian disasters and the rise of non-state foreign actors and hybrids such as the Islamic State can require varying approaches to crisis management. Plus, there are never win-win options that come without some negative consequences in the near or long term. Those who have demanded President Obama create and employ a consistent "Obama Doctrine" in today's complex world call to mind the beginning of Emerson's famous maxim, "A foolish consistency is the hobgoblin of little minds."

Drawing red lines in the sand makes good sound bites but can limit presidential action later. The idea of an ultimatum came up during White House meetings in virtually every crisis, but the dangers of an unfulfilled threat or unwelcome, unintended consequences usually quieted that impulse, save for Kennedy and Obama. (Both erred in making unscripted remarks in election years.) Conversely, though, Kennedy ultimately learned that before taking the first step, he had to understand what the last step would yield. Obama acknowledged the first-step, last-step connection after Libya descended into chaos in the years following his intervention. Bush 43 appeared to have had no credible last step in mind when he invaded Iraq.

Preventing leaks preoccupied most presidents during the crisis meetings covered in this analysis. But the handmaidens to secrecy are insularity and groupthink. The loyalty and discretion of a small group of advisers can give way to sycophancy, just as the exclusion of military experts can create false expectations for military operations. Reasoned advocates of alternate actions are not always devils. White House civilians and Pentagon generals rarely understand the intricate challenges that the other group faces during a crisis.

Finally, there have been attempts by staff members in some administrations to anticipate crises. Obama asked his staff to think through possible solutions to problems involving humanitarian crises in countries important to US national interests. President Reagan authorized the creation of the Crisis Pre-Planning Group to develop contingency plans for likely international flare-ups. The staff of the Crisis Management Center supported the CPPG, which essentially was a deputies committee under the principals, by creating sets of alternative reactions to potential crises. (The CMC was a short-lived extension of the Situation Room that operated from 1983 to 1989 in the Old Executive Office Building.) The idea was that an administration could war-game a scenario—the communists take control of Nicaragua, or the Islamic State seizes part of Iraq—and try to determine what would likely happen if the United States were to become involved. Then later, just pull the folder off the shelf if such a scenario were to develop. The trouble with the idea, at least during the Reagan years, was that it depended on experts at State, Defense, and the CIA and NSC staff members to simulate the crisis and fashion a set of options to deal with it. But they were always too busy with the daily grind to participate routinely, and the principal national security advisers never would have had time even to listen to the gaming results. Any administration that sought to develop this sort of crisis management preplanning would likely find the same pressures working against it. As a result, when something did happen, national security teams would rely on what they did the last time, trust their instincts, or cautiously muddle through.

NOTES

page	**Introduction**
xvii	**This is a national disgrace**: Lou Cannon, "Reagan: Action to Rescue Hostages 'Long overdue,'" *Washington Post*, May 1, 1980.
xvii	**I'm not a jingo thinking about**: Lou Cannon, "Reagan Rejects Military Action to Free Iran Hostages," *Washington Post*, March 28, 1980.
xviii	**Reagan the Gunslinger**: Lou Cannon, "What Happened to Reagan the Gunslinger?" *Washington Post*, July 7, 1985.
xviii	**Everybody wants to be a striding titan**: David Brooks, "Wise Muddling Through," *New York Times*, July 31, 2009.
xx	**Well, I think in the first place**: http://www.presidency.ucsb.edu/ws/?pid=9060.
xx	**The group locks itself in; galloping consensus**: James David Barber, *Politics by Humans* (Durham, NC: Duke University Press, 1988), 20–21.
xx	**weed out ruthlessly**: George E. Reedy, *The Twilight of the Presidency* (New York: New American Library, 1970).
xxi	**presidential rite of passage**: R. W. Apple, "War: Bush's Presidential Rite of Passage," *New York Times*, December 21, 1989.
xxi	**Situations do not create crises**: Denise Bostdorff, *The Presidency and the Rhetoric of Foreign Crisis* (Columbia: University of South Carolina Press, 1994), 9.
xxii	**wanton misdeed**: "Text of President's Statement," *Washington Post*, September 2, 1983.
xxii	**attack on all citizens**: "Transcript of President Reagan's News Conference," *Washington Post*, June 19, 1985.

xxii **clandestine, reckless, and provocative**: Haynes Johnson, "'62 Crisis with Russia Differed from Today's, *Washington Post*, May 9, 1972.

xxii **We're kind of boxed in**: David Sanger, "US Shifting Its Warning on Syria's Chemical Arms," *New York Times*, December 7, 2012.

xxii **The president meeting his advisers**: Michael K. Bohn, *Nerve Center: Inside the White House Situation Room* (Washington: Brassey's, Inc., 2003), 116.

xxiii **I believe that the fact that the president meets**: Ibid.

xxiii **After President Nixon's fall in the Watergate**: Charlie Cook, "What Will We Expect of the Next President?" *National Journal*, February 6, 1999.

xxiv **Our definitions of what**: Mark Rozell, interview with author, April 2014.

xxiv **Wise muddling through**: Brooks, "Wise Muddling Through," July 31, 2009.

xxv **That may not always be sexy**: Juliet Eilperin, "Obama Lays Out His Foreign Policy Doctrine," *Washington Post*, April 29, 2014.

xxv **hedging your bets**: David Ignatius, "Life After Containment— Muddling Through," *Washington Post*, April 9, 1989.

xxv **The doctrinal approach**: http://fareedzakaria.com/2011/07/06/stop-searching-for-an-obama-doctrine/.

xxviii **Jesus Christ**: Bohn, *Nerve Center*, 74.

Chapter 1: Harry Truman

1 **Mr. President**: Robert J. Donovan, *Tumultuous Years* (New York: W. W. Norton, 1996), 191; David McCullough, *Truman* (New York: Simon & Schuster, 1992), 775.

2 **None of us got much sleep**: Margaret Truman, *Harry S. Truman* (New York: Avon, 1972), 455.

2 **IT WOULD APPEAR**: McCullough, *Truman*, 776.

2 **Dean, we've got to stop**: Alonzo Hamby, *Man of the People* (New York: Oxford University Press, 1995), 534.

2 **The boss is going to hit**: Donovan, *Tumultuous Years*, 196.

2 **Mrs. Truman was calm but serious**: Anthony Leviero, "Don't Be Alarmist, Truman Bids Press," *New York Times*, June 26, 1950.

3 **Communism was acting in Korea**: Harry S. Truman, *Memoirs: Years of Trial and Hope* (Garden City: Doubleday, 1956), 333.

3   **Malik's absence surprised US diplomats**: For a full analysis of Stalin's motives, please see John Lewis Gaddis, *We Now Know* (New York: Oxford University Press, 1997), 76.

3   **By God, I'm going**: Donovan, *Tumultuous Years*, 197.

4   **darkening; We must draw the line; Russia is not yet**: Dean Acheson, *Present at the Creation* (New York: W. W. Norton, 1969), 456. Omar N. Bradley, *A General's Life* (New York: Simon & Schuster, 1983), 535–36. Memorandum of Conversation, "Korean Situation," June 25, 1950, http://www.trumanlibrary.org/whistlestop/study_collections/korea/large/documents/pdfs/ki-12-1.pdf#zoom=100.

4   **Can we knock out their bases; It might take some time**: Ibid.

5   **Instructions to General MacArthur**: Bradley, 536.

5   **stuffed shirt**: Margaret Truman, *Harry S. Truman*, 260.

5   **Now let's all have; I have hoped and prayed**: John D. Hickerson oral history, http://www.trumanlibrary.org/oralhist/hickrson.htm.

6   **What is striking**: Gaddis, *We Now Know*, 70.

6   **The West had stymied communist expansion**: For a detail analysis of Stalin's reasoning, please see Vladislav M. Zubok, *A Failed Empire* (Chapel Hill: University of North Carolina Press, 2007), 79–80.

7   **America would never participate**: Gaddis, *We Now Know*, 74.

7   **If you should get kicked**: Ibid.

7   **Tanks entering the capital**: Harry Truman, *Memoirs*, 337.

8   **Let's wait a few days**: Bradley, *A General's Life*, 536.

8   **the bungling and inconsistent**: Robert C. Albright, "Taft Sees Acheson Reversed and Calls for Resignation," *Washington Post*, June 29, 1950.

8   **Mr. President, everybody is asking; Yes. That is exactly what**: http://teachingamericanhistory.org/library/document/the-presidents-news-conference-of-june-29-1950/.

8   **He was not good in the fast**: Acheson, *Present at the Creation*, 192.

9   **Push the North Koreans back**: Harry Truman, *Memoirs*, 341.

9   **Frank Pace called at**: http://www.trumanlibrary.org/exhibit_documents/index.php?tldate=1950-06-30&groupid=3433&pagenumber=1&collectionid=korea.

9   **The only assurance of holding**: Douglas MacArthur, *Reminiscences* (New York: McGraw-Hill, 1964), 334.

9   **I just had to act**: Hamby, *Man of the People*, 538.

10   **saw eye-to-eye on Formosa**: Harry Truman, *Memoirs*, 354.

10   **Nothing could be more fallacious**: Bradley, *A General's Life*, 551.

10   **weasel out of the task**: Ibid.

11   **close to the last straw**: Margaret Truman, *Harry S. Truman*, 479–80.

11   **Louis Johnson was causing; When he came in**: George M. Elsey, *An Unplanned Life* (Columbia: University of Missouri Press, 2005), 195.

11   **extend his operations north**: Harry Truman, *Memoirs*, 359.

13   **no threat by Russian or Chinese**: Donovan, *Tumultuous Years*, 542.

13   **We want you to feel**: Harry Truman, *Memoirs*, 360.

13   **all appropriate steps**: Richard E. Neustadt, *Presidential Power and the Modern Presidents* (New York: Free Press, 1990), 103.

13   **continue the action as long**: Ibid., 115.

13   **They may get so dizzy**: Gaddis, *We Now Know*, 78.

13   **The situation of our Korean; Should we fear this**: Ibid., 79.

14   **80,000 soldiers of the Chinese Fourth Field Army**: http://www.history.army.mil/books/PD-C-13.HTM.

14   **He was itching to overrun**: Elsey, An Unplanned Life, 197.

14   **I begged to be excused**: Acheson, *Present at the Creation*, 456.

14   **What are the chances**: Harry Truman, *Memoirs*, 366; Bradley, *A General's Life*, 575.

15   **Hell no! I want to get out**: Dean Rusk, *As I Saw It*, as told to Richard Rusk (New York: W. W. Norton, 1990), 169.

15   **The San Francisco report**: Elsey, *An Unplanned Life*, 199.

15   **The Korean War only temporarily restored**: Richard Ned Lebow, *Between Peace and War* (Baltimore, MD: Johns Hopkins University Press, 1981), 174.

16   **The pressures on the administration**: Ibid., 175.

17   **Unfortunately, we reached drastically wrong**: Bradley, *A General's Life*, 594.

17   **To lure a big fish**: Gaddis, *We Now Know*, 81.

17   **our last real chance to stop MacArthur's proposed**: Bradley, *A General's Life*, 596.

18   **If this operation is successful**: Donovan, *Tumultuous Years*, 303.

18   **We face an entirely new war**: Ibid., 305.

18   **We've got a terrific situation**: John Hersey, "Profiles: Mr. President," *The New Yorker*, April 14, 1951. All of the quotes in this segment are from this article.

19   **get out with honor**: Memorandum of Conversation, NSC Meeting November 28, 1950. http://www.trumanlibrary.org/whistlestop/study_collections/koreanwar/documents/index.php?documentdate=1950-11-28&documentid=ki-15-12&pagenumber=1.

19   **Mr. President, will the United Nations**: John Hersey, "The Wayward Press," *The New Yorker*, December 16, 1950, 78–90. All of the dialogue in this segment is from this article. See also http://trumanlibrary.org/publicpapers/viewpapers.php?pid=985.

20   **WA10A WASHINGTON NOV 30**: Hersey, "The Wayward Press," 87.

20   **correct a state of affairs; You can relieve**: Matthew Ridgway, *The Korean War* (New York: Da Capo, 1967), 62.

22   **the psychological drive for consensus**: Irving Janis, *Groupthink* (Boston: Houghton Mifflin, 1982), back cover.

22   **the intoxication of success**: Janis, *Groupthink*, 48.

22   **By God, I'm going**: Donovan, *Tumultuous Years*, 197.

23   **No one went to Truman**: Neustadt, *Presidential Power*, 121.

23   **We were all deeply apprehensive**: Acheson, *Present at the Creation*, 468.

Chapter 2: Dwight Eisenhower

24   **FLASH-FLASH-FLASH**: William M. Rountree, oral history, The Association for Diplomatic Studies and Training Foreign Affairs Oral History Project, Library of Congress.

24   **All right Foster, you tell 'em**: Donald Neff, *Warriors at Suez* (New York: Linden Press, 1981), 365.

25   **It is far more serious than that**: Ibid., 366. See also http://history.state.gov/historicaldocuments/frus1955-57v16/d411. All quotations in this segment are from these sources.

25   **any of these states was preparing**: Dean Acheson, *Present at the Creation* (New York: W. W. Norton, 1969), 396.

26   **unabashed believer in conciliation and compromise**: Emmet John Hughes, *The Ordeal of Power* (New York: Dell, 1963), 311.

26   **With many of our citizens**: Dwight D. Eisenhower, *Waging Peace: 1956–1961* (Garden City: Doubleday, 1965), 74.

27   **Political scientists Edward Drachman and Alan Shank**: Edward R. Drachman and Alan Shank, *Presidents and Foreign Policy* (Albany: State University of New York Press, 1997), 55-60.

29 **a strategy of delay, cooling off**: Ibid., 62

30 **I just can't figure out what**: Hughes, *The Ordeal of Power*, 185–86. All dialogue from Hughes.

31 **His face drawn, eyes heavy**: Hughes, *The Ordeal of Power*, 187.

31 **There's the danger of our being drawn**: http://history.state.gov/historicaldocuments/frus1955-57v16/d419. See also Neff, *Warriors at Suez*, 372f, and David A. Nichols, *Eisenhower 1956* (New York: Simon & Schuster, 2011), 205.

32 **assume temporary control of the canal**: http://history.state.gov/historicaldocuments/frus1955-57v16/d432.

32 **deep concern at the prospect**: Neff, *Warriors at Suez*, 374.

32 **They may be planning**: http://history.state.gov/historicaldocuments/frus1955-57v16/d435. See also Neff, *Warriors at Suez*, 375.

32 **Well it looks as if**: John S. D. Eisenhower, *Strictly Personal* (Garden City: Doubleday, 1974), 189.

33 **would do everything we can**: Nichols, *Eisenhower 1956*, 210.

33 **at an absolute dead end**: Robert C. Albright, "Stevenson Says American Policy in Middle East Is at Dead End," *Washington Post*, November 2, 1956.

33 **has been a dismal and desperate**: Joseph and Stewart Alsop, "Matter of Fact: Failure of a Policy," *Washington Post*, October 31, 1956.

33 **We go past 6:00 still dictating; Boy, this is taking it right**: Hughes, *The Ordeal of Power*, 191–92.

34 **It seems to me that; I believe these powers**: http://history.state.gov/historicaldocuments/frus1955-57v16/d455. See also Neff, *Warriors at Suez*, 390f.

35 **Eisenhower wrote later**: Dwight Eisenhower, *Waging Peace*, 89.

35 **If this war is not stopped**: http://history.state.gov/historicaldocuments/frus1955-57v16/d505.

35 **We have to be positive and clear**: Hughes, *Ordeal of Power*, 194.

36 **In London, Eden was under attack**: Neff, *Warriors at Suez*, 409. See also Jean Edward Smith, *Eisenhower in War and Peace* (New York: Random House, 2012), 702.

36 **First of all, I can't tell you; If you don't get out of Port Said tomorrow**: Smith, *Eisenhower*, 704.

37 **I am quite certain that unless**: Nichols, *Eisenhower, 1956*, 263.

37   **Nikita Khrushchev, the first secretary**: Gaddis, *We Now Know*, 236; Nichols, *Eisenhower 1956*, 263; Zubok, *A Failed Empire*, 191; and Anthony Nutting, *No End of a Lesson: The Story of Suez* (London: Constable, 1967), 144.

38   **Over the longer term, however**: Please see Drachman and Shank, *Presidents and Foreign Policy*, 75–80 for details on the impact of the war on all parties.

39   **He understood the principle**: Richard A. Melanson and David Mayers, *Reevaluating Eisenhower* (Urbana: University of Illinois Press, 1987), 28.

39   **In retrospect, I believe that**: Richard Nixon, *The Memoirs of Richard Nixon* (New York: Grosset & Dunlap, 1978), 179.

39   **major foreign policy mistake**: Keith Kyle, *Suez* (New York: St. Martin's Press, 1991), 612, n1; Peter Rodman, *Presidential Command* (New York: Alfred Knopf, 2009), 298, n28.

39   **Either way, we'll back 'em up**: Rodman, *Presidential Command*, 28.

39   **Why didn't you go through**: Herbert S. Parmet, *Eisenhower and the American Crusades* (New York: Macmillan, 1972), 487.

40   **Minister of Defense Marshal Malinovsky reporting**: Nikita Khrushchev, *Khrushchev Remembers* (Boston: Little, Brown, 1974), 443.

41   **Jesus, I wonder what's**: Michael R. Beschloss, *Mayday* (New York: Harper & Row, 1986), 42.

42   **Mr. President**: Dwight Eisenhower, *Waging Peace*, 543.

43   **Shame to the aggressor**: Beschloss, *Mayday*, 44.

43   **At the direction of the president**: Ibid., 49.

43   **It is worth a try; apprehension over a surprise attack**: Ibid., 248.

43   **This is a sad and perplexed capital**: James Reston, "Flights Stopped," *New York Times*, May 9, 1960.

43   **Well, we're just going to have to take**: Beschloss, *Mayday*, 255. See also George B. Kistiakowsky, *A Scientist at the White House* (Cambridge: Harvard University Press, 1976), 321.

44   **No one wants another Pearl Harbor**: "Transcript of President's News Conference," *Washington Post*, May 12, 1960.

44   **Eisenhower's stand canceled any opportunity**: Khrushchev, *Khrushchev Remembers*, 448.

44   **The Russians are trying to get us to grovel**: Beschloss, *Mayday*, 248–49.

45   **The acoustics in this room; I have been overflown; Bog minya vidit**: Vernon A. Walters, *Silent Missions* (Garden City: Doubleday, 1978), 344.

45   **Do not let K interrupt you**: Beschloss, *Mayday*, 286.

46   **That was no way to deal**: William Taubman, *Khrushchev* (New York: W. W. Norton, 2003), 468.

46   **The big error**: Dwight Eisenhower, *Waging Peace*, 558.

47   **the lie we told about the U-2**: Evan Thomas, *Ike's Bluff* (New York: Little, Brown, 2012), 386.

Chapter 3: John Kennedy

49   **Let me just say a little**: Ernest R. May and Philip D. Zelikow, ed., *The Kennedy Tapes* (Cambridge: Harvard University Press, 1997), 175; Sheldon M. Stern, *Averting 'The Final Failure'* (Stanford, CA: Stanford University Press, 2003), 121.

49   **We don't have any choice; I don't think they're going**: Stern, *Averting*, 123.

50   **I think that a blockade**: Ibid., 126. See also Michael Dobbs, *One Minute to Midnight* (New York: Alfred Knopf, 2008), 22.

50   **These brass hats have one**: Kenneth P. O'Donnell and David F. Powers, with Joe McCarthy, *"Johnny, We Hardly Knew Ye"* (Boston: Little, Brown, 1972), 318.

50   **the most dangerous moment**: Arthur Schlesinger, "Bush's Thousand Days, *Washington Post*, April 24, 2006.

52   **Eisenhower Calls President**: Tom Wicker, "Eisenhower Calls President Weak on Foreign Policy," *New York Times*, October 16, 1962.

52   **range of 1,292 nautical miles**: Dobbs, *One Minute*, 282.

52   **He can't do this to me**: Barbara Leaming, *Jack Kennedy* (New York: W. W. Norton, 2006), 401.

52   **Supplies**: Ibid., 392.

53   **Were it to be otherwise**: Ibid., 395. See also Dobbs, *One Minute*, 16.

53   **The air strike advocates; There was real concern**: Richard Lebow and Janice Stein, *We All Lost the Cold War* (Princeton, NJ: Princeton University Press, 1994), 107.

53   **Put it back in the box**: Aleksandr Fursenko and Timothy Naftali, *One Hell of a Gamble* (New York: W. W. Norton, 1997), 204.

53   **do-nothing**: "Two More Senators Urge Intervention to Defeat Castro, *Washington Post*, September 3, 1962.

54   **Rash talk is cheap; an offensive military base**: "Transcript of President Kennedy's News Conference, *Washington Post*, September 14, 1962.

54   **I woulda been impeached**: Stern, *Averting*, 204.

54   **I don't think there is a**: http://history.state.gov/historicaldocuments/frus1961-63v11/d21.

55   **On October 17, there were**: The Soviet order of battle is drawn from Raymond L. Garthoff, *Reflections on the Cuban Missile Crisis* (Washington, DC: The Brookings Institution, 1989), 18.

55   **The missile deployment plan**: Garthoff, *Reflections*, 36–40; http://www.wilsoncenter.org/sites/default/files/CWIHP_Bulletin_14-15.pdf.

55   **I was dying to confront him**: O'Donnell, *"Johnny,"* 319.

55   **that lying bastard**: Stern, *Averting*, 117.

56   **Khrushchev's aim was to prevent**: For details on Khrushchev's motives, please see Lebow and Stein, *We All Lost the Cold War*, 19f.

56   **political explosion**: Bruce J. Allyn, James G. Blight, and David A. Welch, "Essence of Revision: Moscow, Havana, and the Cuban Missile Crisis," *International Security*, vol. 14, no. 3 (Winter, 1989–1990), 148.

56   **was a probe, a test**: Bostdorff, *Presidency*, 53.

57   **Gentlemen, today we're going**: Stern, *Averting*, 133.

57   **I shall never forget that scene**: Edward A. McDermott, unpublished personal journal, 151.

57   **We will have to make a deal**: Arthur Schlesinger, *Robert Kennedy and His Times* (New York: Houghton Mifflin Harcourt, 2012), 516.

57   **All twelve in the room sat; I know each of you is hoping I didn't**: McDermott journal, 151.

58   **Everybody was given a specific**: Edward A. McDermott oral history, Kennedy Library, family copy, 45.

59   **We're either a world-class power**: Dobbs, *One Minute*, 41.

59   **We do think this first step**: May, *Kennedy Tapes*, 258.

59   **Dobrynin aged at least ten years**: Rusk, *As I Saw It*, 235.

59   **rub it in**: Garthoff, *Reflections*, 61–62.

59   **probably the most dramatic**: Bostdorff, *Presidency*, 40.

59   **I call upon Chairman Khrushchev**: Haynes Johnson, "'62 Crisis with Russia Differed From Today's," *Washington Post*, May 9, 1972.

59   **More so than any other president**: Bostdorff, *Presidency*, 46.

60   **If Soviet missiles in Cuba were attacked**: Sergei Khrushchev, *Nikita Khrushchev* (University Park: Pennsylvania State University, 2000), 582.

60   **Khrushchev responded directly**: Lebow, *We All Lost*, 112f.

61   **We've just received information; We're eyeball to eyeball**: Dobbs, *One Minute*, 86–88; O'Donnell, et. al., *"Johnny,"* 332.

61   **I repeat my regret that these events**: Laurence Chang and Peter Kornbluh, eds., *The Cuban Missile Crisis* (New York: The New Press, 1998) 183.

62   **unofficial**: Max Frankel, "Blockade Starts," *New York Times*, October 25, 1962.

62   **If she's not important enough to save**: McDermott journal, 150; "Aiming Missiles, and Dodging Them," *New York Times*, August 13, 1980.

62   **While you're safe with the president**, O'Donnell, et al., *"Johnny,"* 324.

62   **That's OK**: "A Near Tragedy of Errors," *Time*, February 13, 1989.

63   **Well, our quarantine itself**: May, *Kennedy Tapes*, 464.

63   **Bobby Kennedy and Dobrynin held a significant meeting**: Garthoff, *Reflections*, 87; James Blight, Bruce Allyn, and David Welch, *Cuba on the Brink* (Lanham: Rowman & Littlefield, 2002), 283.

63   **I had a slight feeling of optimism**: Robert F. Kennedy, *Thirteen Days* (New York: W. W. Norton, 1971), 69.

64   **It was like a dose of cold water**: James Blight and David Welch, *On the Brink* (New York: Noonday Press, 1990), 162.

64   **Most early analysis of the two letters was wrong**: Lebow, *We All Lost*, 133.

64   **Haggle**: McGeorge Bundy, *Danger and Survival* (New York: Random House, 1988), 439–40.

64   **absolutely forbidding**: Blight, *Cuba on the Brink*, 353; http://www.wilsoncenter.org/sites/default/files/CWIHP_Bulletin_14-15.pdf.

65   **A Soviet SA-2 surface-to-air missile**: Dobbs, *One Minute*, 237.

65   **It isn't the first step**: Kennedy, *Thirteen Days*, 74.

65   **We can't very well invade Cuba**: Stern, *Averting*, 367.

65   **He and Kennedy devised a back-up plan**: Bundy, *Danger and Survival*, 435; Lebow, *We All Lost*, 127.

66   **In 1989, Dobrynin verified his conversation with Bobby**: Allyn, "Essence of Revision," 163; Lebow, *We All Lost*, 11.

66 **The plane violating our airspace; Today one general had decided**: Sergei Khrushchev, *Khrushchev*, 608, 609.

66 **I feel like a new man**: O'Donnell, *"Johnny,"* 341.

67 **We've been had; It's the greatest defeat in our history**: Stern, *Averting*, 385.

67 **the bellicose premier of**: "The Backdown," *Time*, November 2, 1962.

67 **that bludgeon consisted of more**: Garthoff, *Reflections*, 73.

68 **Both leaders made concessions**: Lebow, *We All Lost*, 110–111.

68 **Adlai wanted a Munich**: Stewart Alsop and Charles Bartlett, "In Time of Crisis," *Saturday Evening Post*, December 18, 1962, 20. See also Dobbs, *One Minute*, 338, regarding Khrushchev's letter.

68 **We misled our colleagues**: Bundy, *Danger and Survival*, 434.

68 **The Americans will make a fuss**: Max Frankel, *High Noon in the Cold War* (New York: Ballantine, 2004), 11.

69 **Compromise is not a word**: Leslie Gelb, "The Myth That Screwed Up 50 Years of U.S. Foreign Policy," *Foreign Policy*, October 8, 2012. http://www.foreignpolicy.com/articles/2012/10/08/the_lie_that_ screwed_up_50_years_of_us_foreign_policy.

Chapter 4: Lyndon Johnson

70 **Mr. Secretary, Soviet Prime Minister Kosygin**: Robert McNamara, interview with author, 2002; See also McNamara oral history at the Johnson Library, http://www.lbjlibrary.net/assets/documents/archives/ oral_histories/mcnamara_r/McNamara-SP1.PDF, and http://www. gwu.edu/~nsarchiv/coldwar/interviews/episode-17/mcnamara2.html. The whole conversation is from these three sources.

71 **They look upon anything less**: Rusk, *As I Saw It*, 381.

74 **All to create an alibi**: Tom Segev, *1967: Israel, the War, and the Year That Transformed the Middle East* (New York: Metropolitan Books, 2007), 256–57.

74 **We think it is probably a gambit**: http://history.state.gov/ historicaldocuments/frus1964-68v19/d61.

74 **Around sundown I'm going**: Michael Oren, *Six Days of War* (New York: Oxford University Press, 2002), 112–113. All dialogue in this segment is from this source.

74 **Do you have the will and determination**: Ibid., 114.

75 **will support a plan to use**: Ibid., 115.

75   **If [Egypt] attacks, you will**: Lyndon Baines Johnson, *The Vantage Point* (New York: Holt, Rinehart and Winston, 1971), 293.

75   **If your cabinet decides**: Oren, *Six Days*, 115; William Quandt, *Decade of Decisions* (Berkeley: University of California Press, 1977), 53.

75   **I don't think it's our business**: Oren, *Six Days*, 153.

75   **Meir, if you crush Nasser**: William Quandt, author interview, July 2014.

75   **The United States won't go into mourning**: Segev, *1967*, 332.

76   **If they had not done so**: William Quandt, *Peace Process* (Washington, DC: Brookings Institution Press, 2005), 39.

76   **Rusk will fiddle while Israel**, Ibid., 40.

76   **I understand that if you act alone**: Oren, *Six Days*, 153.

76   **war of choice; We decided to attack him**: John Mearsheimer and Stephen Walt, *The Israel Lobby and US Foreign Policy* (New York: Farrar, Straus and Giroux, 2007), 85.

77   **We hope that the Government of the United States**: http://history. state.gov/historicaldocuments/frus1964-68v19/d156.

77   **Comrade Kosygin**: Memorandum of conversation between Llewellyn Thompson and Nathaniel Davis; Johnson Library, NSC Histories, Middle East Crisis, vol. 7, appendix G.

77   **We feel it is very important**: http://history.state.gov/historical documents/frus1964-68v19/d157.

77   **making fun of them in some way**: Thompson and Davis MemCon.

78   **We have tried to steer an even-handed**: http://history.state.gov/ historicaldocuments/frus1964-68v19/d164.

78   **McCloskey's statement was killing**: Ibid.

79   **It would neutralize the 'neutrality' statement**: http://history.state. gov/historicaldocuments/frus1964-68v19/d198.

79   **You Zionist dupe**: Joseph Califano, *The Triumph & Tragedy of Lyndon Johnson* (New York: Simon & Schuster, 1991), 205.

79   **Johnson was much loved and greatly hated**: http://www.pbs.org/ newshour/character/essays/johnson.html.

79   **I didn't believe them**: Rusk, *As I Saw It*, 388.

80   **Critics of Israel's claim of an accident**: See an account by a naval officer aboard *Liberty*, James Ennes, Jr., *Assault on the Liberty* (New York: Ivy Books, 1979).

80   **On the morning of June 10**: Johnson, *The Vantage Point*, 301.

81 **went silent as abruptly**: Richard Helms, *A Look Over My Shoulder* (New York: Random House, 2003), 302. See also Johnson, *Vantage Point*, 301–03; and http://history.state.gov/historicaldocuments/frus1964-68v19/d243.

81 **Tension in the room**: Helms, *A Look*, 303.

81 **Where is the Sixth Fleet now**: Johnson, *Vantage Point*, 302. All dialogue in this segment is from this source.

81 **The Kremlin did not actually plan**: Anatoly Dobrynin, *In Confidence* (New York: Times Books, 1995), 161.

82 **President Johnson says it is time**: Nicholas deB. Katzenbach, *Some of It Was Fun* (New York: W. W. Norton, 2008), 252.

82 **The Hot Line proved a powerful tool**: Johnson, *Vantage Point*, 303.

82 **I'm glad the circuit**: Walt Rostow, interview with the author, 2002.

83 **watch closely, watch against escalation**: http://www.lbjlibrary.net/assets/documents/archives/oral_histories/mcgeorge_b/Bundy%20Dallek%202%20web.pdf.

83 **wishful thinking**: Quandt, *Decade of Decisions*, 55.

83 **cautious, at times ambiguous**: Ibid., 39.

84 **temporary and hasty**: Johnson, *Vantage Point*, 303.

84 **Same old shit isn't it**: Roger Morris, *Uncertain Greatness* (New York: Harper & Row, 1997), 12.

86 **COMPANY OUTSIDE**: http://www.nsa.gov/public_info/_files/cryptologic_histories/on_watch.pdf. All of the dialogue, signal flag messages, and radio transmissions in this segment are drawn from a declassified National Security Agency report posted at the preceding URL.

87 **Twelve F-105 Thunderchief fighter-bombers launched**: For details, see Mitchell Lerner, *The Pueblo Incident* (Lawrence: University Press of Kansas, 2002), 93–95.

88 **Hitting the North Koreans with US forces**: http://history.state.gov/historicaldocuments/frus1964-68v29p1/d213.

88 **unclear whether or not the ship**: Ibid.

89 **Were there no planes available**: http://history.state.gov/historicaldocuments/frus1964-68v29p1/d218.

89 **Why wasn't air cover sent**: "Hill Calls for Action to Recover Seized Ship," *Washington Post*, January 24, 1968.

90 **How do we get the ship; But this still leaves us**: http://history.state.gov/historicaldocuments/frus1964-68v29p1/d225.

90   **I think a measured show of force; The simple answer to that**: http://history.state.gov/historicaldocuments/frus1964-68v29p1/d226.

91   **often cried uncontrollably**: Robert Mann, *A Grand Delusion* (New York: Basic Books, 2001), 601.

91   **In that period**: Editorial, "Turnabout," *Washington Post*, February 5, 1968.

92   **still another failure**: Mitchell Lerner, *The Pueblo Incident*, 200.

92   **If you really make it clear beforehand**: Trevor Armbrister, *A Matter of Accountability* (Guilford: Lyons Press, 2004), 334.

93   **false hopes, self-generated illusions**: Robert Dallek, *Flawed Giant* (New York: Oxford University Press, 1998), 626.

94   **not only uninvolved in the planning but they**: http://www.wilsoncenter.org/publication/nkidp-e-dossier-no-5-new-romanian-evidence-the-blue-house-raid-and-the-uss-pueblo.

Chapter 5: Richard Nixon

96   **This is very important for our relationship**: Henry Kissinger, *Crisis* (New York: Simon & Schuster, 2003), 15.

96   **We may have a Middle East war; Okay**: All of the dialogue in this segment is drawn from Kissinger, *Crisis*, 27–28. See also Patrick Tyler, *A World of Trouble* (New York: Farrar Straus Giroux, 2009), 138.

97   **Deceptively calm; In the absence of acute crises**: Quandt, *Peace Process*, 103.

97   **I had to win back honor**: Anwar Sadat, *In Search of Identity: An Autobiography* (New York: Harper & Row), 1978. This quotation was drawn from a translation of the 1992 revised edition, page 232, which was translated by Lieutenant Colonel Jack Rives at the National War College in September 1992. See http://www.dtic.mil/dtic/tr/fulltext/u2/a440784.pdf.

98   **We could all wake up one day**: Henry Kissinger, *Years of Upheaval* (Boston: Little, Brown, 1982), 463.

99   **Don't ever preempt!**: Marvin Kalb and Bernard Kalb, *Kissinger* (Boston: Little, Brown, 1974), 460.

99   **It would be an act of folly**: Quandt, *Peace Process*, 105.

100   **If he returns early**: Kissinger, *Crisis*, 51.

100   **I would urge you to keep any**: Tyler, *A World*, 139. See also Walter Isaacson, *Kissinger* (New York: Simon & Schuster, 1992), 514.

100 **He preferred to let his advisers**: Alexander Haig interview with author, 2002.

100 **He basically hated people**: Alistair Horne, *Kissinger: 1973, the Crucial Year* (New York: Simon & Schuster Paperbacks, 2009), 25.

100 **Our major problems are**: http://history.state.gov/historicaldocuments/ frus1969-76v25/d112.

101 **One thing that we have to have**: Kissinger, *Crisis*, 89.

101 **I hope to God this is not a week**: Ibid., 124.

102 **The best result**: Isaacson, *Kissinger*, 514.

103 **overtly niggardly and covertly forthcoming**: Elmo R. Zumwalt, Jr., *On Watch* (New York: Quadrangle, 1976), 434–35.

103 **I told him that I believed Israel**: Ibid., 435.

103 **national policy**: Leslie Gelb, "Kissinger and Schlesinger Deny Rift in October War," *New York Times*, June 23, 1974.

103 **shock troops**: Edward Sheehan, *The Arabs, Israelis, and Kissinger* (New York: Reader's Digest Press, 1976), 34.

105 **Senator J. William Fulbright called on Dobrynin**: Dobrynin, *In Confidence*, 291–92.

105 **The trick would be to get a cease-fire**: Quandt, *Peace Process*, 118.

106 **Dr. Kissinger speaks with my full authority**: http://history.state.gov/ historicaldocuments/frus1969-76v25/d217.

106 **I want you to know**: http://history.state.gov/historicaldocuments/ frus1969-76v25/d218.

106 **during the night while I'm flying**: http://www2.gwu.edu/~nsarchiv/ NSAEBB/NSAEBB98/. See also Matti Golan, *The Secret Conversations of Henry Kissinger* (New York: Quadrangle, 1976), 86.

107 **Brezhnev would never understand**: Robert Dallek, *Nixon and Kissinger* (New York: Harper Collins, 2007), 518.

107 **My honest opinion is that is a cheap stunt**: Kissinger, *Crisis*, 297.

107 **This is absolutely unacceptable**: http://history.state.gov/historical documents/frus1969-76v25/d241.

107 **We were now in a serious predicament**: Kissinger, *Years*, 571.

108 **Too much is at stake**: http://history.state.gov/historicaldocuments/ frus1969-76v25/d246.

108 **I will say it straight**: http://history.state.gov/historicaldocuments/ frus1969-76v25/d267.

108   **I just had a letter from Brezhnev; All right**: Kissinger, *Crisis*, 343–47; Kissinger, *Years*, 585.

109   **They decided to take several immediate actions**: http://history.state.gov/historicaldocuments/frus1969-76v25/d269.

110   **sent in Nixon's name**: Kissinger, *Crisis*, 353.

110   **a frightening story of Nixon**: Horne, *Kissinger*, 303.

110   **not part of the decision-making**: Isaacson, *Kissinger*, 532.

110   **I don't know; I can't rule it out**: Horne, *Kissinger*, 302.

111   **It is a symptom of what**: Carroll Kilpatrick, "President's Leadership Questioned," *Washington Post*, October 26, 1973.

111   **This town is seething with doubt**: James Reston, "A Crisis a Day," *Washington Post*, October 26, 1973.

111   **The Soviets subsided as soon as**: Kissinger, *Years of Upheaval*, 980.

111   **They portray a different Soviet reaction**: Lebow, 265–282.

112   **The American alert was for home consumption**: Lebow, *We All Lost*, 267.

112   **It is not reasonable to become**: Ibid., 279.

112   **Nixon is overreacting**: Victor Israelyan, *On the Battlefields of the Cold War* (University Park: Pennsylvania State University Press, 2003), 252.

112   **hostile act**: Dobrynin, *In Confidence*, 297.

112   **had made a mistake**: Ibid., 300.

112   **Our military efforts brought**: Sadat, *In Search of Identity*, 238.

113   **A president, any president, expects**: Stephen Ambrose, *Nixon: Ruin and Recovery 1973–1990* (New York: Simon & Schuster, 1991), 3:257.

114   **Any attempt to fine-tune the course**: Zumwalt, *On Watch*, 433.

Chapter 6: Gerald Ford

116   **MAYDAY, MAYDAY, MAYDAY**: Roy Rowan, *The Four Days of Mayaguez* (New York: W. W. Norton, 1975), 66.

117   **Would you go in there and bomb**: Ron Nessen, *Making the News, Taking the News* (Middletown, CT: Wesleyan University Press, 2011), 161.

117   **Well, we'll find out soon enough**: Rowan, *The Four Days*, 39.

117   **Speak English**: Ibid.

118   **At last report; At some point the United States**: http://history.state.gov/historicaldocuments/frus1969-76v10/d285. See also Gerald R. Ford, *A Time to Heal* (New York: Harper & Row, 1979), 276.

119 **He had a very straightforward**: William Doyle, *Inside the Oval Office* (New York: Kodansha International, 1999), 201.

121 **No worry**: Rowan, *The Four Days*, 95.

121 **We were all haunted**: Robert Hartman, *Palace Politics* (New York: McGraw-Hill, 1980), 326.

121 **I think the first two steps can be done**: http://history.state.gov/ historicaldocuments/frus1969-76v10/d291.

122 **The Pentagon dutifully assembled the forces**: Henry Kissinger, *Years of Renewal* (New York: Simon & Schuster, 1999), 558.

122 **Hey, Skipper**: Rowan, *The Four Days*, 132.

123 **I can't breathe**: Ibid., 148.

123 **We do not have much time; Tell them to sink the boats**: http:// history.state.gov/historicaldocuments/frus1969-76v10/d295.

124 **to take strong, decisive action**: Richard Head, Frisco Short, and Robert McFarlane, *Crisis Resolution* (Boulder, CO: Westview Press, 1978), 118.

124 **Welcome to Cambodia; Why did so many planes come**: Rowan, *The Four Days*, 160–163.

124 **Wait till morning**: Ibid., 169.

125 **The Cambodians have apparently**: http://history.state.gov/histori- caldocuments/frus1969-76v10/d298. See also Ford, *A Time*, 276.

125 **Last night**: Ibid.

126 **I thought we were going to use; We have a government of**: Ron Nessen, *It Sure Looks Different from the Inside* (Chicago: Playboy Press, 1978), 124.

126 **It can be argued that Ford**: John Robert Greene, *The Presidency of Gerald R. Ford* (Lawrence: University of Kansas Press, 1995), 150.

128 **Is there any reason for the Pentagon; No, but tell them to bomb**: Nessen, *It Sure Looks*, 128–29.

130 **The president's political neck**: Robert Pfaltzgraff, Jr. and Jacquelyn Davis, ed., *National Security Decisions* (Lexington: Lexington Books, 1990, 276–77.

130 **Used a "sledgehammer to swat a fly**": "The Mayaguez Affair," *Washington Post*, May 29, 1975. Both headlines from this source.

131 **Neither Ford, nor Schlesinger and the military**: Richard Neustadt and Ernest May, *Thinking in Time* (New York: Free Press, 1986), 64.

Chapter 7: Jimmy Carter

132   **It would be a sign of weakness; It makes no sense to bring him here**: Hamilton Jordan, *Crisis* (New York: G. P. Putnam's Sons, 1982), 29.

133   **Fuck the shah**: Terence Smith, "Why Carter Admitted the Shah," *New York Times*, May 17, 1981.

133   **Mr. President, if the shah dies; To hell with Henry Kissinger**: Jordan, *Crisis*, 31.

133   **What are you guys going to advise**: Ibid., 32. See also David Harris, *The Crisis* (Boston: Little, Brown, 2004), 193.

134   **would be a sharp reaction in the country**: Jimmy Carter, *Keeping Faith* (New York: Bantam Books, 1982), 455.

134   **You're opening Pandora's Box**: Smith, "Why Carter Admitted."

134   **a reign of terror in Iran**: Harris, *The Crisis*, 28.

135   **Don't be afraid**: Ibid., 204.

136   **Don't forget, the press will**: Jordan, *Crisis*, 19.

137   **They have us by the balls**: Gary Sick, *All Fall Down* (New York: Random House, 1985), 209.

137   **Get our people out of Iran**: Ibid., 210

137   **By the way, Cy and Jody**: Jordan, *Crisis*, 34.

138   **resented their exclusion**: Sick, *All Fall Down*, 216.

138   **Mr. President, you can't allow; And Johnson wasn't in the middle**: Jordan, *Crisis*, 44–45.

139   **that almost every recommendation**: Stansfield Turner, *Burn Before Reading* (New York: Hyperion, 2005), 172.

140   **The president has to do something**: Jordan, *Crisis*, 60.

140   **Ham whispered to me**: Zbigniew Brzezinski, *Power and Principle* (New York: Farrar, Straus, Giroux, 1983), 483.

140   **I will not sit here as president**: Sick, *All Fall Down*, 234.

141   **Carter had inflated the importance**: Betty Glad, "Personality, Political and Group Process Variables in Foreign Policy Decision-Making," *International Political Science Review*, vol. 10, no. 1 (1989), 42.

141   **reinforced his public image as a passive leader**: Bostdorff, *The Presidency*, 161.

141   **transformed the strategic environment**: Sick, *All Fall Down*, 282.

141   **the State Department was controlled**: Jordan, *Crisis*, 105.

142   **What choice do we have?**: Ibid., 126.

142   **diddling along**: Ibid., 283.

142   **may also have influenced his views**, Ibid., 253.

143   **What the hell are you doing**: Walter Mondale, *The Good Fight* (New York: Scribner, 2010), 252.

143   **we shall be taking additional non-belligerent**: Sick, *All Fall Down*, 273.

143   **We look foolish**: Jordan, *Crisis*, 246.

144   **A look back over the past ten weeks**: David Broder, "Jimmy Carter's 'Good News' Strategy," *Washington Post*, April 2, 1980.

145   **If the rescue team could get to the walls**: Sick, *All Fall Down*, 285.

145   **Gentlemen**: Jordan, *Crisis*, 250.

146   **Mr. Secretary; But we really don't have much choice**: Jody Powell, *The Other Side of the Story* (New York: William Morrow, 1994), 228.

146   **I went to see the president**: Cyrus Vance, *Hard Choices* (New York: Simon & Schuster, 1983), 409.

146   **I feel strongly that now is not the time; There was an awkward silence**: Jordan, *Crisis*, 253.

146   **I think we have an abort situation**: Brzezinski, *Power*, 497.

147   **Yes, Dave; Mr. President**: Jordan, *Crisis*, 272–73; Mark Bowden, *Guests of the Ayatollah* (New York: Grove, 2006), 468.

147   **lance the boil**: George Wilson, "Carter's Judgment," *Washington Post*, May 4, 1980. See also Brzezinski, *Power*, 494.

147   **Manageable enough; Poor choice of words**: Jordan, *Crisis*, 287.

148   **little-boy-cries-wolf**: Harris, *The Crisis*, 399.

148   **made a concerted effort**: Sick, *All Fall Down*, 319.

149   **We had to play it down the middle**: Jordan, *Crisis*, 363.

151   **Carter . . . provided somewhat better management**: http://www.foreignpolicy.com/articles/2010/01/21/the_real_jimmy_carter#sthash.wpMo7k3c.dpbs.

151   **there are limits even on our nation's great**: Terence Smith, "Putting the Hostages' Lives First," *New York Times*, May 17, 1981.

Chapter 8: Ronald Reagan

152   **Let terrorists be aware**: Hedrick Smith, "An Assertive America, *New York Times*, January 28, 1981.

152   **Hit the deck! Hit the deck**: David Martin and John Walcott, *Best Laid Plans* (New York: Harper & Row), 1988.

153   **He looked like a man; How could this happen**: Robert McFarlane and Zofia Snardz, *Special Trust* (New York: Cadell & Davies, 1994), 263.

153   **Those sons of bitches**: Robert Timberg, *The Nightingale's Song* (New York: Simon & Schuster, 1995), 337.

154   **Mr. President, I have to leave; I didn't know I had that kind of power**: Michael Deaver, with Mickey Herskowitz, *Behind the Scenes* (New York: William Morrow, 1987), 165–66.

156   **cautious and uncertain leader**: Lou Cannon, *President Reagan* (New York: Public Affairs, 2000), 291.

156   **This trait invited middle-ground solutions**, Ibid., 351.

157   **The first thing I want to do**: David Wills, *The First War on Terrorism* (Lanham, MD: Rowman & Littlefield, 2003), 63.

157   **I'm not an eye-for-an-eye man; As I understand it, Mr. President**: Ibid., 64.

158   **If they were put there to fight**: Cannon, *President Reagan*, 389–90.

158   **lovely little war**: Richard Reeves, *President Reagan* (New York: Simon & Schuster, 2005), 190–91. See also http://www.pbs.org/wgbh/americanexperience/features/general-article/reagan-grenada/.

158   **The events in Lebanon and Grenada**: Lou Cannon, "In Speech, Reagan Offers No Deadlines, *Washington Post*, October 28, 1983.

158   **Not only was Weinberger against**: McFarlane, *Special Trust*, 268.

159   **Well, I have decided that we really; Gosh, that's really disappointing**: Ibid., 270–71; Wills, *The First War*, 74.

159   **I cancelled them because our experts**: Ronald Reagan, *Ronald Reagan: An American Life* (New York: Threshold Editions, 1990), 463–64.

159   **Absurd**: Caspar Weinberger, *Fighting for Peace* (New York: Warner Books, 1991), 161.

160   **Bud, what is the light at the end**: Cannon, *President Reagan*, 397.

160   **What are you trying to do**: McFarlane, *Special Trust*, 326.

160   **It was probably the closest Ronald Reagan**: Martin, *Best Laid*, 150.

160   **Often he held the reins of power**: Cannon, *President Reagan*, 118.

161   **Lebanon . . . became the arena**: Ibid., 339.

163   **For their own safety, they better**: Bernard Weintraub, "President Issues A Veiled Warning," *New York Times*, June 17, 1985.

165   **We implore you**: Martin, *Best Laid*, 185.

166   **Retaliation . . . might just entail striking a blow**: Transcript of President Reagan's News Conference, *Washington Post*, June 19, 1985.

166 **What can we expect Israel**: George Shultz, *Turmoil and Triumph* (New York: Charles Scribner's Sons, 1993), 659.

166 **Once the TWA hostages are released**: http://www.pbs.org/wgbh/pages/frontline/shows/target/interviews/oakley.html.

167 **We don't have the luxury of waiting**: Wills, *The First War*, 122.

167 **I have to wait it out; whatever actions are necessary**: Lou Cannon and John Goshko, "Captors Told President's Patience 'Not Limitless,'" *Washington Post*, June 26, 1985; Martin, *Best Laid*, 195–96.

167 **thugs, murderers, and barbarians**: Martin, *Best Laid*, 198.

168 **What Happened to Reagan the Gunslinger**: Lou Cannon, "What Happened to Reagan the Gunslinger?" *Washington Post*, July 7, 1985.

168 **with a ransom of shame**: Norman Podhoretz, "Ransom of Shame," *Washington Post*, July 2, 1985.

170 **most dangerous man in the world**: Allen Cowell, "U.S. and Libya: Are the Views in Both Directions Distorted?" *New York Times*, November 28, 1981.

171 **steadily increasing pressures**: Howard Teicher and Gayle Teicher, *Twin Pillars to Desert Storm* (New York: William Morrow, 1993), 343.

171 **against international law**: Jo Thomas, "Britain Rules Out Joining Sanctions," *New York Times*, January 17, 1986.

171 **Could this lead into trouble**: Richard Stengel, "Sailing in Harm's Way," *Time*, April 7, 1986.

171 **You and Cap better come over here**: William Crowe, with David Chanoff, *The Line of Fire* (New York: Simon & Schuster, 1993), 131.

172 **Tripoli will be happy when**: Wills, *The First War*, 196.

172 **We had emphatically put down a marker**: Shultz, *Triumph*, 686–87.

174 **The president's involvement in foreign affairs**: Martin, *Best Laid*, 139.

175 **embarrassing bumbles**: Editorial, "Shovels in the White House," *New York Times*, November 21, 1986.

175 **flustered**: Tom Shales, "Tough Rounds for Reagan," *Washington Post*, November 20, 1986.

Chapter 9: George H. W. Bush

177 **Mr. President; I don't have any problem**: Colin Powell, with Joseph Persico, *My American Journey* (New York: Random House, 1995), 521.

177 **In what was probably too cute by half**: George Bush and Brent Scowcroft, *A World Transformed* (New York: Vintage Books, 1999), 486.

178   **You have got to be shitting me**: Michael Gordon and Bernard Trainor, *The General's War* (Boston: Little, Brown, 1995), 423.

178   **We have a lot to do to finish**: Jeffrey Engel, ed., *Into the Desert* (New York: Oxford University Press, 2013), 138.

178   **I can't think of another case**: "The Day We Stopped the War, *Newsweek*, January 19, 1992.

178   **This restraint would have seemed prudent**: Engel, *Into the Desert*, 109.

179   **A triumph for American diplomacy**: James Baker, III, *The Politics of Diplomacy* (New York: G. P. Putnam's Sons, 1995), 2.

179   **A triumph without victory**: *Triumph Without Victory* (New York: Time Books, 1993). Written by the staff of *U.S. News and World Report*.

179   **An incomplete success**: Gordon, *The General's War*, xii.

179   **Strategically inconclusive**: Zbigniew Brzezinski, *Second Chance* (New York: Basic Books, 2007), 183.

179   **Politically, it was a botched war**: Theodore Draper, "The True History of the Gulf War," *New York Review of Books*, January 30, 1992. http://www.nybooks.com/articles/archives/1992/jan/30/the-true-history-of-the-gulf-war/?pagination=false#fnr28-138654329.

179   **A 'nothing war'**: Stephen Graubard, *Mr. Bush's War* (New York: Hill and Wang, 1992), xv.

180   **the high-water mark of our efforts**: Baker, *The Politics of Diplomacy*, 267.

180   **perceived himself within Washington's crosshairs; Saddam Hussein believed the time**: Engel, *Into the Desert*, 23–24.

181   **By God, we will make the fire**: Jean Edward Smith, *George Bush's War* (New York: Henry Holt, 1992), 46.

181   **direct aggression; Disputes should be settled**: Baker, *The Politics of Diplomacy*, 271.

181   **bolster a friend and lay down**: Michael Gordon, "U.S. Deploys Air and Sea Forces After Iraq Threatens 2 Neighbors," *New York Times*, July 25, 1990.

181   **There is no place for coercion; If Iraq seizes a small amount**: Nora Boustany and Patrick Tyler, "U.S. Pursues Diplomatic Solution in Persian Gulf Crisis, Warns Iraq," *Washington Post*, July 25, 1990.

182   **a modern-day version of gunboat**: Engel, *Into the Desert*, 58–59.

182   **Repeated American statements; I know you need funds**: "Confrontation in the Gulf," *The New York Times*, September 23, 1990.

182   **I believe we would be well-advised**: Gordon, *The General's War*, 22.

183   **The war was a stunning failure**: Ibid., xiii.

183   **This ain't our show**: "Iraq Force Invades Kuwait," *Washington Post*, August 2, 1990.

183   **I'm not contemplating such action**: Bob Woodward, *The Commanders* (New York: Simon & Schuster, 1991), 225.

183   **Hey too bad about Kuwait**: Dan Goodgame, "What If We Do Nothing?" *Time*, January 7, 1991, 22.

183   **I was frankly appalled at**: Bush, *A World*, 317.

184   **If Iraq wins, no small state is safe**: Ibid., 319.

184   **Remember,   George**:   http://www.politifact.com/truth-o-meter/statements/2013/apr/10/dick-cheney/dick-cheney-margaret-thatcher-go-wobbly/.

184   **I was about to be defeated**: Kevin Phillips, *American Dynasty* (New York: Viking, 2004), 308.

184   **Under these circumstances**: Gordon, *A General's War*, 37.

185   **There's a deterrence piece and a war-fighting piece; The navy's not a problem**: Woodward, *The Commanders*, 248–49.

185   **If you want to deter**: Ibid., 251.

185   **Our defense of Saudi Arabia**: Ibid., 253.

186   **What's emerging is nobody is; Please believe me, there are**: "The Iraqi Invasion: Transcript of News Conference Remarks by Bush on Iraq Crisis," *New York Times*, August 6, 1990.

186   **He had listened quietly to his advisers**: Powell, *My American*, 466–67.

187   **He led with his gut, with his instincts**: http://www.youtube.com/watch?v=nzkOlNlb7KI.

187   **appeasement does not work**: "If History Teaches Us Anything," *Washington Post*, August 9, 1990.

187   **Are we at war**: "We've Taken This First Significant Step to Defend Saudi Arabia," *Washington Post*, August 9, 1990.

188   **Vuono leaked the true size**: Smith, *George Bush's War*, 105.

188   **our jobs, our way of life**: R. W. Apple, "U.S. May Send Saudis A Force of 50,000," *New York Times*, August 16, 1990.

188   **I would advise Iraqi ships**: R. W. Apple, "U.S. Says Its Troops in the Gulf Could Reach 100,000 in Months," *New York Times*, August 11, 1990. See also Bush, *A World Transformed*, 345, and Nicholas M. Horrock, "U.S. Starts Enforcing Embargo Against Iraq, *Chicago Tribune*, August 13, 1990.

188   **Well, all right George**: Bush, *A World Transformed*, 352.

189   **I don't yet see fruitful negotiations**: Dan Balz, "Bush Expresses Pessimism On Diplomatic Solution," *Washington Post*, August 28, 1990.

189   **gone too far in terms; oppressive and reactionary**: E. J. Dionne, Jr., "Conservatives Are Leading Murmurs of Dissent to Bush Actions in Mideast," *Washington Post*, August 24, 1990.

190   **Air power is the only answer**: John Broder, "U.S. War Plan in Iraq," *Los Angeles Times*, September 16, 1990.

190   **Given the extreme delicacy and sensitivity**: John Broder, "Air Force Chief Fired by Cheney," *Los Angeles Times*, September 18, 1990.

190   **But perhaps his greatest transgression**: John Broder, "News Analysis: Dugan's Sin," *Los Angeles Times*, September 20, 1990.

190   **Prepare for economic pain at home**: Andrew Rosenthal, "Pivotal Moment for Bush," *New York Times*, October 3, 1990.

191   **There is a case here for containment; I don't think**: Woodward, *The Commanders*, 42.

192   **We've just seen a first cut**: Powell, *My American Life*, 485.

192   **The briefing made me realize**: Bush, *A World Transformed*, 381.

192   **Hitler revisited; systematic assault on the soul**: Dan Balz, "President Warns Iraq of War Crimes Trials," *Washington Post*, October 16, 1990.

192   **There's a parallel between what Hitler**: Thomas Friedman, "No Compromise on Kuwait, Bush Says," *New York Times*, October 24, 1990.

192   **Our original strategy wasn't working; were a box to check**: Elizabeth Drew, "Letter From Washington," *The New Yorker*, December 31, 1990, 87–88.

193   **If that's what you need**: Woodward, *The Commanders*, 320.

193   **What's going on**: Ibid., 312.

194   **would focus the issue for Congress**: Walter Pincus, "Bush Is Said to Want U.N. Assent on Force Before Seeking Hill's," *Washington Post*, November 21, 1990.

194   **rape, pillage, and plunder, hostages**: Ann Devroy and Dan Balz, "Bush Says Time Is Limited For Peaceful Gulf Solution," *Washington Post*, November 11, 1990.

194   **It was an embarrassing display**: Tom Mathews et al., "The Road to War, *Newsweek*, January 28, 1991, 64.

194   **Every time we score with one**: Ibid., 65.

195   **To go the extra mile for peace**: "Bush's Statement: 'We Are Not Alone. . . . It Is Iraq Against the World," *Los Angeles Times*, December 1, 1990.

195   **Patsies**: Elizabeth Drew, "Letter From Washington," *The New Yorker*, February 4, 1991, 86.

195   **Exercises**: Woodward, *The Commanders*, 345.

195   **domestic reasons**: Drew, "Letter," February 4, 1991, 84.

195   **If we get into an armed situation**: John Goshko and Dan Balz, "Time for Talks Running Out, Iraq Warned," *Washington Post*, December 21, 1990.

195   **little boy who shines shoes**: Smith, *George Bush's War*, 232, footnote. See also, http://www.sfgate.com/entertainment/article/Fightin-words-There-are-hidden-meanings-in-how-2665077.php.

195   **You don't talk to Arabs**: Drew, "Letter," February 4, 1991.

196   **Evan Thomas said the term grew**: Evan Thomas and Rich Thomas, http://www.newsweekmemories.org/e-thomas.html.

196   **Lapdog**, George Will, "The Sound of a Lapdog," *Washington Post*, January 30, 1986.

196   **We all know instinctively; to the exclusion of everything else**: Drew, "Letter," February 4, 1991, 83.

196   **A lot of people here think that the president**: Ibid., 84.

196   **that was the plan all along**: Drew, "Letter," December 31, 1990, 87.

196   **Don't vote for this**: Drew, "Letter," February 4, 1990, 88.

197   **Perhaps if, in President Bush's rhetoric**: Lawrence Freedman and Efraim Karsh, *The Gulf Conflict 1990–1991* (Princeton, NJ: Princeton University Press, 1993), 439.

197   **It must be said that US policymaking**: Engel, *Into the Desert*, 76.

197   **had killed 158,001 Iraqis**: Barton Gellman, "Census Worker Who Calculated '91 Iraqi Death Toll Is Told She Will Be Fired," *Washington Post*, March 6, 1992.

198   **Finlandization**, Engel, *Into the Desert*, 67–69.

198   **Not all of Bush's actions and decisions**: Please see the following assessments of President Bush's handling of the crisis: Stephen J. Wayne, "President Bush Goes to War," in Stanley Renshon, ed., *The Political Psychology of the Gulf War* (Pittsburgh: University of Pittsburgh Press, 1993), 29–48; Stephen Sestanovich, *Maximalist* (New York: Alfred A. Knopf, 2014), 250–256; and Goodgame, "What If We Do Nothing," *Time*, 22–26.

Chapter 10: Bill Clinton

200   **Gayle, Sit Room calling; No, that's the right list**: Bohn, *Nerve Center*, xv–xvi.

201   **First, rescue; The senior officer from each CSG**: Richard Clarke, *Against All Enemies* (New York: Free Press, 2004), 181–83.

201   **The president wanted to talk**: Bohn, *Nerve Center*, xvii.

202   **chronic disagreements and tensions**: Steve Coll, *Ghost Wars* (New York: Penguin Press, 2004), 406.

202   **set up a large and complex set**: *The 9/11 Commission Report* (New York: W. W. Norton, 2004), 57.

203   **Al-Qaeda affiliates led the resistance**: For information on the 1993 US intervention in Somalia, please see the book *Blackhawk Down* by Mark Bowden.

203   **no connection**: http://www.informationclearinghouse.info/article7204.htm.

203   **A decade's worth of research**: Paul Pillar, "A Scapegoat Is Not a Solution," *New York Times*, June 4, 2004.

203   **Crusaders and Jews**: Peter Bergen, *The Longest War* (New York: Free Press, 2011), 29.

204   **We ate cake, we drank iced tea**: "First Lady, Staffers Team to Catch President Off Guard with Party," *Los Angeles Times*, August 15, 1998.

204   **This one is a slam dunk**, Clarke, *Against*, 184.

204   **You thinking what I'm thinking**: Ibid.

205   **Don't you fucking tell me**: Jane Mayer, "The Search for Osama," *The New Yorker*, August 4, 2003, 32.

205   **simple housing, firing ranges**: Paul Pillar, *Terrorism and U.S. Foreign Policy* (Washington, DC: Brookings Institution Press, 2001), 103.

206   **The FBI has left a bad taste**: Seymour Hersh, "The Missiles of August," *The New Yorker*, October 12, 1998, 38.

207   **Early that afternoon**: Coll, *Ghost Wars*, 411.

207   **Today I ordered our armed forces**: "Clinton's Words: There Will Be No Sanctuary for Terrorists," *New York Times*, August 21, 1998.

207   **We also had received at that point; Let me be very clear about this**: Press Briefing by Secretary of State Madeleine Albright and National Security Advisor Sandy Berger, August 20, 1998, http://www.presidency.ucsb.edu/ws/?pid=48285.

207   **criminal act**: Howard Schneider, Nora Boustany, "A Barrage of Criticism In Mideast," *Washington Post*, August 21, 1998.

207 **I think the president did exactly**: Barton Gellman and Dana Priest, "U.S. Strikes Terrorist-Linked Sites In Afghanistan, Factory in Sudan," *Washington Post*, August 21, 1998.

208 **I just hope and pray**: Todd Purdam, "Critics of Clinton Support Attacks," *New York Times*, August 21, 1998.

208 **I couldn't believe my ears**: Hersh, "The Missiles," October 12, 1998, 35.

208 **they had no evidence directly linking**: Tim Weiner and James Risen, "Decision to Strike Factory in Sudan Based on Surmise Inferred from Evidence," *New York Times*, September 21, 1998.

208 **It's fairly commonly known**: Paul Richter, "Sudan Attack Claims Faulty, US Admits," *Los Angeles Times*, September 1, 1998.

209 **Officials are still troubled; I would say the director**: James Risen, "To Bomb Sudan Plan, or Not: A Year Later, Debates Rankle," *New York Times*, October 27, 1999.

209 **The best post-facto intelligence**: Mayer, "The Search for Osama," August 4, 2003, 32.

209 **Tell the Americans that we aren't afraid**: Lawrence Wright, *The Looming Tower* (New York: Alfred A. Knopf, 2006), 286.

209 **Life is back to normal**: Peter Bergen, *Holy War, Inc.* (New York: Free Press, 2001), 122.

209 **twenty or thirty al-Qaeda operatives were killed**: Wright, *Looming Tower*, 285.

210 **timidity, hypersensitivity to public reaction**: Dick Morris, *Because He Could* (New York: ReganBooks, 2004), 100–01.

211 **wholly new kind of president; The way Clinton arrived at decisions**: Nigel Hamilton, *Bill Clinton* (New York: Public Affairs, 2007), 109.

211 **They turned bin Laden**: Bergen, *Holy Wars*, 125.

211 **By the grace of God**: Wright, *Looming Tower*, 285.

Chapter 11: George W. Bush

212 **What I'm telling you, buddy**: Lynn Spencer, *Touching History* (New York: Free Press, 2008), 158.

212 **Sir, we have to leave now**: Stephen Hayes, *Cheney* (New York: Harper Collins, 2007), 333.

213 **Someone from the Secret Service**: *60 Minutes II*, CBS, September 11, 2002. http://www.cbsnews.com/news/the-presidents-story-11-09-2002/.

213   **The Situation Room staff**: Rob Hargis interview with author, 2011.

214   **Rob Hargis called me at 8:50 a.m.; Thank you Captain**: Deborah Loewer interview with author, 2011.

214   **A second plane has hit the Trade Center**: Ibid.

214   **A second plane hit the second tower**: *9/11 Commission Report*, 38.

215   **A . . . girl . . . got**: Bill Sammon, *Fighting Back* (Washington: Regnery, 2002), 86.

215   **DON'T SAY ANYTHING**: Ibid.

215   **Who would you like to speak with first**: Loewer interview.

215   **Mark my words**: Hayes, *Fighting Back*, 2.

215   **Am I the evil genius**: Judy Keen, "Cheney says it's too soon to tell on Iraqi arms," *USA Today*, January 19, 2004.

215   **Ladies and gentlemen**: Sammon, *Fighting Back*, 96–97.

216   **The tarmac was swarming with tense people**: Loewer interview.

216   **We're at war, Dick**: Hayes, *Cheney*, 335.

216   **So I urged him**: Ibid., 336.

218   **At 9:26 a.m., the command center**: Linda Schuessler, interview with author, 2011.

218   **You bet**: Dan Balz and Bob Woodward, "America's Chaotic Road to War; Bush's Global Strategy Began to Take Shape in First Frantic Hours After Attack," *Washington Post*, January 27, 2002.

219   **John, can you confirm that**: Hargis interview.

220   **I know, I've seen them**: Hargis interview.

220   **You don't have to worry; For one moment, I had this**: http://www.independent.co.uk/arts-entertainment/tv/reviews/911-state-of-emergency--sat-channel-4brdavid-jason-the-battle-of-britain--sun-itv1b-ralberts-memorial--sun-itv1-2077487.html.

220   **a direct threat to Angel**: Balz and Woodward, January 27, 2002; Hargis interview.

220   **It was a B-52 base**: Tom Vanden Brook, "Air Force One pilot's 9/11 Mission: Keep President Safe," *USA Today*, updated 9/7/2011.

221   **We never received a threat**: Hargis interview.

221   **I was in the president's cabin**: Loewer interview.

221   **Make no mistake** : http://georgewbush-whitehouse.archives.gov/news/releases/2001/09/20010911-1.html.

221   **I want to go back home ASAP; The right thing to do is let the dust settle**: Sammon, *Fighting Back*, 119.

222   **Get your ears up; We will find these people**: Balz and Woodward, January 27, 2002.

222   **We're gonna get those bastards**: Sammon, *Fighting Back*, 126.

222   **It was a horrible sight**: Loewer interview.

223   **Good evening. Today, our fellow**: http://georgewbush-whitehouse. archives.gov/news/releases/2001/09/20010911-16.html.

223   **I want you all to understand; I don't care what the international lawyers**: Clarke, *Against All Enemies*, 24.

224   **I think I was unprepared for war**: Dan Eggen, "Reflecting on His Tenure, Bush Shows New Candor," *Washington Post*, December 2, 2008.

224   **That's just PR**: http://archives.cnn.com/TRANSCRIPTS/0109/15/ cg.00.html.

225   **Until his speech last night**: Dan Balz, "Bush Confronts a Nightmare Scenario," *Washington Post*, September 12, 2001.

225   **I can hear you**: Edward Walsh, "Bush Encourages N.Y. Rescuers," *Washington Post*, September 15, 2001.

225   **Fierce . . . eloquent . . . powerful; I thought it was A-plus**: Tom Shales, "From President Bush, a Speech Filled With Assurance and Reassurance," *Washington Post*, September 21, 2001.

225   **It is critical how we define; I want to get moving**: Dan Balz and Bob Woodward, "We Will Rally the World," *Washington Post*, January 28, 2002.

226   **We're prepared to launch in short order; When we're through with them**: Bob Woodward, *Bush at War* (New York: Simon & Schuster, 2002), 50–53.

226   **This conflict has begun on the timing**: http://georgewbush-white-house.archives.gov/news/releases/2001/09/20010914-2.html.

227   **Going to War; That's okay with me**: Woodward, *Bush at War*, 75. See also Bergen, *The Longest War*, 54–56; and Kurt Eichenwald, *500 Days* (New York: Touchstone, 2012), 72–75.

227   **It starts today**: Dan Balz and Bob Woodward, "Combating Terrorism: 'It Starts Today,'" *Washington Post*, February 1, 2002.

227   **I believe Iraq was involved**: Woodward, *Bush at War*, 97–99.

227   **We're going to rain holy hell**: Balz and Woodward, "Combatting," February 1, 2001.

229   **In the end there were probably**: Bergen, *The Longest War*, 81.

229   **From January 2002 on**: Seymour Hersh, "The Other War," *The New Yorker*, April 12, 2004, 44.

229   **From the very beginning**: http://www.cnn.com/2004/ALLPOLITICS/01/10/oneill.bush/.

230   **Go massive**: http://www.cbsnews.com/news/plans-for-iraq-attack-began-on-9-11/ (CBS News, September 4, 2002).

230   **I know you have a lot to do; Wolfowitz got to him**: Clarke, *Against All Enemies*, 32.

230   **What the hell, what are these guys**: Dan Balz and Bob Woodward, "Afghan Campaign's Blueprint Emerges," *Washington Post*, January 29, 2002.

230   **What kind of war plan do you have for Iraq**: Bob Woodward, *Plan of Attack* (New York: Simon & Schuster, 2004), 1–2.

231   **States like these**: George W. Bush, "Our War on Terror . . . Is Only Begun," *Washington Post*, January 30, 2002.

231   **Many of us are convinced**: Colum Lynch and Walter Pincus, "Iraq Calls Weapons Inspections Irrelevant," *Washington Post*, August 30, 2002.

231   **solid intelligence; remains determined to acquire**: Colin Powell, *Vital Speeches of the Day*, 69.9, February 15, 2003, 276–288.

231   **They still don't get it; They aren't going to send**: Clarke, *Against All Enemies*, 241.

232   **The issue got away from the president**: Glenn Kessler, "U.S. Decision on Iraq Has Puzzling Past," *Washington Post*, January 12, 2003.

232   **Those weapons of mass destruction**: Jennifer Frey, "George Bush, Entertainer In Chief," *Washington Post*, March 25, 2004.

233   **Too many assumptions**: David Rothkopf, *Running the World* (New York: Public Affairs, 2005), 408.

233   **Defense had their thumb on the scale**: Ibid., 407.

233   **three bites of the apple; behind two and a half to one**: Ibid., 408.

233   **at being able to achieve**: Hersh, "The Other War," 42.

234   **Bush II was the vigilante**: Brzezinski, *Second Chance*, 179.

234   **Just as bin Laden made a large**: Bergen, *The Longest War*, 155.

Chapter 12: Barack Obama

235   **fight until the last man; thousands of deaths**: http://www.alarabiya.net/articles/2011/02/21/138515.html.

235 **We're talking here a matter; I wasn't talking about it**: http://www. whitehouse.gov/the-press-office/2011/03/07/corrected-press-briefing-press-secretary-jay-carney-372011.

236 **have his head examined**: http://www.defense.gov/Speeches/Speech. aspx?SpeechID=1539.

237 **Will this no-fly zone stop; That's the only thing we're going**: The dialogue in the two March 15 meetings is drawn from several sources and combined. See James Mann, *The Obamians* (New York: Viking, 2012), xi–xiii; David Corn, *Showdown* (New York: William Morrow, 2012), 202–08; Michael Lewis, "Obama's Way," *Vanity Fair*, October 2012, 260.

237 **Obama structures meetings**: Lewis, "Obama's Way," 260.

238 **a foreign policy sensibility**: David Remnick, "Going the Distance," *The New Yorker*, January 27, 2014.

238 **to seek a new beginning between**: http://www.whitehouse.gov/the-press-office/remarks-president-cairo-university-6-04-09. For a recent and detailed analysis of Obama's foreign policy, see Marin Indyk, Kenneth Lieberthal, and Michael O'Hanlon, *Bending History* (Washington: Brookings, 2012).

238 **No system of government can**: http://www.whitehouse.gov/the-press-office/remarks-president-cairo-university-6-04-09.

239 **no longer driven by ideology and politics**: Corn, *Showdown*, 152–53.

239 **ditherer in chief**: John Bolton, "Ditherer in chief," *Los Angeles Times*, October 18, 2009.

239 **It was a calculated political act**: Marc Lynch, *The Arab Spring* (New York: Public Affairs, 2012), 75.

240 **Egypt is a strong ally**: Scott Wilson and Joby Warrick, "As Arabs Protest, U.S. Speaks Up," *Washington Post*, January 27, 2011.

240 **Mubarak's prospects for survival**: Lynch, *The Arab Spring*, 92.

240 **I hope Mubarak, President Mubarak**: http://www.pbs.org/newshour/bb/politics-jan-june11-biden_01-27/.

241 **I'm going upstairs to call Mubarak**: Corn, *Showdown*, 167.

241 **With all due respect**: Ibid., 168. See also Mann, *The Obamians*, 263.

241 **What is clear, and what**: Mark Landler, Helene Cooper and David Kirkpatrick, "A Diplomatic Scramble as an Ally Is Pushed to the Exit," *New York Times*, February 2, 2011.

242   **Extremists, like the Muslim Brotherhood**: http://www.newsmax.
      com/InsideCover/donald-rumsfeld-egypt-muslim/2011/02/08/id/
      385426/.

242   **Only *six* days after Egypt's protests**: Marc Lynch, *The Arab Spring*
      (New York: Public Affairs, 2012), 95.

243   **I wished we had better options**: Hillary Clinton, *Hard Choices* (New
      York: Simon & Schuster, 2014), 360.

243   **did not want to be friends**: http://news.bbc.co.uk/2/hi/africa/7599479.
      stm.

243   **First, we are doing everything**: http://www.whitehouse.gov/
      the-press-office/2011/02/23/remarks-president-libya.

244   **We can't risk allowing Qaddafi**: http://nypost.com/2011/03/07/
      libyas-fiercest-fight/.

244   **Fiddling While Libya Burns**: Anne-Marie Slaughter, "Fiddling While
      Libya Burns," *New York Times*, Match 14, 2011.

244   **I believed that what was happening in Libya**: Robert Gates, *Duty*
      (New York: Alfred A. Knopf, 2014), 511–12.

244   **Don't give the White House staff**: Ibid., 512.

245   **especially any options to take out Qaddafi**: Ibid., 515.

245   **The violence must stop**: http://www.whitehouse.gov/blog/2011/03/
      03/president-libya-violence-must-stop-muammar-gaddafi-has-lost-
      legitimacy-lead-and-he-m.

245   **I'm one of those who believes**: Karen DeYoung and Edward Cody,
      "U.S. plans to send aid team to Libya," *Washington Post*, March 11,
      2011.

246   **We knew we didn't have**: Lewis, *Vanity Fair*, 260.

246   **Our goal is to protect civilians**: Clinton, *Hard Choices*, 317.

246   **the spectator-in-chief; as indecisive as I've ever seen**: Howard
      Kurtz, "Critics have slammed Obama for everything . . .," *Daily Beast*,
      March 19, 2011.

247   **consequences**:http://www.whitehouse.gov/the-press-office/2011/03/18/
      remarks-president-situation-libya.

247   **You are the biggest micromanagers**: Gates, *Duty*, 522.

247   **For those of us who have decried**: David Rothkopf, "Master of Cer-
      emonies," *Washington Post*, March 20, 2011.

247   **On Libya, is Congress going**: http://www.cbsnews.com/news/
      boehner-gop-want-obama-to-consult-with-congress-on-libya.

248   **He's tentative, indecisive, timid; It is impossible to make sense**: Doyle McManus, "The GOP's Libya Dilemma," *Los Angeles Times*, March 24, 2011.

248   **leading from behind; the US is reviled in many parts**: Ryan Lizza, "The Consequentialist," *The New Yorker*, May 2, 2011. http://www.newyorker.com/reporting/2011/05/02/110502fa_fact_lizza?currentPage=all.

248   **provided an Aha! moment**: http://www.newyorker.com/online/blogs/newsdesk/2011/10/where-leading-from-behind-has-led.html.

249   **The president is not a king; It's time to stop shredding**: Charlie Savage, "Libya Effort Is Called Violation of War Act," *New York Times*, May 26, 2011.

251   **Syria's terrain was far less favorable**: Lynch, *The Arab Spring*, 190.

251   **wicked problem; Do nothing**: Clinton, *Hard Choices*, 461.

252   **The idea was to put a chill**: Peter Baker, et al., "Off-the-Cuff Obama Line Put U.S. in Bind on Syria," *New York Times*, May 5, 2013.

252   **We have been very clear**: http://www.whitehouse.gov/the-press-office/2012/08/20/remarks-president-white-house-press-corps.

252   **What the president said in August**: Baker, "Off-the-Cuff," May 5, 2013.

253   **totally unacceptable; This is a red line for the United States**: Peter Finn and Anne Gearan, "Obama Sternly Warns Syria," *Washington Post*, December 4, 2012.

253   **We're kind of boxed in**: David Sanger and Eric Schmitt, "U.S. Shifting Its Warning on Syria's Chemical Arms," *New York Times*, December 7, 2012.

253   **We have to make sure that**: Karen DeYoung, "Obama Again Warns Syria on Chemical Arms," *Washington Post*," March 21, 2013.

253   **President Obama evaded, ducked**: Jennifer Rubi, "Obama Erases His 'Red Line,'" *Washington Post*, April 29, 2013.

253   **When it comes to Syria**: Susan Glasser, "Redlines," *Washington Post*, May 5, 2013.

253   **impose consequences**: Mark Mazzetti et al., "Obama's Uncertain Path Amid Syrian Bloodshed," *New York Times*, October 22, 2013.

253   **The president has said that the**: Karen DeYoung and Anne Gearan, "U.S., Citing Use of Chemical Weapons by Syria," *Washington Post*, June 14, 2013.

254   **U.S. credibility is on the line**: Ibid.

254 **The Obama team has clearly struggled**: Thomas Friedman, "Arm and Shame," *New York Times*, September 4, 2013.

254 **Look, you wrestle with it**: Remnick, "Going the Distance," January 27, 2014, 58.

255 **Denis, if you had met the rebels**, Mazzetti, "Obama's Uncertain Path," October 22, 2013.

255 **I haven't made a decision yet on military**: Mark Landler, "President Pulls Lawmakers into Box He Made," *New York Times*, September 1, 2013.

255 **shot across the bow; We don't have good options**: Ibid.

255 **There's a broad naiveté in the political; I can't believe the president**: Ernesto Londono, "Many Officers Concerned about Strategy, Impact," *Washington Post*, August 30, 2013.

256 **I have a big idea I want to run**: Adam Entous, "Inside White House, a Head-Spinning Reversal on Chemical Weapons," *Wall Street Journal*, September 15, 2013.

256 **We don't want them to have their cake**: Scott Wilson, "In the Oval Office, a Debate about Whether to Involve Lawmakers," *Washington Post*, September 1, 2013.

257 **He knows we will vote it down**: Shashank Bengali, et al., "The Syria Crisis," *Los Angeles Times*, September 1, 2013.

257 **President Obama is abdicating his responsibility**: Ernesto Londono, "Syria Attack Is Put on Hold," *Washington Post*, September 1, 2013.

257 **He appeared to want to disappear**: Mark Landler, "Photographs Tell Tale of Anguished Debate," *New York Times*, September 7, 2013.

257 **He's compelled Republicans**: Harold Myerson, "A 'Red Line' for the GOP," *Washington Post*, September 5, 2013.

257 **Sure . . . he could turn over**: Anne Gearan et al., "Syria Welcomes Russian Plan to Avert Strike," *Washington Post*, September 10, 2013.

258 **obsolete**: "Syria's Crisis Averted? Not So Fast," *Washington Post*, October 21, 2013.

258 **Everybody was sort of breathing; Congress . . . served its role**: Stacy Kaper, "A Sigh of Relief from Lawmakers on Syria," *National Journal Daily*," September 11, 2013.

258 **the threat of US action and the pressure**: Gearan, "Syria Welcomes Russian Plan," September 10, 2013.

258　**I have reason to believe that we**: Thomas Pickering interview with the author, March 2014.

259　**The two agreed that Russian**: Walter Pincus, "Groundwork on Syria Deal Began Months Ago," *Washington Post*, September 9, 2013.

259　**We don't have a strategy yet**: "Transcript: President Obama's Aug. 28 Remarks on Ukraine, Syria and the Economy," *Washington Post*, August 28, 2014.

260　**In the foreign policy establishment**: Remnick, "Going the Distance," January 27, 2014, 55.

260　**So that's a lesson**: Thomas Friedman, "Obama on the World," *New York Times*, August 9, 2014.

261　**a large-scale disaster for the**: Gerald Seib, "The Risks Holding Back Obama on Syria," *Wall Street Journal*, May 6, 2013.

261　**The political price he'll pay**: Amy Davidson, "Harder Answers," *The New Yorker*, September 23, 2013, 41.

261　**always been a fantasy**: Friedman, "Obama on the World," August 8, 2014.

262　**Well, I don't know the answer**: Jeffrey Goldberg, "Hillary Clinton: 'Failure' to Help Syrian Rebels Led to the Rise of ISIS," *Atlantic*, August 10, 2014. http://www.theatlantic.com/international/archive/2014/08/hillary-clinton-failure-to-help-syrian-rebels-led-to-the-rise-of-isis/375832/?single_page=true.

262　**I can't sit here today and say**: Ibid.

262　**needs to burn itself out**: Rod McDaniel, interview with author, March 2013.

BIBLIOGRAPHY

Books

Acheson, Dean. *Present at the Creation*. New York: W. W. Norton, 1969.

Ambrose, Stephen. *Nixon*. Vol. 3, *Ruin and Recovery 1973–1990*. New York: Simon & Schuster, 1991.

Armbrister, Trevor. *A Matter of Accountability*. Guilford: Lyons Press, 2004.

Baker, James, III. *The Politics of Diplomacy*. New York: G. P. Putnam's Sons, 1995.

Barber, James David. *Politics by Humans*. Durham, NC: Duke University Press, 1988.

Bergen, Peter. *The Longest War*. New York: Free Press, 2011.

Beschloss, Michael R. *Mayday*. New York: Harper & Row, 1986.

Blight, James, and David Welch. *On the Brink*. New York: Noonday Press, 1990.

Blight, James, Bruce Allyn, and David Welch. *Cuba on the Brink*. Lanham, MD: Rowman & Littlefield, 2002.

Bohn, Michael K. *Nerve Center: Inside the White House Situation Room*. Washington: Brassey's, Inc., 2003.

Bostdorff, Denise. *The Presidency and the Rhetoric of Foreign Crisis*. Columbia: University of South Carolina Press, 1994.

Bowden, Mark. *Guests of the Ayatollah*. New York: Grove, 2006.

Bradley, Omar N. *A General's Life*. New York: Simon & Schuster, 1983.

Brzezinski, Zbigniew. *Power and Principle*. New York: Farrar, Straus, Giroux, 1983.

———. *Second Chance*. New York: Basic Books, 2007.

Bundy, McGeorge. *Danger and Survival*. New York: Random House, 1988.

Bush, George, and Brent Scowcroft. *A World Transformed*. New York: Vintage Books, 1999.

Califano, Joseph. *The Triumph & Tragedy of Lyndon Johnson*. New York: Simon & Schuster, 1991.

Cannon, Lou. *President Reagan*. New York: Public Affairs, 2000.

Carter, Jimmy. *Keeping Faith*. New York: Bantam Books, 1982.

Chang, Laurence, and Peter Kornbluh, eds., *The Cuban Missile Crisis*. New York: New Press.

Clarke, Richard. *Against All Enemies*. New York: Free Press, 2004.

Clinton, Hillary. *Hard Choices*. New York: Simon & Schuster, 2014.

Coll, Steve. *Ghost Wars*. New York: Penguin Press, 2004.

Corn, David. *Showdown*. New York: William Morrow, 2012.

Crowe, William. *The Line of Fire*. With David Chanoff. New York: Simon & Schuster, 1993.

Dallek, Robert. *Flawed Giant*. New York: Oxford University Press, 1998.

———. *Nixon and Kissinger*. New York: Harper Collins, 2007.

Deaver, Michael. *Behind the Scenes*. With Mickey Herskowitz. New York: William Morrow, 1987.

Dobbs, Michael. *One Minute to Midnight*. New York: Alfred Knopf, 2008.

Dobrynin, Anatoly. *In Confidence*. New York: Times Books, 1995.

Donovan, Robert J. *Tumultuous Years*. New York: W. W. Norton, 1996.

Doyle, William. *Inside the Oval Office*. New York: Kodansha International, 1999.

Drachman, Edward R., and Alan Shank. *Presidents and Foreign Policy*. Albany: State University of New York Press, 1997.

Eichenwald, Kurt. *500 Days*. New York: Touchstone, 2012.

Eisenhower, Dwight D. *Waging Peace: 1956–1961*. Garden City: Doubleday, 1965.

Eisenhower, John S. D. *Strictly Personal*. Garden City: Doubleday, 1974.

Elsey, George M. *An Unplanned Life*. Columbia: University of Missouri Press, 2005.

Engel, Jeffrey, ed. *Into the Desert*. New York: Oxford University Press, 2013.

Ennes, James, Jr. *Assault on the Liberty*. New York: Ivy Books, 1979.

Ford, Gerald R. *A Time to Heal*. New York: Harper & Row, 1979.

Frankel, Max. *High Noon in the Cold War*. New York: Ballantine, 2004.

Freedman, Lawrence, and Efraim Karsh. *The Gulf Conflict 1990–1991*. Princeton, NJ: Princeton University Press, 1993.

Fursenko, Aleksandr, and Timothy Naftali. *One Hell of a Gamble*. New York: W. W. Norton, 1997.

Gaddis, John Lewis. *We Now Know*. New York: Oxford University Press, 1997.

Garthoff, Raymond L. *Reflections on the Cuban Missile Crisis*. Washington, DC: The Brookings Institution, 1989.

Gates, Robert. *Duty*. New York: Alfred A. Knopf, 2014.

George, Alexander, ed. *Avoiding War*. Boulder, CO: Westview Press, 1991.

Golan, Matti. *The Secret Conversations of Henry Kissinger*. New York: Quadrangle, 1976.

Gordon, Michael, and Bernard Trainor. *The General's War*. Boston: Little, Brown, 1995.

Graubard, Stephen. *Mr. Bush's War*. New York: Hill and Wang, 1992.

Greene, John Robert. *The Presidency of Gerald R. Ford*. Lawrence: University of Kansas Press, 1995.

Hamby, Alonzo. *Man of the People*. New York: Oxford University Press, 1995.

Hamilton, Nigel. *Bill Clinton*. New York: Public Affairs, 2007.

Harris, David. *The Crisis*. Boston: Little, Brown, 2004.

Hartman, Robert. *Palace Politics*. New York: McGraw-Hill, 1980.

Hayes, Stephen. *Cheney*. New York: Harper Collins, 2007.

Head, Richard, Frisco Short, and Robert McFarlane. *Crisis Resolution*. Boulder, CO: Westview Press, 1978.

Helms, Richard. *A Look Over My Shoulder*. New York: Random House, 2003.

Horne, Alistair. *Kissinger: 1973, the Crucial Year*. New York: Simon & Schuster, 2009.

Hughes, Emmet John. *The Ordeal of Power*. New York: Dell, 1963.

Indyk, Martin, Kenneth Lieberthal, and Michael O'Hanlon. *Bending History*. Washington: Brookings, 2012.

Isaacson, Walter. *Kissinger*. New York: Simon & Schuster, 1992.

Israelyan, Victor. *On the Battlefields of the Cold War*. University Park: Pennsylvania State University Press, 2003.

Johnson, Lyndon Baines. *The Vantage Point*. New York: Holt, Rinehart and Winston, 1971.

Johnson, Lyndon Library. National Security Council Histories, Middle East Crisis, vol. 7, appendix G.

Jordan, Hamilton. *Crisis*. New York: G. P. Putnam's Sons, 1982.

Kalb, Marvin, and Bernard Kalb. *Kissinger*. Boston: Little, Brown, 1974.

Katzenbach, Nicholas deB. *Some of It Was Fun*. New York: W. W. Norton, 2008.

Kennedy, Robert F. *Thirteen Days*. New York: W. W. Norton, 1971.

Khrushchev, Nikita. *Khrushchev Remembers*. Boston: Little, Brown, 1974.

Khrushchev, Sergei. *Nikita Khrushchev*. University Park: Pennsylvania State University, 2000.

Kissinger, Henry. *Crisis*. New York: Simon & Schuster, 2003.

———. *Years of Renewal*. New York: Simon & Schuster, 1999.

———. *Years of Upheaval*. Boston: Little, Brown, 1982.

Kistiakowsky, George B. *A Scientist at the White House*. Cambridge: Harvard University Press, 1976.

Kyle, Keith. *Suez*. New York: St. Martin's Press, 1991.

Leaming, Barbara. *Jack Kennedy*. New York: W. W. Norton, 2006.

Lebow, Richard Ned. *Between Peace and War*. Baltimore, MD: Johns Hopkins University Press, 1981.

Lebow, Richard Ned, and Janice Stein. *We All Lost the Cold War*. Princeton, NJ: Princeton University, 1994.

Lerner, Mitchell, *The Pueblo Incident*. Lawrence: University Press of Kansas, 2002.

Lynch, Marc. *The Arab Spring*. New York: Public Affairs, 2012.

MacArthur, Douglas. *Reminiscences*. New York: McGraw-Hill, 1964.

Mann, James. *The Obamians*. New York: Viking, 2012.

Mann, Robert. *A Grand Delusion*. New York: Basic Books, 2001.

Martin, David, and John Walcott. *Best Laid Plans*. New York: Harper & Row, 1988.

May, Ernest R., and Philip D. Zelikow, eds., *The Kennedy Tapes*. Cambridge: Harvard University Press, 1997.

McCullough, David. *Truman*. New York: Simon & Schuster, 1992.

McDermott, Edward A. Unpublished personal journal, family copy.

McFarlane, Robert, and Zofia Snardz. *Special Trust*. New York: Cadell & Davies, 1994.

Mearsheimer, John, and Stephen Walt. *The Israel Lobby and US Foreign Policy*. New York: Farrar, Straus and Giroux, 2007.

Melanson, Richard A., and David Mayers. *Reevaluating Eisenhower*. Urbana: University of Illinois Press, 1987.

Mondale, Walter. *The Good Fight*. New York: Scribner, 2010.

Morris, Dick. *Because He Could*. New York: ReganBooks, 2004.

Morris, Roger. *Uncertain Greatness*. New York: Harper & Row, 1997.

National Commission on the Terrorist Attacks Upon the United States. *The 9/11 Commission Report*. New York: W. W. Norton, 2004.

Neff, Donald. *Warriors at Suez*. New York: Linden Press, 1981.

Nessen, Ron. *It Sure Looks Different from the Inside*. Chicago: Playboy Press Paperbacks, 1978.

———. *Making the News, Taking the News*. Middletown, CT: Wesleyan University Press, 2011.

Neustadt, Richard E. *Presidential Power and the Modern Presidents*. New York: Free Press, 1990.

Neustadt, Richard, and Ernest May. *Thinking in Time*. New York: Free Press, 1986.

Nichols, David A. *Eisenhower 1956*. New York: Simon & Schuster, 2011.

Nixon, Richard. RN: *The Memoirs of Richard Nixon*. New York: Grosset & Dunlap, 1978.

Nutting, Anthony. *No End of a Lesson: The Story of Suez*. London: Constable, 1967.

O'Donnell, Kenneth P., and David F. Powers. *"Johnny, We Hardly Knew Ye."* With Joe McCarthy. Boston: Little, Brown, 1972.

Oren, Michael. *Six Days of War*. New York: Oxford University Press, 2002.

Parmet, Herbert S. *Eisenhower and the American Crusades*. New York: Macmillan, 1972.

Pfaltzgraff, Robert Jr., and Jacquelyn Davis, ed. *National Security Decisions*. Lexington: Lexington Books, 1990.

Phillips, Kevin. *American Dynasty*. New York: Viking, 2004.

Pillar, Paul. *Terrorism and U.S. Foreign Policy*. Washington, DC: Brookings Institution Press, 2001.

Powell, Colin. *My American Journey*. With Joseph Persico. New York: Random House, 1995.

Powell, Jody. *The Other Side of the Story*. New York: William Morrow, 1994.

Quandt, William. *Decade of Decisions*. Berkeley: University of California Press, 1977.

———. *Peace Process*. Washington, DC: Brookings Institution Press, 2005.

Reagan, Ronald. *Ronald Reagan: An American Life*. New York: Threshold Editions, 1990.

Reedy, George E. *The Twilight of the Presidency*. New York: New American Library, 1970.

Reeves, Richard. *President Reagan*. New York: Simon & Schuster, 2005.

Renshon, Stanley, ed. *The Political Psychology of the Gulf War*. Pittsburgh: University of Pittsburgh Press, 1993.

Ridgway, Matthew. *The Korean War*. New York: Da Capo, 1967.

Rodman, Peter. *Presidential Command*. New York: Alfred Knopf, 2009.

Rothkopf, David. *Running the World*. New York: Public Affairs, 2005.

Rowan, Roy. *The Four Days of Mayaguez*. New York: W. W. Norton, 1975.

Rusk, Dean. *As I Saw It*. As told to Richard Rusk. New York: W. W. Norton, 1990.

Sammon, Bill. *Fighting Back*. Washington: Regnery, 2002.

Schlesinger, Arthur. *Robert Kennedy and His Times*. New York: Houghton Mifflin Harcourt, 2012.

Segev, Tom. *1967: Israel, the War, and the Year that Transformed the Middle East*. New York: Metropolitan Books, 2007.

Sestanovich, Stephen. *Maximalist*. New York: Alfred A. Knopf, 2014.

Sheehan, Edward. *The Arabs, Israelis, and Kissinger*. New York: Reader's Digest Press, 1976.

Shultz, George. *Turmoil and Triumph*. New York: Charles Scribner's Sons.

Sick, Gary. *All Fall Down*. New York: Random House, 1985.

Smith, Jean Edward. *Eisenhower in War and Peace*. New York: Random House, 2012.

———. *George Bush's War*. New York: Henry Holt, 1992.

Spencer, Lynn. *Touching History*. New York: Free Press, 2008.

Stern, Sheldon M. *Averting 'The Final Failure.'* Stanford, CA: Stanford University Press, 2003.

Taubman, William. *Khrushchev*. New York: W. W. Norton, 2003.

Teicher, Howard, and Gayle Teicher. *Twin Pillars to Desert Storm*. New York: William Morrow, 1993.

Thomas, Evan. *Ike's Bluff*. New York: Little, Brown, 2012.

Timberg, Robert. *The Nightingale's Song*. New York: Simon & Schuster, 1995.

Truman, Harry S. *Memoirs: Years of Trial and Hope*. Garden City: Doubleday, 1956.

Truman, Margaret. *Harry S. Truman*. New York: Avon, 1972.

Turner, Stansfield. *Burn Before Reading*. New York: Hyperion, 2005.

Tyler, Patrick. *A World of Trouble*. New York: Farrar Straus Giroux, 2009.

U.S. News and World Report. *Triumph Without Victory*. New York: Time Books, 1993.

Vance, Cyrus. *Hard Choices*. New York: Simon & Schuster, 1983.

Walters, Vernon A. *Silent Missions*. Garden City: Doubleday, 1978.

Weinberger, Casper. *Fighting for Peace*. New York: Warner Books, 1991.

Wills, David. *The First War on Terrorism*. Lanham, MD: Rowman & Littlefield, 2003.

Woodward, Bob. *Bush at War*. New York: Simon & Schuster, 2002.

———. *Plan of Attack*. New York: Simon & Schuster, 2004.

———. *The Commanders*. New York: Simon & Schuster, 1991.

Wright, Lawrence. *The Looming Tower*. New York: Alfred A. Knopf, 2006.

Zubok, Vladislav M. *A Failed Empire*. Chapel Hill: University of North Carolina Press, 2007.

Zumwalt, Elmo R. Jr. *On Watch*. New York: Quadrangle, 1976.

Articles, Newspapers, Periodicals

Allyn, Bruce J., James G. Blight, and David A. Welch. "Essence of Revision: Moscow, Havana, and the Cuban Missile Crisis." *International Security*, vol. 14, no. 3 (Winter, 1989–1990); 136–172.

Foreign Policy, 2012.

Glad, Betty. "Personality, Political and Group Process Variables in Foreign Policy Decision-Making," *International Political Science Review*, vol 10, no. 1 (1989); 35–61.

Los Angeles Times, 1990–2013.

Newsweek, 1991–1992.

New York Review of Books, 1992.

New York Times, 1950–2014.

Powell, Colin. *Vital Speeches of the Day*, 69.9, February 15, 2003, 276–288.

The New Yorker, 1950–2014.

Time Magazine, 1986–1991.

USA Today, 2004–2011.

Vanity Fair, 2012.

Wall Street Journal, 2013.

Washington Post, 1950–2014.

Oral Histories

McDermott, Edward A. John F. Kennedy Library, family copy.

McNamara, Robert. Lyndon Johnson Library.

Rountree, William M. The Association for Diplomatic Studies and Training Foreign Affairs Oral History Project, Library of Congress.

Author Interviews

Bostdorff, Denise, 2014.

Brzezinski, Zbigniew, 2013.

Bush, George H. W., 2001.

Ford, Gerald R., 2001.

Gates, Robert, 2001.

Goodpaster, Andrew, 2001.

Haass, Richard, 2001.

Haig, Alexander, 2001.

Hargis, Rob, 2011.

Kissinger, Henry, 2001.

Lake, Anthony, 2001.

Loewer, Deborah, 2011.

McDaniel, Rod, 2013.

McFarlane, Robert, 2001.

McNamara, Robert, 2001.

Pickering, Thomas, 2014.

Quandt, William, 2014.

Rostow, Walt, 2001.

Rozell, Mark, 2014.

Saunders, Harold, 2001.

Schuessler, Linda, 2011.

Scowcroft, Brent, 2001.

Sick, Gary, 2001.

Smith, Gayle, 2001.

Sorenson, Theodore, 2001.

Steinberg, James, 2001.

Teicher, Howard, 2014.

Internet

Al Arabya. http://www.alarabiya.net/articles/2011/02/21/138515.html.

American Presidency Project. http://www.presidency.ucsb.edu/ws/?pid=9060.

American Presidency Project. http://www.presidency.ucsb.edu/ws/?pid=48285.

BBC News. http://news.bbc.co.uk/2/hi/africa/7599479.stm.

Bush, George W. White House Archives. http://georgewbush-whitehouse.
archives.gov/news/releases/2001/09/20010911-1.html.

———. White House Archives. http://georgewbush-whitehouse.archives.
gov/news/releases/2001/09/20010911-16.html.

———. White House Archives. http://georgewbush-whitehouse.archives.
gov/news/releases/2001/09/20010914-2.html.

CBS News. http://www.cbsnews.com/news/boehner-gop-want-obama-to-
consult-with-congress-on-libya.

———. http://www.cbsnews.com/news/plans-for-iraq-attack-began-on-9-11/.

———. *60 Minutes II*. http://www.cbsnews.com/news/the-presidents-story-
11-09-2002.

CNN. http://archives.cnn.com/TRANSCRIPTS/0109/15/cg.00.html.

———. http://www.cnn.com/2004/ALLPOLITICS/01/10/oneill.bush/.

George Washington University. The National Security Archive, Cold War
Interviews. http://www.gwu.edu/~nsarchiv/coldwar/interviews/episode-17/
mcnamara2.html.

———. The National Security Archive, The October War and U.S. Policy.
http://www2.gwu.edu/~nsarchiv/NSAEBB/NSAEBB98/.

Independent. http://www.independent.co.uk/arts-entertainment/tv/reviews-
/911-state-of-emergency--sat-channel-4brdavid-jason-the-battle-of-brit-
ain--sun-itv1bralberts-memorial--sun-itv1-2077487.html.

Information Clearing House. http://www.informationclearinghouse.info/
article7204.htm.

Johnson Library. Online Documents, Oral Histories. http://www.lbjlibrary.
net/assets/documents/archives/oral_histories/mcgeorge_b/Bundy%20
Dallek%202%20web.pdf.

National Security Agency. Public Information, "On Watch." http://www.nsa.
gov/public_info/_files/cryptologic_histories/on_watch.pdf.

The New Yorker. http://www.newyorker.com/reporting/2011/05/02/
110502fa_fact_lizza?currentPage=all.

Truman Library. Online Documents, Korea. Memorandum of Conversation, "Korean Situation," June 25, 1950. http://www.trumanlibrary.org/
whistlestop/study_collections/korea/large/documents/pdfs/ki-12-1.
pdf#zoom=100.

———. Online Documents, Korea. Memorandum of Conversation,
NSC Meeting November 28, 1950. http://www.trumanlibrary.

org/whistlestop/study_collections/koreanwar/documents/index.
php?documentdate=1950-11-28&documentid=ki-15-12&pagenumber=1.

———. The Cold War Turns Hot, Personal memo of Harry S. Truman, June 30, 1950. http://www.trumanlibrary.org/exhibit_documents/index.php?tl-date=1950-06-30&groupid=3433&pagenumber=1&collectionid=korea.

———. Oral Histories, John D. Hickerson. http://www.trumanlibrary.org/oralhist/hickrson.htm.

New York Post. http://nypost.com/2011/03/07/libyas-fiercest-fight/.

Newsmax. Inside Cover. http://www.newsmax.com/InsideCover/donald-rumsfeld-egypt-muslim/2011/02/08/id/385426.

Newsweek Memories. http://www.newsweekmemories.org/e-thomas.html.

PBS. *American Experience, 25 years,* The Invasion of Grenada. http://www.pbs.org/wgbh/americanexperience/features/general-article/reagan-grenada/.

———. Frontline. http://www.pbs.org/wgbh/pages/frontline/shows/target/interviews/oakley.html.

———. *Newshour.* http://www.pbs.org/newshour/bb/politics-jan-june11-biden_01-27/

———. http://www.pbs.org/newshour/character/essays/johnson.html.

PolitiFact. http://www.politifact.com/truth-o-meter/statements/2013/apr/10/dick-cheney/dick-cheney-margaret-thatcher-go-wobbly/.

SFGate. Fightin' words: There are hidden meanings in how we pronounce foreign words and names. Like Saddam. http://www.sfgate.com/enter-tainment/article/Fightin-words-There-are-hidden-meanings-in-how-2665077.php.

Teaching American History. Harry S. Truman, The President's News Conference of June 29, 1950. http://teachingamericanhistory.org/library/document/the-presidents-news-conference-of-june-29-1950/.

US Army Center of Military History. http://www.history.army.mil/books/PD-C-13.HTM.

US Defense Technical Information Center. http://www.dtic.mil/dtic/tr/fulltext/u2/a440784.pdf

US Department of Defense. Speeches. http://www.defense.gov/Speeches/Speech.aspx?SpeechID=1539.

US Department of State. Foreign Relations of the United States, 1950, Korea, volume VII. http://digicoll.library.wisc.edu/cgi-bin/FRUS/FRUS-idx?-type=header&id=FRUS.FRUS1950v07.

———. 1955–1957, Suez Crisis, July 26–December 31, 1956, volume XVI. http://history.state.gov/historicaldocuments/frus1955-57v16/ch1.

———. 1961–1963, volume XI, Cuban Missile Crisis and Aftermath. http://history.state.gov/historicaldocuments/frus1961-63v11.

———. 1964–1968, volume XIX, Arab-Israeli Crisis and War, 1967. http://history.state.gov/historicaldocuments/frus1964-68v19/comp1.

———. 1964–1968, volume XXIX, Part 1, Korea, Pueblo Crisis. http://history.state.gov/historicaldocuments/frus1964-68v29p1/ch2.

———. 1969–1976, volume XXV, Arab-Israeli Crisis and War, 1973. http://history.state.gov/historicaldocuments/frus1969-76v25/comp1.

———. 1969–1976, volume X, Vietnam, January 1973–July 1975. The SS *Mayaguez* Incident, May 12–15, 1975. http://history.state.gov/historicaldocuments/frus1969-76v10/ch4.

White House. Briefing Room, Press Briefings. http://www.whitehouse.gov/the-press-office/2011/03/07/corrected-press-briefing-press-secretary-jay-carney-372011.

White House. Briefing Room, Speeches and Remarks. http://www.whitehouse.gov/the-press-office/remarks-president-cairo-university-6-04-09.

———. http://www.whitehouse.gov/the-press-office/2011/02/23/remarks-president-libya.

———. http://www.whitehouse.gov/the-press-office/2011/03/18/remarks-president-situation-libya.

———. http://www.whitehouse.gov/the-press-office/2012/08/20/remarks-president-white-house-press-corp.

White House. The White House Blog. http://www.whitehouse.gov/blog/2011/03/03/president-libya-violence-must-stop-muammar-gaddafi-has-lost-legitimacy-lead-and-he-m.

Wilson Center. Cold War International History Project, Publications. http://www.wilsoncenter.org/sites/default/files/CWIHP_Bulletin_14-15.pdf.

———. North Korea International Documentation Project. http://www.wilsoncenter.org/publication/nkidp-e-dossier-no-5-new-romanian-evidence-the-blue-house-raid-and-the-uss-pueblo.

YouTube. H. W. Bush on Policing the World: Opposing Iraqi Aggression. http://www.youtube.com/watch?v=nzkOlNlb7KI.

Zakaria, Fareed. http://fareedzakaria.com/2011/07/06/stop-searching-for-an-obama-doctrine/.

INDEX

All references to China in this index are to Communist China; references to Nationalist China have that modifier. All dates are in Washington time.